100+ Solutions in Java

2nd Edition

Everything you need to know to develop Java applications

Dhruti Shah

www.bpbonline.com

First published: 2021

Second published: 2024

Published by BPB Online
WeWork
119 Marylebone Road
London NW1 5PU

UK | UAE | INDIA | SINGAPORE

ISBN 978-93-5551-571-1

www.bpbonline.com

Dedicated to

My beloved Parents:

Late Dr. Jyotikant S. Shah
Mrs. Ushakiran J. Shah
&
My little ***Swara, Aaria & Madhav***

About the Author

Dhruti Shah is a multi-skilled, tech-savvy person with over 15 years of experience as a software trainer, technical writer, and manager in the IT education industry. She has been working extensively with Java technology for the last 10 years. She is also a Microsoft Certified Training Specialist who has trained over 2000 candidates worldwide on more than 10 technologies.

She has been appreciated as a model representative for India for flawlessly managing two prestigious international projects to set up and upgrade the Centre of Excellence in Information Technology in Panama and Costa Rica, Central America (a collaboration project of the Indian government with the governments of Panama and Costa Rica).

Acknowledgement

Writing a book on a technology that I have been obsessed with since I first learned about it, years ago, was a gratifying experience. However, it could never have been possible without the support of all my family members and friends. They always believed in me, encouraged me to follow my dreams, and gave me the confidence to face my struggles.

I would like to thank my mother, Mrs. Ushakiran Shah, who is my friend, philosopher, and guide. Her belief in me and my aspirations has given me the courage to face challenges head on and emerge a victor. Further, I would like to thank all my readers whose valuable feedback has helped me while writing this revised edition of my book.

Finally, I would like to extend my gratitude to the entire team of BPB publications for their support and appreciation of my work.

Preface

Java is a programming language that has been around for decades and has proved its potential ever since as a versatile programming language. Over the years, Java has advanced tremendously and has become one of the preferred programming languages for the development of applications ranging from standalone to Web applications as well as mobile apps. It is no longer a simple client-side language but is more dynamic and supports development for application servers, embedded devices, and much more.

This book is a result of several years of application development in Java and the experience gained by using different features introduced with each new version of Java. The goal of this book is to give a beginner enough knowledge to start application development in Java. Java is an evolving technology, and this book attempts to introduce the readers to basic features of Java and the new features of Java 8 to Java 19. It aims to gradually introduce the reader to a new programming approach called modular programming. The book presumes that the reader has a basic idea about programming and aspires to begin development using Java. It has been written after extensive research and provides ample examples and demonstrations to help you take the first step to learn new technology. This book will prove to be a great reference for beginners as well as professionals to begin development in Java. Over the 14 chapters of this book, you will learn the following:

Chapter 1: Introduction to Java- introduces the concept of object-oriented programming and explains how Java has evolved as object-oriented programming (OOP) language. It explains the versions and features of Java and steps to create an application by using JDK 8 and JDK 10.

Chapter 2: Java Programming Constructs - discusses the different programming constructs of Java language such as comments, variables, datatypes, and operators. It then shows you the use of decision-making constructs, looping constructs, and branch statements.

Chapter 3: Java Application Components - introduces Java classes, objects, variables, methods, access specifiers, and constructors. It explains the implementation of polymorphism, creation of packages and use of keywords such as static, final, and this keyword.

Chapter 4: Java Reference Types - discusses different types of Arrays and String class. It then shows you the use of StringBuilder and StringTokenizer classes, command-line arguments, and wrapper classes.

Chapter 5: Subclasses and Interfaces - discusses the concept of inheritance in Java in-depth and different ways of implementing inheritance by using abstract classes, nested classes, and so on. It then explains the interfaces and lambda expressions.

Chapter 6: Exceptions and Regular Expressions - describes exception handling with built-in exception classes and custom exceptions. It further introduces the important classes of java.lang and java.util.regex packages.

Chapter 7: Collections and Stream API - introduces the more advanced features such as Collections framework with the different utility classes and interfaces of the java.util package.

Chapter 8: Generics and Time API - describes the use of generics in Java to create generic classes, methods, and collections. It also introduces the Time API that provides better support for date and time.

Chapter 9: File Manipulation in Java - describes different types of streams of java.io package for file management. Further, it introduces the different classes of the java.util.zip and java.nio package.

Chapter 10: Threads and JDBC - explains the creation of thread and multithreading to improve the performance of applications. It then describes how to connect to databases by using JDBC API.

Chapter 11: Design Patterns and Internationalization - explains the use of design patterns as solutions to common problems encountered during software development. It also describes the internationalization and localization of an application.

Chapter 12: More about JDK 8, 9 and 10 - describes some prominent new features of Java 8 to 10, such as Java Platform Module System (JPMS), JShell, JLink tool, Local Variable Type Inference, and so on.

Chapter 13: Java 11 (LTS) and New Updates - introduces the new feature of Java 11 (LTS), such as string and file methods, HTTPClient, Garbage Collectors, etc. It also describes the different JDK providers and the new features launched in Java 12 to 16.

Chapter 14: Java 17 (LTS) and New Updates - explains Java 17 and the new features added to the JDK, such as pattern matching for switch. It also describes the new features and enhancements in Java versions 18 and 19.

Code Bundle and Coloured Images

Please follow the link to download the
Code Bundle and the ***Coloured Images*** of the book:

https://rebrand.ly/e3qa9xg

The code bundle for the book is also hosted on GitHub at **https://github.com/bpbpublications/100Plus-Solutions-in-Java-2nd-Edition**. In case there's an update to the code, it will be updated on the existing GitHub repository.

We have code bundles from our rich catalogue of books and videos available at **https://github.com/bpbpublications**. Check them out!

Errata

We take immense pride in our work at BPB Publications and follow best practices to ensure the accuracy of our content to provide with an indulging reading experience to our subscribers. Our readers are our mirrors, and we use their inputs to reflect and improve upon human errors, if any, that may have occurred during the publishing processes involved. To let us maintain the quality and help us reach out to any readers who might be having difficulties due to any unforeseen errors, please write to us at :

errata@bpbonline.com

Your support, suggestions and feedbacks are highly appreciated by the BPB Publications' Family.

Piracy

If you come across any illegal copies of our works in any form on the internet, we would be grateful if you would provide us with the location address or website name. Please contact us at **business@bpbonline.com** with a link to the material.

If you are interested in becoming an author

If there is a topic that you have expertise in, and you are interested in either writing or contributing to a book, please visit **www.bpbonline.com**. We have worked with thousands of developers and tech professionals, just like you, to help them share their insights with the global tech community. You can make a general application, apply for a specific hot topic that we are recruiting an author for, or submit your own idea.

Reviews

Please leave a review. Once you have read and used this book, why not leave a review on the site that you purchased it from? Potential readers can then see and use your unbiased opinion to make purchase decisions. We at BPB can understand what you think about our products, and our authors can see your feedback on their book. Thank you!

For more information about BPB, please visit **www.bpbonline.com**.

Join our book's Discord space

Join the book's Discord Workspace for Latest updates, Offers, Tech happenings around the world, New Release and Sessions with the Authors:

https://discord.bpbonline.com

Table of Contents

CHAPTER 1
Introduction to Java

Introduction

This chapter introduces the concept of object-oriented programming and explains how Java has evolved as an **Object-Oriented Programming (OOP)** language. You will learn about the various versions and features of Java and the steps to install a **Java Development Kit (JDK)**. You will also learn to create an application by using JDK 8 and JDK 10.

Structure

Following are the topics that are covered in this chapter:

- Introduction to object-oriented programming
- Java programming language
- Java platform and editions
- Java SE platform components
- Java SE version history
- Features of Java SE 9 and Java SE 10
- Download and install JDK 8 and JDK 10
- Setting up the path for JDK
- Java application development

- Structure of a Java program
- Java code compilation and execution
- Create and execute a Java program using JDK 8
- Create and execute a Java program using JDK 10
- Creating and executing a Java 8 project in NetBeans
- Creating and executing a Java 10 project in NetBeans

Objectives

In this chapter, you will learn the concept of object-oriented programming. You will also learn to download and install JDK 8 and JDK 10. Finally, you will understand the structure of a Java program and learn to develop a Java project in NetBeans. You will learn to download and install JDK 8 and JDK 10

1.1 Introduction to object-oriented programming

With the advancement in technology and the increasing complexity of software, a requirement for new and flexible modes of programming was observed. A need to make reliable software and reduce the overall development and maintenance cost, and deliver completed software on decided timelines, resulted in the development of the object-oriented programming model.

The primary focus of object-oriented programming is on objects. Any real-world entity that has certain characteristics and behavior that can be used to describe it is considered as an object. There are several objects that have certain common characteristics. These can be grouped into categories or classes. Thereby, every object of a class will be considered as an instance of that class. Programmatically, a class is a structure that contains the data (characteristics) and methods (behavior) to work on that data.

For example, a class `Vehicle` can have characteristics such as color, type, and behavior such as start, stop, accelerate, and so on. The following image shows a **Unified Modeling Language (UML)** class diagram representation of the Vehicle class:

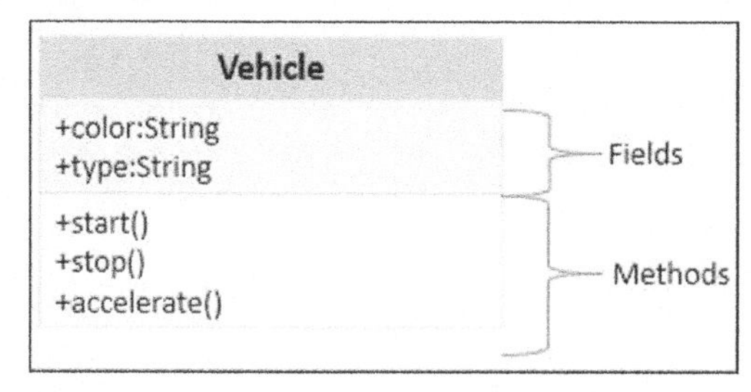

Figure 1.1: *Class diagram*

Here, the **Fields** represent the characteristics, and **Methods** represent the behavior of the object. The Vehicle class can then have instances of type Vehicle, such as bike, bicycle, car, and so on. This is explained in detail in the following figure:

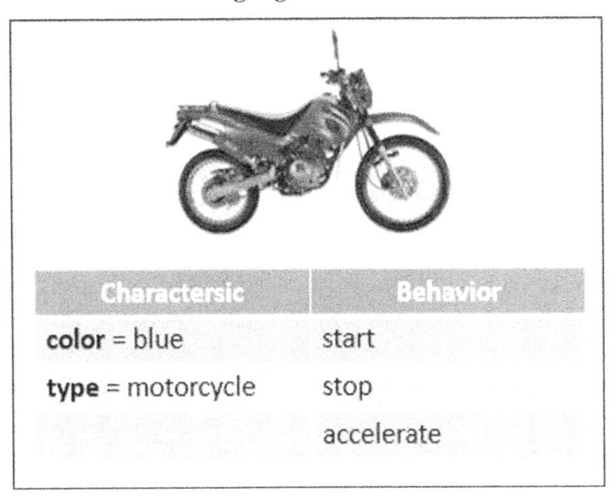

Figure 1.2: *Object of Vehicle class*

Here, the object bike has the characteristics **color=blue** and **type=motorcycle** with the behavior including start, stop, and accelerate. Similarly, there can be other instances of class Vehicle such as car, bicycle, and so on. with the same or different values for characteristics and similar behavior.

An object-oriented programming language is based on the following principles:

- **Encapsulation**: To encapsulate means to enclose. Hence, encapsulation allows enclosing the data members and methods into a closed structure called a class. Encapsulation ensures data security through data hiding so that a user cannot access the members of a class directly.
- **Abstraction**: Abstraction is a programming concept in which the non-essential details of an entity are hidden from user view. For example, in the case of a washing machine, the user only presses the button on a digital panel to set up the process and start the machine. However, the internal functioning of the washing machine is not known to the user. This means that the non-essential aspect of how the washing machine washes the clothes is abstracted from the user. Similarly, abstraction can also be implemented in code to hide the unnecessary details from the user.
- **Inheritance**: To inherit means to acquire some feature or asset from an ancestor. For example, a child acquires certain aspects of physical appearance and certain behavior of his/her biological parents. In programming also, inheritance plays a similar role. It allows us to combine the common characteristics and behavior of objects into a parent class also called a superclass. This class can then be inherited by other classes that allow a developer to extend and reuse the feature of existing classes. The new/inherited classes are called child classes, derived classes, or subclasses.

- **Polymorphism**: Polymorph is a combination of words *poly* which means many and *morph* which means forms. This polymorph is an object that can have multiple forms/ behavior. For example, a chameleon can change its color as per the environment to protect itself from predators. In programming, polymorphism is the ability of an object to behave in different ways based on requirements. Polymorphism can be implemented in several ways in programming based on the programming language used.

1.2 Java programming language

Java is a popular object-oriented, platform-independent programming language. It allows the development of a variety of applications that can run on different hardware and operating systems. Java also provides a runtime environment for executing Java applications on different devices.

Java was originally developed in 1991 by *James Gosling* and a team of engineers at *Sun Microsystems* which was later acquired by *Oracle Corporation*. It was initially designed for consumer devices such as washing machines, television, and so on. For such devices, it was necessary to have a language that was small, efficient, fast, and platform-independent. Languages such as C and C++ were not preferred due to the compiler's dependence on specific CPUs and also high development time and cost. Thus, Java was developed as a portable and platform-independent language that could execute codes on any platform. Initially, it was named *Oak* but later renamed to Java.

Even though Java was developed to cater to the programming needs for smaller devices, it was found to be able to address larger problems including Web and mobile applications. It gained instant popularity and was adopted all over the world for the development of applications ranging from embedded, desktop, Web, and mobile applications. Java can be used to create applications for small to large businesses and even for supercomputers.

1.2.1 Features and advantages of Java

Following are some features and advantages of Java programming language:

- **Simple and robust:** Java syntax is derived from its predecessor programming languages like C, C++. This makes it easy for developers to learn Java quickly. Further, the complexity of pointers, operator overloading, multiple inheritances and other such features has been removed in Java. Instead, it has been made more robust through efficient memory management and exception handling features.
- **Object-oriented:** Java is based on the object-oriented programming paradigm. Thereby, it is well suited for the development of real-world applications.
- **Platform independent**: Java provides a solution to a major problem faced by earlier languages, that is, code portability. During compilation, it converts the source code into an intermediate, architecture-neutral format called bytecode. This bytecode can be executed on any platform which has a **Java Virtual Machine (JVM)** installed. Further, even the language specifications, such as the size of primitive data types and operators,

have been defined to be independent of the hardware. This ensures that the code will function properly in case of a change in the operating system, processor, or system resources.

- **Secure:** Security is an important issue in Java applications since they are designed for multiple and distributed platforms. Java provides security checks at different levels during application development. The JVM is designed to apply its security features during code execution to ensure that the code is well-formed and written as per Java standards.
- **Multithreaded**: Java supports the development of multithreaded applications to perform multiple tasks concurrently. In a multithreaded application, a single program can have multiple threads performing tasks independently and concurrently. Java allows creating thread pools that can be used to obtain threads when required.
- **Distributed and dynamic**: Java supports distributed programming to deploy and access resources across the network. It provides several **Application Programming Interfaces (APIs)** to handle remote transmission and requests over a network. Java also allows dynamic execution of classes by storing them in a separate location and loading the necessary classes dynamically at runtime.
- **Modular**: The concept of modularity has been introduced since Java 9. It was supposed to be incorporated in Java 7 and Java 8 but was not accomplished. Until Java 1.8, the packages were bundled into JAR files that were the final executable for a Java application. But, with Java 9, a new construct called *Module* has been introduced. A module is similar to the JAR file but unlike the JAR file, it also contains configuration information in the form of a `module-info.java` file. This allows a module to be more powerful and flexible as compared to a JAR file since all dependencies are specified in the `module-info.java` file. While using a JAR, the entire JAR is loaded during application execution, but with the module, only those modules that are part of the dependency list will be loaded. This allows applications to remain light weight as well as execute faster.

1.3 Java platform and editions

The Java platform is a development and execution environment for Java applications which is a mixture of software and hardware components. Following image shows the components of a Java platform:

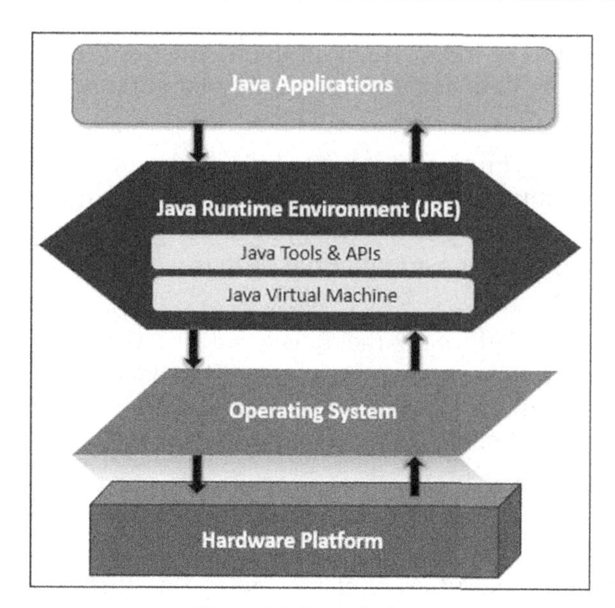

Figure 1.3: *Java platform*

The above figure depicts the components of a Java platform. It is formed of the **Java Runtime Environment** (**JRE**) which contains the Java library (Java API) and **Java Virtual Machine** (**JVM**). In languages such as C and C++, the compiled code is platform dependent as it is in the form of executable binary code. However, the Java compiler converts the code into an intermediate bytecode which is an optimized set of instructions that can be executed on any machine that has the appropriate JVM. Thus, JVM provides platform independence to Java code. Each operating system such as Windows, Linux, Mac, and so on. has its JVM. Thus, Java code follows the principle of write-once use many.

The Java API/library is a collection of ready-to-use components such as calluses and interfaces, that can be used to create applications. For example, the Swing library is used to create a **User Interface** (**UI**) of a Java application. Java is released under several editions to meet the requirements of a specific type of device and application. Following is a brief description of the different Java Editions:

- **Java Standard Edition (Java SE)**: Java SE is the base for creating applications that are console or network-based applications, mainly for desktop computers. It contains the core APIs, including the basic types and classes for higher-level programming such as networking, security, **Graphical User Interface** (**GUI**), database manipulation, and parsing of XML data. It also provides the virtual machine, development and deployment tools, and other toolkits and libraries for advanced programming.
- **Java Enterprise Edition (Java EE)**: The Java EE platform is an extension of the Java SE platform. It provides the tools and APIs for the creation and deployment of large-scale, distributed, scalable, multi-tier, reliable, and secure enterprise applications with complex business logic.

- **Java Micro Edition (Java ME)**: The Java ME platform is mainly used for creating embedded Java applications for small devices such as mobiles, TV set-top boxes, and so on. It contains a subset of Java SE APIs and a smaller virtual machine to execute Java programs on small devices with lesser memory and storage space. Java ME applications are generally used as clients of Java EE platform services.
- **JavaFX**: The JavaFX platform provides lightweight user-interface APIS for creating rich internet applications that use hardware-accelerated graphics and media engines. Java FX allows the creation of high-performance graphic applications with a modern look-and-feel. It also provides high-level APIs to connect with data sources over the network. JavaFX applications can also be used as clients of Java EE platform services.

1.4 Java SE platform components

The two important Java SE platform components are **Java Runtime Environment** (**JRE**) and **Java Development Kit** (**JDK**). The JRE contains all the Java libraries required to execute a Java program, whereas the JDK contains the libraries required to develop Java programs and is distributed for different platforms like Windows, Mac OS X, Linux, and so on. The JDK comprises the tools required for application development, compilation, debugging, and so on. It also has its own JRE to execute and test Java applications. The figure below shows the different Java SE platform components:

Java Language						
Tools and APIs	java	javac	javadoc	jar	javap	Scripting
	Security	Monitoring	JConsole	VisualVM	JMC	JFR
	JVM T1	IDL	RMI	Deployment	Java DB	
	Internationalization		Web Services		Troubleshooting	
Deployment	Java Web Start			Applet/Java Plug-in		
User Interface Toolkits	Java FX					
	Swing	Java 2D	AWT	Accessibility	Drag and Drop	
	Input Methods		Print Service		Image I/O	Sound
Integration Libraries	IDL	JDBC	JNDI	RMI	RMI/IIOP	Scripting
Other Base Libraries	Beans	XML JAXP	Date and Time		Extension Mechanism	
	JMX	Security	Networking		Override Mechanism	
	JNI	Serialization	Input/Output		Internationalization	
Lang and util Base Libraries	lang and util		Concurrency Utilities		Collections	JAR
	Logging	Management	Preferences API		Ref Objects	
	Regular Expressions		Reflection	Instrumentation	Versioning	Zip
Java HotSpot Client and Server Virtual Machine						

JDK | JRE | Java SE API

Figure 1.4: *Java SE platform*

The brief descriptions of the tools and libraries are given below:

- **Development tools and APIs**: The tools and utilities form the base for Java development. The development tools include **javac** compiler, **java** launcher, a Javadoc documentation tool, and so on. The Java APIs are ready-to-use classes and interfaces for different functionalities such as networking, XML parsing, GUI creation, database manipulation, and many more.

- **Deployment tools**: The JDK provides software for deploying applications on target machines. Java Web Start and Java Plug-in are examples of deployment tools.
- **User interface toolkits**: The JDK comes bundled with UI toolkits such as Swing, Java2D, and **Abstract Window Toolkit** (**AWT**) for the development of graphical user interfaces in Java applications.
- **Integration libraries**: Integration libraries such as **Java Database Connectivity** (**JDBC**), **Java Naming and Directory Interface** (**JNDI**), and so on. provide access to databases and remote objects for data manipulation and network access.
- **Other base libraries**: These libraries include APIs for file manipulation, networking, XML parsing, security, internationalization, and so on.
- **Language and utility libraries**: These libraries include Math, Collections, Logging, Regular Expressions, and so on. that allow us to perform manipulation of data in a Java program.

1.5 Java SE version history

The **Java Standard Edition** (**Java SE**) is a platform for the development of robust, reliable, and secure applications with the development tools, APIs, utilities, and runtime environment provided by the JDK. The JDK has undergone several modifications over the years with some major enhancements and new features added with every new release. The following table lists the different releases of JDK with the corresponding features and enhancements:

Features and enhancements	Code name	Release date	Features and enhancements
JDK 1.0	**Oak**	**January 1996**	Package and class creation in a standard library.
JDK 1.1	**-**	**February 1997**	AWT with event delegation, JDBC API, JavaBeans.
J2SE 1.2	**Playground**	**December 1998**	New GUI API named Swing, Reflection API, and Collection framework.
J2SE 1.3	**Kestrel**	**May 2000**	JNDI for remote lookup.
J2SE 1.4	**Merlin**	**February 2002**	Exception chaining, API for XML parsing, regular expressions, channel based I/O, and assertions.
J2SE 5.0	**Tiger**	**September 2004**	The new program constructs like a for-each loop, annotations, generics, and auto-boxing.

Features and enhancements	Code name	Release date	Features and enhancements
Java SE 6	**Mustang**	**December 2006**	Included script language, visual basic language support, and improvements in the GUI.
Java SE 7	**Dolphin**	**July 2011**	Switch statement with `String` cases, an integer can store a binary number, use of underscore (_) between the digits, try-with-resources statement, type arguments provided to the constructor of a generic class declaration replaced with an empty set of parameters (<>), single `catch` block to handle one or more exceptions.
Java SE 8 (LTS)		**March 2014**	Inclusion of `forEach()` method in Iterable interface, Lambda Expressions, Time API, support for default and static methods in Interfaces, Improvements in Collection API, Functional Interfaces, Bulk operations on collections with Java Stream API, Concurrency API, Java I/O and Core APIs.
Java SE 9		**September 2017**	**Java Platform Module System (JPMS)**, interactive Java REPL named JShell, improved Javadoc, jlink tool for Linking, Multi-release JARs, Collection factory methods, Stream API improvements, HTTP/2 support, and Private interface methods.
Java SE 10		**March 2018**	Application Data-Class Sharing, Local-Variable Type Inference, Thread Callbacks, Time-Based Release Versioning, and Root Certificates.
Java SE 11 (LTS)		**September 2018**	Features such as Java applets, Java Web Start, JavaFX, and so on. were dropped.Few new methods added to Strings and Files.Local-Variable Type Inference (`var`) for lambda parameters. Final, non-preview version of the HttpClient from Java 9. Deprecated features: Flight Recorder, No-Op Garbage Collector, Nashorn-Javascript-Engine
Java SE 12		**March 2019**	Some new features and clean-ups such as Unicode 11 support and a preview version of the new switch expression.

Features and enhancements	Code name	Release date	Features and enhancements
Java SE 13		**September 2019**	Unicode 12.1 support. Two preview features: Switch expressions can now return a value. A lambda-style syntax for expressions, without the fall-through/break issues: Multiline Strings
Java SE 14		**March 2020**	Preview versions of switch expressions in versions 12 and 13 were now standardized. Preview version of record classes introduced to alleviate the effort of writing a lot of boilerplate with Java. `NullPointerExceptions` describe exactly which variable was null. Preview version of Pattern Matching for `InstanceOf`. Introduction of jpackage tool for packaging Java applications into platform-specific packages along with its dependencies. **Garbage collectors**: **Concurrent Marks Sweep (CMS)** garbage collector removed and Z garbage collector added.
Java SE 15		**September 2020**	The preview version of multiline Strings of Java 13 is now production-ready. Preview version of Sealed classes introduced. Records and Pattern Matching features of Java 14 are still not finalized. **Nashorn JavaScript Engine** - Deprecated feature of Java 11, the Nashorn JavaScript Engine finally removed in JDK 15. The Z Garbage Collector made production-ready.
Java SE 16		**March 2021**	Pattern Matching for `instanceof` Unix-Domain Socket Channels Preview version of Foreign Linker API – a replacement for **Java Native Interface (JNI)** for binding with native libraries (think C). Records and pattern matching features made production-ready Sealed classes are still in preview version.

Features and enhancements	Code name	Release date	Features and enhancements
Java SE 17 (LTS)		**September 2021**	It is a **long-term support (LTS)** release of Java, after Java 11. Preview version of pattern matching for switch: Allows passing Objects to switch functions and check for a particular type.Preview version of Sealed Classes of Java 15 are finalizedForeign Function & Memory API (Incubator) - A replacement for the **Java Native Interface (JNI)** to call native functions and access memory outside the JVM.Security Manager available since Java 1.0 is not deprecated.
Java SE 18		**March 2022**	UTF-8 encoding by Default Simple Web Server – Rudimentary HTTP server introduced that can be started with `jwebserver` command.
Java SE 19		**September 2022**	Features such as virtual threads, foreign function & Memory API, structured concurrency, and the Vector API are all in preview mode.

Table 1.1: *Versions of Java*

1.6 Features of Java SE 9 and Java SE 10

The release, Java 8, was full of various new features that had made a significant impact on application development with Java. Until JDK 8, every JRE had all the classes for the runtime bundled into a single **Java Archive (JAR)** called **`rt.jar`** that was present in the **`lib`** directory. This led to a large number of unnecessary classes getting added to the runtime leading to overhead for the JVM. Thus, the JAR becomes bulky in size and the execution environment is forced to deal with all the classes whether or not they are used.

But Java SE 9 comes with more versatility and customization and a hoard of new features. The most important of them is the Jigsaw project which applies the new module system to break the JRE into reusable and interoperable components. The programming code is divided into modules that contain the tasks to be executed by them. This makes programs reusable and easier to manage and debug.

Another advantage of modularity is that it makes the Java platform more lightweight and scalable so that programs can run on smaller devices with fewer resources. The modular JRE can be used even with embedded systems allowing IoT apps to be coded by using Java.

Listed below are some new and exciting features of Java SE 9:

- **Java Platform Module System (JPMS):** This is the most important feature of Java SE 9. The important issues encountered with the growing codebase of a system are:
  - o Difficulty to encapsulate code
  - o Lack of clarity of dependencies among the various aspects (JARs)
  - o Easy access of public classes on the CLASSPATH leading to injudicious usage
  - o Lack of surety about the availability of all required JARs on the CLASSPATH

All these issues are addressed by the module system by using a module descriptor within the modular JARs. In this file, a module can define the list of all other modules on which it is dependent by using the **`requires`** statements. Further, to make packages of a module accessible to other modules, the **`exports`** keyword is used. If **`exports`** keyword is not used with a package, it is encapsulated in that module by default as shown in the image below:

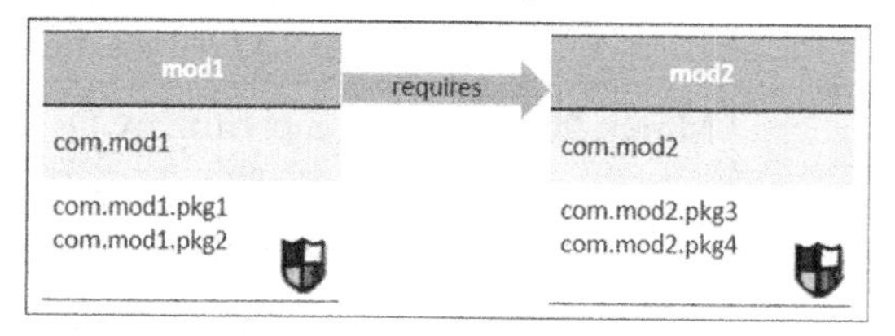

Figure 1.5: Module dependencies

Note that module **`mod1`** requires the module **`mod2`.** Both modules have packages that are encapsulated (as indicated by the shield symbol) as they are not exported. This ensures that the classes of the packages do not get accessed accidentally. Programmatically, this can be depicted as shown below:

```
module mod1 {
  exports com.mod1;
  requires mod2;
}
```

Similarly, the entire Java platform has been modularized by encapsulating the internal classes of JDK, thereby, making it more secure and flexible. Unlike, JARs, the JVM verifies the CLASSPATH for the existence of all dependent modules specified by using the **`requires`** statement. This avoids unexpected errors and code crash during execution encountered earlier due to missing JARs.

- **Linking**: You can create a minimal runtime by adding only the modules that are needed to execute and application. This can be done by using the new **`jlink`** tool provided with Java 9. The modularized JDK and the module descriptor file, which contains explicit dependencies mentioned in it, make it possible to create such minimal runtime. Thus, you can create a minimal and optimized runtime and avoid a bulky JDK installation.
- **JShell**: JShell is a new **Read-Eval-Print-Loop (REPL)** interactive terminal of JDK 9. You can launch the jshell from the console and type and execute Java code directly

from it. When a code is executed, it gives immediate feedback, which allows trying and exploring new APIs and language features. You can also test regular expressions in Java by using the interactive shell.

- **Enhanced Javadoc**: Javadoc now provides a built-in search facility in the API documentation. Further, the new Javadoc is HTML5 compliant and every page includes information about the JDK module to which a class or interface belongs.
- **Collection Factory Methods**: Java SE 9 brings a new feature with factory methods for collections such as `List`, `Set`, and so on. This helps a developer to quickly populate collections in one statement instead of using several `add` calls. For example,

```
Set<Integer> set1 = Set.of(3,4,5);
```

These collections are immutable, that is, items cannot be added to these collections after creation, or else it will throw the `UnsupportedOperationException` exception. The use of factory methods makes the code shorter and avoids section of a specific implementation of the collection type.

- **Enhancements in Stream API**: Java SE 9 adds more features to the Streams API by allowing declarative pipelines of transformations on collections. It adds new methods to the `Stream` interface namely, `dropWhile, takeWhile, ofNullable`, and provides an overloaded version of the iterate method to provide an expression to stop iterating. This is shown in the following example:

```
IntStream.iterate(1, num -> num < 10, num -> num + 1).forEach(System.
out::println);
```

The lambda expression in the second argument returns true until `num` becomes 100 and prints the integers from 1 to 99.

Further, it is possible to convert an `Optional` object to a `Stream` object.

```
Stream<Integer> num = Optional.of(1).stream();
```

- **Private interface methods**: Java SE 8 introduced the concept of default methods for interfaces. But interfaces were allowed only method signatures without any implementation. With Java SE 9, interfaces can also have methods with behavior and private helper methods to implement shared code that can be invoked from multiple default methods. This is explained in the code below:

```
public interface Interface1 {
  void interfaceMethodWithOnlySignature();
  default void interfaceDefaultMethod() {  initProcess(); }
  default void interfaceDefaultMethod1() { initProcess(); }
 // Private method that is not part of the public API exposed by Interface1
  private void initProcess() {
    System.out.println("Initializing the Process");
  }
}
```

Thus, private interface methods can help to structure the implementation of APIs with default methods.

- **HTTP/2:** Java 9 introduces a new way of performing HTTP calls by using the HTTPClient API as a replacement for the old **HttpURLConnection** API which also supports **WebSockets** and **HTTP/2:**

  ```
  HttpClient client = HttpClient.newHttpClient();
  ```

- **Multi-release JARs**: Java SE 9 brings the feature of multi-release JARs as a solution to bulky JARs resulting from deprecated libraries retained for backward compatibility. This feature allows the creation of alternate versions of classes that will be used only when the library is run on a specific version of Java.

  This is explained in the image below:

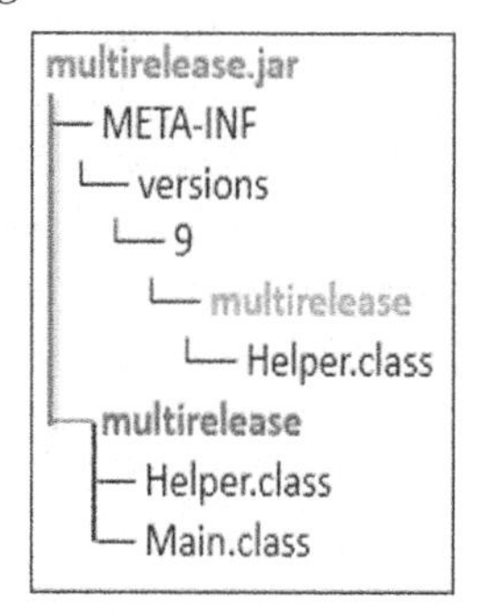

Figure 1.6: Multi-release JAR

  The image shows a **multirelease.jar** file with a **Helper** class at the top level as well as the Java 9 specific version. This indicates that while working with Java 9, the **multirelease. Helper** class under the **META-INF/versions/9** folder will be used, that can use Java 9 features and libraries. The JAR will, however work with earlier versions as well in which case, the top-level **multirelease. Helper** class will be used.

JDK 10 follows the modular model of JDK 9 and provides enhancements on the features and functionalities of JDK 9. JDK 10 does not bring any major changes or improvements over JDK 9 but it does act as the first release in the new, six-monthly release cadence announced by Oracle. Slated to be just a short-term release, the public updates for JDK 10 will end in six months. The next version, JDK 11 is scheduled for release in September 2018 and it will be a **Long-Term Support** (**LTS**) version of Java.

Listed below are the new features and enhancements in Java SE 10:

- **Application Data-Class Sharing (CDS)**: This **JDK Enhancement Proposal** (**JEP**) is an extension to the existing CDS feature to allow storing the application classes into a shared archive to improve startup.
- **Parallel full GC for G1**: A full parallel GC improves the worst-case latencies of the F1 garbage collector.
- **Garbage collector interface**: JDK 10 introduces the **Garbage Collector (GC)** interface to improve the source code isolation of different garbage collectors.

- **Combine the multiple JDK repositories into a single repository**: This feature is incorporated to simplify and streamline development.
- **Local-variable type inference**: This enhancement allows to extend type inference to declarations of local variables with initializers. It also introduces `var` to Java.
- **Thread callbacks**: JDK 10 introduces the possibility to stop individual threads instead of all threads or none by executing a callback on threads without performing a global VM safepoint.
- **Time-based release versioning**: It introduces a new time-based release versioning for the version-string scheme of the Java SE Platform and the JDK.
- **Other features**: Several other high-level features include:
    - o A default set of root **Certification Authority** (**CA**) certificates in the JDK.
    - o Enabling heap allocation on alternative memory devices specified by the user.
    - o Using Graal, the Java-based JIT compiler, as an experimental JIT compiler on the Linux/x64 platform.
    - o Enhanced `java.util.Locale` and related APIs to implement additional Unicode extensions.

1.7 Download and install JDK 8 and JDK 10

In order to understand the difference between the old JAR based and new module based JDK, download and install JDK 8 and JDK 10 for Windows from Oracle's official download page.

JDK 8 downloads page is shown in the below screenshot:

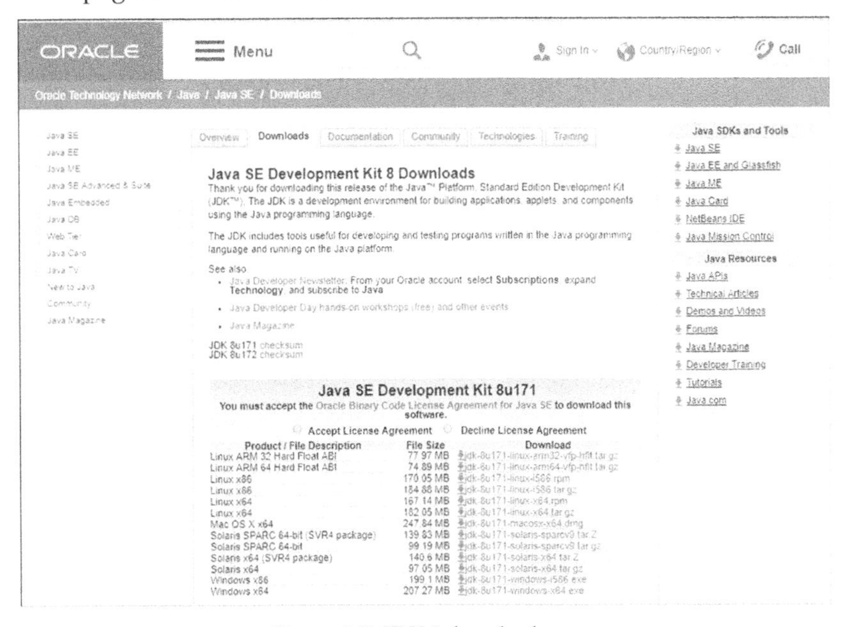

Figure 1.7: JDK 8 download page

Download the JDK 8 installer for Windows x64 and install JDK 8 by double-clicking the downloaded installer executable. Steps to download and install JDK 10 are as under:

1. Open the JDK 10 **Downloads** page. JDK 10 download page is shown in the screenshot below:

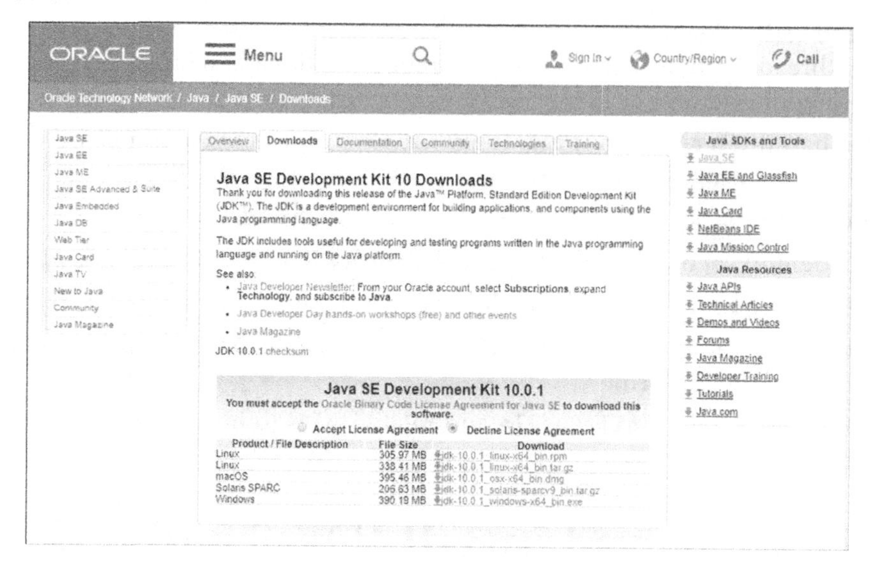

Figure 1.8: JDK 10 download page

2. Select the **Accept License Agreement** radio button.
3. Download the JDK 10 installer executable for Windows 64-bit OS as shown in the below screenshot:

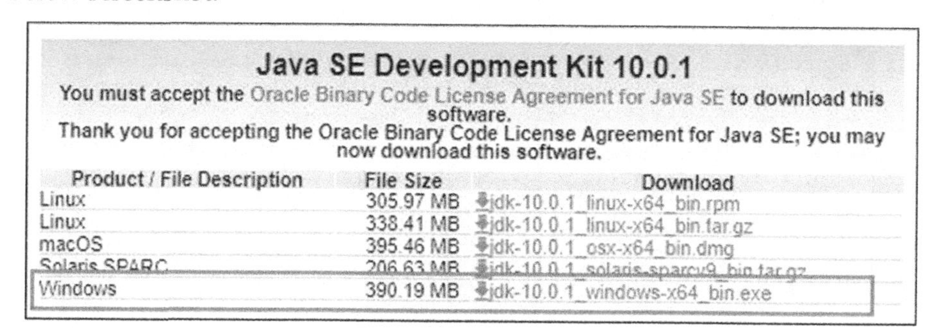

Product / File Description	File Size	Download
Linux	305.97 MB	jdk-10.0.1_linux-x64_bin.rpm
Linux	338.41 MB	jdk-10.0.1_linux-x64_bin.tar.gz
macOS	395.46 MB	jdk-10.0.1_osx-x64_bin.dmg
Solaris SPARC	206.63 MB	jdk-10.0.1_solaris-sparcv9_bin.tar.gz
Windows	390.19 MB	jdk-10.0.1_windows-x64_bin.exe

Figure 1.9: JDK 10 download link

4. Once downloaded, double-click the installer executable to begin the installation and follow the instructions of the installation wizard:

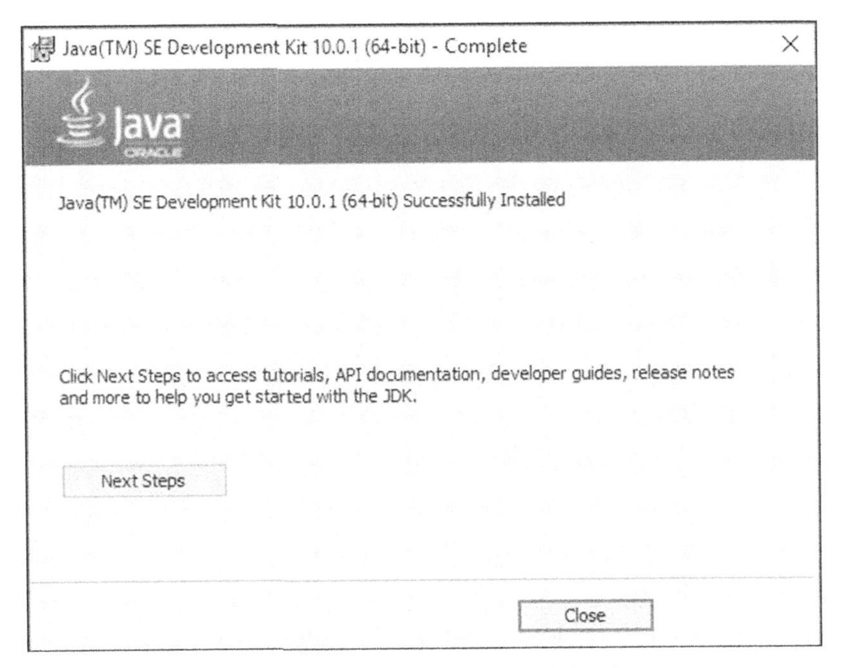

Figure 1.10: JDK 10 Installation Wizard

5. Click **Next** to begin the installation process.

   By default, the installer installs all the development tools, source code, and the JRE in the **`C:\Program Files\Java directory.`**

   The following screenshot shows the Java directory with JDK 8 and JDK 10 installation folders along with the respective JRE folders:

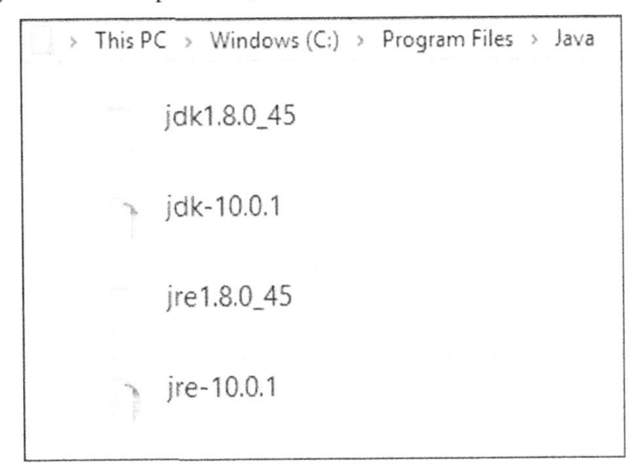

Figure 1.11: JDK 8 and JDK 10 installation folders

Following screenshot shows the subfolders of JDK 8 and JDK 10 directories:

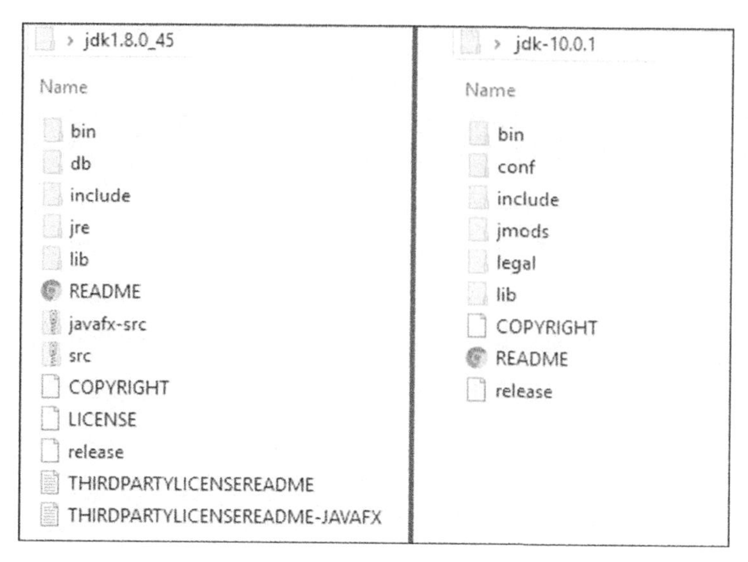

***Figure 1.12**: JDK 8 and JDK 10 installation folder structure*

Following table provides a brief description of the common directories of a typical JDK 8 installation:

Directory	Contents	Description
`bin`	**Development tools**	It contains the tools and utilities required to develop, execute, test, debug, and document Java applications.
`db`	**Java DB**	It contains Oracle's distribution of the Apache Derby relational database.
`include`	**C header files**	It contains header files that support native-code programming in C language with **Java Native Interface** (**JNI**) and the JVM tool interface.
`jre`	**Runtime Environment**	Contains an implementation of the **Java Runtime Environment** (**JRE**) used by the JDK. It includes class libraries, other files to support the execution of Java programs, and a **Java Virtual Machine** (**JVM**).
`lib`	**Additional libraries**	Contains additional class libraries and support files necessary for the working of development tools.
`Javafx-src.zip`	**JavaFX tools**	It contains various tools that are specific to JavaFX programming.
`src.zip`	**Source code**	It contains the source files for Java core API classes such as `java.*`, `javax.*`, and so on. These files are only for informational purposes to learn Java and cannot be used to rebuild the class libraries.

***Table 1.2:** Contents of JDK 8 installation directory*

Following table provides a brief description of the common directories of a typical JDK 10 installation:

Directory	Contents	Description
`bin`	**Executables**	It contains an implementation of the JRE used by the JDK. It includes class libraries, other files to support the execution of Java programs, and a JVM. It also contains the tools and utilities required to develop, execute, test, debug, and document Java applications.
`conf`	**Configuration files**	These files contain user-configurable options and can be edited to configure security algorithms, modify access permissions, and set the **Java Cryptography Extension** (**JCE**) policy files to limit the cryptographic strength of the JDK.
`include`	**C header files**	It contains header files that support native-code programming in C language with JNI and the JVM Debugger Interface.
`jmods`	**Compiled Java modules**	It contains the compiled Java modules to be used by jlink for creating custom runtimes.
`legal`	**Copyright and license files**	It contains the license and copyright files for each module as well as the third-party notices in the form of `.md` (markdown) files.
`lib`	**Additional libraries**	It contains additional class libraries and support files necessary for the functioning of the JDK. These cannot be used externally.

Table 1.3: *Contents of JDK 10 installation directory*

1.8 Setting up the path for JDK

To work with JDK, the path of the **`bin`** folder must be set in the system environment variable named **`PATH`**. The **`PATH`** variable is set to point to the executables (**`javac.exe`** and **`java.exe`**) so that these commands can be executed from any directory without having to specify the full path.

To set the **`PATH`** variable from the command prompt window, type the below command:

```
C:\>set path=<drivename>:\<installation_folder>\bin
```

For example:

```
C:\>set path=C:\Program Files\Java\jdk1.8.0_45\bin
```

Similarly, set the path for the JDK 10 version's **`bin`** directory.

To set the **`PATH`** variable permanently on the system (Windows 10), follow the steps given below:

Right-click **This PC** | **Properties** | **Advanced System Settings** | **Advanced Tab** | **Click Environment Variables:**

Figure 1.13: Set the PATH environmental variable

1. In the **System variables** section, select the **PATH** variable and click the **Edit** button to enter the JDK installation folder path.
2. Click **New** to enter a new path and type the below path to the **bin** folder:
3. **C:\Program Files\Java\jdk1.8.0_45\bin**
4. Click OK to save the changes.

Similarly, the path for the JDK 10 version's **bin** folder can also be set permanently in the environment variable **PATH**.

1.9 Java application development

The popularity of Java is on the rise even after more than two decades. Java is still the chosen language for the application of different domains and continues to advance at an accelerated pace. Java language can be used to develop a variety of applications, including:

- Console-based and window-based desktop applications
- Web applications with Web components such as Servlets, **Java Server Pages** (**JSP**), **Java Server Faces** (**JSF**), and so on. that are executed in a browser.
- Enterprise applications with components such as **Enterprise JavaBeans** (**EJB**) are used for distributed computing.
- Web servers and application servers to host and deploy web and enterprise applications.
- Apps that are created for small devices such as mobile phones.
- Embedded software such as tiny chips, SIM cards, and so on. for electronic devices.
- Scientific applications involving scientific calculations and mathematical operations. For example, applications like **`MATLAB`** use Java for interacting user interface as well as part of the core system.

The applications can be created by using a simple text editor, for example, Notepad or by using an **Integrated Development Environment** (**IDE**) that provides the necessary tools such as editor, compiler, debugger, and so on. for development of Java applications. The popular IDEs include NetBeans, Eclipse, IntelliJ, and Android Studio for mobile apps, and so on.

1.10 Structure of a Java program

Since Java is an object-oriented programming language, the development of an application in Java begins with the creation of a class. The definition of a class is saved in a file with the same name as the class name and a **`.java`** extension. The structure and elements of a class are as shown below:

```
package <package-name>;

import <package-name>;

public class <class-name>{

//variable declarations

// constructor method(s)

// other method definitions

}
```

Figure 1.14: *Structure of a java program*

The words depicted in bold font are keywords of Java language with a predefined meaning in the language. The keywords cannot be used for names of variables, methods, classes, or as any other identifier:

- **The package statement:** A package in Java is similar to a namespace where classes of similar functionalities are saved. The **`package`** keyword is used to indicate that the succeeding text is the name of a package to which the class belongs. In Java, a class is always within a package. If no package is specified, the class belongs to the default package. Examples of built-in packages are **`java.swing`**, **`java.io`**, and so on. The classes related to GUI are stored in the **java.swing** package and those related to input/output functionality are stored in **java.io** package and so on.

- **The import statement:** The import statement is used to include external packages and classes in a Java class. In order to use classes from another package, they must be imported by using the **import** keyword. However, some packages are included by default in a Java program, namely, **java.lang**. These need not be explicitly imported for using the classes of these packages. Further, it is not required to import classes that are in the same package or classes that are used with the fully qualified name of their package. For example, **java.io.File f1 = new java.io.File("myfile");**
- **The class declaration statement**: A Java class declaration is identified with the **class** keyword followed by the name of the class. The use of **public** keyword indicates the visibility of the class to other classes within and outside a package.
- **Variables**: Variables in a Java program represent the attributes of the entity and are also referred to as fields. Instance variables are those for which instance or object of a class has its own copy of that variable.
- **Methods**: Methods in a Java program represent the behavior or functions to be performed by an object on the data. Instance methods can be invoked by creating an object of a class.
- **Constructors**: Constructors in a Java program are special methods with the same name as the name of the class. They are invoked during the creation of an object and are generally used to initialize the data members of a class.

To create a Java program, any text editor such as Notepad can be used. The basic steps to create the Java program are:

1. Create a class and save it with the **.java** extension.
2. Compile the **.java** file.
3. Build and execute the Java program.

The code below demonstrates a simple **Hello World** program in Java. It is written in the Notepad text editor of Windows OS:

```
public class Hello {

  public static void main(String[] args) {

    System.out.println("Hello World!");

  }

}
```

The class declaration is composed of an access modifier, **class** keyword and name of the class followed by the curly braces, **{ }**. Java is a tightly encapsulated language; hence, nothing can be placed outside the class. In the example, the name of the class is **Hello**. Within the class is the **main()** method with is the entry point of the application, that is, execution of every Java program begins by invoking the **main()** method.

Syntax:

```
public static void main(String[] args) {
  // code statements
}
```

Below is a brief description of the important keywords in the program:

- `public`: Enables the JVM to access the `main()` method.
- `static`: Allows accessing a method of a class without creating an instance of the class.
- `void:` Indicates the data type of the value returned by the `main()` method. Data type void means the method will not return any value.
- `args`: A `String` array that stores the arguments passed at the command line.

Note: The String class is a built-in Java class and data type that allows a variable to store a group of characters.

Within the `main()` method, the actual functionality of the program is specified by using the `System.out.println()` statement.

The `println()` method takes a `String` argument and displays it on the console. System class is a predefined class in Java that allows access to system resources such as a console. The keyword `out` represents the output stream connected to the console.

Save the file as `Hello.java`. To save the `Hello.java` program, click **File | Save As** in Notepad and enter `Hello.java` in the **File name** box. The quotation marks avoid saving the file with extension `HelloWorld.java.txt.`

1.11 Java code compilation and execution

A Java program file with the `.java` extension is converted into a bytecode file with the `.class` extension by using the javac compiler. The resulting `.class` file can then be executed on any platform that has its appropriate JVM as shown in the image below:

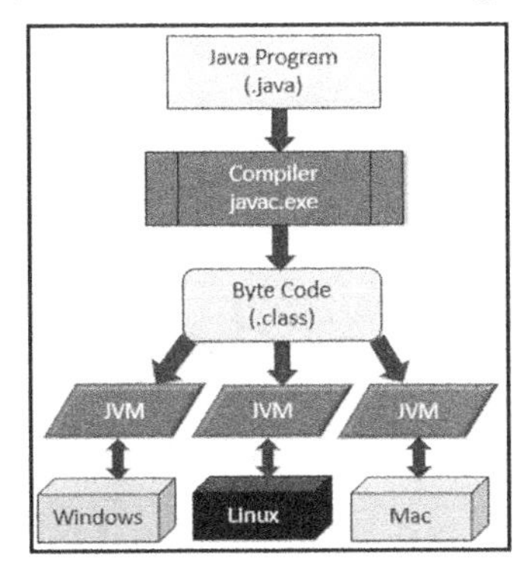

Figure 1.15: *Java code compilation*

The following figure shows the task of the JRE during code execution:

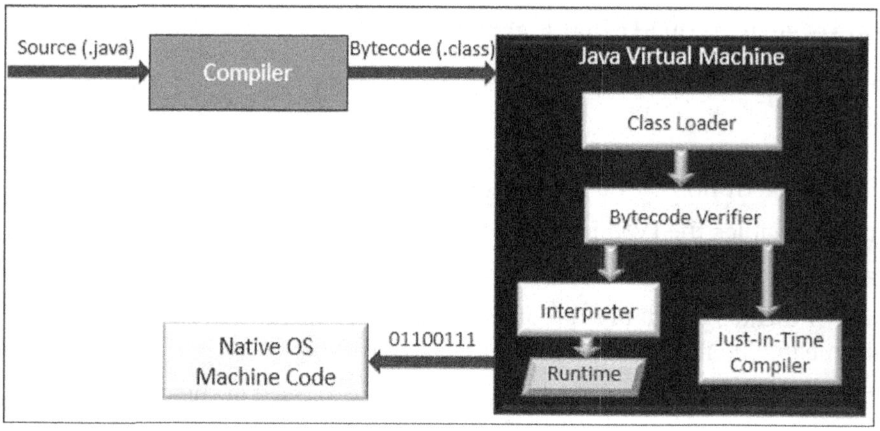

Figure 1.16: Java code execution

The `.class` file generated by the compiler is not dependent on the hardware or software platform of the target system. The `.class` file that contains the main class is passed to the JVM. Within the JVM, the file passes through certain components which are:

- **Class loader**: Once the main class is loaded in the memory by the JVM, the other classes referenced in the program are loaded through the class loader.
- **Bytecode verifier**: The bytecode of the loaded class is checked by the bytecode verifier for the presence of any damaged instructions. The checks performed by the bytecode verifier are:
  - Initialization of variables before usage.
  - Method calls and types of object references should match.
  - There is no violation of the rules for accessing private data and methods.
  - Access to a local variable is within the runtime stack.
  - There should not be any run-time stack overflow.

If any of the above checks fail, the verifier does not allow the class to be loaded. Next, the bytecode is executed by the interpreter.

- **Just-In-Time (JIT) Compiler:** Java 2.0 onwards, the JIT compiler was included at runtime to enhance the speed of execution. The job of the JIT compiler is to convert the bytecode to native code or platform-specific code to increase the performance.

1.12 Creating and executing a Java program using JDK 8

In JDK 8 and earlier versions, compile the source file **`Hello.java`** by using the built-in **`javac.exe`** compiler as shown in the screenshot below:

```
Microsoft Windows [Version 10.0.17134.112]
(c) 2018 Microsoft Corporation. All rights reserved.

C:\Users\Admin3>set path="C:\Program Files\Java\jdk1.8.0_45\bin"

C:\Users\Admin3>F:

F:\>cd pkg1

F:\pkg1>javac Hello.java

F:\pkg1>
```

Figure 1.17: Compiling Java code with the javac compiler

First, move to the folder where the **Hello.java** file is saved and then execute the **javac** command. The command will generate a file named **Hello.class** in the current directory which will be used for execution by the runtime.

Note: The path is set to JDK 8 version's bin folder.

Use the **dir** command on the current directory to view the **.class** file generated by the **javac** command as shown below:

```
F:\pkg1>dir
 Volume in drive F is New Volume
 Volume Serial Number is 30A1-253D

 Directory of F:\pkg1

14-06-2018  17:40    <DIR>          .
14-06-2018  17:40    <DIR>          ..
14-06-2018  17:40               416 Hello.class
14-06-2018  17:39               120 Hello.java
               2 File(s)            536 bytes
               2 Dir(s)  368,896,966,656 bytes free
```

Figure 1.18: Bytecode Hello.class generated

The following table lists some of the options that can be used with the **javac** command:

Option	Description
-classpath	Indicates the location for importing classes and overrides the setting of the `CLASSPATH` environment variable.
-d	Used to specify the destination directory for the class files generated by the javac compiler. For example, `javac -d F:\ Hello.java` will generate and save the `Hello.class` file in the `F:\` drive.
-g	Used to prints the entire debugging information instead of the default line number and file name.

Option	Description
`-verbose`	Used to display messages in real time while the class is being compiled.
`-version`	Displays version information.
`sourcepath`	Indicates the location of the input source file.
`-help`	Displays the list of standard options with usage.

***Table 1.4:** Options for the javac command*

The **`.class`** files allow for *write once, run anywhere* to be possible for Java codes. Now use the Java interpreter program **`java.exe`** to interpret and convert the bytecode to machine code and execute the program. The **`java`** command takes the class file name as an argument for execution.

The following screenshot shows the execution of the **`Hello.class`** file by using the **`java`** command:

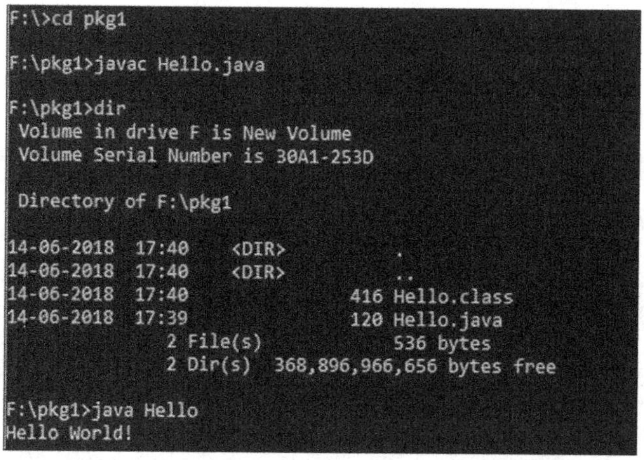

```
F:\>cd pkg1

F:\pkg1>javac Hello.java

F:\pkg1>dir
 Volume in drive F is New Volume
 Volume Serial Number is 30A1-253D

 Directory of F:\pkg1

14-06-2018  17:40    <DIR>          .
14-06-2018  17:40    <DIR>          ..
14-06-2018  17:40               416 Hello.class
14-06-2018  17:39               120 Hello.java
               2 File(s)            536 bytes
               2 Dir(s)  368,896,966,656 bytes free

F:\pkg1>java Hello
Hello World!
```

***Figure 1.19:** Java code executed with the java command*

The following table lists some of the options available with the **`java`** command:

Options	Description
`classpath`	Indicates the location for importing classes and overrides the setting of the `CLASSPATH` environment variable
`-v or -verbose`	Used to display additional information about each loaded class and each compiled source file
`-version`	Displays version information and exits
`-jar`	Uses the name of a JAR file instead of a class file
`-help`	Displays help information and exits
`-X`	Displays non-standard options information and exits

***Table 1.5:** Options for the java command*

1.13 Creating and executing a Java program using JDK 10

Until JDK 8, developers generally used the directory structure **`src/main/java`** for the source directory. For example, the main class file **`Hello.java`** would typically be present in a package **`com.pkg1.app`** and the overall path would be **`src/main/java/com/pkg1/app/Hello.java.`** This has been the traditional mode of organizing code so far. However, with the new JPMS feature from Java SE 9 onwards, the mode of structuring and writing code has been modified.

A Java 9 module is a self-describing collection of code and data. It can contain several packages that in turn may have one or more classes, interfaces, and so on. The module may also contain resource files, property files, and so on. To create a complete application, a collection of such modules need to be integrated. Each module is a building block with a larger structure. In short, instead of creating one huge Java project, now it is possible to create multiple modular functional units that can be integrated to form an application and also can be reused for other applications.

To create and execute a Java program in JDK 10, perform the following steps:

1. Create a module with a unique name, for example, **`moduleone.`**
2. Create a root folder for the module – this needs to be done for each module. The module root folder should have the same name as the module. So, the **`root`** folder for the module in this case would be **`moduleone.`**
3. Add the module code inside the module root folder. Begin with packages from the module root folder onward. For example, create a package hierarchy **`mypkg\util`** inside the **`module`** folder **`moduleone`** and add a class **`Hello.java`** in the **`com.mypkg.util`** package. The folder structure, in this case, is shown below:

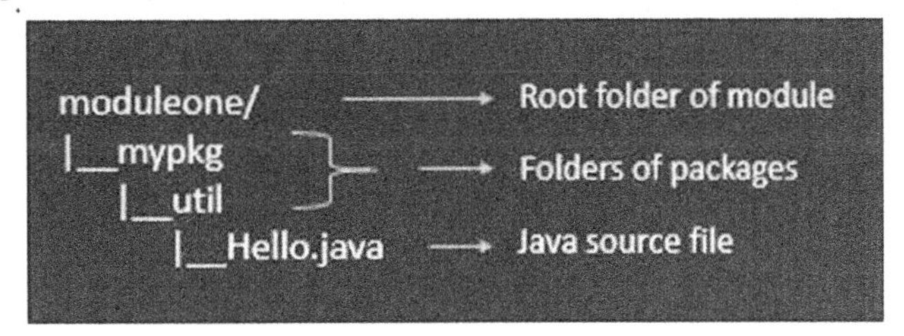

Figure 1.20: *Modular structure of Java application*

Until JDK 8, the packages were directly stored under the source folder whereas JDK 9 onwards, the packages are now stored under a module root folder. From the module root folder, the structure is again the same as earlier versions.

Steps for Java SE 8 and earlier versions are as follows:

1. Create one or more source folders.
2. In a source folder, create package folders to match the package names.
3. Place the **`.java`** source files in the appropriate package folders.

Steps for Java SE 9 onwards are as follows:

1. Create one or more source folders.
2. In each source folder, create a module folder for each module.
3. In the module folders, create package folders to match the package names.
4. Place the **.java** source files in the appropriate package folders.

Create a module descriptor file that has metadata about the module, that it, its exports, and dependencies. Save the file directly in the module root folder with the name **module-info.java.** For example, the module descriptor for the module **moduleone** is shown below:

```
module moduleone {

  // module exports and dependencies

}
```

The file begins with the keyword **module** which indicates that the succeeding text is the name of the module. The module name should be the same as the name of the module root folder. Within the curly braces, the module dependencies and exports are specified.

The final folder structure with the module descriptor is shown below:

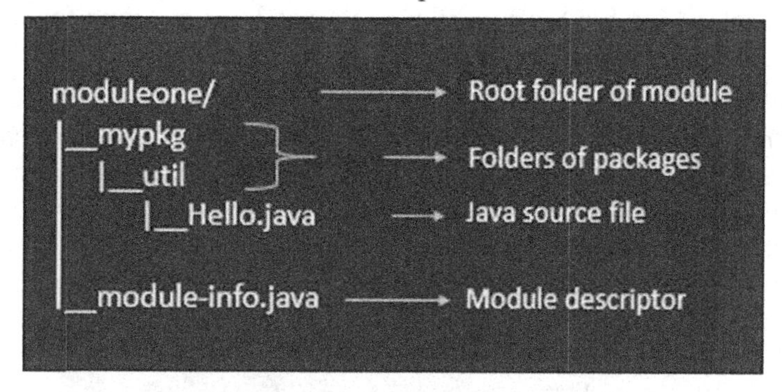

Figure 1.21: *Module descriptor of a Java module*

Note that the module descriptor file is a **.java** file but it does not follow the class naming conventions of Java language. That is, the use of hyphen (-) character is not allowed for a Java type name. Also, the name of the **.java** file should match the name of the public type declared in the file, which is not observed with the module descriptor name. This is similar to the **package-info.java** file used in Java since Java 1.5, though not so widely used. These files have been given invalid Java type names deliberately to indicate their special purpose and distinguish them from the other Java files in the application.

Below is the code for the **Hello.java** source file and the **module-info.java** module descriptor file:

```
//Hello.java

package mypkg.util;
```

```
public class Hello {
  public static void main(String[] args) {
    System.out.println("Hello World!");
  }
}
// module-info.java
module moduleone {
}
```

The following screenshot shows the compilation and execution of the **Hello.java** file using JDK 10:

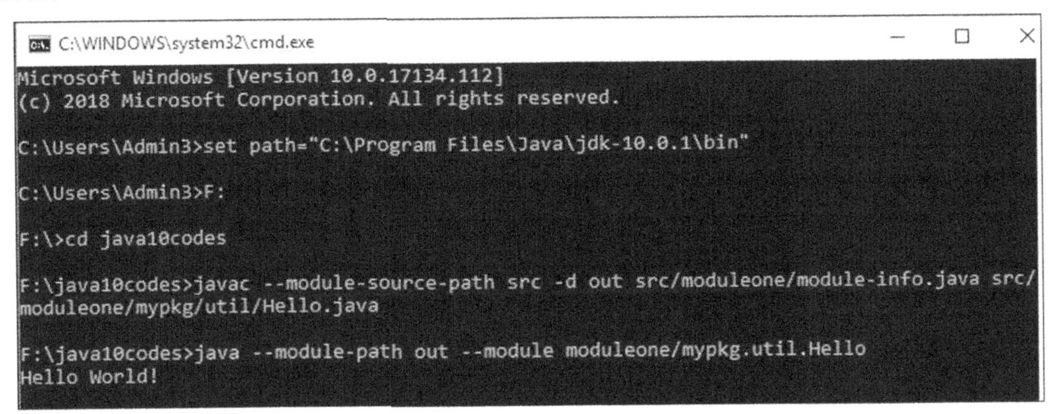

Figure 1.22: Compiling and executing Java code with JDK 10

Note: The module descriptor module-info.java is mandatory for every module. If the file is not available during compilation, then the code will not compile and we will throw error. error: module moduleone not found in module source path.

The module is compiled by using the **javac** command with the **--module-source-path** option which indicates that the modules are present in the **src** folder. The generated **.class** file for **Hello.java** source file will be saved in the **out** folder as mentioned in the **-d** option. The last two paths indicate the location of the module descriptor and the source file to be compiled.

Listed below are the different ways of compiling a module by using the javac command.

```
javac --module-source-path src -d out -m moduleone
javac --module-source-path src -d out --module moduleone
javac --module-source-path src -d out src/moduleone/module-info.java src/moduleone/mypkg/util/Hello.java
javac --module-source-path src -d out F:/java10codes/src/moduleone/module-info.java F:/java10codes/src/moduleone/mypkg/util/Hello.java
```

Next, the java command is used to run the **.class** file **--module-path** option indicating that the compiled module is present in the **out** folder. The **--module** option points to the location of the **Hello.class** file. Finally, the **.class** file is executed and the output **Hello World!** is displayed on the console.

Listed below are the different ways of executing a module by using the **java** command:

- **java --module-path out --add-modules moduleone mypkg.util.Hello**
- **java --module-path out -m moduleone/mypkg.util.Hello**
- **java --module-path out --module moduleone/mypkg.util.Hello**

Following screenshot shows the folder hierarchy of the **src** and **out** folders:

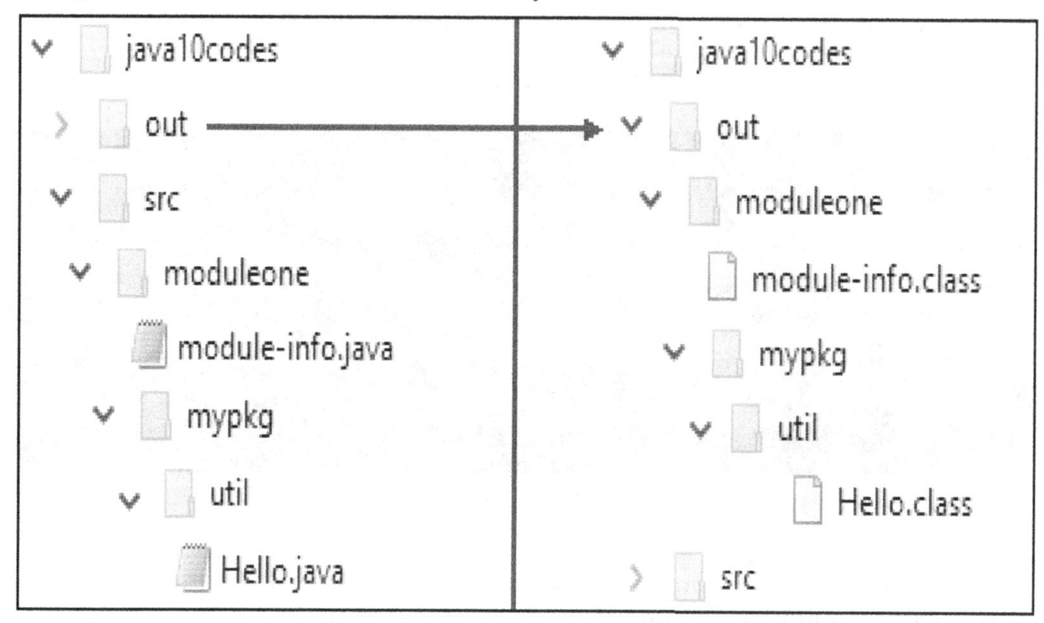

***Figure 1.23:** Source and output folders of a modular Java application*

With the command line, all tasks for project creation, compilation, and execution are done manually which can be time-consuming and prone to errors. To avoid this, JDK 8 and JDK 10 projects can also be created in IDEs like NetBeans, Eclipse, and so on. that have support for the appropriate JDK version.

1.14 Creating and executing a Java 8 project in NetBeans

To create a Java 8 project, perform the following steps:

1. Download and install **NetBeans 8.1** or earlier that has support for JDK 8 from NetBeans official site **https://netbeans.org/downloads/**. Please refer to the following figure:

Figure 1.24: NetBeans IDE 8.1 download page

2. Download the full bundle and install it as per the instructions from the wizard. Ensure to select the correct path of JDK 1.8 during installation.
3. Once installed, start NetBeans 8.1 and click **File | New Project** as shown below:

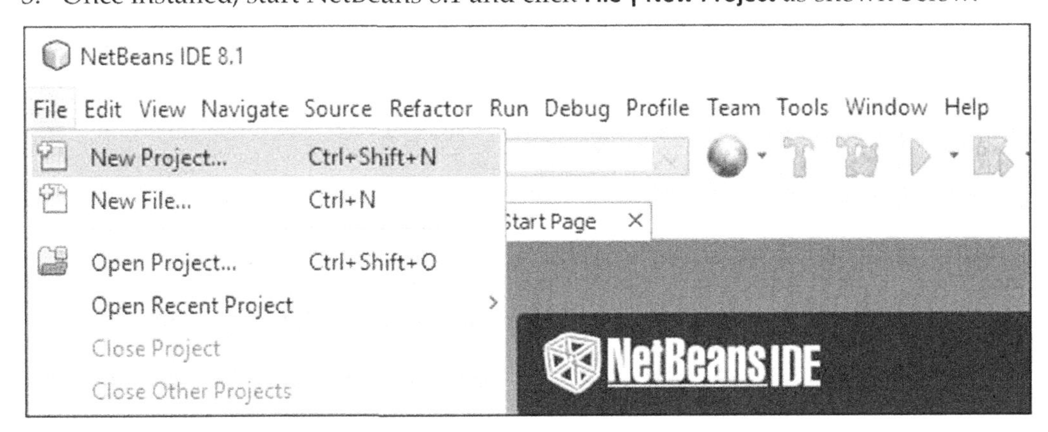

Figure 1.25: Creating a new project in NetBeans 8.1

It will open the **New Project** window.

4. From the **Categories** pane select Java and **Projects** pane select **Java Application** as shown below:

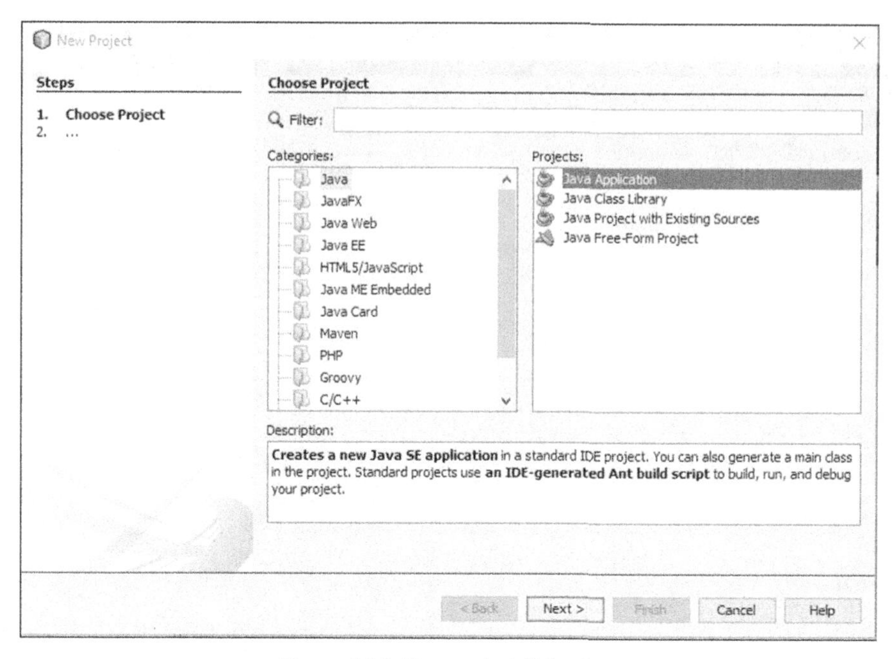

Figure 1.26: New project dialog box

5. Click **Next**.
6. In the **Name and Location** screen, specify the name of the project, the location where it must be saved, and a name for the main class file as shown below:

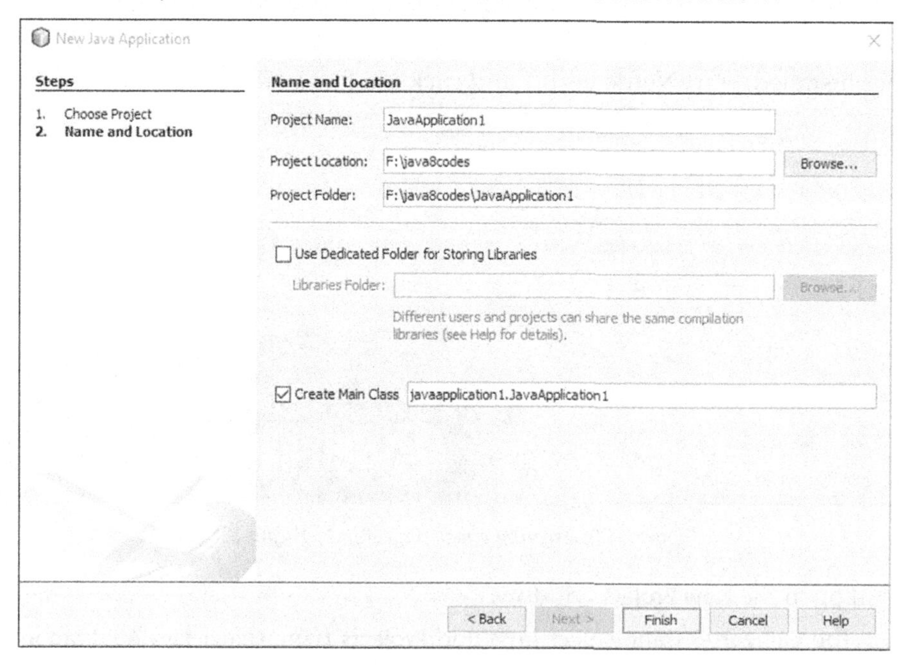

Figure 1.27: New Java application dialog box

By default, it takes the name of the application as the name of the package and main class file. It can be changed as per requirement.

7. Click **Finish.** This will create a new project with the folder hierarchy and **main** class file as shown below:

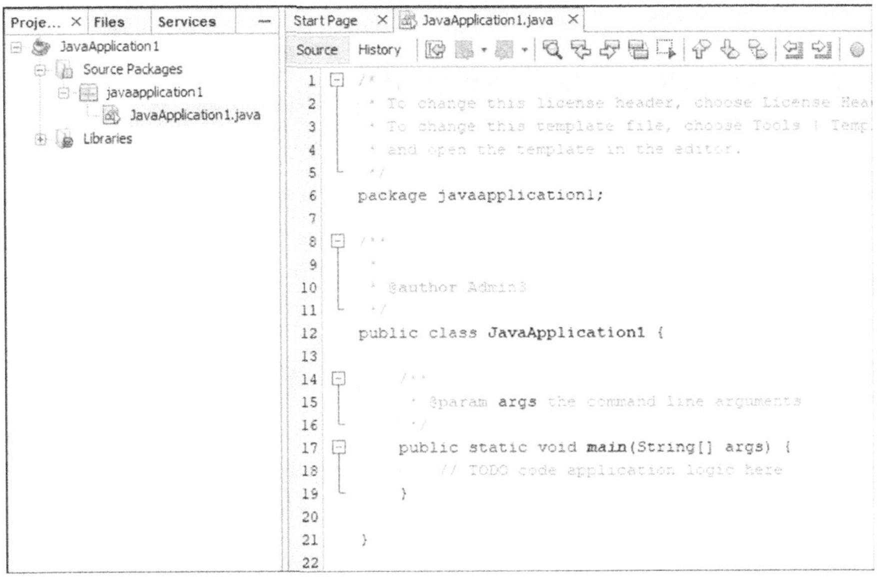

```
/*
 * To change this license header, choose License Hea
 * To change this template file, choose Tools | Temp
 * and open the template in the editor.
 */
package javaapplication1;

/**
 *
 * @author Admin3
 */
public class JavaApplication1 {

    /**
     * @param args the command line arguments
     */
    public static void main(String[] args) {
        // TODO code application logic here
    }

}
```

Figure 1.28: First application in Java SE 8

8. Enter a line of code in the `main()` method in the editor as shown below:

```
package javaapplication1;

/**
 *
 * @author Admin3
 */
public class JavaApplication1 {

    /**
     * @param args the command line arguments
     */
    public static void main(String[] args) {
        // TODO code application logic here
        System.out.println("Hello World!");
    }

}
```

Figure 1.29: Defining the main() method

9. Save the application.
10. Right-click the project and select **Run** as shown below:

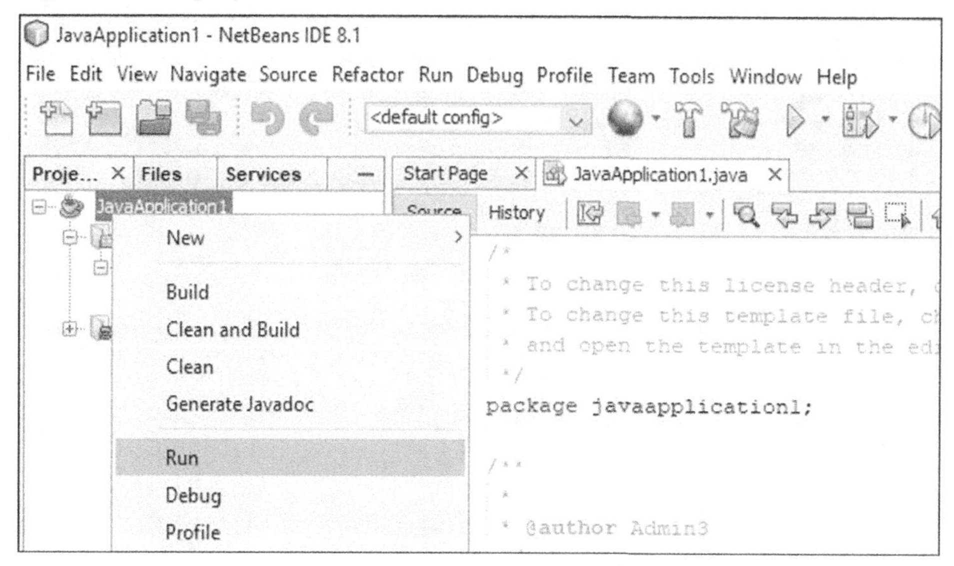

Figure 1.30: Executing the Java 8 Application

The program will be executed and output will be seen in the Output window as shown below:

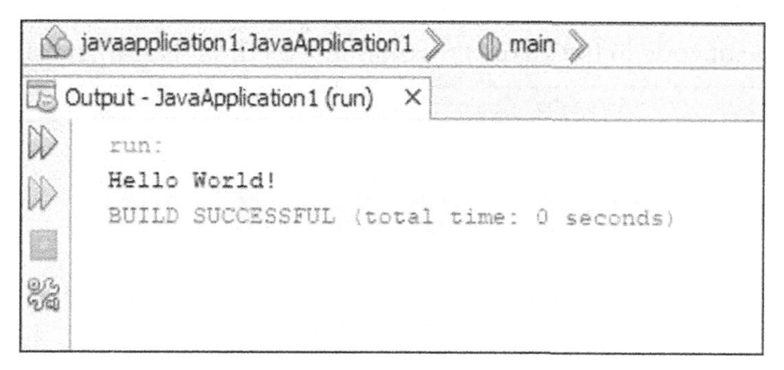

Figure 1.31: Output of the Java 8 application

Similarly, more packages and classes can be created in the **`Source Packages`** folder.

1.15 Creating and executing a Java 10 project in NetBeans

To create a Java project in JDK 10, perform the following steps:

1. Download and install the **NetBeans 8.2** version or higher that has support for JDK 10 from the official download page of **NetBeans**:

Figure 1.32: NetBeans IDE 8.2 download page

2. Once downloaded, install **`NetBeans 8.2`** on the system. Ensure that the location JDK 1.10 is properly selected during installation as shown below:

Figure 1.33: NetBeans 8.2 installation wizard

3. After installation, open the **NetBeans 8.2 IDE**
4. To create a new project, Click **File | New Project**.
5. If this does not work, it means the release version does not have support for JDK 10 yet.
6. In this case, download the early access copy from **http://bits.netbeans.org/download/trunk/nightly/latest/** as shown below:

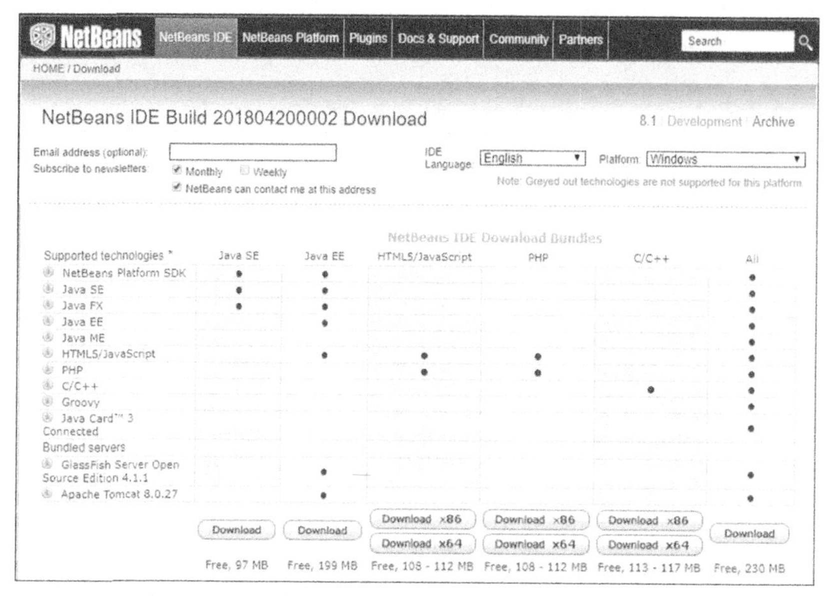

Figure 1.34: NetBeans IDE Build Download Page

7. Once the installer is downloaded, install **NetBeans** and it will be ready to use as shown below:

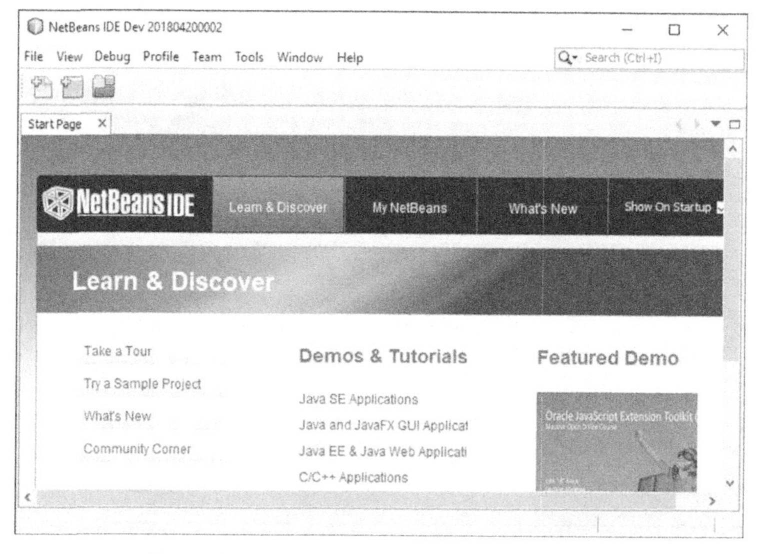

Figure 1.35: NetBeans IDE – Early access version

8. Click **File | New Project** to open the New Project wizard. It shows a new project type in the **Java** category called **Java Modular Project** as shown below:

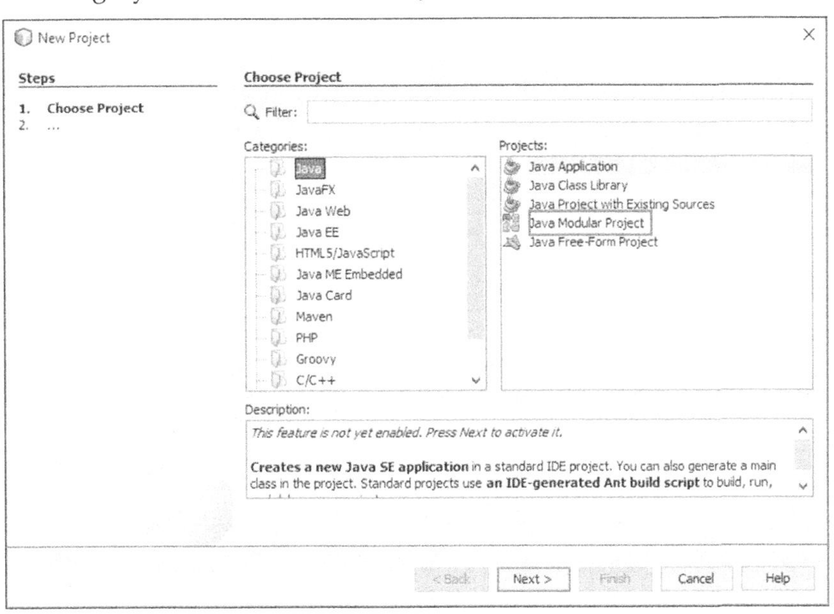

Figure 1.36: New project dialog box

9. Select **Java Modular Project** and click **Next.**
10. In the **Name and Location** screen, specify the project name and location as shown below:

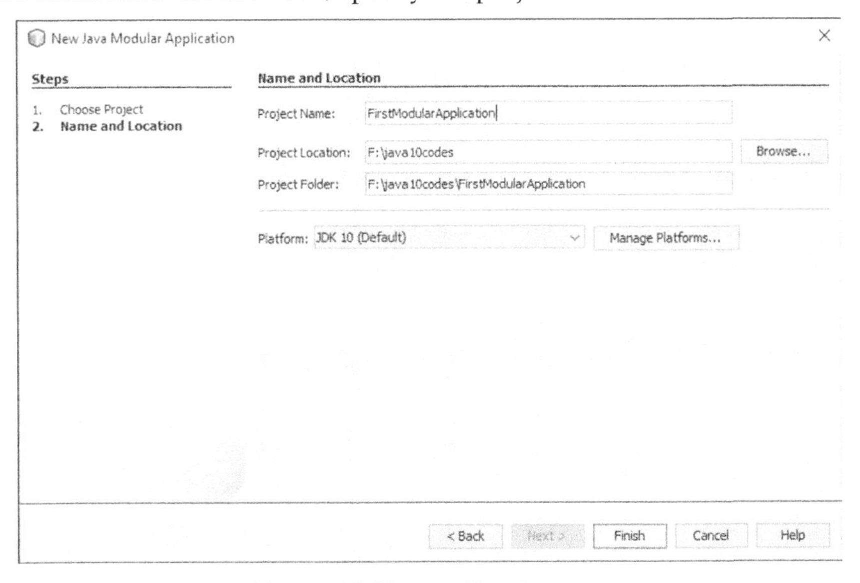

Figure 1.37: Name and location screen

Note that the JDK 10 is selected as the default platform for the modular project.

11. Click **Finish** and the project will be created as shown in the screenshot below:

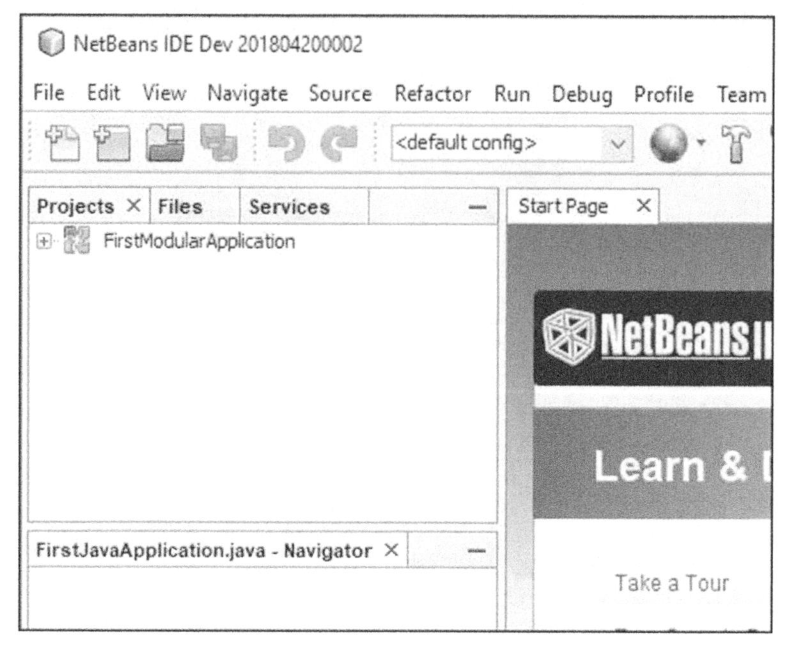

Figure 1.38: First modular Java project in NetBeans IDE

12. To create a new module in the project, right-click the project name in the **Projects** tab and select the **New | Module** as shown below:

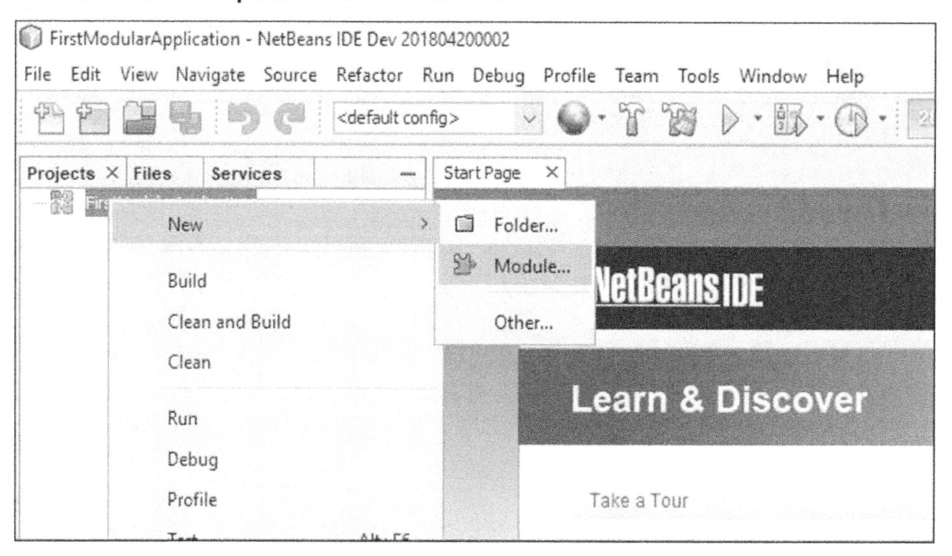

Figure 1.39: Creating a new module

13. In the **New Module** dialog box, specify the name of the module as shown below:

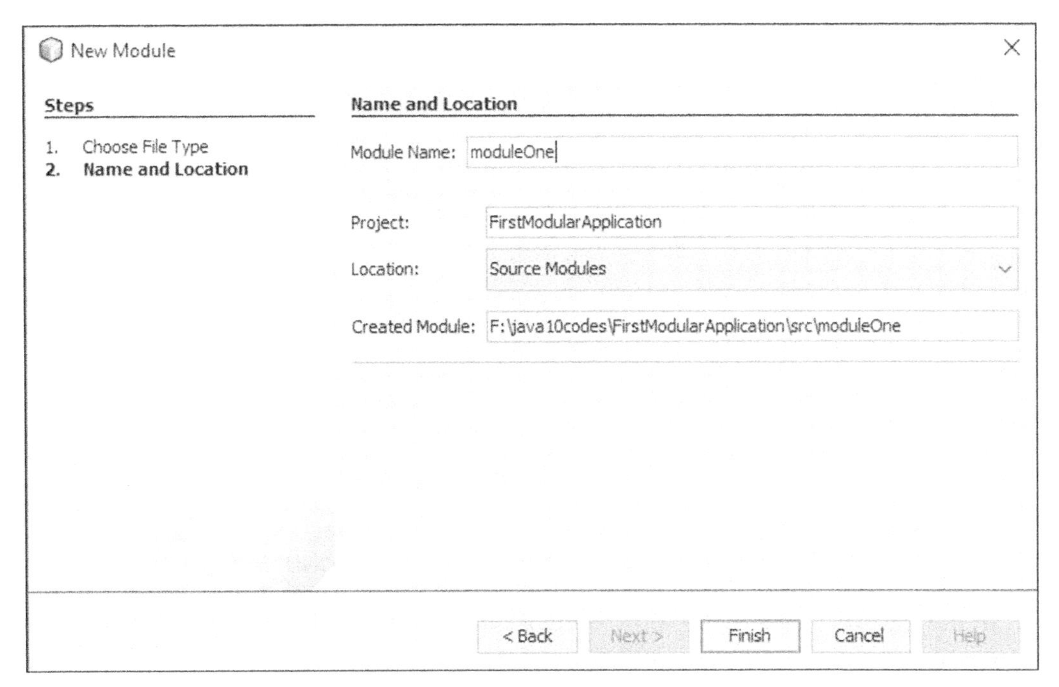

Figure 1.40: Specifying module name

14. Click **Finish**. The new module is added to the project along with the corresponding module descriptor file **`module-info.java`** as shown below:

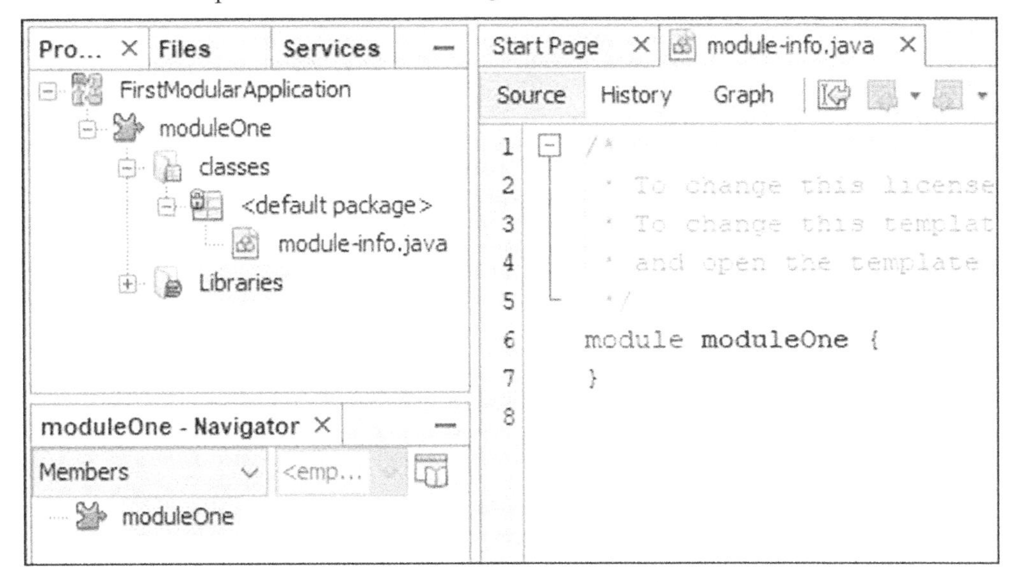

Figure 1.41: Module descriptor file

15. To create the main class file within the module, right-click **`moduleOne`** and select **New | Java Class** as shown below:

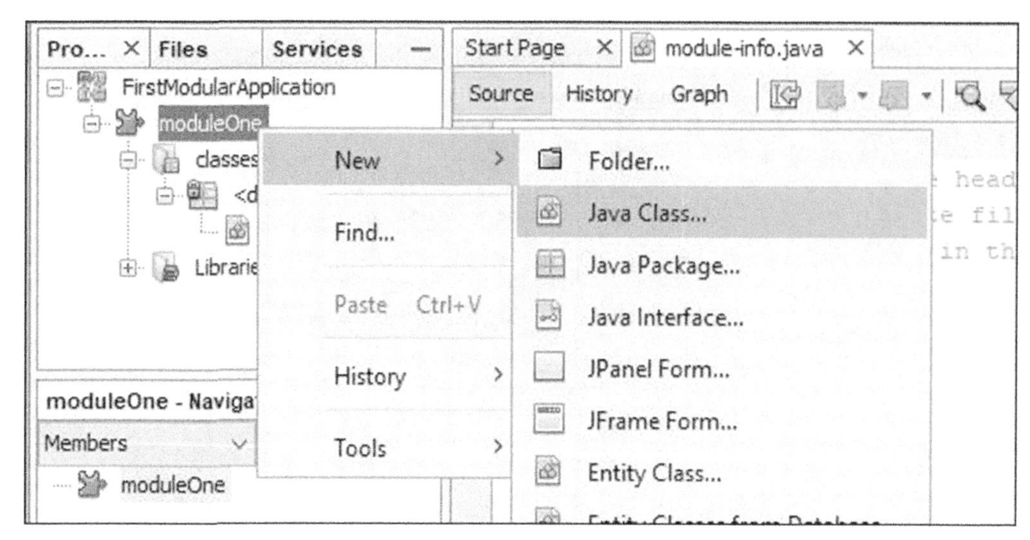

Figure 1.42: Creating a new Java class in the module

16. In the **New Java Class** dialog box, specify the class name and package name as shown below:

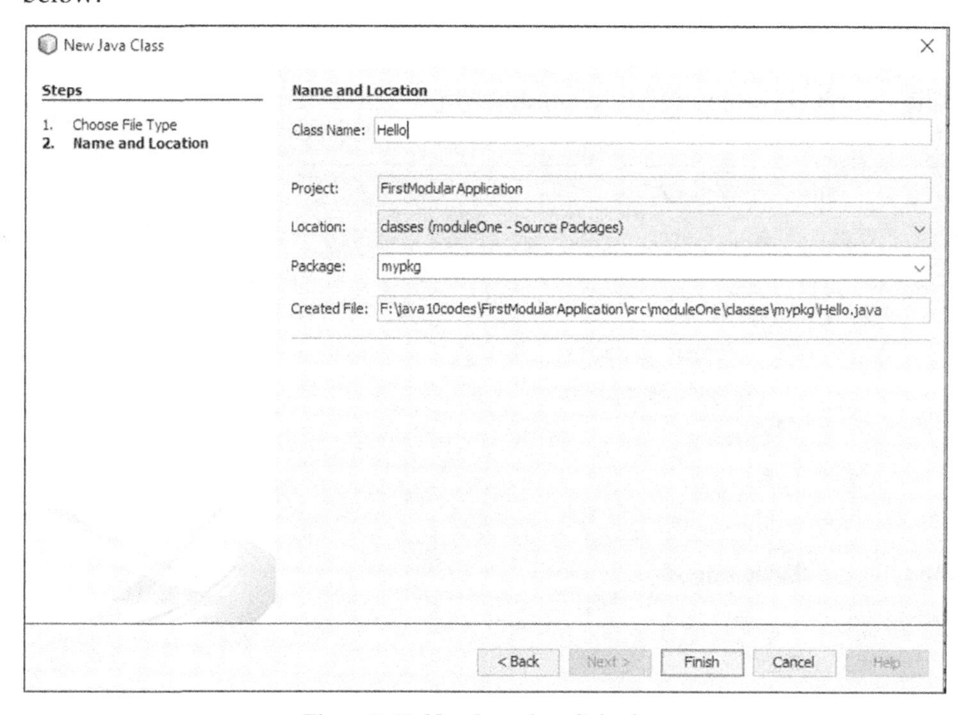

Figure 1.43: New Java class dialog box

17. Click **Finish**. The class will be created as shown below:

Figure 1.44: *Hello.java class*

18. Add the **main** method and a **print** statement within the class **Hello.java** as shown below:

```
package mypkg;

/**
 *
 * @author Admin3
 */
public class Hello {
    public static void main(String[] args) {
        System.out.println("Hello World!");
    }
}
```

Figure 1.45: *Defining the main() method*

19. To execute the application, right-click the project name and select **Run** as shown below:

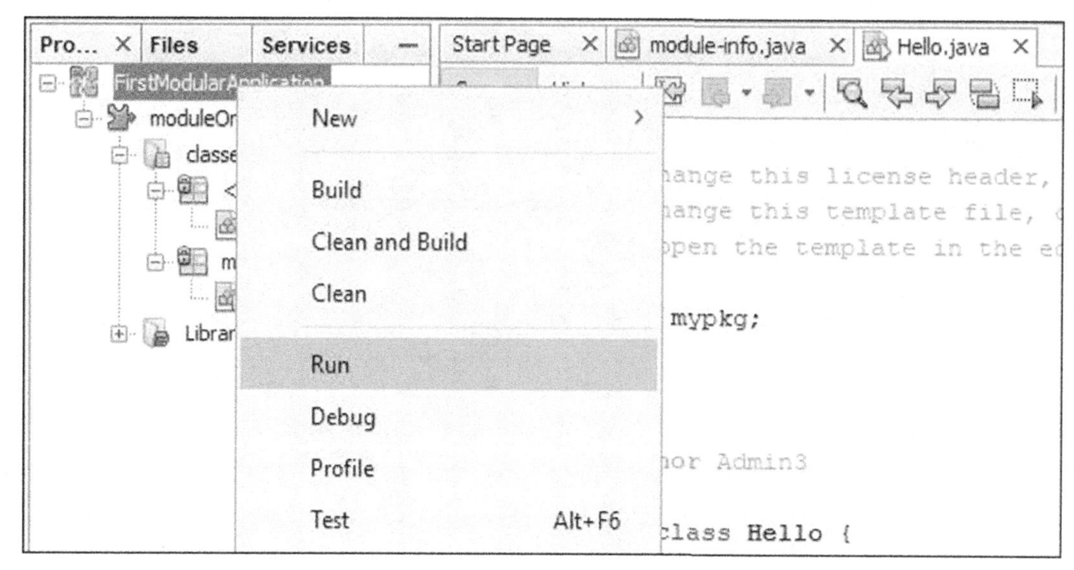

Figure 1.46: Executing the Java 10 application

The **Run Project** dialog box is displayed.

20. Select **mypkg.Hello** and click **OK** as shown below:

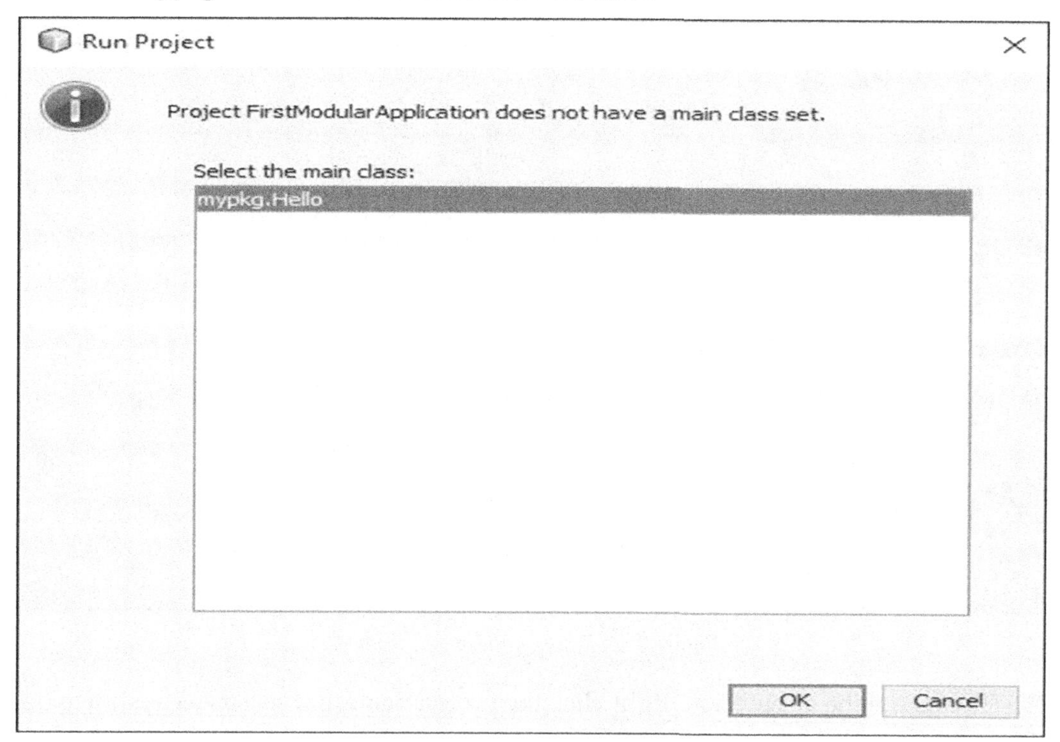

Figure 1.47: Run project dialog box

21. The code will be executed, and the output is displayed in the output window as shown below:

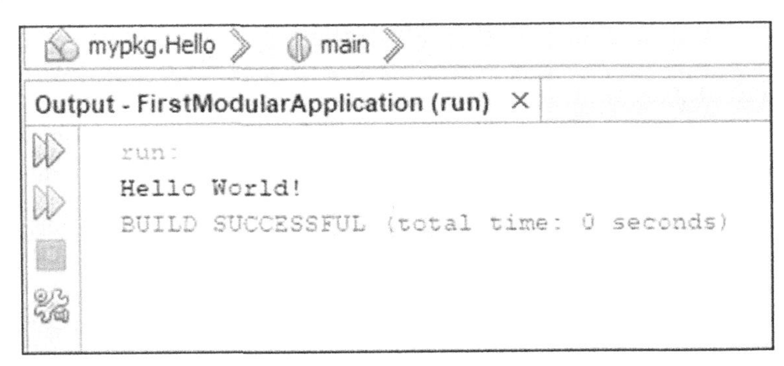

Figure 1.48: *Output of the Java 10 application*

This completes the execution of the first program in Java using JDK 10. This was a module with just one Java class, **`Hello.java`**.

Following screenshot shows the actual location of the source files **`Hello.java`**, **`module-info.java`** and the class files **`Hello.class`**, **`module-info.class`** in the NetBeans Modular Java project:

New Volume (F:) › java10codes › FirstModularApplication › src › moduleOne › classes › mypkg

Name

Hello

New Volume (F:) › java10codes › FirstModularApplication › src › moduleOne › classes

Name

mypkg

module-info

New Volume (F:) › java10codes › FirstModularApplication › build › modules › moduleOne › mypkg

Name

Hello.class

New Volume (F:) › java10codes › FirstModularApplication › build › modules › moduleOne

Name

mypkg

.netbeans_automatic_build

.netbeans_update_resources

module-info.class

Figure 1.49: *Location of source files of the application*

Similarly, more modules and classes can be added to the project as per requirement.

Conclusion

In this chapter you learnt that any real-world entity that has certain characteristics and behavior that can be used to describe it is considered as an object. Java is a popular object-oriented, platform-independent programming language. Java SE is the base for creating applications that are console or network-based applications mainly for desktop computers and the two important Java SE platform components are JRE and JDK.

The JDK has undergone several modifications over the years with some major enhancements and new features added with every new release. The most important feature of JDK 9 is the Jigsaw project which applies the new module system to break the JRE into reusable and interoperable. A Java 9 module is a self-describing collection of code and data. JDK 9 offers a new interactive **Read–Eval–Print Loop (REPL)** terminal called JShell. JDK 10 follows the modular model of JDK 9 and provides enhancements on the features and functionalities of JDK 9.

In the next chapter, you will learn about Java programming constructs.

Multiple choice questions

1. **__________ is programming concept in which the non-essential details of an entity are hidden from user view.**
    a. Encapsulation
    b. Polymorphism
    c. Abstraction
    d. Inheritance
2. **Which of the following is the most important feature of JDK 9?**
    a. JShell
    b. JPMS
    c. REPL
    d. HTTP/2
3. **Match the columns.**

	JDK 10 Installation folder		Content
a.	`bin`	1.	Compiled Java Modules
b.	`conf`	2.	Executables
c.	`include`	3.	Configuration files
d.	`jmods`	4.	C header Files

    a. a-2, b-3, c-4, d-1
    b. a-3, b-4, c-1, d-2

c. a-4, b-1, c-2, d-3

d. a-2, b-4, c-1, d-3

4. **Identify the correct format to compile a module in Java 10.**

   a. `javac --module-source src -d out -m moduleA`

   b. `javac --module-path src -d out -m moduleA`

   c. `javac --module-source-path src -d out --mod moduleA`

   d. `javac --module-source-path src -d out -m moduleA`

5. **Which command is used to execute a `.class` file in Java?**

   a. `javac`

   b. `java`

   c. `javah`

   d. `jmod`

Answers

1. c
2. b
3. a
4. d
5. b

Assignment

1. Research the new features of the latest/upcoming version of JDK.
2. Download and install JDK 10 and NetBeans IDE. Create a new Java Modular Project in NetBeans. Create a new module with the main class file and execute the Java program.

Join our book's Discord space

Join the book's Discord Workspace for Latest updates, Offers, Tech happenings around the world, New Release and Sessions with the Authors:

https://discord.bpbonline.com

CHAPTER 2
Java Programming Constructs

Introduction

This chapter introduces you to the different programming constructs of Java language, such as comments, variables, data types, and operators. It explains how to format output and use Scanner class for taking user input. Further, it introduces you to the different decision-making constructs, looping constructs, and branch statements used for manipulating and processing user input.

Structure

In this chapter, we will go through the following topics:

- Java comments
- Variables in Java
- Data types in Java
- Type casting
- Literals and escape sequences
- Constants and enumerations
- Operators in Java
- Operator precedence and associativity

- Formatting the output
- Scanner class for input
- Decision-making constructs
- Looping constructs
- Jump statements

Objectives

In this chapter you will learn to use comments, variables, constants, and enumeration. You will also work with data types and operators. Further, you will learn to use the different decision-making constructs, looping constructs, and branch statements.

2.1 Java comments

Comments are used to document a program for understanding the code or logic. It is ignored by the compiler and simply used to describe the operations of the program.

Java supports three types of comments which are explained in the following sections.

Single-line comments

A single-line comment is used to describe code in a single line.

Syntax:

```
// Comment text
```

Example:

```
//Defining the main method
public static void main(String args[]){
}
```

Single-line comments can be used in the following two ways:

- Beginning-of-line comment which is placed before the code
- End-of-line comment which is placed at the end of the code on the same line

Example:

```
//Defining the main method
public static void main(String args[]){
} // End of the main method
```

Multi-line comments

A multi-line comment is written over multiple lines. It begins with a `/*` symbol and ends with a `*/` symbol. Everything between the two symbols is ignored by the compiler.

Example:

```
/*
* The main method is the point of
* execution of a Java program
*/
public static void main(String args[]){
}
```

Javadoc comments

The Javadoc commenting style is generally used to document the classes, methods, and so on. of a program. Javadoc comments begin with `/**` and end with `*/` symbols. The comment can span across multiple lines and everything between the symbols is ignored by the compiler. The **`javadoc`** command is used to generate Javadoc comments.

Example:

```
/**
* This is the main method which is the point of execution.
* @param args Not used.
* @return Nothing.
*/
public static void main(String args[]){
}
```

Here, **`@param, @return`** are examples of built-in tags recognized by Javadoc comments.

2.2 Variables in Java

The most basic implementation of any program is to store and manipulate data. Java supports different types of data such as numbers, characters, boolean, and so on. To store these types of values, Java uses a variable which is a name given to a memory location where the data will be stored. A variable can have different data types based on the type of data that it stores. Java is strongly typed, therefore, during compilation, each variable is checked for the type that it stores. If a type mismatch is found, a compilation error is raised.

Syntax:

```
datatype variableName;
```

- **datatype:** Any type supported by Java.
- **variableName:** A valid variable name.

Example:

```
...
int userId;
String password;
...
```

Here, two variables have been declared namely, **userId** and **password**. The **userId** is of type integer and **password** is of type **String**. Based on the datatype, memory is allocated to the variables. It is mandatory to declare a variable before using it in code.

Variable names need to follow some naming conventions, which are:

- A variable name cannot be a Java keyword such as **static, void, public, int**, and so on.
- A variable name can have Unicode letters and digits, underscore (_), and the dollar sign (**$**).
- A variable name must begin with a letter, dollar sign (**$**), or underscore (_).
- A variable name is case sensitive; hence, number is not the same as Number
- A variable name with a single word should begin with lowercase, for example, password.
- A variable name with multiple words should have the first letter of each succeeding word capitalized, for example, **firstName**.

The following table lists some valid and invalid variable names as per Java naming conventions:

Valid	Invalid
firstName	total#score
_15_years	Integer
X3y5_e897	4years
$paid_amount	
$$_a	

Table 2.1: Valid and invalid variable names

Variables can be assigned values during declaration or after declaration as shown below:

```
// Declaring two variables of Integer type
int a,b;
```

```
// Initializing variables, a and b
a=20;
b=10;
// Declaring one variable and initializing two variables in // the same statement
int x = 4, y, z = 10;
// Declaring and initializing a variable
byte age = 20;
// Declaring and initializing multiple variables
// with the same value
int val1 = val2 = 10;
```

Types of variables

Java supports instance, static and local variables. Each one is explained as follows:

- Instance variables can be accessed by using an instance of a class. There exists a separate copy of the instance variable for each instance.
- Static variables do not require an instance to access them as these are class-level variables. The **static** keyword is used to declare a static variable and a common copy of the variable is shared by all instances.
- Local variables are declared inside blocks or methods and cannot be accessed outside of them.

Note: A block begins with '{' and ends with '}' curly braces symbol.

The following figure shows the use of instance and static variables:

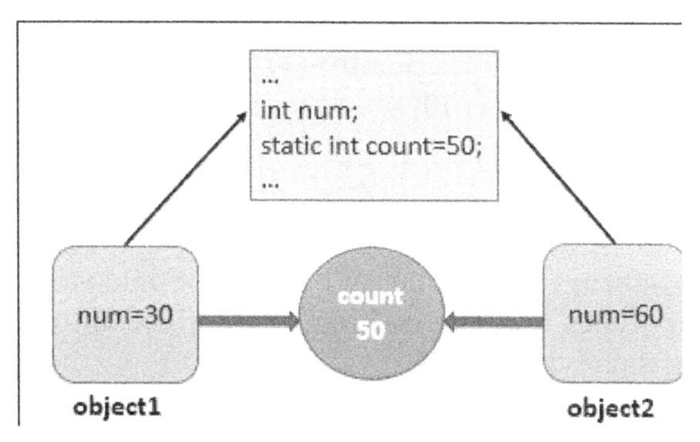

Figure 2.1: Instance and static variables

Here, the variable **num** is an instance variable and **count** is a static variable. The objects **object1** and **object2** have their own copies of values for variable num. But, the value of the **count** variable is the same for both objects since it is a static variable. So, the objects share the same copy of the variable **count**.

Apart from variable type Java also defines a *scope* for each variable. The scope is decided by the location where the variables are declared and at what point they are accessed. Broadly classifying, the variable scope can be class level or method level (local). Class level scope includes '**`instance`**' and '**`static`**' variables whereas '**`local`**' variables are declared within a method or a block.

The lifetime of the instance variable is till the existence of the object and that of static variable is till the existence of the class. The lifetime of method level variables is dependent on the execution of the methods. These variables are allocated memory during method execution and are destroyed after method execution completes. Another set of variables is the parameters passed to methods that hold the values passed to methods during execution.

The following example shows the different scopes of variables in a Java program:

```
public class Calculate{
// variables with the class level scope
int a, b;
static int count;    public static void main(String args[]){
    int x;  // variable with method level scope
    {
      int y=10;  // variable with block level scope
    }
    //Below statement gives error
    // as y is not accessible here
    System.out.println("Value of y is "+y);  } }
```

Note: In the println() method, the statement Value of y is concatenated with the actual variable y by using the concatenation operator (+). If the value of y would be accessible, the output would be the Value of y is 10.

2.3 Data types in Java

The data type is used to inform the compiler of the type of data stored in a variable. Java has support for different data types that can be broadly classified into primitive data types and non-primitive (reference) data types.

Primitive data types

A primitive data type is a built-in type in Java that can store a single value at a time. Java supports several primitive types which are broadly classified into four categories which are:

- **Integer**: These types store signed integers. The types in this category are **`byte, short, int`**, and **`long`**.

Note: Signed integers can store positive as well as negative values such as -20.

The following table describes the four Integer types:

Integer type	Description	Bit size	Default value	Range Default value
`byte`	Stores a small amount of data. Used for streaming data from a network file. Used for processing raw binary data.	8-bit (1 byte)	0	-128 to 127
`short`	The least used data type. Stores smaller numbers such as Id.	16-bit (2 bytes)	0	-32,768 to 32,767
`int`	Most commonly used. Stores whole numbers. Most efficient data type. Used to store salary, invoice amount, and so on.	32-bit (4 bytes)	0	-2,147,483,648 to 2,147,483,647
`long`	Used for a number larger than int type. For example, the results of large scientific calculations.	64-bit (8 bytes)	0L	-9,223,372,036,854,775,808 to 9,223,372,036,854,775,807

Table 2.2: *Integer data types*

Float: Float types store floating-point numbers or real numbers with fractional precision. The float types supported by Java are float and double. The following table gives a brief description of the float types:

Float type	Description	Bit size	Default value
`float`	Supports single-precision value. Used to store numbers will less precision. For example, float PI, area;	32-bit (4 bytes)	0.0f

Float type	Description	Bit size	Default value
`double`	Supports double-precision value. Used for larger mathematical calculations requiring more accuracy. For example, double bigData;	64-bit (8 bytes)	0.0d

Table 2.3: Floating-point data types

Note: In Java, all numeric types are signed, that is, they store both positive and negative values. The size of each type is the same and standardized for all platforms.

- **Character**: The character type is used to store symbols such as letters and numbers. It supports only one type, **`char`**.
- **Bit-size**: 16-bit (2 bytes) Unicode character
- **Range**: 0 ('`\u0000`') to 65,535 ('`\uffff`')
- **Default value**: 0 ('`\u0000`')

  For example,

  ```
  char gender = 'M';
  ```

- **Boolean**: The Boolean type is used to indicate true or false. It supports only one type, Boolean. Its size is 1 bit and the default value is false.

  For example,

  ```
  boolean selected = true;
  ```

Non-primitive data types

Java also supports several non-primitive and reference types namely, String, Array, Class, Interface, and so on.

- **String**: The **`String`** class is defined in the **`java.lang`** package and is used to store a sequence of characters also called a string. None of the primitive data types had the support for storing more than one character in a variable. The **`String`** class provides this feature.

  For example,

  ```
  String str = "Stores a string";
  ```

  Here, **`str`** is not a primitive type of variable but an object of type **`String`**. The value is specified within double-quotes. The value of the **`str`** variable remains constant throughout. Initializing the variable with a new value, internally creates a new **`String`** object. Thus, **`String`** objects are immutable.

- **Reference types**: A reference type stores the address of an object. In Java arrays and objects represent the reference types. When an object or array is created, the address of the memory assigned to it is stored in the reference variable.

- o **Array**: It is a collection of values of the same type. For example, the score of players can be stored in an array.
- o **Class**: It is a structure that encapsulates data members and methods within it.
- o **Interface**: It is a reference type similar to a class in Java that contains abstract methods default methods, and so on.

The following example shows the use of different data types:

```
package mypkg;
public class Customer {
  public static void main(String[] args) {
    // Declaring variables
    int custId;  // variable of type Integer
    float payableAmt; // variable of type Float
    // Declaring and initializing the variables
    double creditScore = 456790.897; // variable of type Double
    char premiumCust = 'Y'; // variable of type Character
    boolean paymentStatus = false; // variable of type Boolean
    String address = "10, NorthDriven Park"; // variable of type String

    // Initializing the declared variables
    custId = 1007;
    payableAmt = 10487.50f;

    // Displaying the values of variables on the console
    System.out.println("Customer Id: " + custId);
    System.out.println("Address: " + address);
    System.out.println("Order Amount: " + payableAmt);
    System.out.println("Premium Customer?: " + premiumCust);
    System.out.println("Credit Score: " + creditScore);
    System.out.println("Payment Status: " + paymentStatus);
  }
}
```

Here, different types of variables are declared and initialized with appropriate values. Note that the meaningful names have been used for variables based on the type of value they store.

The following screenshot shows the output of the code:

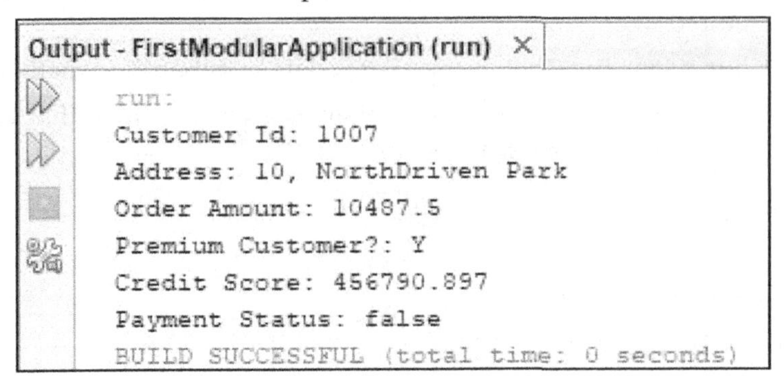

***Figure 2.2:** Variables of different data types*

2.4 Type casting

Java supports the conversion of one type into another by using the type casting feature. Type casting can be of two types, which are:

- **Implicit type casting**: When data of a type is assigned to a variable of the similar or larger type, it leads to implicit or automatic conversion of the smaller type to larger. This is also called type promotion, in which even if one operand of an expression is larger, the result of the whole expression is promoted to the larger type.

  For example,

  ```
  int num = 20;
  double numD = num; // assigning integer value to double type
  ```

- **Explicit type casting**: Java supports conversion of a higher type to a lower type, however, at the cost of loss of precision. This is called explicit casting.

  For example,

  ```
  float numF = 45.65f;
  int num = (int) numF; // converting a float value to integer type
  ```

  Here, the fractional part of the number `numF` will be lost and the result will be saved in integer type variable `num`.

2.5 Literals and escape sequences

The values assigned to variables are called literals. Listed below are the different types of literals assigned to variables of the corresponding type:

- **Integer literals**: Integer literals can be any whole number. Decimal values with base 10 from 0 to 9, such as 40, binary values with base 2, that is 0 and 1, such as 0c01001, hexadecimal values with base 16, that is numbers 0 to 9 and letters A to F, such as 0x1d.

- **Floating-point literals**: Floating-point literals are numbers with fractional components such as 2.9, 2.11, and so on. The use of `E` or `e` at the end of the number indicates exponentiation. For example, 8.37E6, e+394, and so on.
- With Java SE 7, the support for underscore (_) character in numeric literals was added to improve the readability of large data. However, a number cannot begin or end with an underscore. Underscore cannot be placed beside the decimal point in a floating-point number, before a suffix, `L` or `F`, before or after binary/hexadecimal symbols like `b` or `x`. Some examples of valid use of underscore are 9449_3848_3948_2944L, 2.43_37F, 0b11010111_11100100_00010111. Examples of invalid use of underscore are _3837, 2_.43_37F, 0x_83.
- **Character literals**: Character literals can be symbols such as letters or numbers and are enclosed in single quotes, for example, `c`, `$`, and so on. For characters that cannot be enclosed in single quotes, escape sequences are used.
- **Boolean literals**: Boolean literals have only two values, true and false.
- **Null literals**: The `null` literal is assigned to a reference variable that does not point to any memory address. That is, the variable still does not refer to any object. For example, `Vehicle bike = null`;
- **String literals**: A `String` literal is a sequence of characters within double-quotes, for example, "`This is a string literal", "One\nTwo`", and so on.

Escape sequences

An escape sequence is used to represent characters that cannot be passed as values directly to a string. It is symbolized by the backslash (\) character which indicates everything succeeding it has a special meaning. An example is the new line character or tab character. Similarly, characters that have special meaning in Java such as \ or ", also need escape sequences. They are also used to provide formatted output. Listed below are the escape sequences supported by Java:

- `\b`: Backspace
- `\t`: Horizontal tab
- `\n`: New line
- `\'`: Single quote
- `\\`: Backslash
- `\r`: Carriage return
- `\"`: Double quotes
- `\f`: Form feed
- `\xxx`: Octal value xxx between 000 and 0377
- `\uxxxx`: Unicode with encoding xxxx with one to four hexadecimal digits

The following code shows the use of different escape sequences:

```
package mypkg;
public class EscapeSequenceEx {
  public static void main(String[] args) {
  System.out.println("Using \t Escape Sequence Tab and \n New Line");
  System.out.println("This is Escape Sequence for \"Double Quotes\" in Java");
  // Printing 'JAVA' using hexadecimal escape sequences
    System.out.println("\u004A\u0041\u0056\u0041");
  // Printing 'Year' using octal escape sequence for  // character 'a'
  System.out.println("Ye\141r \"2018\" ");
}
```

The output of the code is shown below:

```
run:
Using    Escape Sequence Tab and
 New Line
This is Escape Sequence for "Double Quotes" in Java
JAVA
Year "2018"
BUILD SUCCESSFUL (total time: 0 seconds)
```

***Figure 2.3:** Using escape sequences*

Note: The hexadecimal escape sequence contains a \u symbol followed by 4 hexadecimal digi The octal escape sequence contains a backslash followed by three digits.

2.6 Constants and enumerations

Java constants are variables whose value cannot change once it has been assigned. Constants are declared by using the **final** keyword.

Syntax:

```
final <variable-name> = <value>;
```

Example:

...

```
final int discount = 10;
```

...

Here, the value of the variable **discount** is fixed at **10**. It cannot be modified later since the variable is constant as indicated by the **final** keyword.

Note: When the final keyword is applied to methods, they cannot be overridden and if applied to a class, it cannot be extended.

Enumeration is a class type that contains collection of constant values. It can also contain instance variables and constructors. It is defined using the **enum** keyword.

Syntax:

```
enum <enum-name> {
  constant1, constant2, . . . , constantN
}
```

Unlike a class that is instantiated by using the new operator, the enumeration is used by creating a variable of type **enum**, similar to a primitive type. Enumerations are generally used with decision-making constructs such as **switch-case**.

Example:

```
public class EnumDays {
  // Defining an enumeration of days of the week
  enum Days {
    Sun, Mon, Tue, Wed, Thu, Fri, Sat
  }
  public static void main(String[] args) {
    // Declaring a variable of type Days
    Days day;
    // Instantiating the enum Days
    day = Days.Fri;
    // Printing the value of enum
    System.out.println("Today is: " + day);
  }
}
```

The output of the code is shown below:

```
Today is: Fri
```

2.7 Operators in Java

Java provides operators to perform operations on the data stored in the variables. The symbols used for performing operations are called **operators** and the variables on which the operation is performed are called **operands**.

For example:

```
c = a + b;
```

Here, **c = a + b** is an expression in which, **+** is the operator for addition and **a** and **b** are the operands. Java supports different types of operators which can be seen in the following sections.

Assignment

The assignment operator **=** is used to assign the value of the operand on its right to the operand on its left. More than one variable can be assigned a value simultaneously.

For example:

```
int a =10;
int b = c = 20;
```

Java also supports compound assignment to assign the result of an expression to a variable. For example:

```
int a = 10;
a += 6;  // this is resolved as a = a + 6;
```

Arithmetic

Arithmetic operators operate on numeric data. However, they can be used with character data as well. These are binary operators which means that they operate on two operands.

Listed below are the arithmetic operators in Java:

- **Addition (+)**: Performs the addition operation on the operands.
- **Subtraction (-)**: Performs subtraction operation on the operands.
- **Multiplication (*)**: Performs multiplication operation on the operands.
- **Division (/)**: Performs division operation on the operands.
- **Modulo (%)**: Returns the remainder of a division operation.

The following example shows the use of assignment and arithmetic operators:

```
public class OperatorsDemo {
  public static void main(String[] args) {
    int add, sub, mul, div, mod;
    add = 3 + 5;     sub = 6 - 4;     mul = 2 * 2;     div = 6 / 3;
    mod = 4 % 2;     System.out.println("Addition is " + add);
    System.out.println("Subtraction is " + sub);
    System.out.println("Multiplication is " + mul);
```

```
    System.out.println("Division is " + div);
    System.out.println("Modulo is " + mod);
  }
}
```

The output of the code is shown below:

```
Addition is 8
Subtraction is 2
Multiplication is 4
Division is 2
Modulo is 0
```

Figure 2.4: *Using Arithmetic operators*

Note that the **modulo** operation returned a **0** because **4** is directly divisible by **2**.

Unary

Unary operators operate on a single operand. Java supports different types of unary operators which are:

- **Unary plus (+)**: Indicates a positive value.
- **Unary minus (-)**: Negates an expression.
- **Increment (++)**: Increments the value of a variable by 1.
- **Decrement (--)**: Decrements the value of a variable by 1.
- **Logical complement (!)**: Inverts a boolean value.

There are two ways of using increment and decrement operators, that is, prefix or postfix notation. Both will increment the value of a variable by **1**. However, the prefix version will first increment the value and then assign it, whereas, the postfix version will first assign the value and then increment it.

The following code shows the use of unary operators:

```
public class OperatorsDemo {
  public static void main(String[] args) {
    int x = 3;
    int y = x++;
     int z = ++x;     x = -x;     boolean answer = false;     answer = !answer;
System.out.println("Value of y after postfix increment of x is "+ y);
    System.out.println("Value of z after prefix increment of x is "+ z);
    System.out.println("Value of x after negation is "+ x);
    System.out.println("Logical complement of answer is "+ answer);
```

```
    }
}
```

The output of the code is shown below:

```
Value of y after postfix increment of x is 3
Value of z after prefix increment of x is 5
Value of x after negation is -5
Logical complement of answer is true
```

***Figure 2.5:** Using unary operators*

Conditional/Relational

The conditional operators work on two operands to test the relationship between them. The result of a conditional operator will either be true or false. Listed below are the conditional operators supported in Java:

- **Equal to (==)**: Returns true if the two values are equal, else returns false.
- **Not Equal to (!):** Returns true if the two values are equal, else returns false.
- **Greater than (>)**: Returns true if the value on the left is greater than the value on the right, else returns false.
- **Less than (<)**: Returns true if the value on the left is lesser than the value on the right, else returns false.
- **Greater than or equal to (>=)**: Returns true if the value on the left is greater than or equal to the value on the right, else returns false.
- **Less than or equal to (<=)**: Returns true if the value on the left is less than or equal to the value on the left, else returns false.

Logical

Logical operators work on two boolean expressions. The logical operators supported in Java are:

- **Logical AND (&&)**: Returns true if both the boolean expressions are true, else returns false.
- **Logical OR (| |)**: Returns true if either or both the operations are true, else returns false.

Short-circuit behavior

The logical operator **&&** will test the second expression only if the first expression is true. If the first expression is false, it will not check the second expression. Similarly, the logical operator | | will test the second expression only if the first expression is false. If the first expression is true, it will not check the second expression. This is called short-circuit behavior.

The following example shows the use of conditional and logical operators:

```
public class OperatorsDemo {
  public static void main(String[] args) {
    int num1 = 30, num2 = 23;
    // Using conditional operators
    System.out.println("num1 == num2? "+ (num1==num2));
    System.out.println("num1 != num2? "+ (num1!=num2));
    System.out.println("num1 > num2? "+ (num1>num2));
    System.out.println("num1 < num2? "+ (num1<num2));
    System.out.println("num1 >= num2? "+ (num1>=num2));
    System.out.println("num1 <= num2? "+ (num1<=num2));

    // Using logical operators
   System.out.println("Result of logical AND is "+((num1>num2) && (num1==num2)));
   System.out.println("Result of logical OR is "+((num1>num2) || (num1==num2)));
  }
}
```

The output of the code is shown below:

```
num1 == num2? false
num1 != num2? true
num1 > num2? true
num1 < num2? false
num1 >= num2? true
num1 <= num2? false
Result of logical AND is false
Result of logical OR is true
```

Figure 2.6: *Using relational operators*

Note: The result of logical && and | | operation on the same set of expressions is different.

Bitwise

The bitwise operators operate on the binary form of data to modify the individual bits in a value. Java supports the following bitwise operators:

- **Bitwise AND (&)**: Operates on two values. Returns 1 if both bits are 1 else, it returns 0.
- **Bitwise OR (|)**: Operates on two values. Returns 1 if either or both bits are 1 else, returns 0.

- **Exclusive OR (^)**: Operates on two values. Returns 1 if the bits are complementary else, returns 0.
- **Complement (~)**: Operates on a single value and inverts all of the bits of the value.
- **Right-shift (>>)**: Operates on a single value. Shifts all bits to the right by the number of bits specified in the position. Retains the sign of negative numbers.
- **Left-shift (<<)**: Operates on a single value. Moves all the bits to the left by the number of bits specified in the position.

The following figure shows the bit representation of values in an 8-bit system:

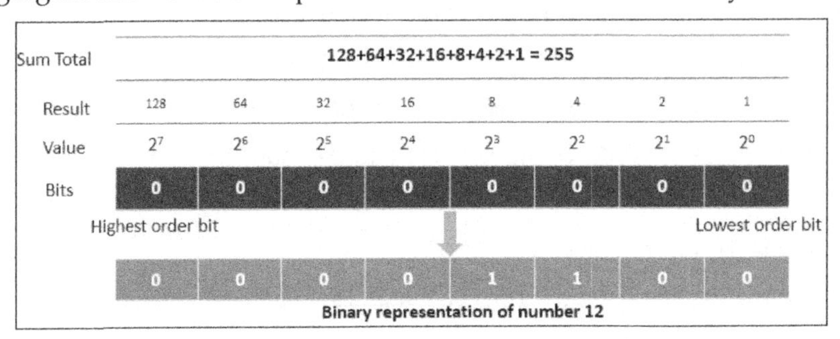

Figure 2.7: *8-Bit representation of number 12*

In an 8-bit system, every letter, number, symbol, and so on. is represented in an 8-bit format as shown in the image. The right-most bit is the lowest order bit and the left-most bit is the highest-order bit. The value for each bit is 2 to the power of 0, 1, 2, ... 7. Hence, the value of the right-most bit is 20 which is 1 and that of the left-most bit is 27 which is 128. The total of all bit values is 255. Since the lowest value is 00000000 and the highest value is 11111111, you can represent 256 characters with the 8-bit system.

The following figure shows a logical & operation on the numbers 12 and 20:

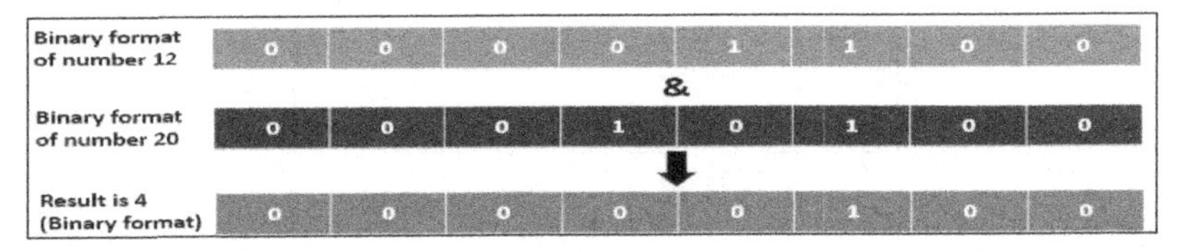

Figure 2.8: *Logical & operation*

The image shows the use of logical & operator. In this case, if both the bits are 1, the result is 1, else the result is 0.

The following figure shows a right-shift operation on the number 12 by 2 positions:

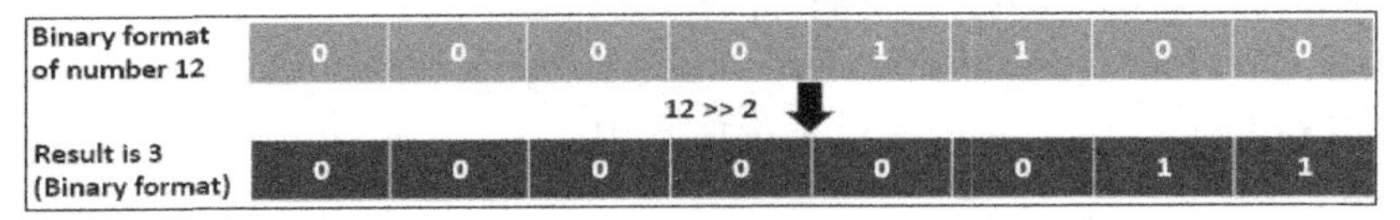

Figure 2.9: *Right shift operation*

The image shows a right-shift of 12 by 2 positions. In this case, the right-most two bits are dropped, and all remaining bits are moved forward by 2 positions. The left-most two-bit positions which will become empty due to right-shift will be set to 0.

The following code shows the use of different bitwise operators:

```
public class OperatorsDemo {
  public static void main(String[] args) {
    int x = 12;  // 00001100
    int y = 20;  // 00010100
    System.out.println("x & y: " + (x & y));  // 00000100 = 4
    System.out.println("x | y: " + (x | y));  // 00011100 = 28
    System.out.println("x ^ y: " + (x ^ y));  // 00011000 = 24
   System.out.println("Logical complement of x is : " + (~x)); // 00001101 = -13
   System.out.println("Right shift of x by 2 is  " + (x >> 2)); // 00000011 = 3
   System.out.println("Left shift of x by 2 is: " + (x << 2)); // 00110000 = 48
  }
}
```

The output of the code is shown below:

```
x & y: 4
x | y: 28
x ^ y: 24
Logical complement of x is : -13
Right shift of x by 2 is  3
Left shift of x by 2 is: 48
```

Figure 2.10: *Using bitwise operators*

Explanation of the result of the logical complement (~) operator:

The bitwise complement operator (~) performs a bitwise negation of the value of variable x. This means, that each bit of the number is inverted so that all binary 0s become 1s and all 1s become 0s:

```
x = 12;  //00001100
y = ~x;
```

So, **y = -13**, however, as per the inversion, the generated value should be 11110011 = 243. But, integer numbers whose highest order bit is set to 1 is considered a negative number. Since the bitwise complement inverts all the bits including the high order bit (which is the sign bit), the high order bit becomes 1 which makes the number negative. Since the number becomes negative, it will be in the 2's complement form. Hence, to know its decimal value, first, subtract 1 from the number, that is 243 -1 = 242 (11110010) and then perform a 1's complement on this value by converting all 1s to 0s and vice-versa. So, the result will be 00001101 = 13 and since it was a negative value, the final result will be -13.

The following figure shows the bitwise complement operation on **x =12**:

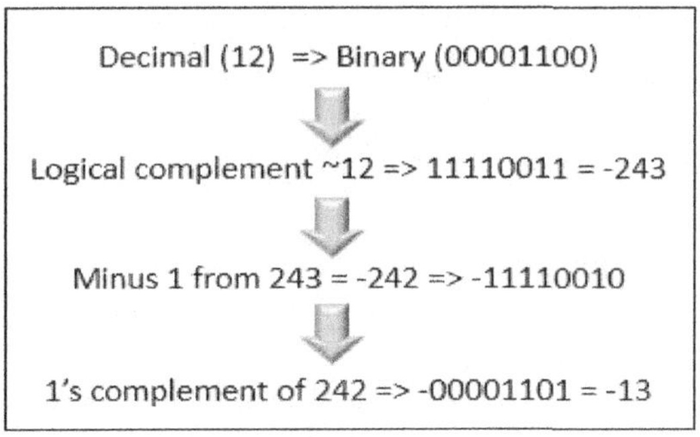

Decimal (12) => Binary (00001100)

Logical complement ~12 => 11110011 = -243

Minus 1 from 243 = -242 => -11110010

1's complement of 242 => -00001101 = -13

Figure 2.11: *Bitwise complement operation*

Ternary

The ternary operator **(?:)** is used as a short alternative for the decision-making construct if-else. It saves lines of code and makes it easy to understand.

Syntax:

```
<expr1> ? <expr2> : <expr3>
```

expr1: An expression that evaluates to true or false.

expr2: An expression that will be executed if **expr1** returns true.

expr3: An expression that will be executed if **expr1** returns false.

The following code shows the use of the ternary operator:

```
public class OperatorsDemo {
  public static void main(String[] args) {
    int a = 10, b=20;
    String result;
    result = (a>b) ? "a is greater" : "b is greater";
    System.out.println(result);
  }
}
```

Here, the expression (**a>b**) is evaluated. Since the expression evaluates to false, the second statement after the colon (**:**), that is, **b is greater** is stored in the variable result.

The output of the code is shown below:

```
run:
b is greater
BUILD SUCCESSFUL (total time: 0 seconds)
```

Figure 2.12: *Using ternary operator*

2.8 Operator precedence and associativity

Operator precedence defines the priority of operators for evaluating a mathematical expression that may have more than one operator. The following table shows the sequence of operator precedence:

<table>
<tr><th>Sequence</th><th>Operators</th></tr>
<tr><td>1.</td><td>Parentheses ( )</td></tr>
<tr><td>2.</td><td>Unary Operators +, -, ++, --, ~, !</td></tr>
<tr><td>3.</td><td>Arithmetic and Bitwise Shift operators *, /, %, +, -, >>, <<</td></tr>
<tr><td>4.</td><td>Relational Operators >, >=, <, <=, ==, !=</td></tr>
<tr><td>5.</td><td>Bitwise and Logical Operators &, ^, |, &&, ||</td></tr>
<tr><td>6.</td><td>Ternary and Assignment Operators ?:, =, *=, /=, +=, -=</td></tr>
</table>

Table 2.4: *Operator precedence*

As per the operator precedence order, anything within parentheses will be evaluated first. Consider the following expression:

```
1*2+6/3 > 2 && 2<4 || 6<5
```

Here, the expression does not have anything in parentheses nor any unary operators. So, as per precedence, the arithmetic operators will be evaluated first:

```
1*2+6/3
```

In arithmetic operators, multiplication and division will be evaluated before addition. Result is:

```
3+2
```

Result is:

```
5
```

So, now the expression is:

```
3>2 && 2<4 || 6<5
```

Now, as per precedence, the relational operators have more priority than logical operators. They will be evaluated from left to right.

So, the result is:

True && True || False

Finally, the logical operators are evaluated where **&&** takes precedence over **||**. So, the result is:

True || False

Final result of logical || is:

True

Operator associativity helps to evaluate an expression with multiple operators having the same precedence. The following table shows the operator associativity of different operators having the same precedence:

Operators	Associativity
(), ++, --	Left to Right
++, --, +, -, !,~	Left to Right
*, /, %, +, -	Right to Left
<<, >>	Left to right
<, <, >=, <=, ==, !=	Left to right
&, ^, |	Left to right
&&, ||	Left to right
?:	Left to right

Table 2.5: Operator associativity

Consider the following expression:

5+12-4*3

Since * has higher precedence, **4*3** is solved first. Result:

5+12-12

Since + and - have the same precedence, the left associativity will be applied. Result:

17-12

Result:

5

2.9 Formatting the output

Java provides methods to format the output using the **print(), println(), printf()**, and **format()** methods. The **print()** and **println()** methods use the **toString()** method to display strings and numeric values in the string format. The **println()** method adds the new line character **\n** at the end of the printed statement.

The following example shows the use of **print()** and **println()** methods:

```
public class PrintMethods {
  public static void main(String[] args) {
    int a = 5;
    System.out.println("The value of a is " + a + ".");
    System.out.print("The value of a is ");
    System.out.print(a);
    System.out.print(".");
    System.out.println("Done");
  }
}
```

The output of the code is shown below:

```
run:
The value of a is 5.
The value of a is 5.Done
BUILD SUCCESSFUL (total time: 0 seconds)
```

Figure 2.13: *Using print methods*

Note the last line prints beside the previous **print** statement. This is because **print()** method does not add a new line character at the end of the statement whereas **println()** adds a new line character so that the second line gets printed in a new line.

The **printf()** method is used to format numeric data to be displayed on the console by using built-in format specifiers which are:

- **%d**: Format the number as a decimal integer
- **%f**: Formats the number as a real number
- **%o**: Formats the number as an octal number
- **%e**: Formats the number as a decimal number in scientific notation
- **%n**: Displays output in a new line

The following example shows the use of **printf()** method:

```
import java.util.Math;
public class PrintMethods {
  public static void main(String[] args) {
    int num = 78 / 33;
    // Using %d for decimal integer
    System.out.printf("Result of 78/33 is %d %n", num);
```

```
        // Using %f with extra zeros
        double val = 3.0 / 2.0;
        System.out.printf("Result of 3.0/2.0 is %09.3f %n", val);
        // Using %e for scientific notation
        val = 7000.0 / 2.0;
        System.out.printf("Result of 7000/2.0 is %7.2e %n", val);
        // Using %e wiht negative infinity
        val = -20.0 / 0.0;
        System.out.printf("Result of -20.0/0.0 is %7.2e %n", val);
        // Using multiple format specifiers
       System.out.printf("Value of PI is %4.2f and E is %4.3f %n", Math.PI, Math.E);
    }
}
```

Note the import statement for the **java.util.Math** class to use the constants, **PI**, and **E** of the **Math** class.

The output of the code is shown below:

```
Result of 78/33 is 2
Result of 3.0/2.0 is 00001.500
Result of 7000/2.0 is 3.50e+03
Result of -20.0/0.0 is -Infinity
Value of PI is 3.14 and E is 2.718
```

Figure 2.14: *Formatted output*

2.10 Scanner class for input

Java provides the **Scanner** class to accept user input from the keyboard. It breaks the input into tokens based on the data type. The **Scanner** object is initialized with the **InputStream** object as a parameter to its constructor as shown below:

```
Scanner input = new Scanner(System.in);
```

Listed below are the methods of **Scanner** class used to accept different types of data:

- **nextByte()**: Returns a byte value
- **nextInt()**: Returns an **int** value
- **nextLong()**: Returns a long value
- **nextFloat()**: Returns a float value
- **nextDouble():** Returns a double value

The following code shows the use of the Scanner class to accept user input:

```
public class ScannerDemo {
  public static void main(String[] args) {
    Scanner s = new Scanner(System.in);
    System.out.println("Enter an integer value:");
    int intValue = s.nextInt();
    System.out.println("Enter a decimal value:");
    float floatValue = s.nextFloat();
    System.out.println("Enter a String value");
    String strValue = s.next();
    System.out.println("Values you entered are: ");
    System.out.println(intValue + " " + floatValue + " " + strValue);
  }
}
```

The output of the code is shown below:

```
Enter an integer value:
30
Enter a decimal value:
45.6
Enter a String value
Hello
Values you entered are:
30 45.6 Hello
```

***Figure 2.15**: Using scanner class*

2.11 Decision-making constructs

Java provides decision-making constructs to execute statement(s) based on the evaluation of a condition. Following are the decision-making constructs supported by Java:

'if' statement

The `if` statement will evaluate a condition and will execute the statements in the `if` block if the condition evaluates to true.

Syntax:

```
if (condition) {
  // execution statements;
}
```

- `condition`: A boolean expression.
- `statements`: Statements to be executed if the condition evaluates to true.

Note: If there is only one statement to be executed, the curly braces are not required. But if there are multiple statements, the curly braces are mandatory.

Listed below are some variations of '`if`' statement:

- **'if-else' statement**: In the **`if-else`** statement, if the condition evaluates to true, the statements within the **`if`** block is executed else, the statements within the **`else`** block are executed:

  Syntax:

  ```
  if (condition) {
    // execution statements;
  }
  else {
    // execution statements;
  }
  ```

- **'if-else-if' ladder**: The multiple **`if`** construct, also called the **`if-else-if`** ladder evaluates multiple **`if`** conditions till a true result is found. If all **`if`** conditions return false, the **`else`** block is executed. Evaluation is done sequentially from the top of the if-else-if ladder.

  Syntax:

  ```
  if(condition) {
    // execution statements
  }
  else if (condition) {
    // execution statements
  }
  else {
    // execution statements
  }
  ```

- **Nested-if statement**: An **`if`** statement can also have a nested **`if`** statement or even a nested **`if-else-if`** ladder within the **`if`** and **`else`** blocks at any level.

  Syntax:

  ```
  if(condition) {
    if(condition) {
      // execution statements;
    }
  ```

```
        else
    // execution statements;
  }
}
else {
  // execution statement;
}
```

The following example shows the use of different **if-else** variations:

```
public class IfElseDemo {
  public static void main(String[] args) {
    int age = 43;
    char gender = 'F';

    if (age >= 60) {
      System.out.println("Elibible for membership.");
      System.out.println("Discount 50%");
    } else if (age >= 18) {
      System.out.println("Elibible for membership.");
      if (gender == 'F') {
        System.out.println("Discount 10%");
      } else {
        System.out.println("Discount 5%");
      }
    } else {
      System.out.println("Not eligible for membership.");
    }
  }
}
```

Here, if the **age** is greater than or equal to 60, the person is eligible for membership with a 50% discount on the membership fee. If **age** is 18 or higher but less than 60, the person is eligible for membership. But, if the person is a female, the discount will be 10% else it will be 5%. If **age** is less than 18, the person is not eligible for membership.

The output of the code is shown below:

```
Elibible for membership.
Discount 10%
```

Figure 2.16: Using if-else construct

switch-case statement

Java provides the switch-case statement as an alternative to complicated multiple **if-else** statements. It compares the value of a variable/expression against a set of pre-defined values. The statements within the exact match are executed. Java **switch**-case supports numbers, **String**, enumerations as well as objects of Wrapper classes such as **Character, Byte, Short**, and **Integer** as variable/expression for a switch-case. The switch statement is created using the **switch** keyword followed by a variable/expression in parentheses **()**. Based on the value of the expression, the appropriate case is executed which is indicated by the **case** keyword. Each case is terminated by the **break** keyword. If none of the cases match the expression, the **default** case is executed.

Syntax:

```
switch (<expression>) {
  case expr1:
    // execution statement
    break;
  case expr2:
    // execution statement
    break;
. . .
  case exprN:
    // execution statement
    break;
  default:
    // execution statement
    break;
}
```

Listed below are some variations of switch-case statement:

- Java also allows using multiple **case** statements with a single **break** statement.

  Syntax:

  ```
  switch (<expression>) {
  ```

```
  case expr1:
  case expr2:
  case expr3:
  case expr4:
  // execution statement
  break;
. . .
  case exprN:
    // execution statement
    break;
  default:
    // execution statement
    break;
}
```

- It is also possible to create nested **switch-case** in Java by embedding one or more **switch-case** statements within a specific case in the parent **switch-case** statement.

  Syntax:

```
switch (<expression>) {
  case expr1:
    switch (<expression>){
      case exprA:
        //execution statements
        break;
      …
       case exprN:
         // execution statements
         break;
    }
    break;
    case expr2:
      // execution statement
      break;
. .
    case exprN:
      // execution statement
```

```
        break;
      default:
        // execution statement
        break;
}
```

The following example shows the use of different types of **switch** cases:

```
public class SwitchCaseDemo {
  enum Days {
    Mon, Tue, Wed, Thu, Fri, Sat, Sun
  }
  public static void main(String[] args) {
    Days today = Days.Tue;
    String hour = "am";
    int week = 2;
    switch (today) {
      case Mon:
      case Tue:
      case Wed:
      case Thu:
      case Fri:
        System.out.println("Discount scheme for Weekdays");
        switch (week) {
          case 1:
          case 3:
            System.out.println("No discount in week 1 and 3");
            break;
          case 2:
          case 4:
            System.out.println("20% disocount in week 2 and 4");
            break;
        }
        break;
        case Sat:
          case Sun:
            switch (hour) {
              case "am":
```

```
                System.out.println("Discount is 40%");
                break;
              case "pm":
                System.out.println("Discount is 20%");
            }
            break;
            default:
              System.out.println("Day does not exist");
               break;
        }
    }
}
```

Here, the main switch-case has been created over an **enum** of days of the week. For weekdays **Mon** to **Fri**, there is a common case and for **Sat-Sun** there is one common case. Now, for weekdays, there is a nested switch case over an integer value which represents the week of the month. For weeks 2 and 4 the discount is 20% and for weeks 1 and 3, there is no discount. Similarly, for Sat-Sun, another nested switch-case is used over String values for the hour of the day. If the hour is **am,** discount is 40% and if it is **pm**, discount is 20%. The default case is for the main **switch-case** when an incorrect value for the day is specified.

The output of the code is shown below:

```
Discount scheme for Weekdays
20% disocount in week 2 and 4
BUILD SUCCESSFUL (total time: 0 seconds)
```

***Figure 2.17:** Using the switch-case construct*

2.12 Looping constructs

Java allows executing a set of statements repeatedly to meet a specified condition. For example, to display the numbers from 1 to n, where n could be any value specified by user or summation of 1 to 'n' numbers. To accomplish such repeated calculations, Java provides looping constructs called loops or iterations.

The different types of loops supported by Java are:

while loop

The **while** statement is used to execute one or more statements until the condition is true.

Syntax:

```
while (<expression>) {
  // execution statement(s)
}
```

Note: If there is only a single statement to be executed, the curly braces {} can be omitted. The value of the variables must be initialized before the execution of the loop. For example, int i = 1; The loop must have an expression to modify the value of the variable used in the loop's expression, such as i++; or i--;

Listed below are some variations of the while loop:

- **Infinite loop:** An infinite loop runs indefinitely when the conditional expression or the increment/decrement expression of the loop is not provided. For example:

  ```
  while (true) {
    System.out.println("This is an infinite loop");
  }
  ```

- **Empty loop:** A loop without any execution statement, that is, an empty body is called an empty loop or null statement loop. It is terminated with a semicolon after the conditional expression. For example:

  ```
  int i = 5;
  int j = 20;
  while (++num1 < --num2);
  System.out.println("Value at the mid-point is : " + i);
  ```

do-while statement

Unlike `while` statement, the `do-while` statement checks the condition at the end of the loop. This allows the loop to execute at least once even if the condition is false.

Syntax:

```
do {
  // execution statement(s);
}
while (<expression>);
```

Note: Both while and do-while loops can have nested loops and decision-making constructs within them. The nested code will be executed for each iteration of the outer loop.

The following example shows the use of `while` and `do-while` loops:

```
public class WhileDoWhileDemo {
  public static void main(String[] args) {
    int num1=10;
```

```
        // while loop with nested-if construct
    while(num1<15){
      System.out.println("Number is: "+num1);
      if(num1==12){
        System.out.println("Warning!! The number " + num1 +" is not allowed");
      }
      num1++;
    }
    System.out.println("---------------------");
    // null statement loop
    int num2=20;
    while(++num1 < --num2);
    System.out.println("Mid-point of num1 and num2 is "+num1);
   System.out.println("---------------------");
    int num3=20;
    // do-while loop that will execute at least once
    // even though condition is false
    do{
      System.out.println("The value of num3 is "+num3);
    }while(num3>21);
    System.out.println("---------------------");
    //infinite while loop
    while(true){
      System.out.println("This is infinite loop");
    }
  }
}
```

The code creates a simple **while** loop with a nested if statement that prints the numbers from 10 to 14. If the number is 12, it prints a warning before moving to the next iteration. Next, the null-statement loop prints the mid-point of **num1** and **num2**. Note, at this point, the value of **num1** has been incremented to 15 because of the **num1++** statement of the first **while** loop.

Next, the **do-while** statement is used to print the value of **num3** which will be printed only once since the condition **num3>21** is false. Finally, an infinite **while-loop** is created to print a statement indefinitely.

Note: The program will have to be stopped manually to stop the infinite execution of the while loop.

The output of the code is shown below:

```
Number is: 10
Number is: 11
Number is: 12
Warning!! The number 12 is not allowed
Number is: 13
Number is: 14
----------------------
Mid-point of num1 and num2 is 18
----------------------
The value of num3 is 20
----------------------
This is infinite loop
This is infinite loop
This is infinite loop
This is infinite loop
```

Figure 2.18: *Using while and do-while loops*

for statement

The `for` loop is similar to the while loop and executes the statements until the condition is true. It is used when the user number of iterations is known. The condition is checked before the statements are executed.

Syntax:

```
for(initialization; condition; increment/decrement) {
  // execution statement(s)
}
```

Here, the initial value of the variable, the terminating condition, and the iteration expression are specified in one statement.

Listed below are some variations of for statement:

- **Multiple expressions in 'for'**: The `for` statement allows more than one initialization or increment expressions separated by using the *comma* (`,`) operator and evaluated from left to right. For example:

  ```
  int x, y, n=10;
  for (x = 0, y = n; x <= y; x++, y--) {
    // execution statement(s)
  }
  ```

- **Declaring control variable within the loop statement**: The scope of control variables can be restricted by declaring them at the time of initialization in the **for** statement. For example:

```
for (int x = 1; x<= 5; x++) {
  // execution statement(s)
}
```

- **Modified for statement declarations**: The **for**-loop allows modifying the declaration statement by declaring any of the three parts of the **for** loop outside the declaration statement. It allows conditional expression to be used to test boolean expressions. The initialization or the iteration section can be left empty in the **for**-loop declaration statement. For example:

```
int x = 10;
boolean check = false;
for (; !check; x--) {
  // execution statement(s);
}
```

- **Infinite for loop**: An infinite for loop is created by leaving all the three expressions empty. For example:

```
for( ; ; ) {
  // execution statement(s);
}
```

- **Nested for loop**: Java allows nesting of for loops. The inner loop with execute for every iteration of the outer loop. For example:

```
for(int i=0;i<5;i++){
  for(int j=0;;<2;;++){
    // execution statement(s)
  }
  // execution statement(s)
}
```

The following example shows the use of **for**-loop:

```
public class ForDemo {
  public static void main(String[] args) {
    int i;
    // for loop with all declartion expressions
    for (i = 1; i <= 3; i++) {
      System.out.println("Value of i is " + i);
    }
    // Variable initialization within for statement
    for (int j = 1; j <= 2; j++) {
```

```
        System.out.println("Value of j is " + j);
      }
      //Nested for loop
      for (int x = 0; x < 3; x++) {
        for (int y = 0; y <=x; y++) {
          System.out.print("*");
        }
        System.out.println("");
      }
      // multiple declarations in for loop
      int p, q, n = 3;
      for (p = 0, q = n; p <= n; p++, q--) {
        System.out.println(p + " + " + q + " = " + (p + q));
      }
      int num = 1;
      // Using boolean variable for condition
      boolean check = false;
      for (; !check; num++) {
        System.out.println("Value of num: " + num);
        if (num == 2) {
          check = true;
          System.out.println("Check = true. Loop terminated.");
        }
      }
    }
  }
```

The output of the code is shown below:

```
Value of i is 1
Value of i is 2
Value of i is 3
Value of j is 1
Value of j is 2
*
* *
* * *
0 + 3 = 3
1 + 2 = 3
2 + 1 = 3
3 + 0 = 3
Value of num: 1
Value of num: 2
Check = true. Loop terminated.
```

Figure 2.19: *Using 'for' loop construct*

Enhanced 'for' loop

The enhanced `for` loop or `for-each` loop was introduced in Java SE 5 to improve the readability of `for` loops as well as to traverse and access elements of collection objects.

Note: Collections are classes used to store objects of the same or different types. For example, ArrayList, LinkedList, HashSet, and so on.

Syntax:

```
for (<type> <variable-name>: <collection-object>) {
  // block of statement
}
```

Here, the type indicates the type of the variable that will represent each element of the collection. The collection object represents the collection that has all the values.

The following example shows the use of simple `for`-loop and enhanced `for`-loop:

int num;
//simple for loop
for (int i=0; i<arr1.length; i++){
num = arr1[i];
...
}
	// enhanced for loop
	for (int i : arr1){
	...
	// execution statement(s)
	...
	}

2.13 Jump statements

Jump statements are used to manipulate loop execution at runtime. It allows to transfer of control to different locations in a loop or to skip statements based on a condition. The two keywords that provide this feature are **break** and **continue:**

- **'break'** statement: The **break** statement can be used to terminate a switch case as well as to jump out of a loop to the next statement in the code. In the case of nested loops, the **break** statement jumps out of the current loop to the immediate outer loop.
- **'continue'** statement: The **continue** statement is used to skip statements within a loop and continue to the next iteration.

The following example shows the use of **break** and **continue** statements:

```
public class JumpStmtDemo {
  public static void main(String[] args) {
    int stopVal;
    for (int cnt = 1; cnt <= 10; cnt++) {
      Scanner input = new Scanner(System.in);
      System.out.println("Enter any number or zero to stop:");
      stopVal = input.nextInt();
      if (stopVal == 0) {
        System.out.println("Got zero. Loop terminated.");
        break;
      }
    }
    System.out.println("");
    for (int i = 1; i < 10; i++) {
      if (i % 2 == 0) {
        continue;
      }
```

```
            System.out.println("Value of i is " + i);
        }
    }
}
```

The output of the code is shown below:

```
Enter any number or zero to stop:
3
Enter any number or zero to stop:
5
Enter any number or zero to stop:
0
Got zero. Loop terminated.

Value of i is 1
Value of i is 3
Value of i is 5
Value of i is 7
Value of i is 9
```

Figure 2.20: *Using Jump statements*

Labeled jump statements

Java provides the use of labels with jump statements to transfer control to a specific location in the code. Once the control is transferred to the labeled location, code execution resumes from that point.

Syntax:

```
break label;

continue label;
```

The following code shows the use of a labeled **break** statement:

```
public class BreakWithLabel {
  public static void main(String[] args) {
    outer:
      for (int i = 0; i < 5; i++) {
        for (int j = 1; j < 4; j++) {
          if (j == 2) {
            System.out.println("Found 2. Jumping out.");
            // Break out of inner loop
            break outer;
          }
```

```
            }
        }
        System.out.println("Out of outer loop");
    }
}
```

Here, the **break** statement is provided with a labeled **outer** which will **break** the inner loop and **jump** outside the outer loop. If the label is not provided with the **break** statement, it will break the inner loop and jump outside the inner loop to execute the outer loop again till the condition of the outer loop is true.

The output of the code is shown below:

```
run:
Found 2. Jumping out.
Out of outer loop
BUILD SUCCESSFUL (total time: 0 seconds)
```

Figure 2.21: Using labelled 'break' statement

The following example shows the use of a labeled **continue** statement:

```
public class ContinueWithLabel {
  public static void main(String[] args) {
    outer:
      for (int i = 1; i < 5; i++) {
        for (int j = 1; j < 5; j++) {
          if (j > i) {
            System.out.println();
            continue outer;
          }
          System.out.print(j);
        }
        System.out.println("\nEnd of outer loop.");
      }
  }
}
```

The use of the label **`outer`** with the **`continue`** statement in the inner loop will transfer the control to the outer loop and skip the execution of the remaining statements of the inner loop. If the label is not used with a **`continue`** statement, it will continue in the inner loop until the condition is true.

The output of the code is shown below:

```
run:
1
12
123
1234
End of outer loop.
BUILD SUCCESSFUL (total time: 0 seconds)
```

Figure 2.22: *Using labelled 'continue' statement*

ConclusionIn this chapter you learnt that comments are used to document a program for understanding the code or logic. For storing data, Java uses a variable which is a name given to a memory location where the data will be stored. Static variables are class level variables and do not require an instance to access them. A data type is used to inform the compiler of the type of data stored in a variable. Java provides operators to perform operations on the data stored in the variables. Java provides the Scanner class to accept user input from the keyboard. The **`if`** statement will evaluate a condition. The switch-case statement is an alternative to complicated multiple **`if-else`** statements. Java allows executing a set of statements repeatedly to meet a specified condition by using looping constructs such as **`while`**, **`do-while`**, and **`for`**. The **`break`** statement can be used to terminate a switch case as well as to jump out of a loop to the next statement in the code. The **`continue`** statement is used to skip statements within a loop and continue to the next iteration.

In the next chapter, you will learn about Java application components.

Multiple choice questions

1. **Which of the following is an invalid variable name?**
    a. name
    b. A43b5_e8
    c. while
    d. $amount

2. **Consider the following partial code.**

```
for(int i=0;i<10;i++){
  System.out.println("Hello");
}
```

How many times will the loop print **Hello**?

a. 0
b. 10
c. 9
d. 11

3. **Consider the following partial code.**

```
int week = 5;
switch (week) {
  case 1:
    System.out.println("Week 1"); break;
  case 2:
    System.out.println("Week 2"); break;
  case 3:
    System.out.println("Week 3"); break;
  case 4:
    System.out.println("Week 4"); break;
}
```

Which of the following is the best option to handle a wrong case value entered by the user?

a. Create a default case to handle a wrong input
b. Create an if case to check the value entered by the user
c. Create a separate case for all possible incorrect values
d. Create a loop to allow new input till user enters correct value matching the cases

4. **Consider the following partial code.**

```
int per=60;
if(per > 60){
  System.out.println("Pass");
}else{
  System.out.println("Fail");
}
```

What will be the output of the code?

a. Pass

b. No output

c. Fail

d. Compilation Error

5. **What will be the output of the following expression?**

3*2/2+4*10/5

a. 14

b. 2

c. 0

d. 11

Answers

1. c
2. b
3. a
4. c
5. d

Assignment

Create a Java program with the below specifications:

1. Create a class with the **`main()`** method.
2. Create an infinite **`while-loop`** and within the loop, perform the following:
    - Ask the users if they wish to continue (0/1). Here 0 is for yes and 1 is for no.
    - If the user enters 1, exit the loop.
    - If the user enters 0, display a menu with four options one for each – addition, subtraction, multiplication, division numbered from 1 to 4 respectively.
    - Take input of choice from the user.
    - Take the input of two numbers from the user.
    - Based on the choice, perform the appropriate arithmetic operation on the numbers. (Hint: Use a switch-case for numbers 1 to 4)
    - Display the result to the user.

The expected output is shown below:

```
Do you wish to continue (0/1)?
0
1. Addition
2. Subtraction
3. Multiplication
4. Division
Select an arithmetic operation:
3
Enter first number:
12
Enter second number:
10
Multiplication of 12 and 10 is 120
Do you wish to continue (0/1)?
1
Program Terminated
```

Figure 2.23: *Expected output*

Join our book's Discord space

Join the book's Discord Workspace for Latest updates, Offers, Tech happenings around the world, New Release and Sessions with the Authors:

https://discord.bpbonline.com

Chapter 3
Java Application Components

Introduction

This chapter introduces Java classes and objects. You will learn about members of a class, such as variables, methods, access specifiers, and constructors. You will learn to implement polymorphism by using the concept of method and constructor overloading. You will understand the creation of packages and use different keywords such as **`static`**, **`final`**, and **`this`** keyword.

Structure

In this chapter, the following topics will be discussed:

- Java class and objects
- Access specifiers
- Instance variables and methods
- Constructor
- Initializer block
- Variable argument method (Varargs)
- Method overloading
- Constructor overloading

- '**this**' keyword
- '**final**' keyword
- '**static**' keyword
- Packages

Objectives

In this chapter, you will learn to create Java classes and objects. You will understand the use of different access specifiers to restrict access to the class and its members. You will be introduced to the different class members such as variables, methods, constructors, and so on. and understand how to perform method and constructor overloading. Finally, you will learn to use the **static**, **final** and **this** keywords as well as create packages in Java.

3.1 Java class and objects

A Java class is the construct that facilitates the concept of encapsulation. Java is a tightly encapsulated language, hence, nothing can be declared outside a class, not even the **main()** method. In Java, a class is also a data type, and objects of this type can be created to access and manipulate the class members.

A class is composed of attributes/fields that store data and methods that perform some operation on the attributes.

Syntax:

```
class <class-name> {
  // variable declarations
  // method definitions
}
```

Note that the class members are enclosed within the curly braces **{}**. The name of the class must follow some conventions:

- The class name should be a simple and meaningful noun, for example, **Calculator**.
- Class names can be in mixed case but the first letter of each succeeding word should be capitalized, for example, **ScientificCalculator**.
- Java keywords cannot be used for the class name.
- The class name cannot begin with a digit or symbol except a dollar (**$**) or an underscore (_), for example, **_Calc or $Calc**.

The following code shows declaration of a class named **Calculator**:

```
class Calculator {
  // class members
}
```

Here, the class **Calculator** is also a data type declaration for which multiple objects can be created later. To create an object or instance of a class, the **new** operator is used which allows the JVM to allocate memory for the object and return the reference/memory address to the variable representing the object. This variable is called the reference variable. Syntax:

```
<class-name> <object-name> = new <class-name> ();
```

```
For example:
```

```
Calculator objCalc = new Calculator();
```

Here, the statement **new Calculator()** allocates memory to the object, **objCalc** at runtime, and returns the reference of the memory location to the reference variable **objCalc**. Java allows to declare an object and initialize/allocate memory later. For example:

```
Calculator objCalc;
```

ObjCalc is a reference variable that does not point to any memory location yet. That is, it is null. Any attempt to use this variable at this point will result in an error. To use this variable, it must be initialized first. For example:

```
objCalc = new Calculator();
```

Now, memory is allocated to the object, and its reference is stored in **objCalc** variable. Therefore, it can be used to access the members of **Calculator** class.

3.2 Access specifiers

In Java, apart from encapsulating the data members and methods in a class, further restriction on access can be provided by using access specifiers. Java provides the public, private, and protected access specifiers that provide different levels of visibility to a class, field, and method. When no access specifier is mentioned for a class member, the default accessibility is package or default.

The access specifiers supported by Java are:

- **public:** The **public** access specifier makes a field, method, or class visible to any class in a Java application within the same package or another package. Hence, it is the least restrictive of all access specifiers.

  With the introduction to JPMS in JDK 9, the meaning of the public has been elevated to the module level as well based on the declaration of **exports** in the **module-info.java** file. With modules, the **public** keyword can be applied as:

  - **Public only within the module**: The public classes of a package within a module that are not exported using **exports** keyword, will be accessible only within the module. For example:

    ```
    module com.ModuleA{
    }
    ```

    Here, since no package is exported, all classes are public only within **ModuleA**.

- **Public to everyone**: The public classes of a package within a module that is exported using **exports** keyword will be accessible to classes of other modules. For example:

```
module com.ModuleA{
  exports pkg1.test;
}
module com.ModuleB{
  requires com.ModuleA   // reading ModuleA
}
```

  Here, **pkg1** is being exported so its public class is can be accessed by other modules.

- **Public only to a specific module**: The public classes of a package within a module that is exported only to a specific module, will be accessible only to classes of that module. For example:

```
module com.ModuleA{
  exports pkg1.test to com.ModuleB;
}
module com.ModuleB{
  requires com.ModuleA  // valid
}
module com.ModuleC{
  requires com.ModuleA  // not allowed
}
```

  Here, the **ModuleA** is allowing access only to **ModuleB**. So, **ModuleC** will get an error if it tries to access **ModuleA**.

- **private**: The **private** access specifier is used to prevent access to fields and methods outside of the enclosing class. It is the most restrictive of all access specifiers. It cannot be applied to classes and interfaces. JDK 9 onwards, private methods are allowed in interfaces. The **private**; access specifier is generally used with fields that have important data that cannot be shared directly. All such fields are declared private and public accessor or getter methods are used to access them.
- **protected**: The **protected** access specifier is used when classes have a parent-child relationship. Members declared protected can be accessed by all classes in the same package but only by the subclasses in other packages. The **protected** keyword cannot be applied to classes and interfaces or fields and methods of an interface.
- **Default**: The default access specifier is applied when no access specifier is mentioned. It allows access to class, field, or method only to the classes of the same package.

3.3 Instance variables and methods

The instance variables and methods are members of a class and define the state and behavior of an object respectively. These can be accessed by creating an object of the class. Each instance of a class has its own copy of instance variables but the instance methods are shared by all the objects during execution. Syntax:

```
<access-specifier> <data-type> <instance-variable-name>;
```

For example:

```
private int count;
```

Instance methods are used to perform operations on the instance variables. Syntax:

```
<access-specifier] <return-type> <method-name> ([<parameters-list>,]) {
  // Method definition
}
For example:
public void add(int a, int b){
  System.out.println("Sum of a and b is "+ (a+b));
}
```

Here, the add method is a **public** method and returns nothing, indicated by void. It takes two parameters of type integer. Within the method body, a **print** statement displays the sum of the two parameters whose values will be specified by the user at runtime during method invocation. Naming conventions for a method name are listed below:

- Java keywords cannot be used for the method name.
- Method names cannot contain spaces and cannot begin with a digit.
- Method name should be a simple and meaningful verb that describes its function.
- Method name can begin with a letter, underscore (_) or dollar (**$**) symbol.
- A multi-word method name should have the first word in lowercase and succeeding words with the first letter capitalized, for example, **beginPayment**.

To access instance variables and methods from a class, an object of the class must be created within the **main()** method. The methods must be invoked by using the object name followed by the dot (**.**) operator and the method name. In Java, a method is always invoked/called from within another method called the calling method. Once all statements of the called methods are executed, the control is returned to the calling method. Generally, all methods are invoked from the **main()** method of a class. The **main()** method is the execution point of the program.

The following figure shows the class diagram of the class **Calculator** with its instance variable and instance method:

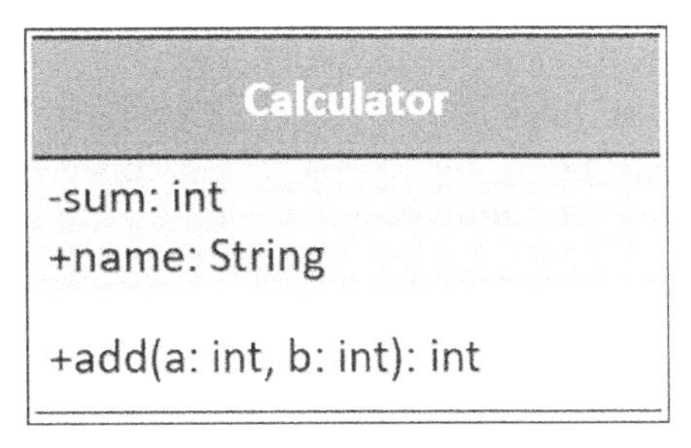

Figure 3.1: *Class diagram*

The following example shows the use of instance variables and methods and invoking methods by using the object of a class:

```
import java.util.Scanner;
public class Calculator {
  private int sum;
  String name;
  public int add(int a, int b) {
    sum = a + b;
    return sum;
  }
  public static void main(String[] args) {
    Calculator objCalc = new Calculator();
    Scanner s = new Scanner(System.in);
    System.out.println("Enter your name: ");
    objCalc.name = s.next();
    System.out.println("Enter first number: ");
    int num1 = s.nextInt();
    System.out.println("Enter second number: ");
    int num2 = s.nextInt();
    System.out.println("Dear, "+objCalc.name);
    System.out.println("Sum of "+num1+" and "+num2 +" is " + objCalc.add(num1,
num2));
  }
}
```

Here, the variable **sum** is a private instance variable, and **add** is a public method that takes two integer arguments. The return type of **add** method is **int**. Hence, a return statement is provided that returns the value of the **sum** of **a** and **b** to the calling method.

Within the **main()** method, an object **objCalc** of class **Calculator** is created by using the **new** keyword. Next, the name of the user is accepted and stored in the **name** variable by using **objCalc.name** statement. Two numbers are accepted from the user with the help of the **Scanner** class. Finally, the sum is calculated by invoking the add method and passing the two values as arguments, that is, **objCalc.add(num1,num2)**. The name of the user and the value returned by the add method is printed on the screen by using the **println()** method.

The output of the code is shown below:

```
Enter your name:
John
Enter first number:
4
Enter second number:
5
Dear, John
Sum of 4 and 5 is 9
```

Figure 3.2: *Instance variables and methods*

3.4 Constructor

A constructor is a method that has the same name as the class name. It may have parameters but cannot have any return type. It can be used to initialize variables with default values and also to instantiate objects. It is executed automatically as soon as an object of the class is instantiated.

A constructor can be default or parameterized.

Syntax:

```
// Default
<class-name>() {
  // Initialization statements
}
// Parameterized
<class-name>([<parameter-list],){
  // Initialization statements
}
```

In case no constructor is defined in a class, the JVM invokes an implicit constructor called the no-argument or default constructor. The default constructor initializes the instance variables of the created object to their default values. For example:

```
Calculator objCalc = new Calculator();
```

The following example shows the use of explicit no-argument constructor and parameterized constructor:

```
public class Calculator {
  private String name;
  public Calculator() {
```

```
    name = "Undefined";
  }
  public Calculator(String username) {
    name = username;
  }
  public static void main(String[] args) {
    Calculator objCalc = new Calculator();
    System.out.println("Your name is " + objCalc.name);
    Calculator objCalc1 = new Calculator("John");
    System.out.println("Your name is " + objCalc1.name);
  }
}
```

Here, there are two constructors, a no-argument constructor that initializes the value of the private variable **name** to a default value. The other constructor takes a **String** argument and assigns it to the **name** variable.

Within the main method, the first object **objCalc**, is instantiated by using the no-argument constructor while the second object **objCacl1** is instantiated by using the parameterized constructor. Next, the value of the **name** variable for both the objects is printed on the screen.

The output of the code is shown below:

```
run:
Your name is Undefined
Your name is John
BUILD SUCCESSFUL (total time: 0 seconds)
```

Figure 3.3: Using constructors

3.5 Initializer block

Java allows using the initializer block as an alternative to constructors to initialize variables with default values. The initializer block is executed before the execution of the constructor during object instantiation.

The following example shows the use of initializer block:

```
public class Calculator {
  private String name;
  {
    name = "Unknown";
```

```
  }
  public static void main(String[] args) {
    Calculator objCalc = new Calculator();
    System.out.println("Your name is " + objCalc.name);
    objCalc.name = "John";
    System.out.println("Your name is " + objCalc.name);
  }
}
```

Here, the initializer **block {}** initializes the value of the variable **name**. Within the main method, the object **objCalc** is instantiated and the value of **name** is printed. Next, the variable **name** is explicitly assigned a value and then printed on the screen.

The output of the code is shown below:

```
run:
Your name is Unknown
Your name is John
BUILD SUCCESSFUL (total time: 0 seconds)
```

***Figure 3.4**: Using initializer block*

3.6 Pass-by-value and pass-by-reference

The variables specified in method declaration are called the parameters while the actual values passed to it during invocation are called arguments. In the case of multiple parameters, the type and order of arguments must be the same as that of the parameters of the method.

Parameters can be of a primitive type such as **int, double**, and so on. and also of reference types such as objects, arrays, and so on.

3.6.1 Passing arguments by value

When arguments are passed by value, a copy of the argument is passed from the calling method to the called method. In this case, any modification done to the argument within the called method will not reflect in the calling method.

The following example shows how to pass the argument by value:

```
public class PassByVal {
  public void modifyVal(int val) {
    val = val + 10;
  }
```

```
  public static void main(String[] args) {
    int val = 10;
    PassByVal obj1 = new PassByVal();
    obj1.modifyVal(val);
    System.out.println("Value of val after method invocation is " + val);
  }
}
```

The output of the code is shown below:

```
run:
Value of val after method invocation is 10
BUILD SUCCESSFUL (total time: 0 seconds)
```

Figure 3.5: Passing arguments by value

Note, the value of variable **val** after passing it to **modifyVal()** method is still 10. This is because **val** was passed by value so only a copy of the value of **val** was passed to **modifyVal()** method. The actual address in memory is not passed hence, the value of **val** remains 10 even after invoking the method **modifyVal()**.

3.6.2 Passing arguments by reference

When arguments are passed by reference, the actual memory address of the argument is passed to the method. This means, if the called method modifies the value of the argument, it will reflect in the calling method also.

There are two references of the same object namely, argument reference variable and parameter reference variable. The following code shows how to pass the argument by reference:

```
public class PassByRef {
  public float areaCircle(CommonVals objPi, float r) {
    float area = objPi.getPI() * r * r;
    objPi.Pi = 3.15f; // modify the value of Pi

    return area;
  }
  public static void main(String[] args) {
    PassByRef p1 = new PassByRef();
    CommonVals c1 = new CommonVals();
    System.out.printf("Area of circle is %03.2f", p1.areaCircle(c1, 3));
```

```
    System.out.printf("\nModified value of PI is %01.2f %n",c1.getPI());
  }
}
class CommonVals {
  float Pi = 3.14f;
  public float getPI() {
    return Pi;
  }
}
```

The class **CommonVals** consists of the **getPI()** method that will return the value of variable **Pi**. Within the **PassByRef** class, the method **areaCircle()** accepts the object of **CommonVals** as a parameter along with the radius. Next, it calculates the area and then modifies the value of **Pi** by using the object **objPi** that was received as an argument from the calling method. Finally, it returns the value of the **area** to the calling method.

In the **main()** method, an object of the **PassByRef** class **p1** and the **CommonVals** class **c1** is created. The **areaCircle** method is invoked with the **p1** object and the **c1** object is passed as the argument. The returned value of the variable **area** is printed by using the **printf()** method.

Next, the value of **Pi** is printed by using the **c1** object. Note that instead of the original value 3.14, now the value of **Pi** is changed to **3.15** for the calling method as well.

The output of the code is shown below:

```
run:
Area of circle is 28.26
Modified value of PI is 3.15
BUILD SUCCESSFUL (total time: 0 seconds)
```

Figure 3.6: *Passing argument by reference*

3.7 Variable argument method

The **Variable argument** (**Varargs**) method allows passing a variable number of arguments when the number of arguments is not known until runtime. It is a shortcut to an array. In a **Varargs** method, the type of the last parameter is followed by an ellipsis (**...**), then, space, followed by the name of the parameter. This method can be called with any number of values for that parameter, including none.

Syntax:

```
<method-name>(type … <variable-name>){
```

```
    // method definition
}
```

The following code shows the use of variable argument method:

```
public class VarArgsMethod {
  public void multiplyVals(int... val) {
    int result = 1;
    for (int x : val) {
      result = result * x;
    }
    System.out.println("Multiplication of numbers is " + result);
  }
  public static void main(String[] args) {
    VarArgsMethod obj = new VarArgsMethod();
    obj.multiplyVals(1, 3, 5, 7);
  }
}
```

Here, the method **multiplyVals()** is a variable argument method that can accept any number of arguments of type integer. The enhanced **for** loop is used to iterate through the collection of values within the **val** variable. The actual values are passed in the **main()** method during the invocation of the **multiplyVals()** method.

The output of the code will be:

```
Multiplication of numbers is 105
```

3.8 Method overloading

Java provides the feature of method overloading to create multiple methods with different method signatures. Method overloading is one of the ways of implementing polymorphism in Java. Method overloading can be implemented in the following three ways:

- Changing the number of parameters
- Changing the sequence of parameters
- Changing the type of parameters

The following example shows the implementation of method overloading:

```
public class Calculator {
  // overloaded method 1
  public void add(int a, int b){
```

```
    System.out.println("Sum is "+ (a+b));
  }

  // overloaded method 2
  public void add(int a, float b){
    System.out.println("Sum is "+ (a+b));
  }

  // overloaded method 3
  public void add(int a, int b, float c){
    System.out.println("Sum is "+ (a+b+c));
  }

  // overloaded method 4
  public void add(float a, int b){
    System.out.println("Sum is "+ (a+b));
  }

  public static void main(String[] args) {
    Calculator c1 = new Calculator();
    c1.add(2.5f, 3);
    c1.add(3, 4, 5.6f);
    c1.add(4, 5);
    c1.add(3, 6, 2.4f);
  }
}
```

Here, four overloaded versions of the add method have been created by modifying the type, number, and sequence of parameters. Note that simply changing the parameter names or the return type does not make the method overloaded.

For example, the below method signatures are not valid for overloading:

```
public int add(int a, int b){
}
public void add(int c, int d){
}
```

Within the **main()** method, the **c1** object of the **Calculator** class is used to invoke the **add()** methods. The compiler will execute the appropriate method that matches the type, sequence, and the number of parameters passed by the user. The output of the code is shown below:

```
Sum is 5.5
Sum is 12.6
Sum is 9
Sum is 11.4
```

Figure 3.7: Method overloading

3.9 Constructor overloading

Java allows the overloading of the class constructor to allow the initialization of different type and number of variables. When the object is instantiated, the compiler invokes the constructor that matches the number, type, and sequence of arguments passed to it. The following example shows the implementation of constructor overloading:

```
public class Customer {
  String custId, address;
  float orderAmt;
  int itemCount;
  public Customer() {
    custId = "C000";
    address = "undefined";
    orderAmt = 0.0f;
    itemCount = 0;
  }
  public Customer(String id, String addr) {
    custId = id;
    address = addr;
  }
  public Customer(String id, float amount, int quantity) {
    custId = id;
    orderAmt = amount;
    itemCount = quantity;
  }
  public void displayDetails() {
    System.out.println("Customer Id: " + custId);
```

```
        System.out.println("Address: " + address);
        System.out.println("Order amount $: " + orderAmt);
        System.out.println("Item count: " + itemCount);
    }
    public static void main(String[] args) {
        Customer c1 = new Customer();
        c1.displayDetails();
        System.out.println("--------------------------");
        Customer c2 = new Customer("C001", "Sandra Park");
        c2.displayDetails();
        System.out.println("--------------------------");
        Customer c3 = new Customer("C002", 456.50f, 30);
        c3.displayDetails();
    }
}
```

Here, three overloaded constructors have been used to initialize the different variables of class **Customer**. In the **main()** method, three objects have been created to invoke the appropriate constructor by passing the arguments according to the respective type, order, and sequence. The output of the code is shown below:

```
Customer Id: C000
Address: undefined
Order amount $: 0.0
Item count: 0
--------------------------
Customer Id: C001
Address: Sandra Park
Order amount $: 0.0
Item count: 0
--------------------------
Customer Id: C002
Address: null
Order amount $: 456.5
Item count: 30
```

Figure 3.8: *Constructor overloading*

Note that the variables for which no values are specified, their default values as per the data type are displayed.

3.10 'this' keyword

The keyword **this** is used to refer to the current object whose method or constructor is being called. It can be used within an instance method or a constructor. The following example shows the use of **this** keyword:

- To assign value to a variable from a parameter that has the same name, that is, to resolve naming conflict.
- To invoke a constructor from another constructor.

```
public class Area {
  int length;
  int width;
  public Area() {
    length = 4;
  }
  public Area(int width) {
    this();  // invoking default constructor
    this.width = width; // resolving name conflict
  }
  public void calcArea() {
    System.out.println("Area is " + (length * width));
  }
  public static void main(String[] args) {
    Area objRect = new Area(3);
    objRect.calcArea();
  }
}
```

In the program, **this** keyword is used in the parameterized constructor to call the default constructor as well as to assign value to variable width from a parameter with the same name. The output of the code is shown below:

```
run:
Area is 12
BUILD SUCCESSFUL (total time: 0 seconds)
```

Figure 3.9: *Using 'this' keyword*

3.11 'final' keyword

The **final** modifier is used to restrict modification of a variable, method, or class. A variable declared final becomes a constant whose value cannot be changed later in the code. For example:

```
final float PI = 3.14;
```

A method declared final cannot be overridden in a subclass to prevent modification of method definition. For example:

```
final float getDiscount(float sales){
  // execution statement(s)
}
```

A final method cannot be declared abstract because then, it cannot be overridden. The abstract keyword is used with a method and class. An abstract method cannot have a body and an abstract class cannot be instantiated and must be inherited. Hence, anything declared abstract cannot use the final modifier.

A class declared final cannot be inherited and the variables and methods of a final class are also implicitly final. Such a class becomes a standard and must be used as it is. For example:

```
public final class Algorithm {
  // class members
}
```

The following code shows the use of the **final** keyword:

```
public class Circle {
  final float PI = 3.14f;
  public void calcArea(int rad) {
    System.out.println("Area of circle is " + (PI * rad * rad));
    PI = 3.15f;  // gives compilation error
  }
  public static void main(String[] args) {
    Circle c1 = new Circle();
    c1.calcArea(2);
  }
}
```

The **Circle** class consists of the **PI** variable which is declared final. Within the **calcarean()** method, an attempt is made to change the value of **PI**. This generates a compile-time error. Despite that, if the code is executed, a runtime exception will be generated as shown below:

```
run:
Area of circle is 12.56
Exception in thread "main" java.lang.RuntimeException: Uncompilable
        source code - cannot assign a value to final variable PI
        at moduleOne/Sess3Codes.Circle.calcArea(Circle.java:17)
        at moduleOne/Sess3Codes.Circle.main(Circle.java:21)
```

Figure 3.10: Using 'final' keyword

3.12 'static' keyword

The **static** keyword is used with variables and methods to provide a class-level scope. Static variables and methods can be accessed directly with the class name without creating an object. For all instances, there exists a single copy of a static/class variable. A static variable declared as final becomes a constant whose value cannot be changed in the code later. For example:

```
static int PI=3.14; // static variable
static final int PI=3.14; // static constant
```

The **static** keyword can also be applied to methods and initializer blocks. However, a static method:

- It can access only static variables.
- It can invoke only static methods.
- It cannot use this or super keywords.

For example:

```
public static void main(String args[]){
   // execution statement(s)
}
```

The **static** keyword can be used with initializer blocks to initialize static variables as soon as the class is loaded. The static block is executed even before the **main()** method is called. There can be more than one static block in a program and they can be placed anywhere in the class. However, a static block can access only those static variables that have been declared before it.

The following example shows the use of static variables, static method, and static block:

```
public class StaticDemo {
  static int staticVar = 0;
  int instanceVar = 0;
  static {
    System.out.println("Static block executed");
  }
  public static void staticMethod() {
```

```
        System.out.println("Static method executed");
    }
    public void display() {
        staticVar++;
        instanceVar++;
        System.out.println("Value of instance variable is:" + instanceVar);
        System.out.println("Value of static variable is:" + staticVar);
    }
    public static void main(String[] args) {
        System.out.println("Main method executed");
        StaticDemo.staticMethod();
        StaticDemo obj1 = new StaticDemo();
        obj1.display();
        StaticDemo obj2 = new StaticDemo();
        obj2.display();
        StaticDemo obj3 = new StaticDemo();
        obj3.display();
    }
}
```

The output of the code is shown below:

```
Static block executed
Main method executed
Static method executed
Value of instance variable is:1
Value of static variable is:1
Value of instance variable is:1
Value of static variable is:2
Value of instance variable is:1
Value of static variable is:3
```

Figure 3.11: *Using the 'static' keyword*

Note that the static block is executed before the **main()** method. Also, the value of the instance variable is **1** for each object. But, the value of the **static** variable is shared by each object, hence, the next object receives the value incremented by the previous object.

3.13 Packages

Packages are used to organize and group related classes, interfaces, and other application resources as one unit. For example, there can be a package for storing all source files, another for images, and yet another for third-party APIs. It is advisable to store classes in packages for easy access and maintenance. Also, it helps to resolve naming conflicts when classes with the same names exist in the application. For example, **pkg1.Test** and **pkg2.Test**. Packages add an extra level of visibility restriction to classes outside of the package.

A package name is usually written in lower case. A package can have sub-packages that can be accessed with the fully qualified name, that is, **<outer-package>.<inner-package>.<class-name>**. Two members of a package cannot have the same name. There can be only one public class in a Java package. Built-in packages in Java begin with the standard **java** or **javax**.

When any class of a package is invoked for the first time, the entire package is loaded in the memory which avoids unnecessary disk I/O for calls to other programs of the same package. The Java platform provides a number of built-in libraries that contain packages and classes used for application development. This library is called the **Application Programming Interface** (**API**). The packages contain classes that are used to perform common programming tasks with ease. These packages are called built-in or predefined packages. For example, the **java.io** package contains classes that allow file manipulation and **java.awt** package contains classes that allow the creation of **Graphical User Interface** (**GUI**) components.

The custom packages created by developers during application development are called user-defined packages. For example, **com.pkg1**. Usually, package names contain the reversed domain name of the company followed by the region and the package name. For example, **com.company.region.pkg1**.

The following example shows the creation of package in JDK 8 without using IDE:

1. Create a class as shown below:

   ```
   package testpkg;
   class Hello{
     public static void main(String[] args){
       System.out.println("Hello World");
     }
   }
   ```

2. Save the source file **Hello.java** in folder/package named **testpkg**.
3. Open the command prompt and set the path for the JDK 8 **bin** folder.
4. Compile the code as follows:

   ```
   javac Hello.java
   ```
   OR
   Compile the code with **-d** option as follows:
   ```
   javac -d . Hello.java
   ```
   where **-d** indicates a directory and **'.'** represents the current directory. The command will create a subfolder named **testpkg** and store the compiled class file inside it.

5. From the parent **testpkg** folder, execute the class file using the fully qualified name as follows:

   java testpkg.Hello

The following screenshot shows the steps to execute a class with the fully qualified name in JDK 8:

```
F:\>set path="C:\Program Files\Java\jdk1.8.0_45\bin"

F:\>cd testpkg

F:\testpkg>javac -d . Hello.java

F:\testpkg>java testpkg.Hello
Hello World
```

Figure 3.12: Using packages in JDK 8

Note, the **testpkg** in **testpkg.Hello** statement indicates the subfolder **testpkg** created after compiling the **Hello.java** file using the **javac** command. To create and execute a program with the fully qualified name using JDK 10, create a source folder named **src**. Within it, create a module folder named **ModuleA** and a module-**info.java** file. Create a package **testpkg** within **ModuleA** folder. In the **testpkg** folder, create a **Hello.java** class.

The following screenshot shows the steps to execute a class with the fully qualified name in JDK 10:

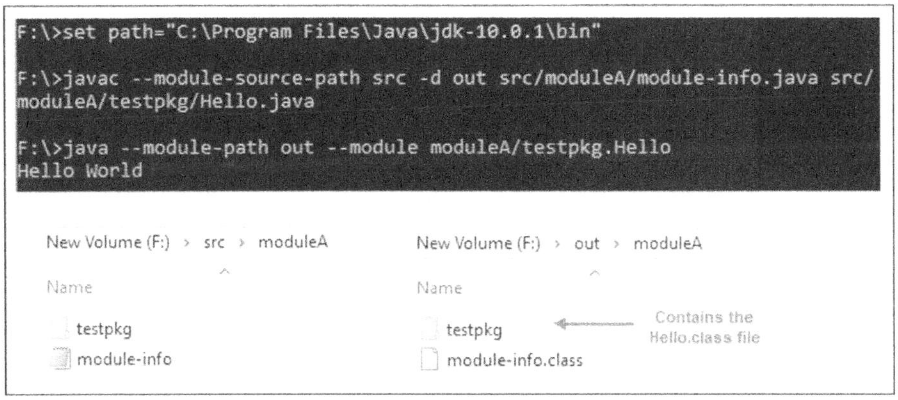

```
F:\>set path="C:\Program Files\Java\jdk-10.0.1\bin"

F:\>javac --module-source-path src -d out src/moduleA/module-info.java src/
moduleA/testpkg/Hello.java

F:\>java --module-path out --module moduleA/testpkg.Hello
Hello World
```

Figure 3.13: Using packages in JDK 10

Note, the **testpkg** in **moduleA/testpkg.Hello** statement of **java** command indicates the subfolder **testpkg** created in the **out** folder after compiling the **Hello.java** file using the **javac** command.

To use the members of built-in and user-defined packages in another class, use the **import** statement. For example, to use the class **Hello** of **testpkg** in a class **Messages** which is in **testpkg1**, the **import** statement must be used as shown below:

[**Assumption**: **testpkg1** and **testpkg** are in the same module, **moduleA**]

```
package testpkg1;
import testpkg.Hello;
import java.util.Calendar;
public class Messages{

  // code statements
}
```

The class **Messages** imports the **testpkg.Hello** user-defined class and the **java.util.Calendar** built-in class.

The module, moduleA must export the classes that it wants to expose to other modules. Further, the access specifiers of the class members will determine if these can be accessed by classes of other packages.

Similarly, packages can be created in an application developed using an IDE. For example. In NetBeans, a new package can be added to a module by simply right-clicking the module name and selecting **New | Java Package** as shown below:

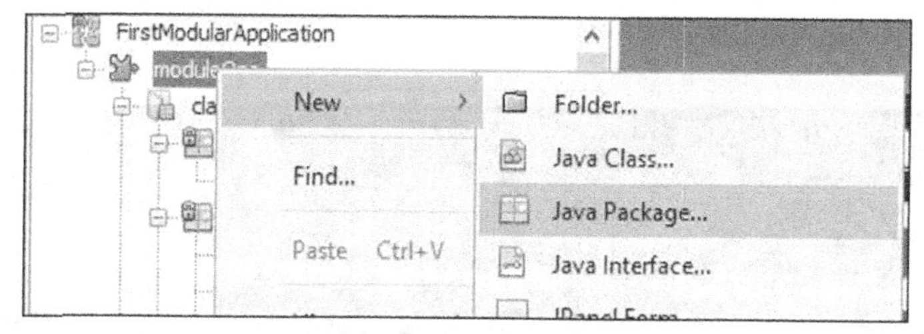

Figure 3.14: Creating package in NetBeans IDE

Conclusion

In this chapter, you learnt that a class is composed of attributes/fields that store data and methods that perform some operation on the attributes. To create an object or instance of a class, the **new** operator is used. Java provides the public, private, and protected access specifiers that provide different levels of visibility to a class, field, and method. A constructor is a method having the same name as the class name and does not have any return type, though, it can have parameters. Java provides the feature of method overloading to create multiple methods with different method signatures. The keyword **'this'** is used to refer to the current object whose method or constructor is being called. The **'final'** modifier is used to restrict the modification of a variable, method, or class. Static variables and methods can be accessed directly with the class name without creating an object. Packages are used to organize and group related classes, interfaces, and other application resources as one unit.

In the next chapter, you will learn about Java reference types.

Multiple choice questions

1. **Which of the following is the most restrictive access specifier?**
   a. public
   b. protected
   c. private
   d. default
2. **Consider the following partial code.**
   ```
   public Rectangle(int width) {
     this();
     this.width = width;
   }
   ```
   What is the purpose of `this()` statement?
   a. To indicate the current object
   b. To invoke the no-argument constructor
   c. To initialize the variables with default values
   d. To override the constructor definition
3. **Which keyword allows accessing data members and methods of a class without creating an instance?**
   a. static
   b. final
   c. this
   d. public
4. **Which of the following statements about packages is false?**
   a. A package name is usually written in lower case.
   b. A package cannot have sub-packages.
   c. Two members of a package cannot have the same name.
   d. There can be only one public class in a Java package.
5. **Consider the following partial code.**
   ```
   // method 1
   public void add(int a, int b){
     System.out.println("Sum is "+ (a+b));
   }
   // method 2
   ```

```
public void add(int c, int d){
  System.out.println("Sum is "+ (a+b));
}
// method 3
public void add(int a, float b){
  System.out.println("Sum is "+ (a+b));
}
```

Which of the method is not a valid overloaded version?

a. method 1
b. method 3
c. method 2
d. method 1 and method 3

Answers

1. c
2. b
3. a
4. b
5. c

Assignment

Create a Java program with the following specifications:

1. Create two packages **pkg1** and **pkg2**.
2. In **pkg1**, create a class named **IncentiveCalculator** and in **pkg2** create a class called **FixedValues**.
3. In the class, **FixedValues** create a constant variable named commission and set its value. The commission variable should be directly accessible using the class name. [Hint: use **static** and **final** keywords]
4. In the **IncentiveCalculator** class, create two private variables **salespersonName** and sales.
5. Create two overloaded constructors, one with a single parameter and one with two parameters.
6. The value of the sales variable must be initialized in the constructor with one parameter named sales. [Hint: use **this** keyword]
7. Create a two-parameter constructor that has parameters with the same name as the variables. It should call the default constructor set the value of the sales variable and also initialize the **salespersonName** variable. [Hint: use **this** keyword and **this(sales)**]

8. Create a method named **calculateIncentive()** to calculate the incentive. If the sales amount is more than or equal to 10000, fand so onh the value of commission from **FixedValues** class and multiply it with sales to get the incentive amount. If sales value is less than 10000, simply print a message that incentive is zero. [Hint: Use **import** statement to access commission variable]
9. In the **main()** method, accept the values of **salespersonName** and sales amount from the user, and pass it to the two-parameter constructor of **IncentiveCalculator** class.
10. Invoke the method **calculateIncentive()** to calculate and display the incentive amount.

The expected output is shown below:

```
Enter Salesperson name:
John
Enter sales amount:
11000
Incentive for sales of 11000.0 is 2200.0
```

```
Enter Salesperson name:
Clara
Enter sales amount:
8000
Incentive for sales of 8000.0 is 0
```

Figure 3.15: *Expected output*

Join our book's Discord space

Join the book's Discord Workspace for Latest updates, Offers, Tech happenings around the world, New Release and Sessions with the Authors:

https://discord.bpbonline.com

CHAPTER 4
Java Reference Types

Introduction

This chapter explains different types of arrays and the **`String`** class. You will learn to work with **`StringBuilder`** and **`StringTokenizer`** classes, command-line arguments, and wrapper classes. You will also understand the concept of autoboxing and unboxing.

Structure

In this chapter, we will learn the following topics:

- Java arrays
- String class in Java
- String arrays
- StringBuilder class in Java
- StringTokenizer class in Java
- Passing arguments to main() method
- Java wrapper classes

Objectives

In this chapter you will learn to create different types of Arrays and work with the String class. You will also learn to use **`StringBuilder`** and **`StringTokenizer`** for manipulating strings. Further, you will learn to work with wrapper classes as well as understand autoboxing and unboxing.

4.1 Java arrays

Java arrays are used for storing multiple values of similar types in the same variable. The number of values in an array is fixed and of a single type stored in the contiguous memory location. The number of values it can store is specified when the array is created and cannot be modified later in code.

Arrays in Java are of the following two types:

- Single-dimensional arrays
- Multi-dimensional arrays

The following figure shows the structure of an array of numbers:

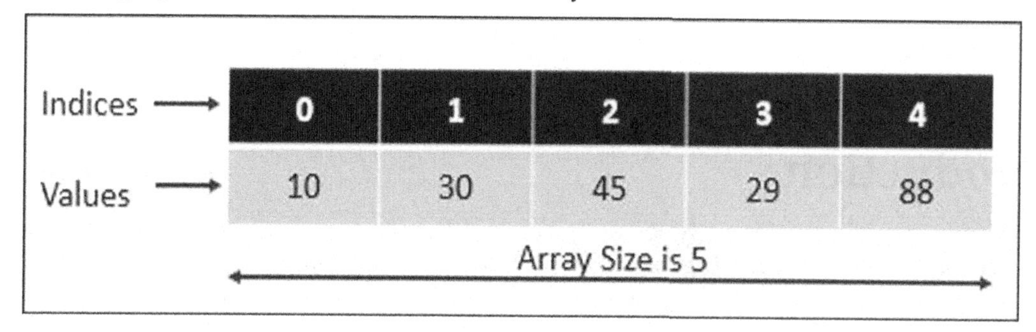

***Figure 4.1:** Array element organization*

As shown in the image, the elements of an array are arranged in contiguous memory locations. Each element of the array is accessed using its index. Array index begins at 0, and the last index is array **`size-1`**. Here, the size of the array is 5, that is, it can store a maximum of 5 elements. Hence, the first element will be at index 0, and the last element will be at index, **`size-1`** = 5-1 = 4. As per the figure, the value at index 4 is 88, which is the last or 5th value of the array.

Arrays are an optimal way of storing multiple elements of the same type because memory is allocated to an array only when the array is used.

4.1.1 Single-dimensional array

A single-dimensional array, when represented vertically, has a single column with multiple rows of data. Each element is accessed with the name of the array and its index. For example, consider the array of students shown below:

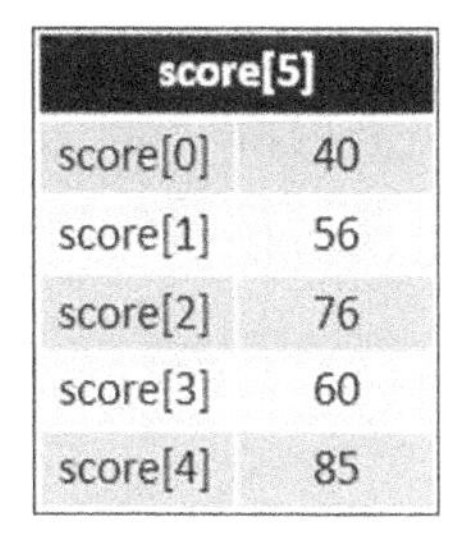

score[5]	
score[0]	40
score[1]	56
score[2]	76
score[3]	60
score[4]	85

Figure 4.2: *Single-dimensional array*

The array score is declared with **`size 5`** in the square brackets **`[]`**. Hence, it can hold a maximum of 5 values. The name of the array with the corresponding index is used to access any value. For example, to access the value 85, the syntax is **`score[4]`**. Note that the last index is 4 that is **`size-1`**. So, an attempt to access **`score[5]`** will raise an error/exception.

Creating a single-dimensional array in Java must be declared, instantiated and initialized.

Declaration syntax:

```
datatype[] <array-name>;
```

Instantiation syntax:

```
datatype[] <array-name> = new datatype[size];
```

Initialization

Array can be initialized in two ways:

During declaration:

```
int[ ] score = {40, 56, 76, 60,85};
```

Note that the size is not specified, and new operator is not used when array is initialized during creation.

After declaration and instantiation:

```
int[] score = new int[5];

score[0] = 40;

score[1] = 56;

score[2] = 76;

score[3] = 60;

score[4] = 85;
```

The following example shows the use of single-dimensional array:

```
public class OneDimenArray {
  int score[];  // declaring the array
```

```
  public OneDimenArray() {
    score = new int[5]; // instantiating the array
    // initializing the array
    score[0] = 40;
    score[1] = 56;
    score[2] = 76;
    score[3] = 60;
    score[4] = 85;
    System.out.println("Scores Added");
  }
  public void viewScores() {
    System.out.println("Scores are listed below:");
     System.out.println(score[0] + "\n" + score[1] + "\n" + score[2] + "\n" +
score[3] + "\n" + score[4]);
  }
  public static void main(String[] args) {
    OneDimenArray obj1 = new OneDimenArray();
    obj1.viewScores();
  }
}
```

Here, a one-dimensional array is declared and then, instantiated and initialized in the constructor. The values of the array are printed by invoking the **viewScores()** method from the **main()** method. The output of the code is shown below:

```
Scores Added
Scores are listed below:
40
56
76
60
85
```

Figure 4.3: *One-dimensional array*

4.1.2 Multi-dimensional array

A multi-dimensional array is an array of arrays, the most common being the two-dimensional array declared with an additional set of square brackets, for example, **int[][] score**. Each element is accessed with an index for each dimension in this case.

The following figure shows a two-dimensional array:

score[5][2]		
Index	0	1
0	40	60
1	56	45
2	76	65
3	60	74
4	85	90

***Figure 4.4:** Multi-dimensional array*

The array score is declared with size 5x2 in the square brackets `[][]`. Hence, it can hold a maximum of 5 rows and 2 columns with values. The name of the array with the corresponding indices of row and column is used to access any value. For example, to access the value 85, the syntax is **`score[4][0]`**. Note that the last index of the row is 4 and of the column is 1 that is **`size-1`**. So, an attempt to access the **`score[5][2]`** will raise an error/exception.

To create a multi-dimensional array in Java, it must be declared, instantiated and initialized.

Declaration and instantiation syntax:

```
datatype[][] <array-name> = new datatype [rows][columns];
```

```
For example:
```

```
int[][] score = new int[5][2];
```

Initialization:

A multi-dimensional array can be initialized in two ways:

During declaration:

```
int[][] score = {{40,60},
{56,45},
{76,65},
{60,74},
{85,90}};
```

Notice that the row elements are specified in a set of curly brackets separated by a comma delimiter. Also, each row is separated by a comma separator.

After instantiation:

A multi-dimensional array can be initialized after creation and instantiation by accessing each element with a row and column subscript.

```
int[][] score = new int[5][2];
score[0][0] = 40; score[0][1] = 60;
score[1][0] = 56; score[1][1] = 45;
score[2][0] = 76; score[2][1] = 65;
score[3][0] = 60; score[3][1] = 74;
score[4][0] = 85; score[4][1] = 90;
```

The following example shows the use of multi-dimensional array:

```
public class MultiDimenArray {
  int score[][];
  public MultiDimenArray() {
    score = new int[5][2];
    score[0][0] = 40; score[0][1] = 60;
    score[1][0] = 56; score[1][1] = 45;
    score[2][0] = 76; score[2][1] = 65;
    score[3][0] = 60; score[3][1] = 74;
    score[4][0] = 85; score[4][1] = 90;
    System.out.println("Scores Added");
  }
  public void viewScores() {
    System.out.println("Scores are listed below:");
    System.out.println("Player 1:" + score[0][0] + "," + score[0][1]);
    System.out.println("Player 2:" + score[1][0] + "," + score[1][1]);
    System.out.println("Player 3:" + score[2][0] + "," + score[2][1]);
    System.out.println("Player 4:" + score[3][0] + "," + score[3][1]);
    System.out.println("Player 5:" + score[4][0] + "," + score[4][1]);
  }
  public static void main(String[] args) {
    MultiDimenArray obj1 = new MultiDimenArray();
    obj1.viewScores();
  }
}
```

Here, a two-dimensional array is declared and then instantiated and initialized in the constructor. The values of the array are printed by invoking the **viewScores()** method from the **main()** method. The output of the code is shown below:

```
Scores Added
Scores are listed below:
Player 1:40,60
Player 2:56,45
Player 3:76,65
Player 4:60,74
Player 5:85,90
```

Figure 4.5: *Two-dimensional array*

4.1.3 Processing arrays with loops

Initializing and accessing individual array elements can be very time-consuming, especially if the array is large in size. To reduce the effort, Java allows using loops to initialize and process the arrays. Following example shows the use of loops to display the elements of a one-dimensional and multi-dimensional array:

```
public class ArrayWithLoops {
  int score[];
  int scores[][];
  public ArrayWithLoops() {
    score = new int[5];
    score[0] = 40; score[1] = 56;
    score[2] = 76; score[3] = 60;
    score[4] = 85;
    System.out.println("Scores Added to One-dimensional Array");
    scores = new int[5][2];
    scores[0][0] = 40; scores[0][1] = 60;
    scores[1][0] = 56; scores[1][1] = 45;
    scores[2][0] = 76; scores[2][1] = 65;
    scores[3][0] = 60; scores[3][1] = 74;
    scores[4][0] = 85; scores[4][1] = 90;
    System.out.println("Scores Added to Two-dimensional Array");
  }
  public void viewScores() {
    System.out.println("Scores of one-dimensional array are:");
    for (int i = 0; i < score.length; i++) {
      System.out.println(score[i]);
```

```
    }
    System.out.println("Scores of two-dimensional array are:");
    for (int row = 0; row < scores.length; row++) {
      System.out.println("Player " + (row + 1));
      for (int col = 0; col < scores[row].length; col++) {
        System.out.println(scores[row][col]);
      }
    }
  }
  public static void main(String[] args) {
    ArrayWithLoops obj = new ArrayWithLoops();
    obj.viewScores();
  }
}
```

Note the use of inner-loop for printing the two-dimensional array. For each iteration of the outer loop, the inner loop will be called and it will iterate until the number of columns available in the array which is retrieved with the statement **`scores[row].length`**.

The output of the code is shown below:

```
Scores Added to One-dimensional Array
Scores Added to Two-dimensional Array
Scores of one-dimensional array are:
40
56
76
60
85
Scores of two-dimensional array are:
Player 1
40
60
Player 2
56
45
Player 3
76
65
Player 4
60
74
Player 5
85
90
```

***Figure 4.6:** Using loops with arrays*

4.2 String class in Java

Java does not provide a primitive type that can store more than one character, that is a string. To accomplish this, an array of characters must be used as shown below:

```
char[] message = {'H','e','l','l','o'}
```

In the case of more than one value, a two-dimensional array is required. But, the array size is fixed during declaration, hence, it is not possible to store string values of different sizes, such as names of persons or addresses, and so on. Moreover, manipulating a character array can be a cumbersome task.

To overcome this, Java provides the **String** data type to store multiple characters without creating an array. A **String** variable is an instance of the **String** class and its value is stored within double-quotes, for example, **Hello**.

An instance of a **String** class can also be created explicitly using the **new** keyword, as shown below:

```
String msg = new String();
```

To concatenate strings, Java provides the plus + operator. For example:

```
String msg = "Hello";
String msg1 = "World";
System.out.println(msg + msg1);
```

A character array can be converted to a string as shown below:

```
char[] msg = {'H', 'e', 'l', 'l','o'};
String message = new String(msg);
```

The **String** class provides several methods for string manipulation. The following tables list the commonly used methods of **String** class. Consider the string **msg="Hello"**:

Method	Description
`length(String str)`	Returns the length of a string. For example, `msg.length(); // will return 5`
`concat(String str)`	Concatenates the string specified as the argument to the end of another string. For example, `msg.concat("World"); // will return 'HelloWorld'`

Method	Description
`substring(int beginIndex, int endIndex)`	Retrieves part of a string, that is, substring from the given string. It accepts the start index and the end index as parameters. If end index is not specified, all characters from the start index to the end of the string will be returned. The substring begins at the specified position denoted by `beginIndex` and extends to the character specified by `endIndex - 1`. Hence, the length of the substring is `endIndex – beginIndex`. The `beginIndex` value is included in the output whereas the `endIndex` value is excluded. For example, **`msg.substring(2,5); // will return 'llo'`**

`toString()`	Returns a `String` object by converting values of other data types into strings. For example,
	`Integer num = 6;`
	`num.toString(); // will return 6`
	Note, that value 6 is now represented as a string instead of an integer. (Integer is a Wrapper class)

`compareTo(String str)`	Compares two String objects based on the Unicode value of each character and returns an integer value as the result. It will return a negative value if the argument string is alphabetically greater than the original string and a positive value if the argument string is alphabetically lesser than the original string. It will return a value of zero if both the strings are equal. For example,
	`msg.compareTo("World"); // will return -15`
	The output is `15` because the letter `W` in the `World` is alphabetically greater than the first character `H` in `Hello`. The difference between the position of `H` and `W` is `15`. Since `H` is smaller than `W`, it returns `-15`.

`charAt(int index)`	Retrieves the character at a specific index. The starts from zero and ranges from zero to `length() - 1` For example, **`msg.charAt(1); // will return 'l'`**
`indexOf(String str)`	Returns the index of the first occurrence of the specified character or string within a string. It returns -1 when the character is not found. For example, **`msg.indexOf("l"); // will return 2`**
`lastIndexOf(String str)`	Returns the index of the last occurrence of a specified character or string from within a string. The search begins from the end of the string backward. For example, **`msg.lastIndexOf("l"); // will return 3`**

Method	Description
`replace(char old, char new)`	Replace all the occurrences of a specified character in the current string with a given new character. For example, `msg.replace('o','a'); // will return "Hella"`
`toUppercase()`	Converts the specified string to upper case. For example, `msg.toUppercase() // will return "HELLO"`
`toLowerrcase()`	Converts the specified string to lower case. For example, `msg.toLowercase() // will return "hello"`
`trim()`	Returns a new string after trimming the leading and trailing whitespace from the current string. For example, `String msg1 = " Hello ";` `msg1.trim()); // will return "Hello" with the spaces removed`
`equals(String str)`	Returns true if the string argument is equal to the value of the `String` object, else return false. For example, `msg.equals("Hello");  // will return true`

Table 4.1: Methods of String class

The following example shows the use of different **String** class methods:

```
public class StringDemo {
  String msg = "Hello";
  Integer num = 6;
  public void display() {
    System.out.println("Length of string is " + msg.length());
   System.out.println("New string after concatenation is " + msg.concat("World"));
    System.out.println("Extracted substring is " + msg.substring(2, 5));
    System.out.println("String format of Integer is " + num.toString());
   System.out.println("Difference after comparison is " + msg.compareTo("World"));
    System.out.println("Character at index 1 is:" + msg.charAt(2));
    System.out.println("First index of character l is:" + msg.indexOf("l"));
    System.out.println("Last index of character l is:" + msg.lastIndexOf("l"));
     System.out.println("New string after replacement is " + msg.replace('o',
'a'));
    System.out.println("Uppercase String is:" + msg.toUpperCase());
    System.out.println("Lowercase String is:" + msg.toLowerCase());
    String msg1 = " Hello ";
```

```
    System.out.println("String before trimming: " + msg1);
    System.out.println("String after trimming:" + msg1.trim());
  }
  public static void main(String[] args) {
    StringDemo obj = new StringDemo();
    obj.display();
  }
}
```

The code uses prints the output of different **String** class methods applied on the string **Hello**. The output of the code is shown below:

```
Length of string is 5
New string after concatenation is HelloWorld
Extracted substring is llo
String format of Integer is 6
Difference after comparison is -15
Character at index 1 is:1
First index of character l is:2
Last index of character l is:3
New string after replacement is Hella
Uppercase String is:HELLO
Lowercase String is:hello
String before trimming:  Hello
String after trimming:Hello
```

Figure 4.7: String class methods

4.3 String arrays

String arrays are used to store multiple strings in the same variable. String array is created in the same manner as arrays of primitive data types. For example:

```
String[] items = new String[5];
```

Here, memory is allocated to store references of 5 strings. To manipulate **String** arrays, loops such as **for, while,** and enhanced **for** can be used.

The following code shows the use of **String** array:

```
public class StringArrayDemo {
  String[] itemId = new String[5];
  public StringArrayDemo() {
    System.out.println("Products Added");
```

```
    for (int count = 0; count < itemId.length; count++) {
      itemId[count] = "Item00" + (count+1);
    }
  }
  public void displayProducts() {
    System.out.println("Products in the inventory are:");
    for (String item : itemId) {
      System.out.println(item);
    }
  }
  public static void main(String[] args) {
    StringArrayDemo obj = new StringArrayDemo();
    obj.displayProducts();
  }
}
```

Here, a string array named **itemId** is created and initialized in the constructor by using the **for** loop. The enhanced **for** loop is used to display the elements of the array. The output of the code is shown below:

```
Products Added
Products in the inventory are:
Item001
Item002
Item003
Item004
Item005
```

Figure 4.8: String array

The **java.lang.String** class cannot be inherited by other classes as it is a final class. **Strings** are immutable hence they can be used when the values are not likely to change later. But, if the string value is likely to change later, it is advisable to use the **StringBuilder** class.

Earlier StringBuffer class was used for creating mutable strings, but it was not efficient as it used thread synchronization. This has been fixed in the enhanced class StringBuilder. It allows modification of the strings without the overhead of synchronization and hence, it is much faster in execution.

4.4 StringBuilder class in Java

Unlike **`String`** objects, **`StringBuilder`** objects are mutable. The different methods of **`StringBuilder`** class allow modification of the string object. StringBuilder offers an advantage of simpler code in some cases, for example, StringBuilder is a more efficient choice to concatenate multiple strings.

Constructors of StringBuilder class:

- **`StringBuilder()`**: This the default constructor that provides space for 16 characters.
- **`StringBuilder(int capacity)`:** This constructor creates an empty object but reserves space for the number of characters specified in the argument, capacity.
- **`StringBuilder(String str)`:** This constructor creates an object that is initialized with the contents of the specified string, **`str`**.

Methods of **`StringBuilder`** class are as follows:

The following table lists the methods of the **`StringBuilder`** class:

Method	Description
`length()`	Returns the length of the character sequence in the class. For example, **`StringBuilder msg = new StringBuilder("JPMS is ");`** **`System.out.println(msg.length(); // returns 8`**
`append()`	Appends values at the end of the `StringBuilder` object. It accepts arguments of different types. For example, **`StringBuilder msg = new StringBuilder("JPMS is ");`** **`System.out.println(msg.append("New "); // returns "JPMS is New"`**
`insert()`	Inserts one string into another at the specified position. The `insert()` method has several versions as follows: **`StringBuilder insert(int position, String str)`** **`StringBuilder insert(int position, char ch)`** **`StringBuilder insert(int position, float f)`** For example, **`StringBuilder msg = new StringBuilder("JPMS is ");`** **`System.out.println(msg.insert(8, "New"); // returns "JPMS is New"`**
`delete()`	Deletes the specified number of characters from the `StringBuilder` object. For example, **`StringBuilder msg = new StringBuilder("JPMS is New");`** **`System.out.println(msg.delete(4,7); // returns "JPMS New"`**

Method	Description

`reverse()`	Reverses the characters of a StringBuilder object.
	For example,
	`StringBuilder msg = new StringBuilder("JPMS is New");`
	`System.out.println(msg.reverse()); // returns "weN si SMPJ"`

Table 4.2: Methods of StringBuilder class

The following code shows the use of different **StringBuilder** methods:

```
public class StringBuilderDemo {
  StringBuilder msg = new StringBuilder("JPMS was introduced in Java ");
  public void display() {
    System.out.println("String length:" + msg.length());
    System.out.println("String after appending: " + msg.append("9"));
    System.out.println("String after insertion: " + msg.insert(28, "SE "));
    System.out.println("String after deletion: " + msg.delete(28, 31));
    System.out.println("Reversed string: " + msg.reverse());
  }
  public static void main(String[] args) {
    StringBuilderDemo obj = new StringBuilderDemo();
    obj.display();
  }
}
```

The code prints the output of different **StringBuilder** class methods applied on the string **JPMS was introduced in Java**. The output of the code is shown below:

```
String length:28
String after appending: JPMS was introduced in Java 9
String after insertion: JPMS was introduced in Java SE 9
String after deletion: JPMS was introduced in Java 9
Reversed string: 9 avaJ ni decudortni saw SMPJ
```

Figure 4.9: StringBuilder class methods

4.5 StringTokenizer class in Java

The **java.util.StringTokenizer** class provides methods to break a string into tokens.

Constructors of **StringTokenizer** class are as follows:

- **StringTokenizer(String str):** Creates **StringTokenizer** with the specified string.
- **StringTokenizer(String str, String delim):** Creates **StringTokenizer** with specified string and delimiter.
- **StringTokenizer(String str, String delim, boolean returnValue)**: Creates **StringTokenizer** with specified string, delimiter, and **returnValue**. If **returnValue** is true, the delimiter character is also considered as a token. If it is false, the delimiter characters are used to separate the tokens.

Methods of **StringTokenizer** class are as follows:

boolean hasMoreTokens(): Checks if there is more tokens available.

boolean hasMoreElements(): Works similar to **hasMoreTokens()** method.

String nextToken(): Returns the next token from the **StringTokenizer** object.

String nextToken(String delim): Returns the next token based on the delimiter.

Object nextElement(): Works similar to **nextToken()** but returns an **Object**.

int countTokens(): Returns the total number of tokens.

The following example shows the use of **StringTokenizer** class:

```
public class StringTokenDemo {
  public static void main(String[] args) {
    StringTokenizer st = new StringTokenizer("East West North South", " ");
    while (st.hasMoreTokens()) {
      System.out.println(st.nextToken());
    }
    StringTokenizer st1 = new StringTokenizer("East,West,North,South");
    // printing next token
    System.out.println("Next token is " + st1.nextToken(","));
  }
}
```

The first object of **StringTokenizer** uses space " " character as delimiter while the second object uses comma "," character as a delimiter. The output of the code is shown below:

```
East
West
North
South
Next token is East
```

Figure 4.10: *Using StringTokenizer*

4.6 Passing arguments to main() method

The **main()** method accepts an array of Strings as arguments. These can be specified from the command line at runtime after the class name. For example:

```
java Customer C001 John
```

Here, **Customer** is a class, and **C001, John** are arguments that will be stored in the **String** array of the **main()** method. The arguments are separated by a space. The size of the **String** array will be set based on the number of arguments passed at the command line.

The following code shows the use of command-line arguments:

```
package testpkg;
public class Customer {
  private String custId, custName;
  public Customer(String custId, String custName) {
    this.custId = custId;
    this.custName = custName;
  }

  public void displayCustomerDetails(){
    System.out.println("Customer Id: "+custId);
    System.out.println("Customer Name: "+custName);
  }
  public static void main(String[] args) {
    String id = args[0];
    String name = args[1];
    Customer c1 = new Customer(id,name);
    c1.displayCustomerDetails();
  }
}
```

Here, the values for **custId** and **custName** variables are accepted from the command line through the **args[] String** array parameter of the **main()** method. The first value is stored in **args[0]** which is assigned to a **String** variable named **id** and the second one stored in **args[1]** is assigned to **String** variable, **name**. Note that the order of arguments is important to ensure that the correct value is assigned to a variable. Save the class as **Customer.java** in package **testpkg**. Store the **testpkg** package in a module named **moduleA** which is in folder **src**.

Execution of the class by passing command-line arguments is shown in the screenshot below:

```
F:\>set path="C:\Program Files\Java\jdk-10.0.1\bin"

F:\>javac --module-source-path src -d out src/moduleA/module-info.java src/moduleA/testpkg/Customer.java

F:\>java --module-path out --module moduleA/testpkg.Customer C001 John
Customer Id: C001
Customer Name: John
```

Figure 4.11: Command line arguments

To run the program from Netbeans IDE perform the following steps:

1. Create a **Modular** application and add a module.
2. Create a package in the module and add the **`Customer`** class within the package.
3. Right-click the project in the **Projects** tab and select **Properties**.
4. Select the **`Main`** class by clicking the **Browse** button and enter the arguments in the **Arguments** box separated by a space as shown below:

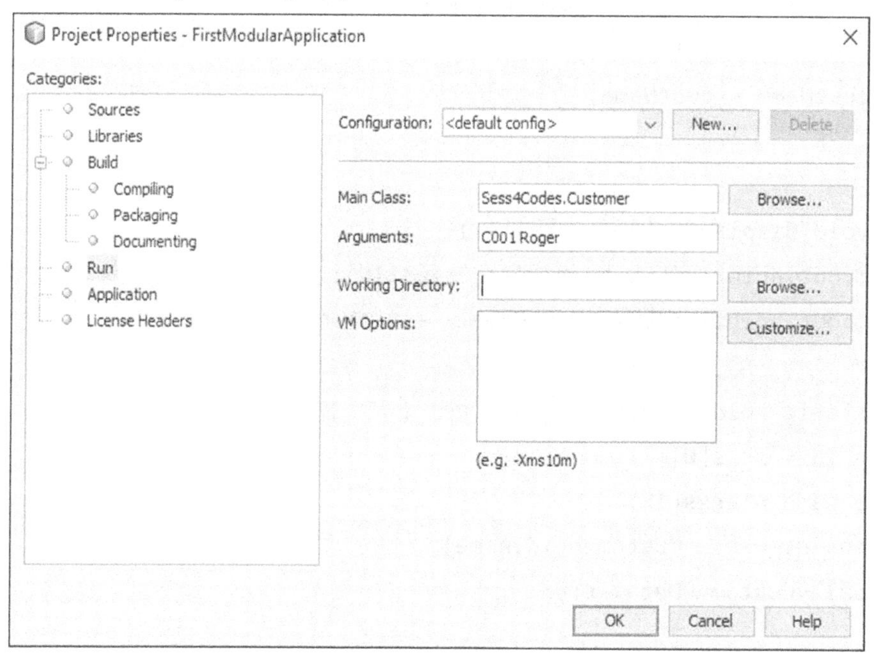

Figure 4.12: Project properties dialog box

5. Click **OK**.
6. Right-click the project and click **Run**. The output of the code is shown below:

```
run:
Customer Id: C001
Customer Name: Roger
```

Figure 4.13: Command line arguments in Netbeans IDE

4.7 Java wrapper classes

Java provides a wrapper class for each primitive type that wraps the primitive type into an object of that class. These classes provide utility methods to manipulate the data of that type. This feature also enables manipulating collections that store objects. Each wrapper class provides the **valueOf()** method to convert a type into another type.

The **valueOf()** method of the **Character** class accepts only char as an argument whereas any other wrapper classes accept the corresponding primitive type or **String** as an argument. The **<type>Value()** method can be used to return the value of an object as its corresponding primitive type. The **parse<type>()** method returns the primitive type of an object.

For example:

```
byte val = Byte.byteValue();
```

The following table lists the primitive types and the corresponding wrapper types:

Primitive type	Wrapper class
byte	Byte
short	Short
int	Integer
long	Long
float	Float
double	Double
char	Character
boolean	Boolean

Table 4.3: Wrapper types

A primitive type holds a value whereas a wrapper type holds the reference/address of memory location.

For example:

```
Primitive type:
int num = 10;
Wrapper type:
Integer num1 = new Integer(20);
```

The reference of the object is assigned to the reference variable **num1**. The following code shows the use of different **Wrapper** classes:

```
public class WrapperDemo {
```

```
  public void useWrappers() {
    byte byteVal = Byte.parseByte("45");
    System.out.println("Byte value is " + byteVal);

    if (Character.isDigit('4')) {
      System.out.println("Character value is a Digit");
    }
    if (Character.isLetter('L')) {
      System.out.println("Character value is a Letter");
    }
  }
  public static void main(String[] args) {
    if (args.length == 2) {
      //parse String to primitive type int
      int a = Integer.parseInt(args[0]);
      int b = Integer.parseInt(args[1]);
      System.out.println("Sum of " + a + " and " + b + " is " + (a + b));
    } else {
      System.out.println("Not enough data to process");
    }
    WrapperDemo obj = new WrapperDemo();
    obj.useWrappers();
  }
}
```

The **useWrappers()** method shows the use of **parseByte(), isDigit()** and **isLetter()** methods. In the **main()** method, the **String** values passed as command-line arguments are parsed to primitive **int** type using the **parseInt()** method. The output of the code is shown below:

```
Sum of 34 and 45 is 79
Byte value is 45
Character value is a Digit
Character value is a Letter
```

Figure 4.14: Methods of wrapper classes

A primitive type can be converted to its respective object type and vice-versa. For example, an int can be converted to Integer and vice-versa. This process is called autoboxing and unboxing.

For example:

Autoboxing

```
Integer num1 = new Integer(4);
Character answer = 'Y';
```

Unboxing

```
int num2 = num1;
char result = answer;
```

Note that both primitive and object type variables give the same output. However, the variable of the wrapper type can use the methods of the wrapper class to manipulate the value which is not available with the primitive type.

Conclusion

In this chapter you learnt that Java Arrays are used for storing multiple values of similar types in the same variable. Java provides the String data type to store multiple characters without creating an array. A String variable is an instance of the String class and its value is stored within double-quotes. The `concat()` method concatenates the string specified as the argument to the end of another string. String arrays are used to store multiple strings in the same variable. If the string value is likely to change later, it is advisable to use the `StringBuilder` class. The `java.util.StringTokenizer` class provides methods to break a string into tokens. Java provides a Wrapper class for each primitive type that wraps the primitive type into an object of that class. The `parse<type>()` method returns the primitive type of an object.

In the next chapter, you will learn about subclasses and interfaces.

Multiple choice questions

1. **The last index of an array is equal to _____.**
   a. 0
   b. size
   c. size-1
   d. undefined
2. **Consider the following partial code.**

```
String msg = "Good Morning";
System.out.println(msg.substring(2,5));
```

What will be the output of the code?

a. od M
b. od
c. ood M
d. oo

3. **Match the columns:**

	StringBuilder method		Description
a.	`length()`	1.	Appends values at the end of the StringBuilder object.
b.	`append()`	2.	Inserts one string into another at the specified position.
c.	`insert()`	3.	Reverses the characters of a StringBuilder object.
d.	`reverse()`	4.	Returns the length of the character sequence in the class.

a. a-2,b-3,c-4,d-1
b. a-3,b-4,c-1,d-2
c. a-4,b-1,c-2,d-3
d. a-2,b-4,c-1,d-3

4. **Consider the below partial code:**

```
int[ ] score = {40, 56, 76, 60,85};
```

What will be the last index of the array?

a. 5
b. 4
c. 0
d. 1

5. **Consider the below partial code:**

```
Integer num1 = new Integer(4);
```

Which concept is depicted here?

a. Autoboxing
b. Unboxing
c. Implicit typecasting
d. Explicit typecasting

Answers

1. c
2. b
3. c
4. b
5. a

Assignment

Create a Java program as per the following specifications:

1. Create a class with the **main()** method.
2. Retrieve username (admin) and password (admin) from command line arguments.
3. If username and password are valid, call two methods, one to accept values and next to display values.
4. Create a method to accept values. Accept the names of the top three players and their scores and store them in arrays. [Hint: Use one-dimensional arrays, **String** array for player names and **int** array for scores, use a single for-loop to accept the values for both arrays at a time.]
5. Create another method to display the player names with their scores. [Hint: Use a single **for**-loop to display values of both arrays at a time]
6. If the username and password are incorrect, display a message to the user and terminate the program.

The expected output is shown below. When valid username and password is passed at the command line:

```
F:\>java --module-path out --module moduleA/testpkg.Assignment admin admin
Enter names of the top three players and their scores
Enter player name:
John
Enter the score:
67
Enter player name:
Mark
Enter the score:
65
Enter player name:
Roger
Enter the score:
58

Names and Scores of the top three players:
Player  Score
John    67
Mark    65
Roger   58
```

Figure 4.15: *Expected output with valid credentials*

When the invalid username and/or password are passed at the command line:

```
F:\>java --module-path out --module moduleA/testpkg.Assignment admin abcde
Invalid credentials
```

Figure 4.16: *Expected output with invalid credentials*

Join our book's Discord space

Join the book's Discord Workspace for Latest updates, Offers, Tech happenings around the world, New Release and Sessions with the Authors:

https://discord.bpbonline.com

CHAPTER 5
Subclasses and Interfaces

Introduction

This chapter introduces the concept of inheritance in Java and the different types of inheritance. You will learn the different ways of implementing inheritance by using abstract classes, nested classes, method overriding, and so on. You will also learn to use interfaces and lambda expressions.

Structure

In this chapter, we will learn the following topics:

- Inheritance in Java
- Abstract methods and abstract classes
- Nested classes
- Interfaces
- Java functional interfaces
- Lambda expressions

Objectives

In this chapter, you will understand the concept of inheritance and implement the different types of inheritance. You will also understand method overriding as well as work with abstract classes and nested classes. Further, you will learn to work with interfaces and lambda expressions.

5.1 Inheritance in Java

Java provides the concept of inheritance to group classes with similar characteristics and creates a class hierarchy. The common characteristics and behavior are combined into a single class termed as the superclass or parent class and all other classes that inherit these characteristics and behavior are termed as subclasses or child classes.

Subclasses inherit all members and methods except the private ones. Constructors of the superclass are not inherited but can be invoked from the child class constructor directly or by using **`super()`**. Subclasses will have its own features along with those inherited from the superclass. Declaring members with similar names in the subclass as that of the parent class will lead to the hiding of members of the parent class.

The following figure shows the different types of inheritance in Java:

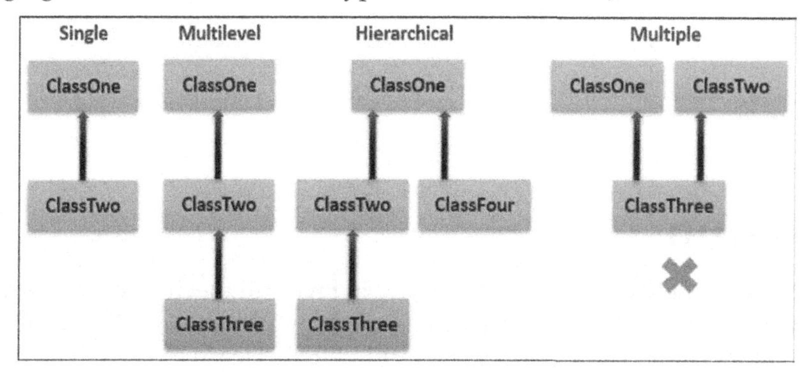

***Figure 5.1:** Types of Inheritance*

The different types of inheritance in Java are as follows:

- **Single inheritance**: In single inheritance, a child class can inherit from only one parent/ superclass.
- **Multilevel inheritance**: In multilevel inheritance, a child class inherits from a single parent, the parent can inherit from another single class itself.
- **Hierarchical inheritance**: In hierarchical inheritance, a parent/superclass can have more than one child classes that in turn may have other child classes at different levels.
- **Multiple inheritance**: In multiple inheritance, a child class can inherit from more than one parent/superclasses. Java does not support multiple inheritance with classes due to an issue called the diamond problem.
- Diamond problem is a situation when there is one abstract class, **`A`** that is inherited by two subclasses, **`B`** and **`C`**. Assume that the abstract class has a method called **`test()`**. This method will be overridden in both subclasses. Now, another class, **`D`** inherits the two subclasses that have the **`test()`** method with the same name and signature. In

this case, a copy of both **`test ()`** methods will be created in the subclass object. When an object of the subclass is created to access the **`test()`** method, the compiler faces an ambiguous situation and cannot decide which method to call. This issue is known as the diamond problem in Java as shown below:

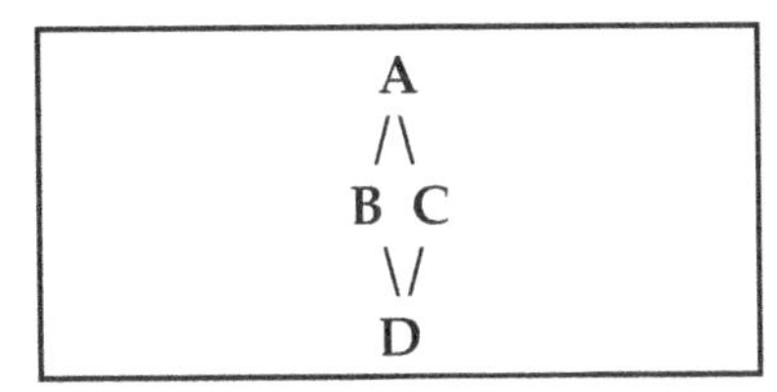

Java offers a solution to the diamond problem in the form of interfaces. Multiple inheritance can be simulated by implementing more than one interface in a class. You can also use default methods introduced in interfaces in Java 8.

5.1.1 Creating subclass

To implement inheritance in Java, a parent-child relationship is created between two or more classes by using the **`extends`** keyword.

Syntax:

```
public class <child-class-name> extends <parent-class-name>{
  // child class members
}
```

To access the superclass constructor, the **`super()`** method is used. The following example shows the implementation of single inheritance in Java:

```
public class Shape {
  private final float PI = 3.14f;
  protected float width;
  private String shape;
  public Shape(String shape) {
    this.shape = shape;
  }
  public void area(float length) {
    switch (shape.toLowerCase()) {
      case "circle":
        System.out.println("Area of Circle is " + (PI * length * length));
        break;
      case "square":
```

```
          System.out.println("Area of Square is " + (length * length));
          break;
        case "rectangle":
          System.out.println("Area of Rectangle is " + 2 * (length + width));
          break;
        case "triangle":
         System.out.println("Area of a Triangle is " + (1 / 2 * (length * width)));
      }
    }
}
```

Class Shape with data members and a method is the parent/superclass. Note the protected variable width:

```
public class Rectangle extends Shape {
  public Rectangle() {
    super("rectangle");
    width = 20;
  }
  public void drawRect(){
    System.out.println("Drawing a Rectangle");
  }
}
```

The **Rectangle** class is the child/subclass that inherits **Shape** class by using the **extends** keyword. It initializes the width variable that it has inherited from the parent class. Note the call to superclass constructor using the **super()** method to set the value of the shape variable. The **drawRect()** method is specific to the **Rectangle** class:

```
public class TestShapes {
  public static void main(String[] args) {
    Rectangle obj = new Rectangle();
    obj.drawRect();
    obj.area(40);
  }
}
```

The **TestShape** class has a **main()** method that creates an object of the **Rectangle** class. The object is used to invoke the **drawRect()** method and the inherited **area()** method to set the value of the **length** variable and display the **area** of the rectangle.

The output of the code is shown below:

```
run:
Drawing a Rectangle
Area of Rectangle is 120.0
```

Figure 5.2: Single inheritance

Similarly, more classes can be inherited from **`Shape`** class such as **`Circle, Triangle`**, and so on. to implement hierarchical inheritance. Also, the subclasses of **`Rectangle`** class can be created to implement multi-level inheritance. The following image describes the concept:

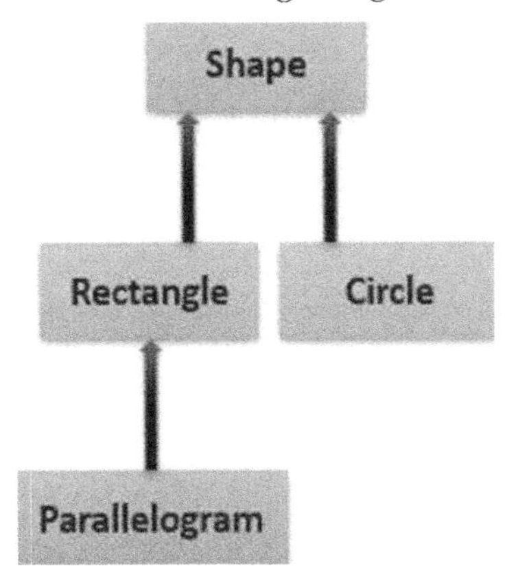

Figure 5.3: Single, hierarchical, and multilevel inheritance

For example:

```
public class Circle extends Shape{
  // class code
}
public class Parallelogram extends Rectangle{
  // class code
}
```

Note: Java does not support multiple inheritance. For example, the following is not allowed.

```
public classA extends classB, classC{
  // class code
}
```

5.1.2 Method overriding

Method overriding is a concept that allows to create a child class method with the same signature and return type as that of the parent class. This allows the child class to modify or enhance the functionality of the parent class method without having to use a new name for it. Method overriding is also one of the ways to implement polymorphism in Java.

Note that the overriding method must have the same signature (name, type, and number of arguments) and return type as that of the parent class method. The access specifier of the overridden method cannot be weaker than that of the superclass method.

At times, the child class might need to use the functionality of the parent class method along with that of its overridden version. This can be done by invoking the parent class method by using the **super** keyword, that is, **super.parentMethodName**. Similarly, if the child class has a data member with the same name as that of a parent class data member, the **super** keyword can be used to access the parent member, that is, **super.parentVariableName**.

The following example shows the use of method overriding and super keyword:

```
public class Employee {

  private String id, name;
  private float salary;
  public Employee(String id, String name, float salary){
    this.id=id;
    this.name=name;
    this.salary=salary;
  }

  public void displayDetails(){
    System.out.println("Employee id: "+ id);
    System.out.println("Employee name: "+ name);
    System.out.println("Salary : $"+salary);
  }
}
```

Employee class is the super class with private variables initialized in the parameterized constructor and a method to display the details:

```
public class ContractEmployee extends Employee{
   int duration;
   public ContractEmployee(String id, String name, float salary, int duration){
    super(id,name,salary);
    this.duration=duration;
  }
```

```
  // overridden method
  @Override
  public void displayDetails(){
    System.out.println("Employee Details");
    super.dispalyDetails();
    System.out.println("Contract duration: "+duration+" months");
  }
}
```

The **ContractEmployee** class inherits the **Employee** class and initializes the superclass variables by calling the superclass constructor by using the **super()** method. It also initializes its own variable, duration. The **displayDetails()** method has been overridden in the **ContractEmployee** class. To use the functionality of the parent method, the super keyword is used to invoke the **dispalyDetails()** method of the superclass.

Note: The @Override is an annotation that informs the compiler that the method is overridden from the parent class.

```
public class TestEmployee {
  public static void main(String[] args) {
    ContractEmployee emp1 = new ContractEmployee("Emp1","John Smith", 4000f, 6);
    emp1.displayDetails();
  }
}
```

The **TestEmployee** class creates an object of **ContractEmployee** class and initializes the variables by passing appropriate arguments to the constructor. The object invokes the **displayDetails()** method. Note that since the object is of **ContractEmployee** class, the **displayDetails()** method of child class is invoked and not of the parent class:

```
Employee Details
Employee id: Emp1
Employee name: John Smith
Salary : $4000.0
Contract duration: 6 months
```

Figure 5.4: Method overriding

5.1.3 Static versus dynamic binding

Binding of methods and method calls during compile time is called static/early binding and at runtime is called dynamic/late binding. All static method calls are resolved at compile-time and for instance methods at runtime. Java variable access also follows static binding.

The following table lists the differences between static and dynamic binding:

Static binding	Dynamic binding
Implemented at compile time.	Implemented at runtime.
Applicable to private, static, and final methods and variables.	Applicable for virtual methods based on the type of runtime object.
Uses a type of object/class for binding.	Uses a type of reference to resolve binding.
Applicable to overloaded methods.	Applicable to overridden methods.

Table 5.1: Difference between static and dynamic binding

Differentiate the type of reference and type of object

The type of object is indicated by the name of the class on the left of the assignment operator, for example, **`Employee objEmp`**. The type of reference is indicated by the class on the right whose constructor is invoked, for example, **`Employee objEmp = new Employee()`**.

In this case, the type of object and type of reference is the same. However, Java allows assigning reference of a different class that is part of the inheritance hierarchy. For example, **`Employee objEmp1 = new ContractEmployee()`**. Here, the type of object is **`Employee`** but the type of reference is **`ContractEmployee()`**. Hence, at runtime, any call to methods or variables will be considered from **`ContractEmployee()`** class and not from **`Employee`** class.

It is possible to cast an instance of a subclass to its parent class which is termed as upcasting. **For example:**

```
ContractEmployee objCE = new ContractEmployee();
Employee objEmp = objCE; // upcasting
```

While upcasting, the parent object cannot access the members that are specific to the child class.

It is also possible to cast the parent reference back to the child type which is termed as **`downcasting`**. However, **`downcasting`** requires explicit type casting by specifying the child class name in parenthesis ().

For example:

```
ContractEmployee emp = (ContractEmployee) objEmp; // downcasting
```

The following example modifies the **`TestEmployee`** class to demonstrate the difference between the type of reference and type of object:

```
public class TestEmployee {
  public static void main(String[] args) {
    Employee emp1 = new Employee("Emp1", "John Smith", 4000f);
    emp1.displayDetails();
```

```
    System.out.println("--------------");
    Employee emp2 = new ContractEmployee("Emp2", "Mark Stevens", 2000f, 6);
    emp2.displayDetails();
  }
}
```

The object **emp1** is of type **Employee** and has the reference of **Employee** as well. Whereas the object **emp2** is of type **Employee** but has the reference of **ContractEmployee** class.

The output of the code is shown below:

```
Employee id: Emp1
Employee name: John Smith
Salary : $4000.0
--------------
Employee Details
Employee id: Emp2
Employee name: Mark Stevens
Salary : $2000.0
Contract duration: 6 months
```

Figure 5.5: *Type of object and type of reference*

5.2 Abstract methods and classes

Java allows creating classes that declare methods to serve as a contract or a standard and simply provide a structure but leave the implementation to the inheriting class. Such methods are called abstract methods and can be created by using the **abstract** keyword.

The abstract methods do not have any method definition, that is the **{}** braces and end with a semicolon.

Syntax:

```
abstract <return-type> <method-name> (<parameter-list>);
```

For example:

```
public abstract void display();
```

A class with abstract methods is considered as an abstract class. It acts as a base for the inheriting classes. The requirement-specific behavior is then implemented by the subclasses.

Syntax:

```
abstract class <class-name>
{
  // fields
```

```
  // concrete methods
  // abstract methods
  // [abstract <return-type> <method-name>(<parameter-list>);]
}
```

The following example shows the creation and implementation of abstract methods in an abstract class:

```
public abstract Shape{
  private float PI = 3.14;
  // concrete method
  public float getPI(){
    return PI;
  }
  // abstract method
  public abstract void calculateArea();
}
```

The **Shape** is an abstract class with one concrete method and one abstract:

```
public class Rectangle extends Shape {
  private float length, width;
  public Rectangle(float length, float width) {
    this.length = length;
    this.width = width;
  }
  @Override
  public void calculateArea() {
    System.out.println("Length: " + length);
    System.out.println("Width: " + width);
    System.out.println("Area of rectangle: " + (length * width));
  }
}
```

The **Rectangle** class inherits abstract class **Shape** and implements the **calculateArea()** method as per its requirement. Similarly, more classes can be inherited from Shape class, such as **Circle, Square**, and so on. and the **calcualteArea()** method can be implemented by each of these classes in their own way:

```
public class TestShapes {
```

```
  public static void main(String[] args) {
    Rectangle obj = new Rectangle(2.3f,4.0f);
    obj.calculateArea();
  }
}
```

The **TestShapes** class creates an object of the **Rectangle** class and initializes the parameters. The **calculateArea()** method is invoked to calculate the area of the rectangle.

The output of the code is shown below:

```
Length: 2.3
Width: 4.0
Area of rectangle: 9.2
```

Figure 5.6: Abstract class and abstract method

5.3 Nested classes

A class defined within another class is called a nested class.

Syntax:

```
class Outer{
...
  class Nested{
...
  }
}
```

Nested classes offer the following advantages:

- Logical grouping of classes based on related functionality.
- Enhanced encapsulation for top-level classes, for example, **ClassA** and **ClassB**. That is, **ClassB** can be nested within **ClassA** so that **ClassB** can access the private members of **ClassA**.
- Increased readability and maintainability of code by placing the code closer to where it will be used.

Nested classes can be broadly classified as:

Non-static nested classes or inner classes: A non-static inner class is declared as a member of the outer or enclosing class. The inner class has direct access to all members including private ones of the outer class. The outer class cannot access any member of the inner class. An inner class can be declared as **public, private, protected, abstract, or final.**

To access the inner class, an instance of the outer class must be created as shown below:

```
OuterClass.InnerClass objInner = objOuter.new InnerClass();
public class OuterClass {
  String outerVariable;
  public void outerMethod(String message) {
    System.out.println("Message received: " + message);
  }
  class InnerClass {
    public String sayHello() {
      // invoke outer class method from inner class
      outerMethod("Good Morning");
      // initialize outer class variable from inner class
      outerVariable = "Hello!!";
      return outerVariable;
    }
  }
}
```

The **InnerClass** has access to all members of the **OuterClass**:

```
public class TestNestedClasses {
  public static void main(String[] args) {
    OuterClass objOuter = new OuterClass();
    // Use OuterClass object to instantiate InnerClass object
    OuterClass.InnerClass objInner = objOuter.new InnerClass();
    System.out.println(objInner.sayHello());
  }
}
```

The **TestNestedClasses** class creates an object of **OuterClass** and uses it to instantiate the object of **InnerClass**.

The output of the code is shown below:

```
Message received: Good Morning
Hello!!
```

Figure 5.7: *Inner class*

Static nested classes: A static nested class is accessed from the outer class in the same manner as static variables and methods. A static nested class cannot directly refer to instance variables or methods of the outer class but only through an object reference. A static nested class is also a top-level class, except that it is nested inside another top-level class. A static nested class can be public, protected, private, default/package-private, final, and abstract. To access a static nested class, use the fully qualified class name.

For example:

```
OuterClass.StaticNestedClass
```

The following example shows the use of the static inner class:

```
public class OuterClass {
  String outerVariable;
  public void outerMethod(String message) {
    System.out.println("Message received: " + message);
  }
  public static void outerMethod1(){
    System.out.println("Outer class static method");
  }
  static class InnerClass {
    public static void sayHello() {
      outerMethod1();
      System.out.println("Greetings from Inner class");
    }
  }
}
```

The static **InnerClass** cannot access the instance methods and variables of the outer class but it can access the static methods and variables:

```
public class TestNestedClasses {
  public static void main(String[] args) {
    OuterClass objOuter = new OuterClass();
    objOuter.outerMethod("Good Morning");
    OuterClass.InnerClass.sayHello();
  }
}
```

The **TestNestedClasses** class creates an object of **OuterClass** to access the static **InnerClass**. The output of the code is shown below:

```
Message received: Good Morning
Outer class static method
Greetings from Inner class
```

Figure 5.8: Static nested class

Local classes: A nested class defined within a block of code such as a constructor, initializer block or method body is called a local class. A local inner class is part of a specific block and not of the outer class. Therefore, it cannot use any access specifier, but it can still access all members of the outer class including final variables declared in the scope in which it is defined:

```
public class OuterClass {
  String outerVariable;
  public void outerMethod(String message) {
    class LocalInner {
      public String getMessage() {
        return "Hello!! ";
      }
    }
    LocalInner obj = new LocalInner();
    System.out.println(obj.getMessage() + "Message received: " + message);
  }
  public static void outerMethod1() {
    System.out.println("Outer class static method");
  }
}
```

The **LocalInner** class is defined within the **outerMethod()** method of **OuterClass** class. The method creates an object of the local class to access the **getMessage()** method:

```
public class TestNestedClasses {
  public static void main(String[] args) {
    OuterClass objOuter = new OuterClass();
    objOuter.outerMethod("Good Morning");
  }
}
```

The **TestNestedClasses** class creates an object of the outer class and invokes the **outerMethod()** method. The output of the code is shown below.

```
Hello!! Message received: Good Morning
```

Anonymous classes: Anonymous class is a class declared without a name. Since it does not have a name, it can be accessed only where it is defined. It cannot use any access specifier. It cannot have static members or constructors. It cannot have a constructor but can have an instance initializer. It can access the members of the outer class.

It is useful for limiting access to another class and the only instance of a special class needs to be created.

Anonymous inner class are mainly created in two ways:

- Class (abstract or concrete)
- Interface

Based on the type of declaration and behavior, there can be three types of anonymous inner classes:

Anonymous inner class that extends a class: Here, the anonymous Inner class extends a class, that is, the `Thread` class:

```
public static void main(String[] args){
  Thread t = new Thread(){
    public void run(){
      System.out.println("Anonymous thread");
    }
  };
  t.start();
  System.out.println("Executing Main Thread");
}
```

Anonymous inner class that implements an interface: Here, the anonymous inner class implements an interface, that is, the Runnable interface:

```
public static void main(String[] args) {
 Runnable r = new Runnable() {
    public void run(){
      System.out.println("Anonymous Thread");
    }
  };
  Thread t = new Thread(r);
  t.start();
  System.out.println("Executing Main Thread");
}
```

Anonymous inner class defined as method/constructor argument: Here, the anonymous inner class is defined as an argument, that is, the constructor argument:

```
public static void main(String[] args) {
 Thread t = new Thread(new Runnable(){
    public void run(){
      System.out.println("Anonymous Thread");
    }
  });
  t.start();
  System.out.println("Executing Main Thread");
}
```

The following example shows the use of the anonymous class:

```
public class OuterClass {

  String outerVariable;

  public void outerMethod(String message) {
    AnonymousInner obj = new AnonymousInner() {
      @Override
      public void displayMessage(String msg) {
        System.out.println("Received message: " + msg);
      }
    };
    obj.displayMessage(message);
  }
}
class AnonymousInner {
  public void displayMessage(String msg) {
  }
}
```

Here, the anonymous inner class within the **outerMethod()** method, extends the **AnonymousInner** class defined outside the **OuterClass** class. The **displayMessage()** method is overridden in the anonymous inner class and then invoked by the **outerMethod()** method.

```
public class TestNestedClasses {
  public static void main(String[] args) {
```

```
    OuterClass objOuter = new OuterClass();
    objOuter.outerMethod("Good Morning");
  }
}
```

The **TestNestedClasses** class creates an object of the **OuterClass** and invokes the **outerMethod()** method. The output of the code is shown below:

```
Received message: Good Morning
```

5.4 Interfaces

An interface is a contract that sets the standards to be followed by the types that implement it. It is a workaround for implementing multiple inheritance. An interface is also a **.java** file saved with the same name as that of the interface. The bytecode of an interface is also converted to **.class** file similar to normal classes.

However, unlike classes, interfaces cannot have constructors and hence, cannot be instantiated. Methods of an interface are implicitly abstract. Fields of an interface must be static and final; it cannot have instance fields. The interface is not extended but implemented by classes. A class can implement multiple interfaces. An interface can extend multiple interfaces.

Until Java SE 7, interface supported only method declarations, that is, methods without a body. However, with Java SE 8, default methods were introduced and in Java 9, private methods have been introduced.

Interfaces are not used for implementing inheritance hierarchy. Rather, they are used to group common methods that can be implemented by different entities as per requirement, even if they are not a type of the interface. As a naming convention, the letter I is generally prefixed with the name of interfaces to differentiate the interface **.java** files from the class **.java** files. Interface names are written in *CamelCase* with the first letter of each word capitalized. The interface name should imply the functionality it performs.

For example:

```
interface IEnumerable

interface IComparable
```

Syntax:

```
<visibility> interface <interface-name> extends <other-interfaces, … >
{
  // declare constants
  // abstract, default, private methods
}
```

For example:

```
public interface ITestInterface extends Interface1{
  static final int num;
  public void interfaceMethod();
}
```

A class implementing an interface must implement all abstract methods else it must be marked abstract. If the class implementing the interface is declared abstract, one of its subclasses must implement the unimplemented methods. If none of the abstract class' subclasses implement the interface methods, the subclasses also must be marked abstract.

Syntax:

```
class <class-name> implements <Interface1>,…
{
  // class members
  // overridden methods of the interface(s)
}
```

To create a new interface in NetBeans, right-click a package and select **New | Java Interface**. Provide the name for it and click **Finish**.

The following example shows the use of interfaces:

```
public interface IProduct {
  static final String PRODUCTZONE = "CA-LA";
  public void addProductDetails();
  public void showProductDetails(String prodID);
}
```

Interface `IProduct` declares a static final variable and two abstract methods:

```
public class TShirts implements IProduct {
  String tshirts[];
  @Override
  public void addProductDetails() {
    tshirts = new String[3];
    tshirts[0] = "T-shirt A, Red color, Brand A";
    tshirts[1] = "T-shirt B, Blue color, Brand B";
    tshirts[2] = "T-shirt C, Black color, Brand C";
    System.out.println("Product details added");
  }
```

```
  @Override
  public void showProductDetails(String prodID) {
    System.out.println("TShirt Details");
    for (String details:tshirts) {
      System.out.println(details);
    }
  }

  public void showTShirtSizes(){
    System.out.println("T-shirt Sizes");
    System.out.println("Large");
    System.out.println("Medium");
    System.out.println("Small");
  }
}
```

The `TShirts` class implements the `IProduct` interface and implements the two methods `addProductDetails()` and `showProductDetails()`:

```
public class TestProducts {
  public static void main(String[] args) {
    System.out.println(IProduct.PRODUCTZONE + " Zone");
    obj = new TShirts();
    obj.addProductDetails();
    System.out.println("------------------");
    obj.showProductDetails("T001");
    System.out.println("------------------");
    obj.showTShirtSizes();
  }
}
```

The `TestProducts` class creates an object of `TShirts` class and invokes the two overridden implemented methods along with the class-specific method. Note that the `PRODUCTZONE` constant is invoked directly with the interface name. The output of the code is shown below:

```
CA-LA Zone
Product details added
--------------------
TShirt Details
T-shirt A, Red color, Brand A
T-shirt B, Blue color, Brand B
T-shirt C, Black color, Brand C
--------------------
T-shirt Sizes
Large
Medium
Small
```

Figure 5.9: *Implementing interface*

Similarly, more classes for any type of products such as toys, materials, stationery, and so on. can be created which can implement the **IProduct** interface.

5.4.1 Implementing multiple interfaces

Java does not support multiple inheritance with classes. As a workaround, it allows implementing multiple interfaces in a class to simulate multiple inheritance.

For example:

```
public class Test implements Interface1, Interaface2{
}
```

The following code shows an implementation of more than one interface in a class:

```
public interface IDistributor {
  public void addDistributor(String detail);
  public void processOrder(String orderId);
}
```

The **IDistributor** interface declares two abstract methods. The modified **TShirts** class is shown below:

```
public class TShirts implements IProduct, IDistributor {
  String tshirts[];
  @Override
  public void addProductDetails() {
    tshirts = new String[3];
    tshirts[0] = "T-shirt A, Red color, Brand A";
    tshirts[1] = "T-shirt B, Blue color, Brand B";
```

```
    tshirts[2] = "T-shirt C, Black color, Brand C";
    System.out.println("Product details added");
  }
  @Override
  public void showProductDetails(String prodID) {
    System.out.println("TShirt Details");
    for (String details:tshirts) {
      System.out.println(details);
    }
  }

  public void showTShirtSizes(){
    System.out.println("T-shirt Sizes");
    System.out.println("Large");
    System.out.println("Medium");
    System.out.println("Small");
  }
  @Override
  public void addDistributor(String detail) {
    System.out.println("Distributor Added: "+detail);

  }
  @Override
  public void processOrder(String orderId) {
    System.out.println("Order Processed: "+orderId);
  }
}
```

The **TShirts** class implements both **IProduct** and **IDistributor** interfaces and implements its methods. The modified **TestProducts** class is shown below:

```
public class TestProducts {
  public static void main(String[] args) {
    System.out.println(IProduct.PRODUCTZONE + " Zone");
    TShirts obj = new TShirts();
    obj.addProductDetails();
```

```
        System.out.println("------------------");
        obj.showProductDetails("T001");
        System.out.println("------------------");
        obj.showTShirtSizes();
        System.out.println("------------------");
        obj.addDistributor("Dress Smart");
        System.out.println("------------------");
        obj.processOrder("O001");
    }
}
```

The **TShirts** object now invokes all the methods implemented from the interfaces as well as its own method. The output of the code is shown below:

```
CA-LA Zone
Product details added
-------------------
TShirt Details
T-shirt A, Red color, Brand A
T-shirt B, Blue color, Brand B
T-shirt C, Black color, Brand C
-------------------
T-shirt Sizes
Large
Medium
Small
-------------------
Distributor Added: Dress Smart
-------------------
Order Processed: O001
```

Figure 5.10: *Implementing multiple interfaces*

Similarly, more interfaces can be created and implemented in class.

5.4.2 Default, static, and private methods of interfaces

The interface design has always been a challenge because any modification/addition to an interface requires changes to all implementing classes. As the application grows, the number of classes implementing an interface also increases which makes it difficult to modify/extend the functionality of the interface without affecting so many classes. A workaround used earlier was the creation of a base implementation class which can then be extended, and its methods could be overridden in other classes as required.

In Java SE 7 and earlier versions, an interface can have only two types of members:

- Static constant variables
- Abstract methods

The method could not have implementations in interfaces. To use both abstract methods and non-abstract/concrete methods (methods with implementation), the abstract class was the only option. With Java 8, Oracle Corporation introduced the default methods and static methods feature which allows methods to have implementations in an interface.

In Java 8, an interface can have:

- Static constant variables
- Abstract methods
- Default methods
- Static methods

The default methods or defender methods allow new methods to be added to the interface without affecting the existing implementation of interfaces. These default methods have a method definition that will be used as default in case an implementing concrete class fails to provide an implementation for that method. The default methods come with a default implementation that can be used, overridden, or ignored without causing any problems to existing classes that have implemented an interface.

Java interface static methods are useful for creating utility methods for common activities such as null check, collection sorting, and so on. They also help in securing the code by preventing implementation classes from overriding them. The default keyword is used to create a default method in an interface as shown below.

The following example shows the use of default and static methods in an interface:

```
public interface ILog {
  String MYSQL_DB_NAME = "MySQLDb";
  // abstract method
  void logMsg(String message);
  // default methods
  default void logWarning(String message) {
    System.out.println("Logging Warning: " + message);
    // Connect to Database
    // Log Warning
    // Close Database connection
  }
  default void logFatalError(String message) {
    System.out.println("Logging Fatal Error: " + message);
```

```
    // Connect to Database
    // Log Fatal Error
    // Close Databse connection
  }
  // static method
  static boolean checkNull(String str) {
    System.out.println("Interface Check for Null");
    return str == null;
  }
}
```

The **ILog** interface declares an abstract method, two default methods, and one static method:

```
public class DBTransaction implements ILog {
  @Override
  public void logMsg(String message) {
    System.out.println(message);
  }
  public static void main(String[] args) {
    System.out.println("Connecting to: " + ILog.MYSQL_DB_NAME);
    DBTransaction obj = new DBTransaction();
    obj.logMsg("Database Connected Successfully");
    obj.logFatalError("Fatal Error while closing DB");
    System.out.println("Null check: " + ILog.checkNull("Hello"));
  }
}
```

The **DBTransaction** class implements the **ILog** interface and overrides the **logMsg** method. Note that it does not implement the default methods and the static method anyways cannot be overridden. Thus, the interface now has the flexibility for classes to not implement all methods of the interface.

The **main()** method creates an object of the class and invokes the **logMsg** method which is the overridden version as well as the default method **logFatalErrror()**. It also accesses the constant variable and static method by directly using the **ILog** interface name. The output of the code is shown below:

```
Connecting to: MySQLDb
Database Connected Successfully
Logging Fatal Error: Fatal Error while closing DB
Interface Check for Null
Null check: false
```

***Figure 5.11:** Default and static methods in interfaces*

In the code, note the redundancy in all the log methods created for establishing the connection and closing database connection. This issue can be solved if a common method is used for database connection, but that would be a public method that is accessible to all other classes. To create a reusable method and make it private, the only option is an abstract class with a private method for the common code.

Java 9 addresses this issue by introducing private methods in interfaces. Java 9 onwards, interfaces can have private methods by using a private access modifier. In Java 9 and later versions, an interface can have the following types of members:

- Static constant variables
- Abstract methods
- Default methods
- Static methods
- Private methods
- Private static methods

So now, the code of **ILog** interface can be optimized for reusability as shown below:

```
public interface ILog {
  String MYSQL_DB_NAME = "MySQLDb";
  // abstract method
  default void logMsg(String message) {
    System.out.println("Logging Information: " + message);
    logData(message, "Information");
  }
  // default methods
  default void logWarning(String message) {
    System.out.println("Logging Warning: " + message);
    logData(message, "Warning");
  }
  default void logFatalError(String message) {
    System.out.println("Logging Fatal Error: " + message);
    logData(message, "Fatal Error");
```

```
  }
  private void logData(String message, String type) {
    // Connect to Database
    // Log Message
    // Close Database connection
  }
  // static method example
  static boolean checkNull(String str) {
    System.out.println("Interface Check for Null");
    return str == null;
  }
}
```

The use of private method **logData()** allows reusability in other log methods and also prevents direct access to implementing classes. The usage of private methods helps to make default methods less bulky and more maintainable.

5.4.3 Issues with default methods

A class can implement multiple interfaces that may have different default methods each. However, if each of the interfaces contains the same default method with same name and signature, the code will fail to compile and raise the following error:

```
java: class ClassWithTwoInterfaces inherits unrelated defaults for defaultMethod()
from types Interface1 and Interface2
```

This is because the compiler fails to determine which default method should be used. To fix this issue, the class can provide an implementation of the default method that overrides the versions of default methods of the interfaces. That overridden version will be used which will remove the ambiguity that resulted in the error.

Further, a class can override the default method of the interface and still invoke the original default method by using the super keyword. However, to resolve ambiguity due to similar names in multiple interfaces, the name of the interface is prefixed before calling super. This is applicable even if only one interface is implemented as the class may extend another class as well.

For example:

```
public class ClassWithTwoInterfaces implements Interface1, Interface2 {
  @Override  public void abstractMethod() {    // some implementation    }
  @Override  public void defaultMethod() {
    // invoke defaultMethod() of interfaces
```

```
    Interface1.super.defaultMethod();
    Interface2.super.defaultMethod();
  }
}
```

Now, an interface can extend another interface. If both contain a default method with the same name, the compiler will consider the implementation from the child interface that is lowest down in the inheritance hierarchy tree.

For example:

```
public interface Interface1 {
  default void defaultMethod() {
    System.out.println("Hello from parent Interface1");
  }
}
public interface IChildInterface extends Interface1 {
  default void defaultMethod() {
    System.out.println("Hello from the IChildInterface");
  }
}
```

Here, both parent and child interfaces have a default method with the same name. When a class will implement the child interface, a call to **`defaultMethod()`** will give the following output:

```
Hello from the IChildInterface
```

That is, the compiler has invoked **`defaultMethod`** of the child interface.

5.5 Java functional interfaces

An interface with exactly one abstract method is called a functional interface. The **`@FunctionalInterface`** annotation has been added to Java to mark an interface as a functional interface. It is not required to use the annotation, but advisable as a best practice to avoid the addition of extra methods accidentally. If more than one abstract method is added to an interface annotated with **`@FunctionalInterface`** annotation, it throws a compiler error.

The most important benefit of functional interfaces is that lambda expressions can be used to instantiate them to avoid bulky anonymous class implementation.

Java 8 Collections API has been rewritten and the new Stream API has been added which uses a lot of functional interfaces. A new package called java.util.function including several functional interfaces has been added to provide target types for lambda expressions and method references. Some of the useful Java 8 functional interfaces are Consumer, Supplier, Function, and Predicate. java.lang.Runnable is a great example of a functional interface with a single abstract method run().]

A functional interface is also referred to as **Single Abstract Method** (**SAM**) Interfaces. It helps to achieve a functional programming approach. Rules for the functional interface:

- A functional interface can declare only one abstract method.
- A functional interface can have any number of default and static methods.
- A functional interface can declare methods of **Object** class.
- A functional interface can extend another interface only if the interface does not have any abstract method.

The following example shows the use of the functional interface:

```
@FunctionalInterface
public interface IPrintable {
  // only one abstract method
  void printMsg(String msg);

  // Functional interface can contain
  // any number of Object class methods.   int hashCode();   String toString();
boolean equals(Object obj);
 default void displayData(){
    System.out.println("Hello!! This is a default method");
  }
}
```

The functional interface **IPrintable** has only one abstract method but has several methods of the implicitly inherited **Object** class. It also has one default method and more can be added.

```
public class Messages implements IPrintable {
  @Override
  public void printMsg(String msg) {
    System.out.println("Received Message: " + msg);
  }
  public static void main(String[] args) {
    Messages obj = new Messages();
```

```
    obj.printMsg("Good Morning");
  }
}
```

The **Messages** class implements the functional interface **IPrintable** and overrides its **printMsg()** method. The output of the code is shown below:

```
Received Message: Good Morning
```

The following example demonstrates an invalid functional interface:

```
interface IParent{   // abstract method
  public void display(String msg);
} @FunctionalInterface interface IChild extends IParent{  public void displayIt();
}
```

The code generates compile-time error as the functional interface **IChild** is extend an interface that has an abstract method. The compilation error is shown below:

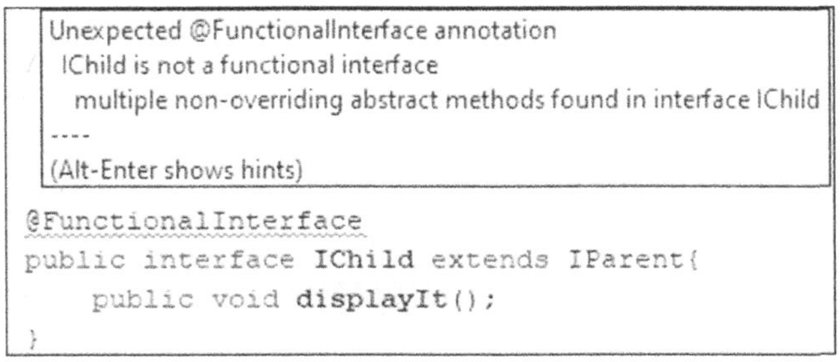

```
Unexpected @FunctionalInterface annotation
 IChild is not a functional interface
  multiple non-overriding abstract methods found in interface IChild
----
(Alt-Enter shows hints)
@FunctionalInterface
public interface IChild extends IParent{
    public void displayIt();
}
```

Figure 5.12: *Compilation error*

The following example demonstrates a valid functional interface as it extending non-functional interface:

```
interface IParent{
  // default method
  default void display(String msg){
    System.out.println("Default method of parent interface");
  }
}
@FunctionalInterface
interface IChild extends IParent{
  // abstract method of child interface
  public void displayIt();
}
```

```
public class TestFunctionalInterface implements IChild{
  @Override
  public void displayIt(){
    System.out.println("Overridden method of child interface");
  }
  public static void main(String[] args) {
    TestFunctionalInterface obj = new TestFunctionalInterface();
    obj.displayIt();
    obj.display();
  }
}
```

The output of the code is shown below:

```
Overridden method of child interface
Default method of parent interface
```

5.6 Lambda expressions

Java being an object-oriented programming language, everything in Java can reside only within a class and can be accessed by its object. This is applicable to functions as well. Some functional languages such as JavaScript, C++, and so on. allow writing functions and using them as required. Some of the languages support both functional as well as object-oriented programming.

Object-oriented programming is desirable but leads to a lot of verbosity in a program. For example, to create an instance of the Runnable class, generally, an anonymous class would be used as shown below:

```
Runnable r = new Runnable(){
  @Override
  public void run() {
    System.out.println("This is Runnable");
  }
};
```

In the above code, the only useful part is the code of the **run()** method. Rest all code is simply because of Java programming rules. With Java 8 Functional Interfaces and Lambda Expressions, the code can be made smaller and cleaner by removing the unnecessary code statements.

Lambda expressions were added to Java in Java SE 8 to introduce functional programming. A Lambda expression is a function that does not belong to any class, and it can be passed as an object or executed as and when required. Lambda Expressions help to visualize functional programming in the object-oriented Java programming world. Common usage of lambda expressions is seen in the implementation of callbacks/event listeners or Streams API. Lambda expressions also help to reduce the bulk code while implementing functional interfaces since they have only one abstract method. With lambda expressions, functionality can be treated as a method argument or code as data.

Syntax:

```
<argument> -> <body>
```

For example:

```
Runnable r1 = () -> System.out.println("This is Runnable");
```

Here, runnable is a functional interface with only one method, `run()` hence, its instance can be created using lambda expression instead of using bulky anonymous class. Since the `run()` method does not accept any argument, the lambda expression will also contain no argument.

Note that if there is only one statement to be processed, curly braces ({}) can be avoided but for multiple statements, braces are mandatory just like `if-else` blocks.

Benefits of Lambda expressions:

- **Reduced lines of code**: Lambda expression reduces lines of code as seen from the creation of functional interface instance using lambda expression rather than using anonymous class.
- **Sequential and parallel execution support**: Benefit from the Stream API sequential and parallel operations support.
- **Passing behaviors into methods**: Allows passing functionality as an argument to methods.

Lambda expression examples

The following table depicts some lambda expressions and their description:

Lambda expression	Description
`() -> {}`	No parameters, an empty body, and void return.
`() -> 42` `() -> null`	No parameters, body with expression, and void return.
`() -> { return 42; }`	No parameters, block body with the return value.
`() -> { System.gc(); }`	No parameters and void block body.

Lambda expression	Description

`() -> {`
`  if (true) return 5;`
`  else {`
`    int val = 10;`
`    for (int i = 1; i <5; i++)`
`      val *= i;`
`    return val;`
`  }`
`}`
	No parameters and complex block body with multiple returns.

`(int x) -> x+1`
Or
`(int x) -> { return x+1; }`
`(String str) -> str.length()`
`(Thread t) -> { t.start(); }`
	A single argument with declared type.

`(x) -> x+1`
Or
`x -> x+1`
`str -> str.length()`
`t -> { t.start(); }`
	Single argument with inferred-type argument.
	The parenthesis is optional.

`(int x, int y) -> x+y`	Multiple arguments with declared types.
`(x,y) -> x+y`	Multiple arguments with inferred types.
`(x, final y) -> x+y`	Illegal: cannot modify parameters with inferred type.
`(x, int y) -> x+y`	Illegal: cannot mix inferred and declared types.

Table 5.2: Examples of lambda expressions

The following example shows the use of lambda expressions for implementing the functional interface:

```
@FunctionalInterface
public interface IPrintable {
  void printMsg(String msg); // only one abstract method

  // Functional interface can contain
  // any number of Object class methods.
```

```
  int hashCode();
  String toString();
  boolean equals(Object obj);

  default void displayData(){
    System.out.println("Hello!! This is a default method");
  }
}
public class LambdaExpDemo {
  public static void main(String[] args) {
    IPrintable obj = (String msg) -> System.out.println(msg);
    obj.printMsg("Hello");
  }
}
```

The class **LambdaExpDemo** implements the **IPrintable** functional interface using Lambda expression and invokes the **printMsg()** method. The output of the code is shown below:

```
Hello
```

Note: The functional interface method can also be implemented with curly braces {} as follows:

```
IPrintable obj = (String msg) -> {
  System.out.println(msg);
};
obj.printMsg("Hello");
```

Note: However, since there is only one statement in the method, the curly braces {} have been avoided in the code.

Method and constructor references

A method reference is used to refer to a method without invoking it. Similarly, a constructor reference is used to refer to a constructor without creating a new instance of its type. The double colon (::) operator was introduced in Java SE 8 and used for method references as a replacement for lambda expressions.

For example:

Method references

```
System::getProperty
System.out::println
```

```
"hello"::length
```

Constructor references

```
ArrayList::new
int[]::new
```

To replace the lambda expression, the double colon (`::`) operator can be used which is a handy short cut in all the cases when the functional interface methods are implemented. This can be accomplished as follows:

- Define a method with a signature similar to the abstract method of the functional interface in a new class and provide a method body as required. Note that signature should be the same but the method name can be changed.
- Replace the lambda expression for implementing the functional interface method with a method reference for the method defined in the class previously with the below syntax.

Syntax:

```
<class-name>::<method-name> if the class method is static
<instance-variable-name>::<method-name> if the class method is non static
```

The following example shows the use of double colon (`::`) operator to refer to a method without invoking it:

```
public class LambdaExpDemo {
  public static void main(String[] args) {
    IPrintable obj = (String msg) -> System.out.println(msg);
    obj.printMsg("Invoking printMsg of IPrintable interface");
    IPrintable obj1 = LambdaExpDemo::displayMsg;
    obj1.printMsg("Invoking displayMsg of LambdaExpDemo class");
  }
   static void displayMsg(String msg){
    System.out.println(msg);
  }
}
```

IPrintable is a functional interface that is implemented by using lambda expression and an instance obj is created to invoke the **printMsg()** method. In the code, a method named **displayMsg()** is created with the same signature as the **printMsg()** method of **IPrintable** functional interface. Next, an instance **obj2** of **IPrintable** is created and the method **displayMsg()** is referenced by using the class name **LambdaExpDemo**. The Java compiler maps the arguments to the called method. The output of the code is shown below:

```
Invoking printMsg of IPrintable interface
Invoking displayMsg of LambdaExpDemo class
```

Conclusion

In this chapter you learnt that Java provides the concept of inheritance to group classes with similar characteristics and creates a class hierarchy. In single inheritance, a child class can inherit from only one parent/superclass. To implement inheritance in Java, a parent-child relationship is created between two or more classes by using the extends keyword. Method overriding is a concept that allows to create a child class method with the same signature and return type as that of the parent class. Abstract classes declare methods to serve as a contract or a standard and simply provide a structure but leave the implementation to the inheriting class. A class defined within another class is called a nested class. Anonymous class is a class declared without a name. An interface is a contract that sets the standards to be followed by the types that implement it. Java allows implementing multiple interfaces in a class. Lambda expressions were added to Java in Java SE 8 to introduce functional programming. The double colon (`::`) operator was introduced in Java SE 8 and used for method references as a replacement for lambda expressions.

In the next chapter, you will learn exceptions and regular expressions.

Multiple choice questions

1. **Java does not support _______ inheritance with classes.**
   a. Single
   b. Multiple
   c. Multilevel
   d. Hierarchical
2. **Consider the following partial code.**
   ```
   Employee emp = new PartTimeEmployee("Emp1", "Mark Stevens");
   ```
   [Assumption: **`Employee`** is superclass and **`PartTimeEmployee`** is subclass]
   Which type of binding is depicted in the code?
   a. Static
   b. Dynamic
   c. Both
   d. None of these
3. **Which of the following types of methods are supported in Java Interfaces in Java 10?**
   a. Abstract
   b. Default
   c. Static
   d. All of these

4. **Which of the following statements about the functional interface is false?**
    a. A functional interface can declare only one abstract method.
    b. A functional interface can have either one default or one static method.
    c. A functional interface can declare methods of Object class.
    d. A functional interface can extend another interface only if the interface does not have any abstract method.
5. **Match the columns.**

	Lambda expression		Description
a.	`() -> {}`	1.	Illegal: cannot mix inferred and declared types.
b.	`() -> { return 42; }`	2.	No parameters, an empty body, and void return.
c.	`(int x, int y) -> x+y`	3.	No parameters, block body with the return value.
d.	`(x, int y) -> x+y`	4.	Multiple arguments with declared types.

    a. a-2, b-3, c-4, d-1
    b. a-3, b-4, c-1, d-2
    c. a-4, b-1, c-2, d-3
    d. a-2, b-4, c-1, d-2

Answers

1. b
2. b
3. d
4. b
5. a

Assignment

Create a Java program with the below specifications:

1. Create a class named **`Employee`** with variables **`id`**, **`name`**, and **`salary`** and initialize them in a constructor.
2. Create a method named **`displayDetails()`** and print values of these variables in the method.
3. Create a functional interface named **`ICalculateCommission`** with one abstract method named **`calcCommission()`** that accepts a float parameter named sales and returns a float value.
4. Create a class named **`PartTimeEmployee`** that inherits from **`Employee`** class.
5. Declare two variables **`shift`** (String) and **`sales`** (float).

6. Create a constructor that accepts all values for **`Employee`** class variables as well as shift and sales.
7. Pass the necessary values to the superclass constructor from child class constructor. Also, initialize the shift and sales variables. [Hint: use **`super()`** method]
8. Override the **`displayDetails()`** method and invoke the superclass **`displayDetails()`** method. Also, print the values of **`shift`** and **`sales`** variables. [Hint: use **`super`** keyword]
9. In the main method, accept input from the user for employee **`id, name, salary, shift`**, and **`sales`** in some local variables. [Hint: Use **`Scanner`** class]
10. Instantiate the **`PartTimeEmployee`** object and pass the arguments to the constructor.
11. Invoke the **`displayDetails()`** method.
12. Implement the functional interface **`ICalcualteCommission`** by using Lambda expression.
13. In the implementation of its abstract method, calculate the commission based on the value of sales. If **`sales>5000`**, the commission is 20% of sales else commission is 5% of sales. Then return the value of the commission.
14. Invoke the **`calcCommission()`** method and pass the sales value received as input from the user to this method.
15. Print the commission value returned by the **`calcCommission()`** method.

The expected output is shown below:

```
Enter employee details
Employee id (E###):
E001
Employee name:
Roger
Salary $:
4000
Shift (AM/PM):
PM
Sales:
6000
------------------
Employee id: E001
Employee name: Roger
Salary $: 4000.0
Shift: PM
Sales: 6000.0
Commission: 1200.0
```

Figure 5.13: *Expected output*

Join our book's Discord space

Join the book's Discord Workspace for Latest updates, Offers, Tech happenings around the world, New Release and Sessions with the Authors:

https://discord.bpbonline.com

CHAPTER 6
Exceptions and Regular Expressions

Introduction

In this chapter, you will learn to handle exceptions in Java by using the different built-in Exception classes. You will also learn to create custom exceptions and work with assertions. Further, you will learn to use the important classes of `java.lang` and `java.util.regex` packages.

Structure

In this chapter, we will learn the following topics:

- Exceptions in Java
- Exception class in Java
- Exception handling in Java
- Using the try-with-resources statement
- Custom exceptions
- Wrapper exceptions
- Assertions in Java
- Classes of the java.lang package
- Regular expressions
- Character classes

Objectives

In this chapter you will learn to perform exception handling in Java and understand the built-in exception classes. You will create custom exceptions and work with assertions in Java. Further, you will learn about the `java.lang` package and also work with regular expressions.

6.1 Exceptions in Java

Any abnormal or unexpected event occurring in a program that disrupts its normal execution is termed as an exception. There can be different types and reasons for exceptions such as an attempt to open a file that does not exist, invalid data specified to a method, network connection error, or out of memory error. The information about the error is stored in the exception object that is passed to the runtime.

An exception occurring in a method can be thrown by using the exception object of the type of exception that occurred. The runtime looks for a handler code that can handle the exception in the same method. If it does not find a handler, it searches the entire method call stack to find an appropriate exception handler. If runtime does not find a handler in the entire call stack, it will eventually terminate the program.

Note: The sequence in which methods are invoked inside another method(s) is called a call stack. A stack trace shows the sequence in which methods were invoked that led to the exception.

For example, consider the following partial code:

```
public void methodOne(){
  methodTwo();
}
public void methodTwo(){
  methodThree();
}
public void methodThree(){
  // code that causes exception
}
```

As seen in the code, `methodOne` calls `methodTwo`, which calls `methodThree`. Here, the `methodThree` has a code that causes an exception but does not have any handler. So, the runtime will look for the handler in `methodTwo` and then `methodOne`. Since none of the methods have a handler, the program will terminate.

In case a handler was found, the exception is passed to the handler which can handle it. Note that an appropriate handler is one that can handle or `catch` the same type of exception as thrown by the method.

Advantages of exception handlers:

- Help to separate normal code from error handling ode.
- Handle errors anywhere within the method call stack.
- Categorize similar error types to have common handlers for them. For example, the **`IOException`** class of java.io package can handle most I/O exceptions. For more specific exceptions, the descendants of **`IOException`** class are used.

6.1.1 Types of exceptions

Java exceptions can be caused by a number of reasons such as user error, logical error, or systemic errors from some system resources. Therefore, exceptions can be broadly categorized as follows:

- Checked exceptions
- Unchecked exceptions

Let us see them in detail.

Checked exceptions

Checked exceptions are anticipated in a program and appropriate handlers are provided. For example, suppose a user is prompted to enter a number but the user specifies a string, this causes a **`java.lang.NumberFormatException`**. However, this will not affect the program fatally as it will have the code to handle this exception and inform the user through an appropriate message. In Java, all exceptions are checked except Error and **`RuntimeException`**.

Listed below are some of the checked exceptions:

- **`InstantiationException`**: This occurs when an attempt is made to create instance of an abstract class.
- **`InterruptedException`**: This occurs when a thread is interrupted.
- **`NoSuchMethodException`**: This occurs when the runtime is unable to resolve which method is to be invoked.

Unchecked exceptions

Errors and runtime exceptions collectively form the unchecked exceptions:

- **Errors**: Errors are not raised by an application but raised externally. For example, **`java.io.IOError`** is raised if the runtime fails to open a file that exists on the system due to some hardware/system issues. The classes for errors are provided in the **`Error`** class hierarchy. An application may catch this exception or leave it to the program to print a stack trace and exit.
- **Runtime exceptions**: The runtime exceptions are caused within an application, but are not anticipated such as logical errors or inappropriate use of an API. Hence, the application does not have any means to recover from such exceptions. For example,

the user passes correct value as a method argument but due to some logical issue, null is passed which leads to an exception. The application may handle this exception or eradicate the error that led to the exception. The classes for runtime exceptions are provided by the **RuntimeException** class hierarchy.

Listed below are some commonly observed unchecked exceptions:

- **ArithmeticException**: This occurs when there is an error in an arithmetic expression, for example, divide by zero.
- **ArrayIndexOutOfBoundsException**: This occurs when an attempt is made to access an array index less than zero or greater than the size of the array.
- **IllegalArgumentException**: This occurs when an illegal argument is passed to a method.
- **NegativeArraySizeException**: This occurs if the array size is less than zero.
- **NullPointerException**: This occurs when an attempt is made to access a null object member.
- **NumberFormatException**: This occurs when an attempt is made to convert a string to a number.
- **StringIndexOutOfBoundsException**: This occurs if the index is negative or greater than the size of the string.

The base class for any class in Java is the **Object** class and for all the exception classes, **Throwable** class is the base class. **Throwable** class is the child class of the **Object** class. The two direct subclasses of **Throwable** class are **Exception** class and **Error** class.

The following figure shows the **Throwable** class hierarchy:

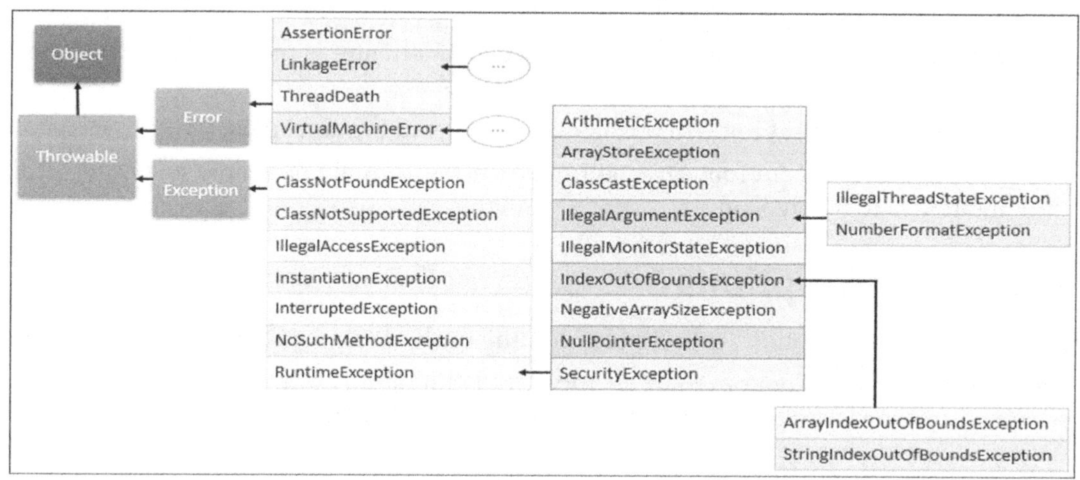

***Figure 6.1:** Throwable class hierarchy*

6.2 Exception class in Java

Exception class is the parent class of all checked exceptions and the **RuntimeException**. It is a subclass of **Throwable** class:

```
public class Exception extends Throwable{
...
}
```

Listed below are the constructors of the **Exception** class:

- **Exception()**: No-argument/default constructor creates an exception with error message set to null.
- **Exception(String message)**: Creates an exception with error message specified in the String argument.
- **Exception(String message, Throwable cause)**: Creates an exception with error message specified in the String argument with the cause.
- **Exception(Throwable cause)**: Creates an exception with the specified cause. If the cause is null, it will return null for message else it will return the **String** representation of the message. The message includes the class name and the detailed information of cause.

Listed below are some of the methods of **Exception** class:

- **public String getMessage()**: Returns the details about the exception that has occurred.
- **public Throwable getCause()**: Returns the cause of the exception indicated by the **Throwable** object.
- **public String toString()**: Returns the result of **getMessage()** method with the name of exception class concatenated to it, if the Throwable object is created with a message string that is not null. Return the name of the actual class of the exception object, if the Throwable object is created with a null message string.
- **public void printStackTrace():** Prints the result of the method, **toString()**, and the stack trace to the error output stream, that is, **System.err**.
- **public StackTraceElement[] getStackTrace()**: Returns an array where each element contains a frame of the method call stack trace with index 0 for the method at the top of the call stack and the last element for the method at the bottom of the call stack.
- **public Throwable fillInStackTrace():** Fills the stack trace of this **Throwable** object with the current stack trace and also, adds to any previous information in the stack trace.

The **Exception** class has several subclasses that represent different types of exceptions such as **ClassNotFoundException, IllegalAccessException**, and so on. The **RuntimeException** subclass of Exception class further contains subclasses which indicate exceptions occurring due to improper use of an API. For example, the **IllegalArgumentException** occurs when an incorrect argument is passed to a method.

6.3 Exception handling in Java

The checked exceptions that a method/constructor is liable to throw must be declared in the throws clause. However, for runtime exceptions, the compiler does not make this a mandate since more than one runtime exception can occur anywhere in a program, and adding code to handle them in every method can affect the clarity of the code.

For example, if a method expects three arguments before execution, instead of throwing a **RuntimeException**, one can check the arguments before invoking the method. Thus, if it is possible to recover from an exception, it can be made a checked exception else it can be unchecked.

To create an exception handler for any code that is liable to cause the error, the **try-catch** block is used.

Syntax:

```
try{
  // statements that may raise exception
  // statement 1
  // statement 2
}
catch(<exception-type> <object-name>){
  // handling exception
}
```

The statements that may throw an exception are enclosed within the **try** block. To handle the exception(s), the appropriate **catch** block is provided with the exception type object as a parameter. The **catch** block can be in the same method or anywhere higher in the method call stack.

To handle multiple types of exceptions, a **try** block can be followed by more than one **catch** block for each specific type of exception.

Syntax:

```
try
{…}
catch (<exception-type1> <object-name>)
{…}
catch (<exception-type2> <object-name>)
```

{...}

To ensure that some important statements can be executed even if an exception occurs, Java provides the **finally** block. The **finally** block is always executed irrespective of whether an exception occurs or not. It is mainly used to execute cleanup code such as closing database connections, file streams, and so on. to avoid resource leaks.

The **finally** block may not execute under the following conditions:

If the JVM exits while executing the **try** or **catch** block.

If a thread executing the **try** or **catch** block gets interrupted or killed.

Syntax:

```
try{
  // statement(s) that may raise exception
  // statement 1
  // statement 2
}
catch(<exception-type> <object-name>){
  // handling exception
}
finally{
  // clean-up code
}
```

The following example shows the use of **try-catch-finally** blocks for handling Java exceptions:

```
import java.util.Scanner;
public class Calculator {
  public static void main(String[] args) {
    Scanner s = new Scanner(System.in);
    System.out.println("Enter first number");
    int num1 = s.nextInt();
    System.out.println("Enter second number");
    int num2 = s.nextInt();
    Calculator obj = new Calculator();
    obj.calculate(num1, num2);
  }
```

```
  public void calculate(int a, int b){
    try{
      int c = a/b; // line 1
      System.out.println("Division of "+a+" and "+b+ " is "+ c);

      int arr[]= new int[c];
      for(int i=0;i<=arr.length;i++){ // line 2
        arr[i]=i+1;
      }
    }catch(ArithmeticException e){
      System.out.println("Exception occurred: "+ e.getMessage());
    }catch(ArrayIndexOutOfBoundsException e){
      System.out.println("Exception occurred: "+ e);
    }
    finally{
      System.out.println("----------------------");
      System.out.println("All resources closed in finally block");
    }
  }
}
```

The **calculate** method contains two statements commented as line 1 and line 2 that can cause an exception. The statement in line 1 can raise an **ArithmeticException** if the user specifies zero as the value of parameter b which is the denominator. In line 2, the loop is iterating till the size of the array which can lead to **ArrayIndexOutOfBounds** exception. Therefore, two catch blocks have been provided to handle the two exceptions. Also, a **finally** block is used to close all resources.

The output of the code when the user passes zero as the denominator is shown below:

```
Enter first number
23
Enter second number
0
Exception occurred: / by zero
----------------------
All resources closed in finally block
```

Figure 6.2: *ArithmeticException*

The output of the code when the user passes a correct value for the denominator is shown below:

```
Enter first number
23
Enter second number
4
Division of 23 and 4 is 5
Exception occurred: java.lang.ArrayIndexOutOfBoundsException: 5
-----------------------
All resources closed in finally block
```

Figure 6.3: ArrayIndexOutOfBoundsException

Note, the value 5 in the exception indicates the index of the array at which the error was raised. Note that, once the exception is thrown, any statements after that statement are not executed except the **finally** block.

6.3.1 'throw' and 'throws' keywords

The **throw** and **throws** clauses are used to explicitly raise exceptions from methods. The throws clause is used to list the exceptions that a method is liable to throw. The **throw** keyword is used to explicitly raise the checked or unchecked exception.

Following example shows the modified **Calculator** class that uses the **throw** and **throws** keywords for explicitly throwing exceptions from the method:

```
import java.util.Scanner;
public class Calculator {
  public static void main(String[] args) {
    Scanner s = new Scanner(System.in);
    System.out.println("Enter first number");
    int num1 = s.nextInt();
    System.out.println("Enter second number");
    int num2 = s.nextInt();
    Calculator obj = new Calculator();
    try {
      obj.calculate(num1, num2);
    } catch (ArithmeticException e) {
      System.out.println("Exception occurred: " + e.getMessage());
    } catch (ArrayIndexOutOfBoundsException e) {
```

```
            System.out.println("Exception occurred: " + e);
        } catch (Exception e){
            System.out.println("Exception occurred:" + e);
        }finally {
            System.out.println("----------------------");
            System.out.println("All resources closed in finally block");
        }
    }
    public void calculate(int a, int b) throws ArithmeticException,
ArrayIndexOutOfBoundsException {
        if (b == 0) {
            throw new ArithmeticException("/ by zero");
        }
        int c = a / b;
        System.out.println("Division of " + a + " and " + b + " is " + c);
        int arr[] = new int[c];
        for (int i = 0; i <= arr.length; i++) {
            if (i == arr.length) {
                throw new ArrayIndexOutOfBoundsException();
            }
            arr[i] = i + 1;
        }
    }
}
```

Here, the **calculate** method throws the **ArithmeticException** and **ArrayIndexOutOfBoundsException** by using the **throw** and **throws** keywords. The exceptions are listed after the method signature and thrown from the method based on some condition.

The **main()** method now executes the **calculate()** method within a **try** block and provides the appropriate **catch** blocks to handle the error. The **finally** block is used for closing the resources as usual.

Note that a third **catch** block with parent class **Exception** object is added to handle any other exceptions that might be raised. This **catch** block should always be placed at the end else it will handle all the exceptions and the specific exception **catch** blocks will never be used.

6.3.2 Single catch block for multiple exceptions

Java SE 7 introduced the concept of a single catch block to handle multiple exceptions. It helps to avoid code duplication when the same/generalized message needs to be displayed for multiple exceptions. To create a single **catch** block for multiple exceptions, specify the exceptions separated by a vertical bar (|).

Syntax:

```
catch (ExceptionType1|ExceptionType2 ex) {
  // handling exception
}
```

The following example shows the modified **Calculator** class to handle multiple exceptions in a single **catch** block:

```
import java.util.Scanner;
public class Calculator {
  public static void main(String[] args) {
    Scanner s = new Scanner(System.in);
    System.out.println("Enter first number");
    int num1 = s.nextInt();
    System.out.println("Enter second number");
    int num2 = s.nextInt();
    Calculator obj = new Calculator();
    try {
      obj.calculate(num1, num2);
    } catch (ArithmeticException | ArrayIndexOutOfBoundsException e) {
      System.out.println("Exception occurred: " + e);
    } finally {
      System.out.println("---------------------");
      System.out.println("All resources closed in finally block");
    }
  }
    public void calculate(int a, int b) throws ArithmeticException,
ArrayIndexOutOfBoundsException {
    if (b == 0) {
      throw new ArithmeticException("/ by zero");
```

```
        }
        int c = a / b;
        System.out.println("Division of " + a + " and " + b + " is " + c);
        int arr[] = new int[c];
        for (int i = 0; i <= arr.length; i++) {
          if (i == arr.length) {
            throw new ArrayIndexOutOfBoundsException();
          }
          arr[i] = i + 1;
        }
    }
}
```

Here, the **catch** block in the **main()** method has been modified to handle both exceptions separated by a vertical bar (**|**).

6.3.3 Best practices for handling exceptions

Listed below are the best practices of handling exceptions:

- A **try** statement must be followed by at least one **catch** or a **finally** block.
- Use the **finally** block to write clean up code.
- Avoid using **java.lang.Exception** or **java.lang.Throwable** class to **catch** exceptions that cannot be handled.
- Always provide an appropriate message along with the default message in a **catch** block when an exception occurs.
- Try to handle the exception as near to the source code as possible so that it is easy to trace the source.
- Avoid repeated re-throwing of the same exception as it may slow down the program.

6.4 Using the try-with-resources statement

A resource is any object that needs to be closed once the program is done using it. For example, a JDBC connection, a **File** resource, or a **Socket** connection. Before Java 7, it was required to explicitly close the resources, usually in the **finally** block as there was no auto resource management. However, this approach used to cause memory leaks and poor performance if one forgot to close the resource.

Java SE 7 introduced the try-with-resources statement to declare more than one resource at a time and also to ensure that all resources are closed after completion of code execution. A resource is any object that implements the **java.lang.AutoCloseable** or **java.io.Closeable** interface.

Note: The Closeable interface extends the AutoCloseable interface.

A **Closeable** resource is a source or destination of data that can be closed and the **AutoCloseable** interface is used to close a resource when it is no longer needed.

close() method

The **close()** method of **Closeable** and **AutoCloseable** interfaces has the following characteristics:

- It releases the resources that the object is holding, for example, open files.
- The **close()** method of the **Closeable** interface throws exceptions of type **IOException**.
- The **close()** method of the **AutoCloseable** interface throws exceptions of type **Exception**.
- The **close()** method can be overridden in the subclasses of the **AutoCloseable** interface. This allows the overridden **close()** method to throw specialized exceptions, such as **IOException,** or no exception at all.

The following example shows the use of **finally** block to close resources:

```
static void readFile(String[] args) {
  BufferedReader br = null;
  try {
    br = new BufferedReader(new FileReader("F:\\myfile.txt"));
    System.out.println(br.readLine());
  } catch (IOException e) {
    e.printStackTrace();
  } finally {
    try {
      if (br != null)
        br.close();
    } catch (IOException ex) {
      ex.printStackTrace();
    }
  }
}
```

Here, the **BufferedReader** object is closed within the **finally** block. The following example shows the use of **try-with-resources** statement to automatically close resources:

```
public static void main(String[] args) {
  try (BufferedReader br = new BufferedReader(new FileReader(
      "F:\\myfile.txt"))) {
    System.out.println(br.readLine());
  } catch (IOException e) {
    e.printStackTrace();
  }
}
```

The following are the benefits of the **try-with-resources** statement:

- Reduces the number of lines of code.
- Code becomes more readable code and easy to maintain.
- Performs automatic resource management.
- The use of **finally** block for explicitly closing resources is avoided.
- Allows to open multiple resources in **try-with-resources** statement separated by a semicolon.

The following example shows the use of **try-with-resources** statement to open multiple resources at a time:

```
try (BufferedReader br = new BufferedReader(new FileReader("F:\\myfile.txt"));
java.io.BufferedWriter writer = java.nio.file.Files.newBufferedWriter(FileSystems.
getDefault().getPath("F:\\myfile.txt"), Charset.defaultCharset())) {
  System.out.println(br.readLine());
  // code to write to file
} catch (IOException e) {
  e.printStackTrace();
}
```

Here, the two resources, **BufferedReader** and **BufferedWriter** are opened together within the **try-with-resources** statement. Note that when multiple resources are opened in **try-with-resources**, they are closed in the reverse order to avoid dependency.

Try with resources exceptions

The method of handling exceptions is different in **try-catch-finally** and **try with resources** statements. For the **try-catch-finally** block, when an exception is thrown from **try** block as well as **finally** block, the method returns the exception thrown by the **finally** block. With **try-with-resources**, if both **try** block and **try-with-resources** throw an exception, the method returns the exception thrown by the **try** block.

6.5 Custom exceptions

Java provides a wide range of built-in exceptions. However, at times, none of the built-in exceptions may fulfill the requirement of a certain code. In such cases, one can create a custom **exception** class. Custom exceptions are also useful when the code is liable to throw more than one related exception or to differentiate from the exceptions thrown from classes created by other vendors.

To create a custom exception, the class must inherit from the built-in **Exception** class.

Syntax:

```
public class <exception-class-name> extends Exception {
   // custom coded
}
```

The following code shows the creation of a custom exception class:

```
public class FileException extends Exception {
  public FileException() {
  }
  // Overriding the getMessage() method
  @Override
  public String getMessage() {
    return "Could not open file";
  }
}
```

The class **FileException** is a custom exception class that extends the built-in **Exception** class and overrides its **getMessage()** method. To raise a custom exception, a method must throw the exception at runtime and must be handled by the caller of the method:

```
public class FileManager {
  String filepath;
  String mode;
  public FileManager() {
  }
  public FileManager(String filepath, String mode) {
    this.filepath = filepath;
    this.mode = mode;
  }
  // creating a method that throws the custom exception
```

```
  public void openFile() throws FileException {
    if (filepath.equals("") || mode.equals("")) {
      throw new FileException();
    } else {
      System.out.println("Openining File...");
    }
  }
}
```

Here, the **openFile()** method of **FileManager** class throws the custom **FileException** if the filepath or mode values are empty:

```
public class TestFileException {
  public static void main(String[] args) {
    FileManager obj = new FileManager("","");
    try{
      obj.openFile();
    }catch(FileException e){
      System.out.println("Exception occurred: " + e.getMessage());
    }
  }
}
```

The **main()** method creates an object of **FileManager** class with empty strings as arguments to the constructor and invokes the **openFile()** method within a **try** block. The **catch** block catches the custom exception **FileException** and invokes the overridden **getMessage()** method. The output of the code is shown below:

```
Exception occurred: Could not open file
```

6.6 Wrapper exceptions

Java allows chaining of exceptions by wrapping one exception inside another without actually swallowing the original exception cause. Exception wrapping indicates catching an exception, wrapping it in a different exception, and throwing the wrapper exception.

Exception chaining was introduced since JDK 1.4 and to support it, Java introduced the **getCause()** and **initCause(Throwable)** in the **Throwable** class with two new constructors **Throwable(Throwable)** and **Throwable(String, Throwable)**. Wrapping exceptions prevents the code at a higher level in the call stack to know about every detail of the exception lower down in the call stack. This is because, the more the exceptions aggregate to the top, the more exception declarations will be required in the top-level methods making it very tedious to manage every time the code changes.

For example, suppose a class has a method that throws **SQLException**. Now, a class using that method will have to catch the exception. Later if the method changes to throw **RemoteException**, **IOException**, and several others, all these exceptions will have to be caught separately in the class that calls this method. Instead, one can create a common exception, say **MyException** that can be thrown every time and caught any of these exceptions are raised. Thus, the code using the method has to deal with just one exception.

The following example shows the use of Wrapper exception:

```
public class StandardException extends Exception {
  public StandardException() {
  }
  public StandardException(Throwable cause) {
    super(cause);
  }
  public StandardException(String message, Throwable cause) {
    super(message, cause);
  }
}
```

Here, the class **StandardException** is a custom exception class with three overloaded constructors. The last constructor accepts a custom message and the **Throwable** object for the cause of the exception:

```
import java.util.Scanner;
public class StandardCalculator {
  public static void main(String[] args) {
    Scanner s = new Scanner(System.in);
    System.out.println("Enter first number");
    int num1 = s.nextInt();
    System.out.println("Enter second number");
    int num2 = s.nextInt();

    try {
      StandardCalculator obj = new StandardCalculator();
      obj.calculate(num1, num2);
    } catch (StandardException e) {
      Throwable t = e.getCause();
```

```
            // print the message and the cause
            System.out.println("Error: " + e.getMessage());
            System.out.println("Cause: " + t);
        } finally {
            System.out.println("----------------------");
            System.out.println("All resources closed in finally block");
        }
    }
    public void calculate(int a, int b) throws StandardException{
        try {
            int c = a / b;
            System.out.println("Division of " + a + " and " + b + " is " + c);
            int arr[] = new int[c];
            for (int i = 0; i <= arr.length; i++) {
                arr[i] = i + 1;
            }
        } catch (ArithmeticException e) {
            throw new StandardException("Divide by zero", e);
        } catch (ArrayIndexOutOfBoundsException e) {
            throw new StandardException("Array Index out of bounds", e);
        }
    }
}
```

The method **calculate()** throws two exceptions, **ArithmeticException** and **ArrayIndexOutOfBounds** exception. But, it does not handle them and rethrows the exceptions. Now, it is the responsibility of the calling method, which is **main()** method to handle both the exceptions. Normally, the actual exception is thrown and a separate **catch** block or single **catch** block for multiple exceptions is used by the calling method. Instead, in this case, the **calculate()** method rethrows the **StandardExeption** with the custom message and exception object. So, the main method only has to have one catch block to catch the **StandardException**. From the **Throwable** object, it can retrieve the custom message and the clause.

6.7 Assertions in Java

An assertion is a statement in Java which allows a developer to test certain assumptions about a code in a program. When an assertion is added to code, it is expected to be true. If the assertion fails, the runtime will throw the **AssertionError**.

The following will be the advantages of assertion are as follows:

- It is an effective way to test code to detect and correct programming errors.
- Used to test for failing of various conditions. If the condition fails, the application can be terminated to view the debugging information.
- Help to document the inner working of the program to simplify code maintenance.

An assertion is composed of a boolean expression which is expected to be true as it confirms the assumption of the behavior of the code being tested. There are two ways of using assertions:

First form:

```
assert <boolean-expression>;
```

Second form:

```
assert <boolean-expression> : <detail-expression> ;
```

Here, the detail-expression has a value. It cannot have the invocation of a method that is declared void. Use the second form of the assertion statement only if the program contains some additional information that might help analyze the failure.

Generally, assertion failures are labeled in the stack trace with the file name and line number similar to all uncaught exceptions. To avoid performance issues in deployed applications, assertions can be enabled or disabled during execution if required. By default, assertions are disabled. Assertions should not be used for checks that need to be done every time at runtime as the assertions may be disabled. Instead, use logic to perform the check in such cases.

Assertions can be enabled by using the following command at the command line:

```
java -ea <class-name>
```

or

```
java -enableassertions <class-name>
```

The following are the steps to enable assertions in NetBeans IDE are as under:

1. Right-click the project in the **Projects** tab and select **Properties** from the menu.
2. In the **Project Properties** dialog box, select **Run**.
3. Click the **Customize** button beside the **VMOptions** box and scroll to the **ea** checkbox.
4. Select it and click **OK** as shown below:

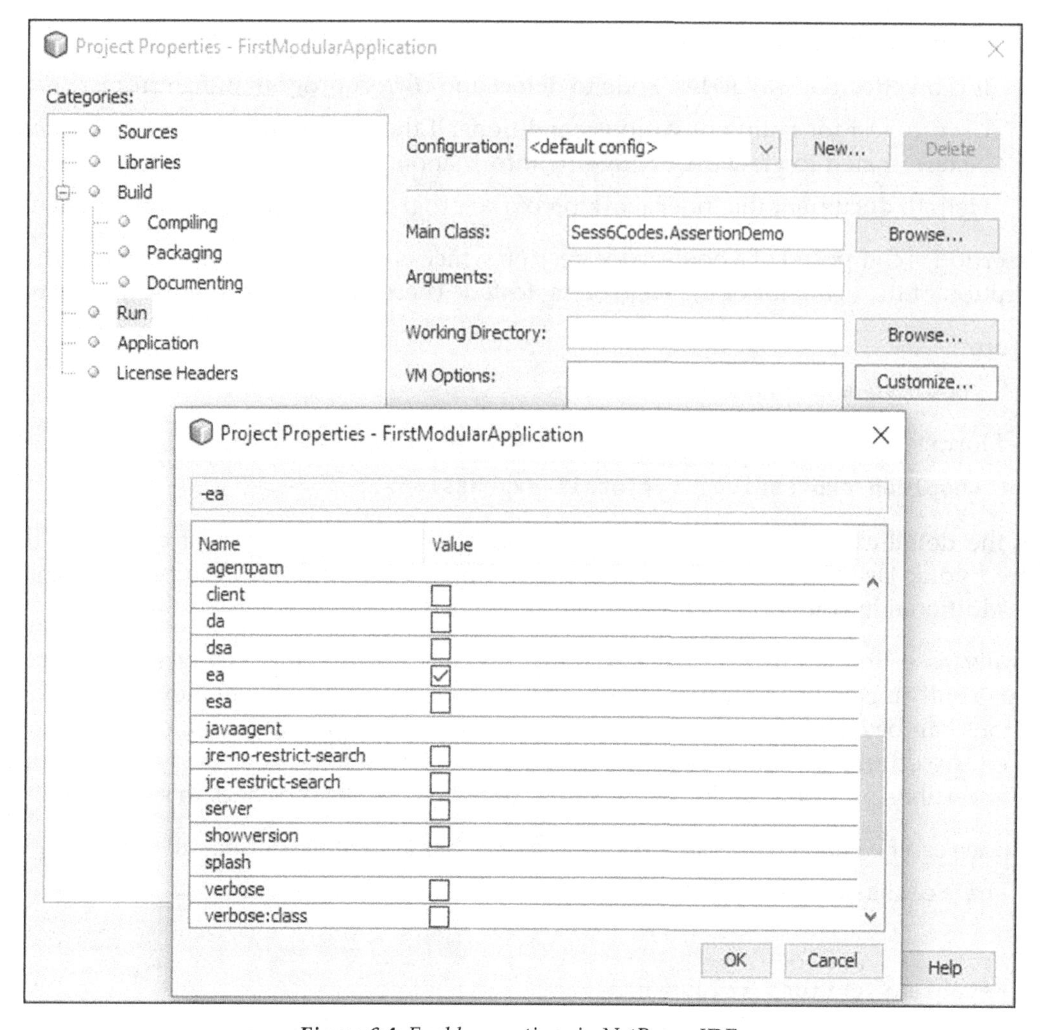

***Figure 6.4**: Enable assertions in NetBeans IDE*

5. Click **OK** to close the **Project Properties** dialog box. Now, assertions will work at runtime in NetBeans IDE.

The following example shows the use of assertion in a program:

```
import java.util.Scanner;
public class AssertionDemo {
  public static void main(String args[]) {
    Scanner s = new Scanner(System.in);
    System.out.print("Enter your age: ");
    int age = s.nextInt();
    assert age >= 18 : "Not valid age";
```

```
    System.out.println("Age is " + age);
  }
}
```

Here, the user is asked to enter his/her age. Before printing the age, it is verified by using an assertion. The assertion checks if **age** is greater than or equal to 18 and expects it to be true. If not, it will raise **AssertionError** and display the message **Not valid age**. The program will be terminated immediately without executing the remaining statements.

The output of the code when the user passes a value less than 18 is shown below:

```
Enter your age: 12
Exception in thread "main" java.lang.AssertionError: Not valid age
        at moduleOne/Sess6Codes.AssertionDemo.main(AssertionDemo.java:22)
C:\Users\Admin3\AppData\Local\NetBeans\Cache\dev\executor-snippets\run.xml:135: The foll
C:\Users\Admin3\AppData\Local\NetBeans\Cache\dev\executor-snippets\run.xml:64: Java retu
BUILD FAILED (total time: 3 seconds)
```

Figure 6.5: *AssertionError*

The **AssertionError** is displayed with the custom message. Different types of assertions that can be used to document and verify the assumptions and internal logic are listed below:

- **Internal invariants**: Used to verify implicit conditions that are not explicitly specified in code.

  For example:

  ```
  public static void main(String[] args){
    int a = -1;
    if(a>0)
      System.out.println("Greater than zero");
    else{
      assert a==0:"Number should not be negative";
      System.out.println("Number is zero");
    }
  }
  ```

  Here, the code expects that the value of a should be either greater than zero or equal to zero. If it is greater than zero, the appropriate message is displayed. In the **else** block, an assert statement verifies that if the value is not greater than it should be equal to zero. If the value is negative, the assertion fails.

- **Control flow invariants**: Control flow invariants such as **switch** statements can also use assertions to implement a default case.

  For example:

  ```
  public static void main(String[] args) {
    String direction = args[0];
  ```

```
    switch (direction) {
      case "east":
        // case code
        break;
      case "west":
        // case code
        break;
      case "north":
        // case code
        break;
      case "south":
        // case code
        break;
      default:
        assert false : direction + " is incorrect";
        break;
    }
}
```

Here, if the user specifies a direction other than the case options, the default case uses an assert to explicitly return false and display the message.

- **Preconditions**: Assertions for preconditions are used to check what must be true when a method is invoked. Do not use assertions for preconditions for checking parameters of a public methods since the method itself will ensure that the arguments are appropriate.

  For example:

```
private void setInterval(int counter) {
  // Verify the precondition in the private method
  assert counter > 0 && counter <= 1500/MAX_SPEED : counter;
  // Set the new counter
  System.out.println("Interval is set to:" + interval);
}
```

  In the code, if the value of `MAX_SPEED` is greater than `1500`, or the value of counter specified by the user is less than zero or greater than the value of the result of the division, the assertion will fail.

- **Postcondition**: Assertions for postconditions are used to check what must be true after a method executes successfully. Postconditions can be checked with assertions in both public and non-public methods.

For example:

```
ArrayList names = new ArrayList();
// code to initialize the ArrayList.
public Object remove(){
  int size = names.size();
  if(size == 0){
    throw new RuntimeException("Empty List");
    Object name = names.remove(0) ;
    // verify postcondition
    assert(names.size() == size-1);
    return name;
  }
}
```

The `remove()` method checks if the size of the array is zero, it throws `RuntimeException`. Next, the element of the array is retrieved. Now, before returning the value, a check is made using assertion, if the `size()` method returns a value equal to `size-1` else, the assertion fails and throws an `AssertionError`.

- **Class invariants**: Assertions for class invariants help to check what must be true about each instance of a class. Call invariant must be true before and after any method completes. For example:

  ```
  // Returns true if the account has balance
  private boolean hasBalance() {
    // code to check if the account has balance
  }
  ```

  The `hasBalance()` method is used to verify a constraint that should be true before and after any method completes. Hence, each public method should contain the line, assert `hasBalance()`; just before it returns.

6.8 Classes of the java.lang package

The `java.lang` package provides several classes to perform basic tasks of data manipulation in classes such as handling exceptions, threading, security, math, and so on. Classes of the `java.lang` are automatically included in every Java source file and do not require an explicit import statement in code.

Listed below are some of the most important classes of the `java.lang` package:

- **Object**: It is the root of the class hierarchy.
- **Class**: Instances of this class represent classes at run time.

- **Enum**: It is the base class for all enumeration classes.
- **Wrapper classes** that encapsulate primitive types as objects.
- **String**: It is the class used for creating and manipulating strings and string literals.
- **StringBuffer and StringBuilder**: These classes are used for performing string manipulation.
- **Math**: This class provides basic math functions such as square root, sine, cosine, and so on.
- **Throwable**: It is the base class of the exception class hierarchy.
- **Error, Exception, and RuntimeException**: These are base classes for each exception type. `Exception` classes are thrown for language-level and other common exceptions.
- **Comparable**: This is an interface that allows generic comparison and ordering of objects.
- **Iterable**: This is an interface that allows generic iteration using the enhanced for loop.
- **Thread**: It is the class that allows manipulation of threads.
- **Process, ClassLoader, Runtime, System, and SecurityManager**: These classes provide system operations for managing the creation of external processes, dynamic loading of classes, making environment inquiries such as the time of day, and enforcing security policies.

6.8.1 Object class

The `Object` class is the root of the Java class hierarchy and hence, every class is an implicit subclass of `Object` class and implements its methods.

Listed below are some of the commonly used methods of the `Object` class.

- `boolean equals(Object obj)`: Returns true if the object invoking the `equals()` method is equal to the object passed as an argument to the `equals()` method, else returns false.
- `protected void finalize()`: It is invoked by the garbage collector on an object when there are no more references to the object.
- `String toString()`: Returns a string representation of the object.
- `Class<? extends Object> getClass()`: Returns the runtime class of an object.
- `protected Object clone()`: Creates and returns a copy of this object.
- `void notify()`: Wakes up a single thread that is waiting on this object's monitor.
- `void notifyAll()`: Wakes up all threads that are waiting on this object's monitor.
- `void wait()`: Causes current thread to wait until another thread invokes the `notify()` or `notifyAll()` method for this object.
- `void wait(long timeout)`: Causes current thread to wait until either the specified amount of time has elapsed or another thread invokes the `notify()` or `notifyAll()` method for this object.

- **`void wait(long timeout, int nanos)`**: Causes current thread to wait until the specified real-time has elapsed or another thread invokes the **`notify()/notifyAll()`** method for this object or some other thread interrupts the current thread.

The following example shows the use of **`Object`** class methods:

```
public class ObjectClassDemo {
  Integer val;
  public ObjectClassDemo() {
  }
  public ObjectClassDemo(Integer val) {
    this.val = val;
  }
  public static void main(String[] args) {
    // creating objects of ObjectClass class
    ObjectClassDemo obj1 = new ObjectClassDemo(4577);
    ObjectClassDemo obj2 = new ObjectClassDemo(4577);
    System.out.println("String form of obj1 is "+obj1.val.toString());
    // check for equality of objects
    if (obj1.equals(obj2)) {
      System.out.println("Objects are equal");
    } else {
      System.out.println("Objects are not equal");
    }
    obj2 = obj1; // assigning reference of obj1 to obj2
    // again, check for equality of objects
    if (obj1.equals(obj2)) {
      System.out.println("Objects are equal");
    } else {
      System.out.println("Objects are not equal");
    }
  }
}
```

Here, the two objects of **`Object`** class are created and checked for equality. The output of the code is shown below:

```
String form of obj1 is 4577
Objects are not equal
Objects are equal
```

***Figure 6.6:** Object class methods*

Note that the first check shows objects are not equal even though the same value is passed in the constructor during object instantiation. But, after assigning the reference of **obj2** to **obj1**, the **equals()** method returns true and prints **Objects are equal**.

6.8.2 Class class

During the execution of a Java program, instances of the **Class** class represent classes and interfaces. The **Class** class has no public constructor and its objects are automatically created by the JVM through the **defineClass()** method calls when classes are loaded by the class loader.

Listed below are some commonly used methods of the **Class** class:

- **static Class forName(String className)**: Returns the **Class** object associated with the class or interface specified in the String argument.
- **Class[]getClasses()**: Returns an array of **Class** objects representing all the public classes and interfaces that are members of the class represented by this **Class** object.
- **String getName()**: Returns the name of the entity (class, interface, array class, a primitive type, or void) represented by this **Class** object, as a **String**.
- **int getModifiers()**: Returns the Java language modifiers for this class or interface, encoded in an integer.
- **Field getField(String name)**: Returns a **Field** object that represents the specified public member field of the class or interface represented by this **Class** object.
- **Method getMethod(String name, Class[] parameterTypes)**: Returns a Method object that represents the specified public member method of the class or interface represented by this Class object.
- **Class[]getInterfaces()**: Returns an array of interfaces implemented by the class or interface represented by this object.
- **URL getResource(String name)**: Finds a resource with the specified name.
- **Class getSuperclass()**: Returns the **Class** representing the superclass of the entity (class, interface, a primitive type, or void) represented by this **Class**.
- **boolean isArray()**: Determines if this **Class** object represents an array class.
- **boolean isInstance(Object obj)**: Determines if the **Object** specified in the argument is assignment-compatible with the object represented by this **Class**.
- **boolean isInterface()**: Determines if the specified **Class** object represents an interface type.
- **String toString()**: Returns the string representation of the object.

6.8.3 Math class

Math class provides methods to perform arithmetic/numeric operations on data. For example, trigonometric functions, logarithmic functions, exponentiation, and so on.

Listed below are some commonly used methods of **Math** class:

- **static <type> abs(<type> a)**: Returns the absolute value of the type specified in the argument. The type could be **double, float, int**, or **long**.
- **static double ceil(double a)**: Returns the smallest double value that is greater than or equal to the argument.
- **static double floor(double a)**: Returns the largest double value that is less than or equal to the argument.
- **static double cos(double a)**: Returns the trigonometric cosine of an angle.
- **static double sin(double a)**: Returns the trigonometric sine of an angle.
- **static double tan(double a)**: Returns the trigonometric tangent of an angle.
- **static double exp(double a)**: Returns Euler's number *e* raised to the power of a double value.
- **static double pow(double a, double b)**: Returns the value of the first argument raised to the power of the second argument.
- **static double log(double a)**: Returns the natural logarithm (*base e*) of a double value.
- **static <type> max(<type> a, <type> b)**: Returns the greater of two values of the specified type. The type could be **double, float, int**, or **long**.
- **static <type> min(<type> a, <type> b)**: Returns the smaller of two values of the specified type. The type could be **double, float, int**, or **long**.
- **static double random()**: Returns a positive double value, greater than or equal to 0.0 and less than 1.0.
- **static long round(double a)**: Returns the closest long to the argument.
- **static int round(float a)**: Returns the closest **int** to the argument.
- **static double sqrt(double a):** Returns the correctly rounded positive square root of a double value.

The following code shows the use of methods of the **Math** class:

```
public class MathDemo {
  static int num1 = 2, num2 = 16;
  public static void main(String[] args) {
    System.out.println("Number 1: " + num1);
    System.out.println("Number 2: " + num2);
    System.out.println("Max value is " + Math.max(num1, num2));
```

```
        System.out.println("Min value is " + Math.min(num1, num2));
        System.out.println("Square root of num2 is " + Math.sqrt(num2));
       System.out.println("Result of num2 to the power of num1 is " + Math.pow(num2,
num1));
        System.out.println("Random value generated is " + Math.random());
    }
}
```

The output of the code is shown below:

```
Number 1: 2
Number 2: 16
Max value is 16
Min value is 2
Square root of num2 is 4.0
Result of num2 to the power of num1 is 256.0
Random value generated is 0.8978670770760632
```

Figure 6.7: Math class methods

6.8.4 ThreadGroup class

A thread in Java, is the path followed when executing a program. All Java programs have at least one thread which is the main thread created by the JVM when the program starts and the **main()** method is invoked with the main thread.

A thread group represents a set of threads and can also include other thread groups. In a thread group hierarchy, every thread group except the initial thread group has a parent. A thread can access information about only its own thread group and cannot access even its parent thread group.

Listed below are some methods of **ThreadGroup** class:

- **int activeCount()**: Returns the number of active threads in this thread group and its subgroups.
- **int activeGroupCount()**: Returns the number of active groups in this thread group and its subgroups.
- **int getMaxPriority()**: Returns the maximum priority of this thread group.
- **String getName()**: Returns the name of this thread group.
- **ThreadGroup getParent()**: Returns the parent of this thread group.
- **void interrupt()**: Interrupts all threads in this thread group.
- **void destroy()**: Destroys this thread group and all of its subgroups.
- **void checkAccess()**: Determines if the currently running thread has access to modify this thread group.

- **`list()`**: Prints information about this thread group to the standard output.
- **`int enumerate(Thread[] list)`**: Copies every active thread in this thread group and its subgroups into the specified array.
- **`int enumerate(ThreadGroup[] list)`**: Copies references to every active subgroup in this thread group and its subgroups into the specified array.
- **`boolean isDaemon()`**: Verifies if this thread group is a daemon thread group.
- **`boolean isDestroyed()`**: Verifies if this thread group has been destroyed.
- **`boolean parentOf(ThreadGroup g)`**: Verifies if this thread group is either the thread group argument or one of its ancestor thread groups.
- **`void setDaemon(boolean daemon)`**: Modifies the daemon status of this thread group.
- **`void setMaxPriority(int pri)`**: Sets the maximum priority of the thread group.
- **`String toString()`**: Returns a string representation of this Thread group.

6.8.5 System class

System class provides several methods for accessing system properties and environment variables, standard I/O and error streams, loading files/libraries, and so on.

Listed below are some of the commonly used methods of the **`System`** class:

- **`static void arraycopy(Object src, int srcPos, Object dest, int destPos, int length)`**: Copies an array from the specified source array, starting at the source position, to the destination position.
- **`static long currentTimeMillis()`**: Returns the current time in milliseconds.
- **`static String getenv(String name)`**: Fetches the value of the specified environment variable.
- **`static Properties getProperties()`**: Returns the current system properties.
- **`static void exit(int status)`**: Terminates the currently running JVM.
- **`static void gc()`**: Runs the garbage collector.
- **`static void loadLibrary(String libname)`**: Loads the system library specified by the **`libname`** argument.
- **`static void setSecurityManager(SecurityManager s)`**: Sets the system security.

The following example shows the use of **`System`** class methods:

```
public class SystemClassDemo {
  static String str1[] = {"Mon", "Tue", "Wed", "Thu"};
  static String str2[] = {"East", "West", "North", "South"};
  public static void main(String[] args) {
        System.out.println("Current time in milliseconds is: " + System.
currentTimeMillis());
```

```
    System.out.println("Value of Path variable is: " + System.getenv("PATH"));
    System.arraycopy(str1, 0, str2, 0, 3);
    System.out.println("Copied array is: ");
    for (int i = 0; i < 4; i++) {
      System.out.println(str2[i]);
    }
  }
}
```

The output of the code is shown below:

```
Current time in milliseconds is: 1531903964884
Value of Path variable is: C:\Program Files (x86)\
Copied array is:
Mon
Tue
Wed
South
```

Figure 6.8: System class methods

6.8.6 Runtime class

To allow a Java application to interact with the system environment, there is always a single instance of the **Runtime** class. However, an application cannot create its own instance of this class.

Listed below are some commonly used methods of the **Runtime** class:

- **static Runtime getRuntime()**: Returns the runtime object associated with the current Java application.
- **void loadLibrary(String libname)**: Loads the dynamic library with the library specified in the argument.
- **long maxMemory()**: Returns the maximum amount of memory that the JVM may use.
- **int availableProcessors()**: Returns the number of processors available to the JVM.
- **long freeMemory()**: Returns the amount of free memory in the JVM.
- **long totalMemory()**: Returns the total amount of memory in the JVM.
- **Process exec(String command)**: Executes the string command specified in the argument in a separate process.
- **void exit(int status)**: Terminates the currently running JVM by initiating its shutdown sequence.

- **`void halt(int status)`**: Forcibly terminates the currently running JVM.
- **`void load(String filename)`**: Loads the filename specified in the argument as a dynamic library.
- **`void gc()`**: Executes the garbage collector.
- **`void runFinalization()`**: Executes the finalization methods of any objects pending finalization.

6.9 Regular expressions

Regular expressions are used to manipulate text and data. They are commonly used to define constraints on strings such as email or password validation. The **`java.util.regex`** API is used to define patterns for searching or manipulating strings. The three main classes of **`java.util.regex`** package that are required for the creation of regular expressions are:

- `Pattern`
- `Matcher`
- `PatternSyntaxException`

6.9.1 Pattern class

An instance of **`Pattern`** class is a compiled form of a regular expression specified in the string format. The **`Pattern`** class does not have any public constructors and hence, it cannot be instantiated. It provides overloaded static **`compile()`** methods to create different patterns.

Syntax:

```
public final class Pattern extends Object implements Serializable
```

The **`Pattern`** class methods accept a regular expression as the first argument and return an instance of **`Pattern`** class. This instance is used to create a **`Matcher`** object that can be used to match different character sequences with a regular expression.

For example:

```
import java.util.regex.Pattern;
import java.util.regex.Matcher;
public class PatternDeo {
  public static void main(String[] args) {
    Pattern pt = Pattern.compile("b*x");
   // create the Matcher object using the Pattern object with the string to match
    Matcher mt = pt.matcher("bbbx");
    // check for a match
```

```
    boolean result = mt.matches();
    System.out.println("Pattern Match: "+result);
  }
}
```

The **matches()** method of the **Matcher** class is used to verify if the pattern specified by the **Pattern** object matches the string specified in the **matcher()** method. Note that the **matches()** method is useful when a regular expression has to be used only once. This method will compile an expression and match it against an input sequence in a single invocation. The output of the code is shown below:

```
Pattern Match: true
```

Listed below are some methods of the **Pattern** class:

- **matches()**: The **Pattern** class also defines the **matches(String, CharSequence)** method to check if a pattern is present in a given input string. For example, the three lines of code used in the previous example can be reduced to just one statement by using the **matches()** method of the **Pattern** class as follows:

  ```
  boolean result = Pattern.matches("b*x", "bbbx");
  ```

  The **matches()** method of **Matcher** class is less efficient for repeated matches as it does not allow the compiled pattern to be reused. Objects of **Pattern** class are immutable and can be used safely **b*y** multiple concurrent threads whereas instances of the **Matcher** class are not safe for such use.

  Another example of **matches()** method of **Pattern** class is shown below:

  ```
  Pattern.matches("\\d","4");
  ```

  Here, **\d** indicates a single digit. The method will return true because the digit **4** matches the regular expression **\d**.

Note: Since the backslash '\' character has a special meaning in Java, it must be used with the escape sequence '\', that is, '\\d' while specifying a pattern.

- **split(String): The split()** method of **Pattern** class is used to extract text that lies on either side of the pattern being matched. The following example shows the use of **split()** method:

  ```
  import java.util.regex.Pattern;
  public class SplitDemo {
    private static final String REGEX = ":";
    private static final String DIRECTION = "East:West:North:South";
    private static final String REGEX1 = "\\d";
    private static final String DIRECTIONS = "East1West2North3South";
    public static void main(String[] args) {
      Pattern objP1 = Pattern.compile(REGEX);
      String[] directions = objP1.split(DIRECTION);
  ```

```
        for (String s : directions) {
          System.out.println(s);
        }

        System.out.println("---------");
        Pattern obj1 = Pattern.compile(REGEX1);
        String[] days = obj1.split(DIRECTIONS);
        for (String s : days) {
          System.out.println(s);
        }
      }
    }
```

The output of the code is shown below:

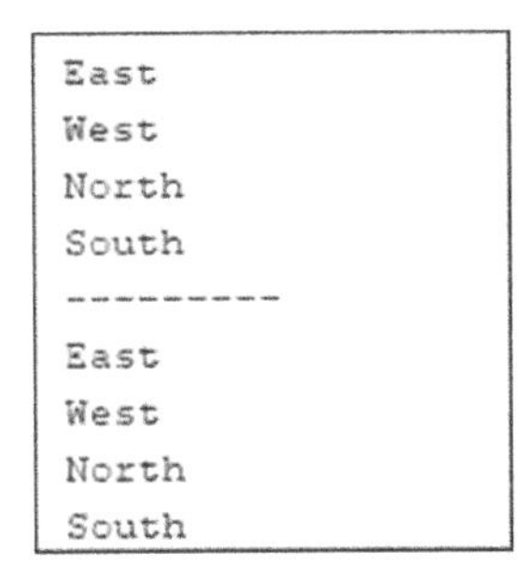

Figure 6.9: Using the split() method

- **`public String toString()`**: Returns the **`String`** representation of this pattern.

6.9.2 Matcher class

A **`Matcher`** object is created by using the **`Pattern`** object and is used to perform match operation of a pattern with an input string. **`Matcher`** class also does not have any public constructors and hence, cannot be instantiated.

A **`Matcher`** object is created by invoking the **`matcher()`** method on the **`Pattern`** object.

Syntax:

`public final class Matcher extends Object implements MatchResult`

The three different types of match operations that can be performed by the **`Matcher`** class are:

- Match the entire input sequence against the pattern by using the **`matches()`** method.
- Match the input sequence, starting at the beginning, against the pattern by using the **`lookingAt()`**.

- Scan the input sequence looking for the next subsequence that matches the pattern by using the **find()** method.

Each of these methods returns a boolean value indicating success or failure. Important points about **Matcher**:

- A matcher finds matches in a subset of its input which is called the region and it contains all of the matcher's input by default.
- The **region()** method can be used to modify the region.
- The **regionStart()** and **regionEnd()** methods can be used to query the region.
- It is possible to modify the manner in which the region boundaries interact with selected pattern constructs.
- The different index methods of **Matcher** class provide index values that can be used to indicate exactly where the match was found in the input string.

The **Matcher** class implements the **MatchResult** interface. Listed below are the important methods of the **Matcher** class:

- **boolean matches()**: Checks whether the regular expression matches the pattern.
- **boolean find()**: Finds the next expression that matches the pattern.
- **boolean find(int start)**: Finds the next expression that matches the pattern from the given start index.
- **String group()**: Returns the matched subsequence.
- **int start()**: Returns the starting index of the matched subsequence.
- **int end()**: Returns the ending index of the matched subsequence.
- **int groupCount()**: Returns the total number of the matched subsequence.

The explicit state of a matcher is initially undefined and an attempt to query any part of matcher's match at this point will cause an **IllegalStateException** to be thrown. The **reset()** method is used to explicitly reset the matcher. For a new input sequence, the **reset(CharSequence)** method can be invoked. When a reset is performed on the **matcher** object, its explicit state information is discarded and the append position is set to zero. It is not advisable to use **Matcher** for concurrent threads.

The following example shows the use of **Matcher** class:

```
import java.util.regex.Pattern;
import java.util.regex.Matcher;
import java.util.Scanner;
public class RegexDemo {
  public static void main(String[] args) {
    String choice;
    while (true) {
      Scanner s = new Scanner(System.in);
```

```
        System.out.println("Enter the pattern:");
        String expression = s.next();
        Pattern pt = Pattern.compile(expression);
        System.out.println("Enter the string to search:");
        String search = s.next();
        Matcher mt = pt.matcher(search);
        boolean found = false;
        while (mt.find()) {
         System.out.println("Found the pattern "+mt.group()+" starting at index "
                             + mt.start()+ " and ending at index "+mt.end());
          found = true;
        }
        if (!found) {
          System.out.println("No match found.");
        }

        System.out.println("Press x to exit or y to continue");
        choice = s.next();
        if (choice.equals("x")) {
          System.exit(0);
        }
      }
    }
  }
```

The output of the code is shown below:

```
Enter the pattern:
abc
Enter the string to search:
abclakdfabcakjdjabc
Found the pattern abc starting at index 0 and ending at index 3
Found the pattern abc starting at index 8 and ending at index 11
Found the pattern abc starting at index 16 and ending at index 19
Press x to exit or y to continue
x
BUILD SUCCESSFUL (total time: 10 seconds)
```

Figure 6.10: *Pattern and Matcher*

6.9.3 PatternSyntaxException

A **PatternSyntaxException** object is an unchecked exception used to indicate a syntax error in a regular expression pattern.

6.10 Character classes

A character class in regular expressions is a set of characters enclosed within square brackets which indicates the characters that will successfully match a single character from a given input string.

The following table lists the supported regular expression constructs in character classes:

Construct	Type	Description
[abc]	Simple class	Matches a, b, or c
[^abc]	Negation	Matches any character except a, b, or c
[a-zA-Z]	Range	Matches any character from a through z, or A through Z (inclusive)
[a-d[m-p]]	Union	Matches any character from a through d, or m through p: [a-dm-p]
[a-z&&[def]]	Intersection	Matches d, e, or f
[a-z&&[^bc]]	Subtraction	Matches any character from a through z, except for b and c, that is, [ad-z]
[a-z&&[^m-p]]	Subtraction	Matches any character from a through z, and not m through p: [a-lq-z]

Table 6.1: Common character classes

Built-in character classes

There are several built-in **Character** classes in the **Pattern** API which provide shortcuts for commonly used regular expressions. The following table lists the pre-defined **Character** classes:

Construct	Description
.	Matches any character (may or may not match line terminators)
\d	Matches any digit, that is, [0-9]
\D	Matches any non-digit, that is, [^0-9]
\s	Matches a whitespace character, that is, [\t\n\x0B\f\r]
\S	Matches any non-whitespace character, that is, [^\s]
\w	Matches any word character, that is, [a-zA-Z_0-9]

Construct	Description
`\W`	Matches any non-word character, that is, [^\w]

Table 6.2: Pre-defined character classes

For example:

`\d\d\d[E-F]`

This will match strings like **`000E`**, **`010F`**, **`384C`**, and so on.

Conclusion

In this chapter, you learnt that any abnormal or unexpected event occurring in a program that disrupts its normal execution is termed as an exception. Checked exceptions are anticipated in a program and appropriate handlers are provided for them. Errors and runtime exceptions collectively form the unchecked exceptions. The base class for any class in Java is the **`Object`** class and for all the exception classes, **`Throwable`** class is the base class. **`Exception`** class is the parent class of all checked exceptions and the **`RuntimeException`**. The **`throw`** and **`throws`** clauses are used to explicitly raise exceptions from methods. Java SE 7 introduced the single catch block to handle multiple exceptions. The **`try-with-resources`** statement allows declaring more than one resource at a time and also ensures that all resources are closed after completion of code execution. Exception wrapping indicates catching an exception, wrapping it in a different exception, and throwing the wrapper exception. An assertion is a statement in Java which allows a developer to test certain assumptions about code in a program. Regular expressions are used to manipulate text and data. An instance of **`Pattern`** class is a compiled form of a regular expression specified in the string format. A **`Matcher`** object is created by using the **`Pattern`** object and is used to perform match operation of a pattern with an input string.

In the next chapter, you will learn about collections and Stream API.

Multiple choice questions

1. **Exception class is the subclass of _________.**
   a. Error
   b. RuntimeException
   c. Throwable
   d. Object
2. **Consider the below partial code.**

```
public static void main(String[] args) {
  try (BufferedReader br = new BufferedReader(new FileReader("F:\\myfile.
txt"))) {
    System.out.println(br.readLine());
```

```
    } catch (IOException e) {
      e.printStackTrace();
    }
}
```

Which concept is depicted in the code?

a. File handling
b. try-with-resources
c. try-catch block
d. Exception

3. **The _____ clause is used to list the exceptions that a method is liable to throw.**
   a. throw
   b. throws
   c. try
   d. catch
4. **Consider the below partial code.**

```
boolean result = Pattern.matches("b*x", "_____");
```

Which of the following strings will match the pattern?

   a. `bxxx`
   b. `bbxx`
   c. `bbbx`
   d. `bxbx`
5. **Consider the below partial code.**

```
public static void main(String args[]) {
  Scanner s = new Scanner(System.in);
  System.out.print("Enter your age: ");
  int age = s.nextInt();
  assert age <= 18 : "Not valid age";
  System.out.println("Age is " + age);
}
```

Assuming that the user passes 12, what will be the output?

   a. Compilation error
   b. AssertionError: Not valid age
   c. No output
   d. Age is 12

Answers

1. c
2. b
3. b
4. c
5. d

Assignment

Create a Java program as per the below specifications:

- Create a custom exception class called **ValidationException** with a parameterized constructor that accepts a custom string message as a parameter.
- Override the **getMessage()** method in the **ValidationException** class.
- Create another class called **Login** with two variables, **empid** and **password**.
- Create a method called **validateEmployeeId()** that accepts **empid** as a parameter and returns a boolean value.
- Inside this method, create a regular expression of your choice to validate the format of employee id. [Hint: use regular expression character classes]
- If the employee ID matches the regular expression, return true else return false.
- Create another method called **validateCredentials()** which accepts **empid** and **password** as parameters and throws the **ValidationException** exception.
- Compare the values against some dummy values and if they match, display a welcome message else throw the **ValidationException** exception.
- Within the **main()** method, create an infinite **while** loop and ask the user to input the employee ID.
- Next, invoke the **validateEmployeeId()** method. If the method returns true, break out of the **while** loop **else** the loop should continue asking for the employee ID until **validateEmployeeId()** returns true.

Once you break out of the loop, ask the user to enter the secret password.

Invoke the **validateCredentials** method and pass the **empid** and **password** values as arguments.

The expected output is shown below. [Assumption: Correct employee id is **E0002** and password is **gatepass**]

The expected output when the user enters employee ID in incorrect format and also incorrect password is shown below:

```
Enter employee id:
ljdf
Enter employee id:
slf
Enter employee id:
lsjdf
Enter employee id:
E0001
Enter secret password
password
Error in login: Incorrect employee id or secret password
```

Figure 6.11: Expected output 1

The expected output when the user enters employee ID incorrect format and also, the employee ID and password are valid. Or, the employee ID format is correct but the employee ID and password fail validation:

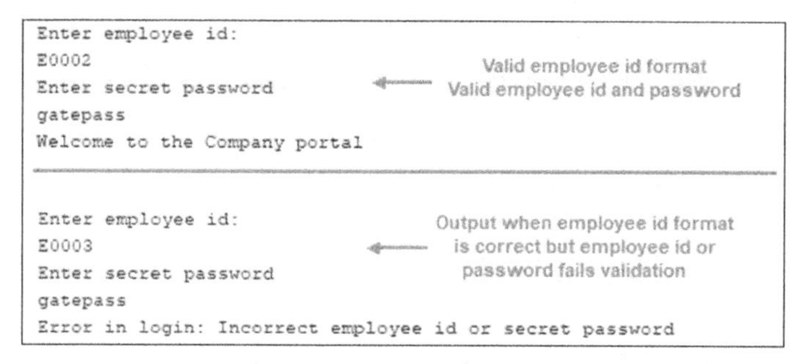

Figure 6.12: Expected output 2

Join our book's Discord space

Join the book's Discord Workspace for Latest updates, Offers, Tech happenings around the world, New Release and Sessions with the Authors:

https://discord.bpbonline.com

CHAPTER 7
Collections and Stream API

Introduction

This chapter introduces the collections framework with the different utility classes and interfaces of the `java.util` package. You will learn to work with `Lists`, `Set`, and `Map` collections. You will also learn, how to use the Arrays class for performing operations such as sorting, searching, and so on. on arrays. Java 8 introduced the `java.util.stream` package which allows parallel processing of elements of Java collections. You will learn about the new additions and enhancements in the Stream API introduced in Java 9.

Structure

In this chapter, we will learn the following topics:

- Collections framework
- Iterable interface
- Collection interface
- List interface
- Queue interface
- Set interface
- Map interface

- Arrays class
- Java Stream API

Objectives

In this chapter you will understand the `java.util` package and the collections framework. You will work with Lists, Set and Map collections as well as the Arrays class. You will learn about collection sorting interfaces and Stream API enhancements.

7.1 Collections framework

The `java.util` package provides several utility classes and interfaces for different functionalities. It contains classes for data and time manipulation, event model, collections framework, internationalization, legacy collection classes, and other utility classes such as `StringTokenizer`, a random-number generator, and a bit array.

A collection is a container object which helps to group multiple elements into a single unit. Some real-world examples of collections include, contacts directory where names are mapped with phone numbers or a stack of plates, and so on. Collections help to store, retrieve, manipulate, and communicate collective data.

A collections framework is used to create and manipulate collections and is composed of the following:

- **Interfaces**: Interfaces are abstract data types and can be used to manipulate collections independently without needing the representation details.
- **Implementations**: These are the concrete implementations of the collection interfaces and are reusable.
- **Algorithms**: Algorithms are a set of methods that are reusable/polymorphic and provide ready computations for processes like sort and search on objects implementing the collection interfaces.

The benefits of the Java collections framework are as follows:

- It provides useful algorithms and data structures that reduce the programming effort and allow interoperability between different APIs.
- The high-performance implementation of these data structures and algorithms increases the quality and speed of a program.
- Reduces the time for learning the use of new APIs as standard collection interfaces allow easy input and output of collections for many APIs.
- Standard collection APIs also reduce the effort to design new APIs.
- Since the new data structures and algorithms that confirm to the standard collection interfaces are reusable by default, the collections framework promotes software reusability.

7.2 Iterable interface

The `Iterable` interface belongs to the `java.lang` package and is the top-level interface for classes and interfaces that need the iterator functionality. Implementing this interface allows an object to be the target of the `foreach` statement. Java SE 8 added the `forEach()` method to the `Iterable` interface.

Methods of `Iterable` interface are as follows:

- `default void forEach(Consumer<? super T> action)`: Performs an action for each element of the `Iterable` until all elements have been processed or the action throws an exception.
- `Iterator<T> iterator()`: Returns an iterator over elements of type `T`.
- `default Spliterator<T> spliterator()`: Creates a `Spliterator` over the elements described by this `Iterable`.

The enhanced for-loop (for-each) and forEach() method both provide the same functionality of looping through elements in a collection. However, the enhanced for-loop is an external iterator whereas the new forEach() method is an internal one. The internal iterator manages the iteration in the background so that the programmer can focus on what is to be done with the elements of the collection instead of managing the iteration and ensuring that all the elements are processed one-by-one. In the case of an external iterator, the programmer has to manually specify how the iteration will be performed. Enumerations, Iterators, and enhanced for-loop are all external iterators with methods such as iterator(), next(), and hasNext() for manipulating collections.]

7.3 Collection interface

The `Collection` interface belongs to the `java.util` package and it is at the top level of the interfaces and classes belonging to the collections framework. The collections can be ordered or unordered. Some collections permit duplicate elements while others do not.

The `Collection` interface is inherited by several specific sub-interfaces such as `Set`, `List`, and `Queue`. These interfaces allow passing and manipulating collections as well as the conversion of a collection type to another. To implement the interfaces, the collections framework provides several abstract and concrete classes in the hierarchy. The `Collection` interface hierarchy is shown below:

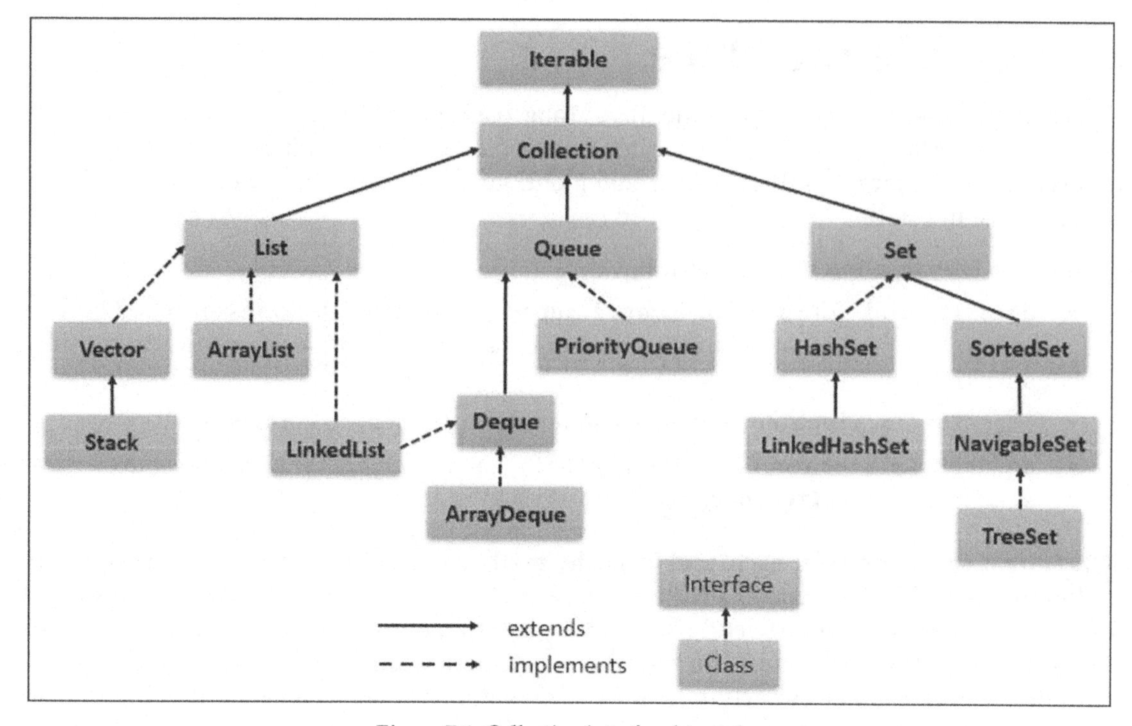

Figure 7.1: Collection interface hierarchy

Common methods of **`Collection`** interface are listed below. These methods can be used by all the implementing classes and sub interfaces:

- **`size()`**: Returns the size (number of elements) in the collection.
- **`isEmpty()`**: Returns true if the collection is empty/has no elements, else returns false.
- **`contains(Object o)`**: Check if a collection contains the specified object.
- **`add(Object o)`**: Used to add an element to the collection
- **`remove(Object o)`**: Removes an element from the collection.
- **`Iterator()`**: Used to traverse a collection.
- **`clear()`**: Clears all the contents from the collection.
- **`toArray()`**: Returns an array containing all the elements of this collection.
- **`equals(Object o)`**: Compares the specified object with this collection to check if they are equal.

Some methods of **`Collection`** interface are provided to perform bulk operations on the entire collection. These methods are listed below:

- **`containsAll(Collection<?> c)`**: Returns true if this collection contains all elements of the specified **`Collection`**.
- **`addAll(Collection<? extends E> c)`**: Adds all the elements of the specified **`Collection`** to this collection.

- `removeAll(Collection<?> c)`: Removes all the elements from this **`Collection`** that are present in the specified collection.
- `retainAll(Collection<?> c)`: Retains only those elements of this collection that are present in the specified collection.

7.3.1 Traversing collections

Traversing collections means iterating through a collection to access/manipulate its elements. In Java, the following two approaches are commonly used to traverse collections:

- **For-each/Enhanced for loop**: The **`for-each`** loop (enhanced for loop), added in Java SE 5, is a control flow statement used to traverse a collection. However, unlike the **`for loop`** construct, the **`for-each`** loop does not maintain an explicit counter, that is, a **`for-each`** loop will *do this for every element in this set* instead of *do this x times*.

  Internally, for-each behaves in the same manner as **`java.util.Iterator`**. Therefore, it is preferred over Iterator when reading each element, one by one and in order, since **`for-each`** is more convenient and concise.

  Syntax:

  ```
  for(Object obj:<collection-object>)
    System.out.println(obj);
  ```

  Since for-each construct does not maintain an explicit index, it does not allow removal of the current element by using the **`remove()`** method.

- **Iterator**: The Iterator interface provides methods to traverse and manipulate collections. To obtain an Iterator for a collection, use the **`iterator()`** method. Listed below are some important methods of **`Iterator`** interface:
  - `hasNext()`: Returns true if the iteration has more elements.
  - `next()`: Returns the next element in the iteration.
  - `remove()`: Removes the last element that was returned from the collection by the **`next()`** method. For every call to the **`next()`** method, the **`remove()`** method can be invoked only once. The **`remove()`** method is the only method that modifies a collection safely during iteration.

7.3.2 Collection factory methods

The factory methods were introduced with Java 9. These are special static methods used to create immutable instances of collections. You can create **`List`**, **`Set`**, and **`Map`** by using these methods for a small set of elements. Each interface has its own factory methods. An attempt to add a new element will throw the **`java.lang.UnsupportedOperationException`**.

7.4 List interface

Lists are collections created by implementing the **List** interface, which is an extension of the **Collection** interface. Lists are ordered collections that allow duplicate values and multiple null elements. Elements of a list can be accessed/searched by using an integer index. Similar to Java arrays, the list index begins at zero and the last index is **size-1**. Collections can be manipulated by the methods of **List** interface through position-based operations. The **List** interface uses an index internally to order the elements that are added to a list. **List** interface also provides methods to add and search elements as well as perform range operations.

The **List** interface provides the **ListIterator** to sequentially access the elements of the list. It is used to insert and replace elements and for bidirectional access along with the normal operations. Listed below are the additional methods of **List** interface apart from those inherited from the **Collection** interface:

- **add(int index, E element)**: Adds the specified element in the list at the position specified by index.
- **addAll(int index, Collection<? extends E> c)**: Adds all the elements of the specified collection, **c**, into the list starting at the given index position.
- **get (int index)**: Retrieves element of this list from the specified index position.
- **set (int index, E element)**: Replaces the element of this list the location specified by index with the specified element.
- **remove(int index)**: Removes the element at a given index position from the list.
- **subList(int start, int end)**: Returns a sub-list containing elements from start to end – 1 of this list.
- **indexOf(Object o)**: Returns the index of the first occurrence of the specified element in the list, or returns -1 is the element is not found in this list.
- **lastIndexOf(Object o)**: Returns the index of the last occurrence of the specified element in the list, or returns -1 is the element is not found in this list.

The **equals()** method helps to check the logical equality of two **List** objects. Two **List** objects are equal if they contain the same elements in the same order. Listed below are the factory methods of **List** interface:

- **static <E> List<E> of()**: Returns an immutable list containing zero elements.
- **static <E> List<E> of(E e1)**: Returns an immutable list containing one element.
- **static <E> List<E> of(E... elements)**: Returns an immutable list containing an arbitrary number of elements.
- **static <E> List<E> of(E e1, E e2)**: Returns an immutable list containing two elements.
- **static <E> List<E> of(E e1, E e2, E e3)**: Returns an immutable list containing three elements.

- **`static <E> List<E> of(E e1, E e2, E e3, E e4)`**: Returns an immutable list containing four elements.

Similarly, there are **`of()`** methods that can create an immutable list containing up to ten elements. The following example shows the use of factory methods of **`List`** interface:

```
import java.util.List;
public class ListDemo {
  public static void main(String[] args) {

    //using the factory method to create an immutable List


   List<String> list1 = List.of("Java","Java EE","Spring","Hibernate","Struts");
    System.out.println("Java Topics");
    for (String l : list1) {
      System.out.println(l);
    }
  }
}
```

Here, an immutable list of strings is created by using the five parameters **`of()`** method. The output of the code is shown below:

```
Java Topics
Java
Java EE
Spring
Hibernate
Struts
```

***Figure 7.2**: List interface factory methods*

7.4.1 ArrayList class

The **`ArrayList`** class implements the **`List`** interface and its methods. It is a solution to fixed-size arrays of primitive types as it allows the creation of a variable-length array of objects which can dynamically grow or shrink in size. While creating an **`ArrayList`** object, an initial size must be specified which can increase or decrease based on manipulations done on the **`ArrayList`** elements.

The **`ArrayList`** class allows all elements including null. **`ArrayList`** class is best suited for random access when insertion/removal of elements is to be done only at the end. Each **`ArrayList`** instance has a capacity which is the size of the array that will increase automatically as elements are added to the list.

Constructors of **ArrayList** class are:

- **ArrayList()**: Creates an empty list having an initial capacity of 10.
- **ArrayList(Collection <? extends E> c)**: Creates a list with the elements of the specified collection stored in the order they were returned by the collection's iterator.
- **ArrayList(int initialCapacity)**: Creates an empty list with the specified capacity.

For example:

```
List<String> list1 = new ArrayList<String> ();
```

Methods of **ArrayList** class:

The **ArrayList** class inherits all the methods of the **List** interface. Some methods are listed below:

- **add(E obj)**: Adds the specified element to the end of this list.
- **contains(Object obj)**: Returns true if this list contains the specified element.
- **size()**: Returns the number of elements in this list.
- **trimToSize()**: Trims the size of the **ArrayList** to the current size of the list.
- **ensureCapacity(int minCap)**: Increases the capacity of the **ArrayList** and ensures that it can hold the least number of specified elements.
- **clear()**: Removes all the elements from this list.

The **ArrayList** index begins at zero and the index of the last element is **size-1**. The following example shows the use of **ArrayList** class:

```
import java.util.List;
import java.util.ArrayList;
public class ArrayListDemo {
  public static void main(String[] args) {
    List<String> list1 = new ArrayList<>();
    System.out.println("List size is : " + list1.size());
    for (int i = 1; i <= 5; i++) {
      list1.add(""+i);
    }
    System.out.println("List of numbers added: "+list1);
    list1.set(4, "20");
    System.out.println("Modified list of numbers: "+list1);
    System.out.println("Value at index 4 is: " + (String) list1.get(3));
  }
}
```

The first **`ArrayList`** object, **`list1`** is created as an empty list, and values are added to it by using the **`for`** loop. The **`set()`** and **`get()`** methods are used to add/retrieve elements at a specific index in the list. The second **`List`** object **`list2`** is an immutable list of fixed values that are printed by using the enhanced **`for`** loop. The output of the code is shown below:

```
List size is : 0
List of numbers added: [1, 2, 3, 4, 5]
Modified list of numbers: [1, 2, 3, 4, 20]
Value at position 4 is: 4
```

Figure 7.3: *ArrayList output*

7.4.2 Vector class

Vector class is similar to the **`ArrayList`** class except that it provides a means to control the capacity increment for storage optimization. The vector list can also grow and shrink dynamically and the elements are accessed by using the index number. Vector also differs from **`ArrayList`** as the methods of **`Vector`** are synchronized and thread-safe. It also contains some legacy methods which do not belong to the collections framework.

Constructors of **`Vector`** class:

- **`Vector()`**: Creates an empty vector with an initial array size of 10.
- **`Vector(Collection<? extends E> c)`**: Creates a vector with elements of the specified collection, c stored in the order it was returned by the collection's iterator.
- **`Vector(int initCapacity)`**: Creates an empty vector with the specified initial capacity.
- **`Vector(int initCapacity, int capIncrement)`**: Creates a vector with the specified initial capacity and increment capacity.

For example:

```
Vector vector1 = new Vector();
```

Protected members of **`Vector`** class are:

- **`int capacityIncrement`**: Stores the increment value.
- **`int elementCount`**: Stores the number of valid components in the vector.
- **`Object [] elementData`**: An array buffer which stores the components of the vector.

Methods of Vector class are:

- **`capacity()`**: Returns the present capacity of the vector.
- **`addElement(E obj)`**: Adds an element at the end of the vector and increases the size of the vector by 1. The capacity of the vector automatically increases if the size is greater than the capacity.
- **`elementAt(int pos)`**: Retrieves the object stored at the specified location.
- **`removeElement(Object obj)`**: Removes the first occurrence of the specified object from the vector.

- **`clear()`**: Removes all the elements of the vector.
- **`toArray()`**: Returns an array containing all elements of the vector in the correct order.

The index of **`Vector`** begins at zero and the index of the last element is **`size-1`**. Following example shows the use of **`Vector`** class methods:

```
import java.util.Vector;
public class VectorDemo {
  public static void main(String[] args) {
    Vector<Object> vector1 = new Vector<>();
    vector1.addElement(3);
    vector1.addElement(8);
    vector1.addElement(4);
    vector1.addElement(5.95);
    vector1.addElement(9.055);
    System.out.println("Vector elements: " + vector1);
    System.out.println("Value at position 3: " + (Object) vector1.elementAt(2));
    vector1.removeElementAt(0);
    System.out.println("Revised Vector: " + vector1);
  }
}
```

Here, a **`Vector`** is created with integer and float types of values. Note that unlike earlier versions, explicit wrapping of primitive values in **`Wrapper`** types is not needed anymore. That is, **`addElement(new Integer(3))`**, is not required. The element of the vector are manipulated by using the **`elementAt()`** and **`removeElementAt()`** methods. The output of the code is shown below:

```
Vector elements: [3, 8, 4, 5.95, 9.055]
Value at position 3: 4
Revised Vector: [8, 4, 5.95, 9.055]
```

Figure 7.4: *Vector class methods*

7.4.3 Stack class

The **`Stack`** class extends the **`Vector`** class and represents a **Last-In-First-Out (LIFO)** stack of objects. It contains five legacy operations that allow a vector to be treated as a stack.

Syntax:

```
public class Stack<E> extends Vector<E>
```

Stack class contains the usual **push** and **pop** operations along with methods to peek at the top item of the stack, a method to search an item in the stack or how far it is from the top, and method to test if the stack is empty. When a stack is first created, it contains no items.

Constructors of **Stack** class are:

- **Stack()**: Creates an empty Stack.

Methods of **Stack** class:

- **push(E item)**: Pushes an item to the top of this stack.
- **pop()**: Removes and returns the object at the top of this stack.
- **peek()**: Looks at the object at the top of this stack without removing it.
- **search(Object o)**: Returns the 1-based position where an object is on this stack. If found, it returns the distance of the first occurrence from the top of the stack. The topmost item on the stack is considered to be at distance 1. The equals method is used to compare object o to the items in this stack.
- **boolean empty()**: Checks if this stack is empty.

The following example shows the use of **Stack** class methods:

```
import java.util.Stack;
import java.util.EmptyStackException;
public class StackExample {
  static void pushValue(Stack st, int val) {
    st.push(val);
    System.out.println("Pushed(" + val + ")");
    System.out.println("Stack: " + st);
  }
  static void popValue(Stack st) {
    System.out.print("Popped -> ");
    Integer val = (Integer) st.pop();
    System.out.println(val);
    System.out.println("Stack: " + st);
  }
  public static void main(String args[]) {
    Stack st1 = new Stack();
    System.out.println("Stack: " + st1);
    pushValue(st1, 24);
    pushValue(st1, 33);
```

```
        pushValue(st1, 45);
        popValue(st1);
        popValue(st1);
        popValue(st1);
        try {
          popValue(st1);
        } catch (EmptyStackException e) {
          System.out.println("Error: Stack is empty");
        }
    }
}
```

Here, a **Stack** is created by using two methods **pushValue()** and **popValue()** which in turn invoke the **push()** and **pop()** methods respectively of the **Stack** class. The output of the code is shown below:

```
Stack: []
Pushed(24)
Stack: [24]
Pushed(33)
Stack: [24, 33]
Pushed(45)
Stack: [24, 33, 45]
Popped -> 45
Stack: [24, 33]
Popped -> 33
Stack: [24]
Popped -> 24
Stack: []
Popped -> Error: Stack is empty
```

Figure 7.5: *Stack class methods*

Note that the **pop** operation removes the last element, 45, first due to the last-in-first-out feature of **Stack**.

7.4.4 LinkedList class

Java **LinkedList** class implements the **List** and **Deque** interfaces. It provides a linked-list data structure and represents a doubly linked-list to store the elements.

A linked-list is a data structure in which data is stored in nodes. A node contains a data part which stores the actual value, followed by the address part which contains the address of the next element in the list sequence. Linked-list allows insertion and deletion of nodes from both ends, but do not permit random access. The different types of linked lists include singly-linked lists, doubly-linked lists, and circularly-linked lists.

A Java **LinkedList**:

- Can contain duplicate elements.
- Maintains insertion order.
- Is non-synchronized.
- Manipulates data faster because no shifting needs to occur.
- It can be used as a list, stack, or queue.

Internally, a **LinkedList** stores object as a separate link, unlike an array that stores objects in consecutive memory locations.

Constructors of **LinkedList** class are:

- **LinkedList()**: Creates an empty linked list.
- **LinkedList(Collection <? Extends E>c)**: Creates a linked list with the elements of a specified collection, in the order, they are returned by the collection's iterator.

For example:

```
LinkedList<String> linkedList1 = new LinkedList<List>();
```

Methods of LinkedList class are:

- **addFirst(E obj)**: Adds the given object at the beginning of this list.
- **addLast(E obj)**: Appends the given object at the end of this list.
- **getFirst()**: Retrieves the first element from this list.
- **getLast()**: Retrieves the last element from this list.
- **removeFirst()**: Removes and returns the first element from this list.
- **removeLast()**: Removes and returns the last element from this list.
- **add(int index, E element)**: Adds the specified element at the specified position in this list.
- **remove(int index)**: Removes the element at the specified position in this list.

The following example shows the use of methods of the **LinkedList** class:

```
import java.util.LinkedList;
public class LinkedListDemo {
  public static void main(String[] args) {
    LinkedList<String> linkedL1 = new LinkedList<>();
    linkedL1.add("Mary Wilson");
```

```
        linkedL1.add("Martin Luther");
        linkedL1.add("Elvis Fetcher");
        linkedL1.add("Jack Dawson");
        linkedL1.add("John Smith");
        System.out.println("Linked list contents: " + linkedL1);
        linkedL1.removeLast();
        System.out.println("Modified Linked list contents: " + linkedL1);
    }
}
```

Here, a **LinkedList** object is created, and some **String** values are added to it. The **removeLast()** method is used to remove the last element and the modified list is displayed. The output of the code is shown below:

```
run:
Linked list contents: [Mary Wilson, Martin Luther, Elvis Fetcher, Jack Dawson, John Smith]
Modified Linked list contents: [Mary Wilson, Martin Luther, Elvis Fetcher, Jack Dawson]
BUILD SUCCESSFUL (total time: 0 seconds)
```

Figure 7.6: *LinkedList output*

7.5 Queue interface

The **Queue** interface extends the **Collection** interface and represents the queue data structure where generally the elements are ordered in **First-In-First-Out** (**FIFO**) order. However, a queue may follow other ordering strategies based on Queue implementation. For example, LIFO queue or stack orders elements in the LIFO pattern. In any case, the **poll()** method always removes the element at the head of the queue. The priority queue orders the element according to their values.

Methods of the Queue class are:

- **offer(E obj)**: Inserts the specified element into this queue. Returns true if the element is added else, returns false.
- **poll()**: Returns the value of the head of the queue and removes it from the queue. Returns null if the queue is empty.
- **remove()**: Returns the value of the head of the queue and removes it from the queue. Throws an exception if the queue is empty.
- **peek()**: Returns the value of the head of the queue but does not remove it from the queue. Returns null if the queue is empty.
- **element()**: Returns the value of the head of the queue but does not remove it from the queue. Throws an exception if the queue is empty.

7.5.1 Deque interface

The **Deque** interface extends the Queue interface and represents a double-ended queue or a deque. A deque (pronounced as the *deck*) is a linear collection that allows the insertion and removal of elements from both ends.

Deque implementations can have an unrestricted number of elements or capacity-restricted deques. Methods of deque interface are inherited from the **Queue** interface. Deque can be implemented with FIFO behavior to simulate a **Queue** or with LIFO structure to simulate a **Stack** (preferred over **Stack** class).

With FIFO structure, elements are added at the end of the deque and removed from the start. With LIFO (Stack) structure, elements are pushed and popped from the beginning of the deque.

Deque is implemented by using the **ArrayDeque** class as shown below:

```
Deque<Integer> stack=new ArrayDeque<>();
```

7.5.2 ArrayDeque class

The **ArrayDeque** class implements the **Deque** interface and is considered to be faster than the **Stack** and **LinkedList** classes when implemented as a queue.

Features of **ArrayDeque** class:

- Does not restrict the capacity.
- Does not allow null values.
- It is not thread safe, that is, it does not support access by multiple threads simultaneously.
- The elements can be accessed in both forward and backward directions.

Constructors of **ArrayDeque** class are:

- **`ArrayDeque()`**: Creates an empty array deque with an initial capacity of 16 elements.
- **`ArrayDeque(Collection<? Extends E> c)`**: Creates a deque containing the elements of the specified collection, in the order, they are returned by the collection's iterator.
- **`ArrayDeque(int initCapacity)`**: Creates an empty array deque with the specified initial capacity.

Methods of **ArrayDeque** class are:

- **`addFirst(E e)`**: Inserts the specified element at the front of this deque.
- **`addLast(E e)`**: Inserts the specified element at the end of this deque.
- **`getFirst()`**: Retrieves, but does not remove, the first element of this deque.
- **`getLast()`**: Retrieves, but does not remove, the last element of this deque.
- **`removeFirst()`**: Retrieves and removes the first element of this deque.
- **`removeLast()`**: Retrieves and removes the last element of this deque.
- **`contains(Object o)`**: Returns true if this deque contains the specified element.

The following code shows the use of **ArrayDeque** class methods:

```
import java.util.ArrayDeque;
import java.util.Iterator;
import java.util.Deque;
public class ArrayDequeDemo {
  public static void main(String[] args) {
    Deque<String> deque1 = new ArrayDeque();
    deque1.addLast("Red");
    deque1.addLast("Green");
    deque1.addFirst("Blue");

    System.out.println("Deque Contents");
    for (Iterator iter = deque1.iterator(); iter.hasNext();) {
      System.out.println(iter.next());
    }
       System.out.println("Reverse Deque");
    for (Iterator iter = deque1.descendingIterator(); iter.hasNext();) {
      System.out.println(iter.next());
    }
    System.out.println("First Color: " + deque1.getFirst());
    System.out.println("Last Color: " + deque1.getLast());
   System.out.println("Deque contains \"Yellow\": " + deque1.contains("Yellow"));
  }
}
```

Here, an object of **Deque** of type **ArrayDeque** is created and three values are added. The **Iterator** object is used to traverse the deque in both directions. Note that the color blue is added as the first element. The output of the code is shown below:

```
Deque Contents
Blue
Red
Green
Reverse Deque
Green
Red
Blue
First Color: Blue
Last Color: Green
Deque contains "Yellow": false
```

Figure 7.7: *ArrayDeque output*

7.5.3 PriorityQueue class

`PriorityQueue` class implements the **`Queue`** interface. It is similar to queues, but it does not follow the FIFO structure. Rather, the elements are ordered as per their natural ordering according to the comparator. It does not support null elements or non-comparable objects. It does not restrict the capacity either and can grow dynamically.

Constructors of PriorityQueue class are:

- **`PriorityQueue()`**: Creates a **`PriorityQueue`** with a capacity of 11 elements and orders its elements according to their natural ordering.
- **`PriorityQueue(Collection<? Extends E> c)`**: Creates a **`PriorityQueue`** with the elements from the specified collection, `c`.
- **`PriorityQueue(int initialCapacity)`**: Creates a **`PriorityQueue`** with the specified initial capacity and orders its elements according to their natural ordering.
- **`PriorityQueue(int initialCapacity, Comparator<? Super E> comparator)`**: Creates a **`PriorityQueue`** with the specified initial capacity and orders the elements according to the specified **`comparator`**.
- **`PriorityQueue(PriorityQueue<? Extends E> c)`**: Creates a **`PriorityQueue`** with elements of the specified **`PriorityQueue`**.
- **`PriorityQueue(SortedSet<? Extends E> c)`**: Creates a **`PriorityQueue`** with the elements of the specified **`SortedSet`**.

Methods of **`PriorityQueue`** class are:

- **`add(E e)`**: Adds the specified element to this priority queue and returns a boolean value.
- **`clear()`**: Removes all elements from this priority queue.

- **comparator()**: Returns the comparator used to order this collection. Returns null if this collection is sorted according to its elements' natural ordering.
- **contains (Object o)**: Checks if this queue contains the specified element.
- **iterator()**: Returns an iterator over the elements in this queue.
- **toArray()**: Returns an array of objects containing all of the elements of this queue.

The following code shows the use of **PriorityQueue** class methods:

```
import java.util.PriorityQueue;
public class PriorityQueueDemo {
 public static void main(String[] args) {
  PriorityQueue<String> pq = new PriorityQueue<>();
  pq.offer("Red");
  pq.offer("Green");
  pq.offer("Blue");
  pq.offer("Yellow");
  System.out.println("Priority queue contents: "+pq);
  System.out.println("1. Removed: " + pq.poll());
  System.out.println("2. Removed: " + pq.poll());
  System.out.println("3. Viewed: " + pq.peek());
  System.out.println("4. Viewed: " + pq.peek());
  System.out.println("5. Removed: " + pq.remove());
  System.out.println("6. Removed: " + pq.remove());
  System.out.println("7. Viewed: " + pq.peek());
  System.out.println("Priority queue contents: "+pq);
  System.out.println("8. Viewed: " + pq.element());
 }
}
```

Here, an object of **PriorityQueue** class is created, and the **offer()** method is used to add values to the queue. The **poll()**, **peek()**, **remove()**, and **element()** methods are used to remove and/or view the values of the priority queue. The output of the code is shown below:

```
Priority queue contents: [Blue, Red, Green, Yellow]
1. Removed: Blue
2. Removed: Green
3. Viewed: Red
4. Viewed: Red
5. Removed: Red
6. Removed: Yellow
7. Viewed: null
Priority queue contents: []
Exception in thread "main" java.util.NoSuchElementException
        at java.base/java.util.AbstractQueue.element(AbstractQueue.java:136)
        at moduleOne/Sess7Codes.PriorityQueueDemo.main(PriorityQueueDemo.java:31)
C:\Users\Admin3\AppData\Local\NetBeans\Cache\dev\executor-snippets\run.xml:135: The following error
C:\Users\Admin3\AppData\Local\NetBeans\Cache\dev\executor-snippets\run.xml:64: Java returned: 1
BUILD FAILED (total time: 0 seconds)
```

***Figure 7.8:** PriorityQueue output*

Note that the **`element()`** method throws an exception when it attempts to view an element from an empty list whereas the **`peek()`** method returns null.

7.6 Set interface

Set is a collection of unordered non-duplicate list of object references. The **`Set`** interface extends the **`Collection`** interface and inherits all the methods except the ones that support duplicate values. The three common implementations of Set interface are **`Hash Set`**, **`LinkedHashSet`**, and **`TreeSet`**. Since **`Set`** does not permit duplication of values, the **`add()`** method returns false if a duplicate value is added to a **`Set`**. The **`Set`** interface is best suited for carrying out bulk operations.

Methods of **`Set`** Interface are:

- **`addAll(Collection<? Extends E> obj)`**: Adds all the elements of the specified collection to this set object.
- **`retainAll(Collection<?> obj)`**: Retains in this set only those elements which are contained in the specified collection.
- **`removeAll(Collection<?> obj)`**: Removes all the elements from this set that are contained in the specified collection.
- **`containsAll(Collection<?> obj)`**: Returns true if this set object contains all the elements of the specified collection.

If two Set instances contain the same elements, they are considered to be equal.

Java **`Set`** interface provides the **`Set.of()`** static factory method for creating an immutable set with the following characteristics:

- It is immutable
- Does not allow null elements
- Does not allow duplicate elements.
- It is serializable if all elements are serializable.
- The iteration order of set elements is unspecified and may change.

Listed below are the factory methods of the **Set** interface:

- **static <E> Set<E> of()**: Returns an immutable set containing zero elements.
- **static <E> Set<E> of(E e1)**: Returns an immutable set containing one element.
- **static <E> Set<E> of(E... elements)**: Returns an immutable set containing an arbitrary number of elements.
- **static <E> Set<E> of(E e1, E e2)**: Returns an immutable set containing two elements.
- **static <E> Set<E> of(E e1, E e2, E e3)**: Returns an immutable set containing three elements.
- **static <E> Set<E> of(E e1, E e2, E e3, E e4)**: Returns an immutable set containing four elements.

Similarly, there are **of()** methods that can create an immutable set containing up to ten elements. The following example shows the use of factory methods of the **Set** interface:

```
import java.util.Set;

import java.util.Set;

public class SetDemo {


  public static void main(String[] args) {
    Set<String> set = Set.of("Java","JavaEE","Spring","Hibernate","Struts");
    System.out.println("Java Topics");
    for(String l:set) {
      System.out.println(l);
    }
  }
}
```

Here, an immutable set of strings is created by using the five parameters **of()** method. The output of the code is shown below:

```
Java Topics
Hibernate
Java
Spring
Struts
JavaEE
```

Figure 7.9: Factory method of SortedSet

7.6.1 HashSet class

The **`HashSet`** class implements the **`Set`** interface and stores its elements in a hash table. It allows the null element but does not guarantee the order of iteration.

A hash table is a data structure used to store information as key-value pairs. Each key is mapped to an index/array position. The key is used to search/access elements of a hash table. Implementation of the key depends on the type of data to be stored. Keys are automatically converted to hash code and the hash table cannot be indexed directly in a program.

Generally, for basic operations, **`HashSet`** class provides a good iteration performance if the initial capacity is not too high or the load factor is not too low.

The load factor is a measure of how full the **`HashSet`** is allowed to get before its capacity is automatically increased. A fill ratio determines the capacity of the set before it is resized upward.

Constructors of the **`HashSet`** class are:

- **`HashSet()`**: Creates a default hash set with an initial capacity of 16 and a load factor of 0.75.
- **`HashSet(Collection<? extends E> c)`**: Creates a hash set with the elements of the specified collection.
- **`HashSet(int size)`**: Creates a hash set of the specified size with a default load factor of 0.75.
- **`HashSet(int size, float fillRatio)`**: Creates a hash set of the specified size and fill ratio.

For example:

```
Set<String> hashset1 = new HashSet<>();
```

7.6.2 LinkedHashSet class

The **`LinkedHashSet`** class extends the **`HashSet`** class and is a linked-list implementation of the **`Set`** interface. It represents a doubly-linked list and iterates through the elements based on their insertion order in the set. A **`LinkedHashSet`** is a combination of hashtable and linked-list and maintains the internal order of the elements added to the **`Set`**. It allows the use of null elements. Performance of the **`LinkedHashSet`** may suffer due to the overhead of maintaining the linked list.

Constructors of **`LinkedHashSet`** class are:

- **`LinkedHashSet()`**: Creates a default linked hash set with an initial capacity of 16 and a load factor of 0.75.
- **`LinkedHashSet(Collection<? extends E> c)`**: Creates a new linked hash set with the elements of the specified collection.

- **`LinkedHashSet(int initial capacity)`**: Creates a new, empty linked hash set with the specified initial capacity.
- **`LinkedHashSet(int initialCapacity, float loadFactor)`**: Creates a new empty linked hash set with the specified initial capacity and load factor.

The following example shows the use of **`LinkedHashSet`**:

```
public class Toy {
  int id;
  String name, color;
  float price;
  public Toy(int id, String name, String color, float price) {
    this.id = id;
    this.name = name;
    this.color = color;
    this.price = price;
  }
}
----------------------------------------------------------------
import java.util.LinkedHashSet;
public class LinkedHashSetDemo {
  public static void main(String[] args) {
    LinkedHashSet<Toy> hs = new LinkedHashSet<>();
    //Creating Toys
    Toy toy1 = new Toy(1001, "Barbie", "Pink", 40.0f);
    Toy toy2 = new Toy(1002, "Teddy Bear", "White", 20.5f);
    Toy toy3 = new Toy(1003, "Aeroplane", "Blue", 50.5f);
    //Adding Toys to hash set
    hs.add(toy1);
    hs.add(toy2);
    hs.add(toy3);
    //Traversing hash set
    for (Toy t : hs) {
      System.out.println(t.id + " " + t.name + " " + t.color + " " + t.price);
    }
  }
}
```

The code creates a class **Toy** with some attributes. Next, the **LinkedHashSet** object is created with type set to **Toy**. Three **Toy** objects are created and added to the hash set and then printed by using the enhanced **for** loop. The output of the code is shown below:

```
1001 Barbie Pink 40.0
1002 Teddy Bear White 20.5
1003 Aeroplane Blue 50.5
```

Figure 7.10: *LinkedHashSet output*

7.6.3 SortedSet interface

The **SortedSet** interface extends the **Set** interface. The elements of a **SortedSet** can be ordered as per natural ordering or by using the **Comparator**. The **SortedSet** interface allows creating sorted lists of non-duplicate elements and its iterator traverses the elements in the ascending order. Internally, the comparison of elements is done by using the **compare()** or **compareTo()** methods.

Methods of **SortedSet** interface are:

- **first()**: Returns the first or lowest element in this sorted set.
- **last()**: Returns the last or highest element in this sorted set.
- **headSet (E endElement)**: Returns a **SortedSet** instance with all the elements from the beginning of the set up to **endElement**, but not including **endElement.subSet (E startElement, E endElement)**: Returns a **SortedSet** instance that includes the elements between **startElement** and **endElement-1**.
- **tailSet (E fromElement)**: Returns a **SortedSet** instance with elements greater than or equal to **fromElement** that are present in this sorted set.

Possible method exceptions are:

- **NoSuchElementException**: When there are no elements in the set.
- **ClassCastException**: When an object is incompatible with the elements in a set.
- **NullPointerException**: When a null object is used.

7.6.4 NavigableSet interface

The **NavigableSet** interface extends the **SortedSet** interface with navigation methods which return the closest matches for given search targets. A **NavigableSet** can be accessed/traversed in either ascending or descending order. The performance of ascending operations and views is likely to be faster than that of descending ones.

Methods **subSet**, **headSet**, and **tailSet** of **NavigableSet** interface differ from the similar **SortedSet** methods as they accept additional arguments indicating if the lower and upper bounds are inclusive or exclusive. However, the **SortedSet** versions of these methods are also retained in **NavigableSet** interface.

The following are the other methods of **NavigableSet** interface:

- **ceiling(E e)**: Returns the smallest element in this set, which is greater than or equal to the given element, or null if there is no such element.
- **floor(E e)**: Returns the greatest element in this set, which is less than or equal to the given element, or null if there is no such element.
- **descendingSet()**: Returns a reverse order view of the elements of this set.
- **higher(E e)**: Returns the smallest element in this set which is greater than the given element, or null if there is no such element.
- **lower(E e)**: Returns the greatest element in this set which is less than the given element, or null if there is no such element.
- **pollFirst()**: Retrieves and removes the first/lowest element, or returns null if this set is empty.
- **pollLast()**: Retrieves and removes the last/highest element, or returns null if this set is empty.

7.6.5 TreeSet class

The **TreeSet** class implements the **NavigableSet** interface. It stores elements in a tree structure and orders elements based on their natural ordering or by using **Comparator** during set creation. Accessing/retrieving elements is faster as they are stored in the ascending order. It is useful for creating a sorted collection.

TreeSet cannot contain a null value. Internally it uses a **TreeMap** to store elements. **TreeSet** class is not thread-safe, hence, explicit synchronization must be done for concurrent access to a **TreeSet** in a multi-threaded environment.

Constructors of **TreeSet** class are:

- **TreeSet()**: Creates an empty **TreeSet** with the elements sorted in ascending order.
- **TreeSet(Collection<? extends E> c)**: Creates a new **TreeSet** with the elements of the specified collection, sorted according to the elements order.
- **TreeSet(Comparator<? super E> c)**: Creates a new, empty **TreeSet** sorted according to the specified **Comparator**.
- **TreeSet (SortedSet<E> s)**: Creates a new **TreeSet** with the elements of the specified **SortedSet** in the same order.

The following example shows the use of **TreeSet**:

```
import java.util.TreeSet;
import java.util.SortedSet;
public class TreeSetDemo {
  public static void main(String[] args) {
    // Creating a TreeSet
```

```
        SortedSet<String> colors = new TreeSet<>();
        // Adding new elements to a TreeSet
        colors.add("Blue");
        colors.add("Pink");
        colors.add("White");
        colors.add("Orange");
        System.out.println("Colors: " + colors);
        // Duplicate elements are ignored
        colors.add("White");
        System.out.println("After adding duplicate element \"White\" : " + colors);
        // This will be allowed because it is in lowercase.
        colors.add("blue");
        System.out.println("After adding \"blue\" : " + colors);
    }
}
```

Here, a **TreeSet** is created with some color names. An attempt is made to add a duplicate value and another value with the same name but lower case. The output of the code is shown below:

```
run:
Colors: [Blue, Orange, Pink, White]
After adding duplicate element "White" : [Blue, Orange, Pink, White]
After adding "blue" : [Blue, Orange, Pink, White, blue]
```

Figure 7.11: TreeSet output

Note that the duplicate value **White** is ignored and the value, **blue** is allowed as it is in the lowercase.

7.6.6 ConcurrentSkipListSet

The **ConcurrentSkipListSet** class belongs to the **java.util.concurrent** package and implements the **NavigableSet** interface. It orders elements as per their natural ordering or based on the specified **Comparator** object. It provides methods to return iterators in ascending or descending order and methods to return the closest matches of elements in a collection.

Constructor of **ConcurrentSkipListSet** class are:

- **ConcurrentSkipListSet()**: Creates an instance of **ConcurrentSkipListSet** with its elements sorted on natural order.

Methods of **ConcurrentSkipListSet** class are:

- **ceiling(E e)**: Returns the smallest element which is greater than or equal to e or null, if there is no such element.

- **floor(E e)**: Returns the greatest element which is less than or equal to e or null, if there is no such element.
- **higher(E e)**: Returns the smallest element which is greater than e or null, if there is no such element
- **lower(E e)**: Returns the greatest element which is less than e or null, if there is no such element

The following example shows the use of **ConcurrentSkipListSet** class:

```
import java.util.concurrent.ConcurrentSkipListSet;
import java.util.Iterator;
public class CSLSdemo {
  public static void main(String args[]) {
    ConcurrentSkipListSet colors = new ConcurrentSkipListSet();
    colors.add("Red");
    colors.add("Green");
    colors.add("Blue");
    colors.add("Yellow");
    Iterator iterator = colors.iterator();
    System.out.print("Ascending CSLS: ");
    while (iterator.hasNext()) {
      System.out.print(iterator.next() + " ");
    }
    System.out.println("\nDescending CSLS: " + colors.descendingSet());
    System.out.println("Lower element: " + colors.lower("Green"));
    System.out.println("Higher element: " + colors.higher("Yellow"));
  }
}
```

Here, an object of **ConcurrentSkipListSet** is created and elements are added to it. The elements are sorted in ascending and descending order and displayed on the screen. The **lower()** and **higher()** methods are used to identify the lower and higher elements for the specified arguments. The output of the code is given below:

```
Ascending CSLS: Blue Green Red Yellow
Descending CSLS: [Yellow, Red, Green, Blue]
Lower element: Blue
Higher element: null
```

Figure 7.12: *ConcurrentSkipListSet output*

Note that the **higher()** method returns null because there is no value greater than **Yellow**.

7.7 Map interface

A **Map** object stores data in the form of key-value pairs where each key is mapped to a single value and can be used to retrieve the value from a **Map** object. Maps can have duplicate values but the keys must be unique. The **Map** interface belongs to the **java.util** package but not extend the **Collection** interface. **Map** interface has its hierarchy as shown below:

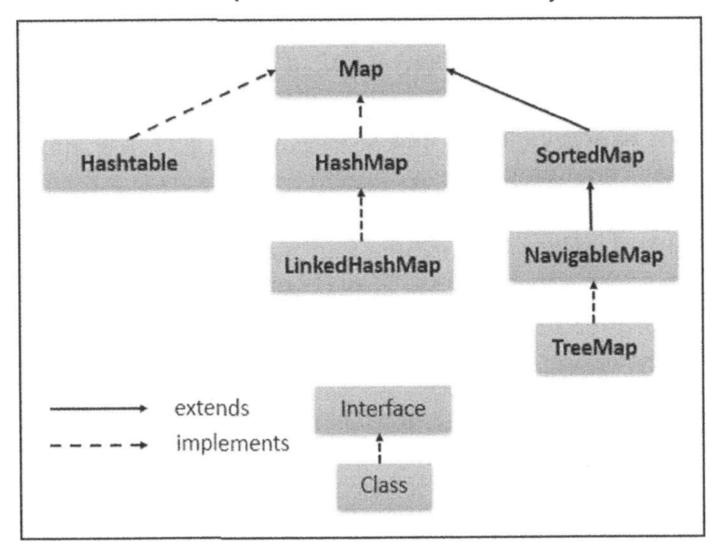

Figure 7.13: Map interface hierarchy

The three common **Map** implementations are **HashMap**, **TreeMap**, and **LinkedHashMap**.

Methods of a **Map** interface are:

- **put(K key, V value)**: Associates the given value with the given key in this map object. It overwrites and returns the previous value associated with the key. Returns null if there was no mapping with the key.
- **get(Object key)**: Returns the value associated with the given key in this map object.
- **containsKey(Object Key)**: Returns true if this map object contains a mapping for the specified key.
- **containsValue(Object Value)**: Returns true if this map object maps one or more keys to the specified value.
- **size()**: Returns the number of key-value mappings in this map.
- **values()**: Returns a collection view of the values stored in this map.

Java **Map** interface provides the **Map.of()** static factory method for creating an immutable map with the following characteristics:

- It is immutable
- Does not allow null keys and values
- It is serializable if all keys and values are serializable

- Rejects duplicate keys at creation time
- The iteration order of mappings is unspecified and may change.

Listed below are the factory methods of the **Map** interface:

- **static <K,V> Map<K,V> of()**: Returns an immutable map containing zero mappings.
- **static <K,V> Map<K,V> of(K k1, V v1)**: Returns an immutable map containing a single mapping.
- **static <K,V> Map<K,V> of(K k1, V v1, K k2, V v2)**: Returns an immutable map containing two mappings.
- **static <K,V> Map<K,V> of(K k1, V v1, K k2, V v2, K k3, V v3)**: Returns an immutable map containing three mappings.
- **static <K,V> Map<K,V> of(K k1, V v1, K k2, V v2, K k3, V v3, K k4, V v4)**: Returns an immutable map containing four mappings.
- **static <K,V> Map<K,V> ofEntries(Map.Entry<? extends K,? extends V>... entries)**: Returns an immutable map containing keys and values extracted from the specified entries.

Similarly, there are **of()** methods that can create an immutable map containing up to ten elements. The following example shows the use of factory methods of **Map** interface:

```
import java.util.Map;
public class MapDemo {
  public static void main(String[] args) {
Map<Integer, String> map1 = Map.of(101, "Java", 102, "Struts", 103, "Hibernate");
    for (Map.Entry<Integer, String> m : map1.entrySet()) {
      System.out.println(m.getKey() + " " + m.getValue());
    }
    System.out.println("Map created by using entries");
    // Creating Map Entry
    Map.Entry<Integer, String> e1 = Map.entry(101, "Java");
    Map.Entry<Integer, String> e2 = Map.entry(102, "Struts");
    // Creating Map by using map entries
    Map<Integer, String> map2 = Map.ofEntries(e1,e2);
    // Iterating Map
    for(Map.Entry<Integer, String> m : map2.entrySet()){
      System.out.println(m.getKey()+" "+m.getValue());
    }
  }
}
```

Here, an immutable map of strings is created by using the three-parameter **of()** method and also by using the **ofEntries()** method. The output of the code is shown below:

```
101 Java
103 Hibernate
102 Struts
Map created by using entries
102 Struts
101 Java
```

Figure 7.14: *Factory method of Map interface*

Note that the order of elements is not maintained.

7.7.1 Hashtable class

The **Hashtable** class implements the **Map** interface. It stores elements as key-value pairs in a hash table in which the keys are converted to hash code. This hash code works as an index that is used to store and retrieve values stored in the **Hashtable**. The **Hashtable** class implements all methods of the **Map** interface.

Constructors of **Hashtable** class are:

- **Hashtable()**: Creates a new, empty **Hashtable**.
- **Hashtable (int initCap)**: Creates a new, empty **Hashtable** with the specified initial capacity.
- **Hashtable (int intCap, float fillRatio)**: Creates a new, empty **Hashtable** with the specified initial capacity and fill ratio.
- **Hashtable (Map<? extends K,? extends V> m)**: Creates a new **Hashtable** with the elements of the given **Map**.

Important methods of **Hashtable** class are:

- **get(Object key)**: Returns the value to which the specified key is mapped. Returns null if this map contains no mapping for the key.
- **isEmpty()**: Checks if this **Hashtable** maps no keys to values.
- **keys()**: Returns an enumeration of the keys in this **Hashtable**.
- **containsKey(Object key)**: Checks if the specified key is present in this **Hashtable**.

The following example shows the use of **Hashtable** class:

```
import java.util.Hashtable;
import java.util.Enumeration;
public class HashTableDemo {
  public static void main(String[] args) {
    Hashtable<String, String> toys = new Hashtable<>();
```

```
        toys.put("T001", "Barbie Doll");
        toys.put("T002", "Teddy Bear");
        toys.put("T003", "Aeroplane");
        String toy = (String) toys.get("T002");
        System.out.println("Selectd toy: " + toy);
        System.out.println("Is hash table empty? " + (toys.isEmpty()?"Yes":"No"));
          System.out.println("Does the hash table contain key T003? " + (toys.
containsKey("T003")?"Yes":"No"));
        Enumeration toyIds = toys.keys();
        while (toyIds.hasMoreElements()) {
          String code = (String) toyIds.nextElement();
          System.out.println(code + ": " + (String) toys.get(code));
        }
    }
}
```

Here, an object of **Hashtable** class is created and some data is added to it. Next, the **get(), isEmpty(), containsKey()**, and **keys()** methods are used to manipulate the **Hashtable**. The **Enumeration** object is used to obtain details of all toys and the keys are retrieved by using the **nextElement()** method of the **Enumeration** interface. Next, the keys are used to fetch the values associated with each key. The output of the code is shown below:

```
Selectd toy: Teddy Bear
Is hash table empty? No
Does the hash table contain key T003? Yes
T003: Aeroplane
T002: Teddy Bear
T001: Barbie Doll
```

***Figure 7.15:** Hashtable class methods*

7.7.2 HashMap class

The **HashMap** class implements the **Map** interface. It has methods that allow adding, removing, and searching elements in a **Map**. It is similar to **Hashtable** in every way except that **HashMap** allows null values for keys and also, it is not synchronized. The order of elements of **HashMap** is unspecified and may change.

Constructors of **HashMap** class are:

- **HashMap()**: Creates an empty **HashMap** with an initial capacity of 17 and a load factor of 0.75.

- **HashMap(int initialCapacity)**: Creates an empty **HashMap** with the specified initial capacity and a load factor of 0.75.
- **HashMap(int initialCapacity, float loadFactor)**: Creates an empty **HashMap** with the specified initial capacity and load factor.
- **HashMap(Map<? extends K,? extends V> m)**: Creates a **HashMap** with the elements of the specified **Map** object.

Note: Initial capacity indicates the number of objects that can be added to the HashMap at the time of creation. The load factor indicates how full the HashMap can get before its capacity is automatically increased.

The following example shows the use of **HashMap** class:

```
public class Toy {
  int id;
  String name, color;
  float price;
  public Toy(int id, String name, String color, float price) {
    this.id = id;
    this.name = name;
    this.color = color;
    this.price = price;
  }
  @Override
  public String toString() {
    return "ID:" + id + ", Name:" + name + ", Color:" + color + ", Price:" +
price+ "\n";
  }
}
```

Here, an object of **HashMap** is created with keys of type string and values of type **Toy** class. Three values are added and the **HashMap** is displayed. Next, the **remove(), put()** and **get()** methods are used to manipulate the **HashMap** and the modified **HashMap** is printed. The output of the code is shown below:

```
1=ID:1001, Name:Barbie Doll, Color:Pink, Price:50.5
 2=ID:1002, Name:Teddy Bear, Color:White, Price:40.3
 3=ID:1003, Name:Aeroplane, Color:Blue, Price:50.6


oy at key 4: ID:1004, Name:Rattles, Color:Multi-color, Price:10.!

odified HashMap
1=ID:1001, Name:Barbie Doll, Color:Pink, Price:50.5
 2=ID:1002, Name:Teddy Bear, Color:White, Price:40.3
 4=ID:1004, Name:Rattles, Color:Multi-color, Price:10.5
```

Figure 7.16: *HashMap class methods*

7.7.3 LinkedHashMap class

LinkedHashMap class extends the **HashMap** class and represents storage as a hash table and the linked-list. Unlike **HashMap**, it maintains the order of its elements and returns them in the same order that they were added to the **Map**.

Constructors of the **LinkedHashMap** class are:

- **LinkedHashMap()**: Creates an empty **LinkedHashMap** with a tan initial capacity of 16 and a load factor of 0.75.
- **LinkedHashMap(int initialCapacity)**: Creates an empty **LinkedHashMap** with the specified initial capacity and a load factor of 0.75.
- **LinkedHashMap(int initialCapacity, float loadFactor)**: Creates an empty **LinkedHashMap** with the specified initial capacity and load factor.

  LinkedHashMap(int initialCapacity, float loadFactor, boolean accessOrder): Creates an empty **LinkedHashMap** with the specified initial capacity, load factor, and ordering mode.

  A true value specifies that the ordering mode is based on access-order and false specifies that ordering mode is based on insertion-order.
- **LinkedHashMap(Map<? extends K,? extends V> m)**: Creates a **LinkedHashMap** with the mappings of the specified **Map** object and ordering mode based on insertion-mode.

Methods of the **LinkedHashMap** class are:

- **get(Object key)**: Returns the value to which the key is mapped.
- **containsValue(Object value)**: Returns true if the map contains the specified value.
- **removeEldestEntry(Map.Entry<K,V> eldest)**: Returns true if the map removes its eldest key.
- **clear()**: Removes all mappings from the invoking map.

The following example shows the use of **LinkedHashMap** class:

```
import java.util.Map;
import java.util.LinkedHashMap;
import java.util.Set;
import java.util.Iterator;
public class LinkedHashMapExample {
  public static void main(String args[]) {
    // Create a hash map
    LinkedHashMap<String,Double> lhm1 = new LinkedHashMap<>();

    // Put elements to the map
    lhm1.put("Barbie Doll", 43.34);
    lhm1.put("Teddy Bear", 23.2);
    lhm1.put("Aeroplane", 58.00);
     // Get a set of the entries
    Set set1 = lhm1.entrySet();
    // Get an iterator
    Iterator i = set1.iterator();
    // Display elements
    while(i.hasNext()) {
      Map.Entry me = (Map.Entry)i.next();
      System.out.print(me.getKey() + ": "+ me.getValue() +"\n");
    }

    // Change price of Aeroplane
    double price = lhm1.get("Aeroplane");
    lhm1.put("Aeroplane", (price + 5.6));

    System.out.println("New price of Aeroplane: " + lhm1.get("Aeroplane"));

    System.out.println("Modified Map: "+lhm1);
  }
}
```

Here, a **LinkedHashMap** object is created with some entries. Methods of **LinkedHashMap** are used to manipulate the data and the modified **Map** is displayed. The output of the code is shown below:

```
Barbie Doll: 43.34
Teddy Bear: 23.2
Aeroplane: 58.0
New price of Aeroplane: 63.6
Modified Map: {Barbie Doll=43.34, Teddy Bear=23.2, Aeroplane=63.6}
```

Figure 7.17: *LinkedHashMap output*

7.7.4 TreeMap class

The **TreeMap** class implements the **NavigableMap** interface and stores the keys in a tree structure in sorted order.

Constructors of the **TreeMap** class:

- **TreeMap()**: Creates a new empty **TreeMap**.
- **TreeMap(Comparator<? super K> c)**: Creates **TreeMap**, where the keys are sorted according to the given comparator.
- **TreeMap(Map<? extends K,? extends V> m)**: Creates a new **TreeMap** with the entries of the given **Map** and orders them according to the natural ordering of its key.
- **TreeMap(SortedMap<K,? extends V> m)**: Creates a new **TreeMap** with the entries of the given **SortedMap** and uses its comparator for ordering the elements.

Methods of **TreeMap** class:

- **firstKey()**: Returns the first key in this sorted map.
- **lastKey()**: Returns the last key in this sorted map.
- **headMap(K toKey)**: Returns a portion of the map whose value is less than the value of **toKey**.
- **tailMap(K fromKey)**: Returns a portion of this map whose keys is greater than or equal to the value of **fromKey**.

The following example shows the use of **TreeMap** class:

```
import java.util.TreeMap;
public class TreeMapDemo {
  public static void main(String[] args) {
    TreeMap<String, Toy> toys = new TreeMap<>();
    toys.put("3", new Toy(1003, "Aeroplane", "Blue", 50.6f));
    toys.put("1", new Toy(1001, "Barbie Doll", "Pink", 50.5f));
    toys.put("2", new Toy(1002, "Teddy Bear", "White", 40.3f));
```

```
        toys.put("5", new Toy(1005, "Bus", "Red", 30.6f));
        System.out.println(toys);
        toys.remove("3");
        toys.put("4", new Toy(1004, "Rattles", "Multi-color", 10.5f));
        System.out.println("Toy at key 4: "+toys.get("4"));
        Object firstKey = toys.firstKey();
        System.out.println("First key: "+firstKey.toString());
        System.out.println("Last key: "+(String) (toys.lastKey()));
        System.out.println("Modified Tree Map: \n"+toys);
    }
}
```

Here, a **TreeMap** object is created and data is added to it. Its methods are used to manipulate the data. The output of the code is shown below:

```
{1=ID:1001, Name:Barbie Doll, Color:Pink, Price:50.5
, 2=ID:1002, Name:Teddy Bear, Color:White, Price:40.3
, 3=ID:1003, Name:Aeroplane, Color:Blue, Price:50.6
, 5=ID:1005, Name:Bus, Color:Red, Price:30.6
}
Toy at key 4: ID:1004, Name:Rattles, Color:Multi-color, Price:10.5

First key: 1
Last key: 5
Modified Tree Map:
{1=ID:1001, Name:Barbie Doll, Color:Pink, Price:50.5
, 2=ID:1002, Name:Teddy Bear, Color:White, Price:40.3
, 4=ID:1004, Name:Rattles, Color:Multi-color, Price:10.5
, 5=ID:1005, Name:Bus, Color:Red, Price:30.6
}
```

Figure 7.18: *TreeMap class methods*

7.7.5 ConcurrentSkipListMap

The **ConcurrentSkipListMap** class implements the **ConcurrentNavigableMap** interface. It belongs to **java.util.concurrent** package. It allows modification without locking the entire map.

Constructor of **ConcurrentSkipListMap** class are:

- **ConcurrentSkipListMap()**: Creates a new empty **Map** with elements sorted according to the natural ordering of the keys.

Methods of **ConcurrentSkipListMap** class are:

- **firstEntry()**: Returns data of the lowest key in the map.
- **lastEntry()**: Returns data of the highest key in the map.
- **ceilingEntry(K key)**: Returns the closest value which is greater than or equal to the specified key, or null if there is no such key
- **put(K key, V value)**: Adds the specified value with the specified key in this map.
- **descendingMap()**: Returns a reverse order view of the elements in this map.

The following example shows the use of **ConcurrentSkipListMap** class:

```
import java.util.concurrent.ConcurrentSkipListMap;
public class CSLMdemo {
  public static void main(String args[]) {
    ConcurrentSkipListMap colors = new ConcurrentSkipListMap();
    colors.put(1,"Red");
    colors.put(2,"Green");
    colors.put(5,"White");
    colors.put(4,"Yellow");
    System.out.println("Descending CSLM: " + colors.descendingMap());
    System.out.println("First entry: " + colors.firstEntry());
    System.out.println("Last entry: " + colors.lastEntry());
  }
}
```

Here, an object of **ConcurrentSkipListMap** class is created and data is added to it as key-value pairs. The map is displayed in the descending order. The first and last entries of the map are displayed. The output of the code is shown below:

```
Descending CSLM: {5=White, 4=Yellow, 2=Green, 1=Red}
First entry: 1=Red
Last entry: 5=White
```

Figure 7.19: ConcurrentSkipListMap output

7.8 Arrays class

The **java.util.Arrays** class provides methods for performing operations such as sorting, searching, and so on. on arrays. All the methods of **Arrays** class throw a **NullPointerExcpetion** if the array reference is null. It provides a static factory that allows arrays to be viewed as lists.

Commonly used methods of **Array** class are:

- **equals(<type> arrObj1, <type> arrObj2)**: Compares the two specified arrays of the same type for equality. Returns true if each array holds the same number of elements and each element of both arrays is the same. There is an overloaded version of this method for each primitive data type and **Object**.
- **sort(<type>[] array)**: Sorts the array in ascending order. There an overloaded version of this method for each primitive data type except boolean.
- **sort(<type> [] array, int startIndex, int endIndex)**: Sorts the elements of the array between the given indices. There is an overloaded version of this method for each primitive data type.
- **fill(<type>[] array, <type> value)**: Initializes an array by assigning the specified value to all elements in the array. There is an overloaded version of this method for each primitive data type and **Object**.
- **fill (type[] array, int fromIndex, int toIndex, type value)**: Initializes the elements of an array by assigning the specified value between the given indices.
- **static int[] copyOf(int[] original, int newLength)**: Copies the specified array and length. Truncates the array if the provided length is smaller and pads if the provided length is larger.
- **static int[] copyOfRange(int[] original, int from, int to)**: Copies the specified range of the specified array into a new array. The initial index of the range (**from**) must lie between zero and **original.length**, inclusive.
- **static List asList(T… a)**: It takes an array as an argument and creates a wrapper that implements **List**, to convert the original array into a list.
- **toString(<type>[] array)**: Returns a string representation of the contents of an array. There is an overloaded version of this method for each primitive data type.

The following example shows the use of **Arrays** class:

```
import java.util.Arrays;
import java.util.List;
public class ArraysDemo {
  public static void main(String[] args)
  {
    int nums[] = {5, 7, 2, 9, 4, 8, 6, 5, 1};
    int nums1[] = {5, 7, 2, 9, 4, 8, 6, 5, 1};

    // check for equality of arrays
    System.out.println("Arrays are equal? "+ Arrays.equals(nums, nums1));
    // Sort a specific range of array in
    // ascending order
```

```
Arrays.
System.
                                        );

// So
// i
Arra
Sys                                       : "
                                       ring(nums));

//
i                                         s.length);
Sy
                                       copyNums));

//
int                                      nums, 1, 4);
Syst                                     " +
                                       ng(rCopyNums));

// Fill a range with                 alue
Arrays.fill(nums, 0, 4, 0);
System.out.println("Array filled with 0 "+
       "from 0 to 4: " + Arrays.toString(nums));
// Fill complete array with a specific value
Arrays.fill(nums, 31);
System.out.println("Array completely filled"+
               " with 31: "+Arrays.toString(nums));

// To print the array in string form
System.out.println("String form of array: "+Arrays.toString(nums));

Integer nums2[] = {5, 7, 2, 9, 4, 8, 6, 5, 1};
// Creates a wrapper list over nums2[]
List<Integer> l1 = Arrays.asList(nums2);
System.out.println("Array as List: "+l1);
```

```
  }
}
```

Here, **int** arrays are created and manipulated by using the different **Arrays** class methods. The output of the code is shown below:

```
Arrays are equal? true
Sorted array in range of 0-3: [2, 5, 7, 9, 4, 8, 6, 5, 1]
Completely sorted array: [1, 2, 4, 5, 5, 6, 7, 8, 9]
Copied array: [1, 2, 4, 5, 5, 6, 7, 8, 9]
Copied subarray: [2, 4, 5]
Array filled with 0 from 0 to 4: [0, 0, 0, 0, 5, 6, 7, 8, 9]
Array completely filled with 31: [31, 31, 31, 31, 31, 31, 31, 31, 31]
String form of array: [31, 31, 31, 31, 31, 31, 31, 31, 31]
Array as List: [5, 7, 2, 9, 4, 8, 6, 5, 1]
```

Figure 7.20: Arrays class methods

7.9 Sorting collections

Collections can be sorted by using the two interfaces, **Comparable** and **Comparator**.

Comparable

This interface belongs to the **java.lang** package and is used to order the objects of the user-defined class. It has only one method named **compareTo(Object)** and supports only a single sorting sequence. That is, elements can be sorted based on single data members only. For example, sorting on id, name, and so on. Lists of objects implementing this interface are automatically sorted by using **Collection.sort** or **Arrays.sort** method.

For example, the boolean result for **e1.compareTo(e2) == 0** is same as **e1.equals(e2)** for every **e1** and **e2** of class **C**. That is, the natural ordering is consistent with equals. Here, null is not considered as an instance of any class. Therefore, **e.compareTo(null)** will throw a **NullPointerException** even when **e.equals(null)** returns false.

Note: It is recommended that the natural ordering of elements should be consistent with equals. This is because, sorted sets and maps without explicit comparators used with elements/keys having natural ordering inconsistent with equals, results in unusual behavior.

The following example shows the use of the **Comparator** interface:

```
public class Student implements Comparable<Student> {
  int id;
  String name;
  int age;
  Student(int id, String name, int age) {
```

```
    this.id = id;
    this.name = name;
    this.age = age;
  }
  @Override
  public int compareTo(Student s) {
    if (age == s.age) {
      return 0;
    } else if (age > s.age) {
      return 1;
    } else {
      return -1;
    }
  }
}
import java.util.Collections;
import java.util.ArrayList;
public class ComparableSort {
  public static void main(String args[]) {
    ArrayList<Student> st = new ArrayList<>();
    st.add(new Student(1, "John", 23));
    st.add(new Student(8, "Mary", 27));
    st.add(new Student(3, "Roger", 21));
    Collections.sort(st);
    for (Student s : st) {
      System.out.println(s.id + " " + s.name + " " + s.age);
    }
  }
}
```

Here, a type, **Student** is created which implements the **Comparable** interface and overrides the **compareTo()** method to perform ordering based on the value of age. The **ArrayList** of type **Student** is created and sorted by using the **Collections.sort()** method. The output of the code is shown below:

```
run:
3 Roger 21
1 John 23
8 Mary 27
```

Figure 7.21: Sorting with Comparable

Note that the list is sorted based on the value of the age attribute.

Comparator

This interface belongs to the **java.util** package and is used to order the objects of the user-defined class. It provides two methods, **compare(Object obj1, Object obj2)** and **equals(Object element)**. It allows multiple sorting sequences, that is, sorting based on any data members such as ID, name, and so on.

The following example shows the use of the **Comparator** interface:

```
public class Students {
  int id;
  String name;
  int age;
  Students(int id, String name, int age) {
    this.id = id;
    this.name = name;
    this.age = age;
  }
}
```

A class **Students** is created with a constructor to initialize its attributes:

```
import java.util.Comparator;
public class AgeComparator implements Comparator<Students> {
  @Override
  public int compare(Students obj1, Students obj2) {
    Students s1 = (Students) obj1;
    Students s2 = (Students) obj2;
    if (s1.age == s2.age) {
      return 0;
    } else if (s1.age > s2.age) {
      return 1;
```

```
    } else {
      return -1;
    }
  }
}
```

A **Comparator** type is created called **AgeComparator** to compare the **Students** objects based on the value of age by using the **compare()** method:

```
import java.util.Comparator;
public class NameComparator implements Comparator<Students> {
  @Override
  public int compare(Students obj1, Students obj2) {
    Students s1 = (Students) obj1;
    Students s2 = (Students) obj2;
    return s1.name.compareTo(s2.name);
  }
}
```

Another **Comparator** type is created called **NameComparator** which overrides the compare method to compare two **Students** objects based on the value of name:

```
import java.util.ArrayList;
import java.util.Collections;
public class ComparatorSort {
  public static void main(String[] args) {
    ArrayList<Students> st = new ArrayList<>();
    st.add(new Students(1, "John", 23));
    st.add(new Students(8, "Roger", 27));
    st.add(new Students(3, "Mary", 21));
    System.out.println("Sorted by age");
    Collections.sort(st, new AgeComparator());
    for (Students s : st) {
      System.out.println(s.id + " " + s.name + " " + s.age);
    }
    System.out.println("Sorted by name");
    Collections.sort(st, new NameComparator());
    for (Students s : st) {
```

```
        System.out.println(s.id + " " + s.name + " " + s.age);
      }
    }
}
```

Here, an **ArrayList** of type **Students** is created and initialized with some data. The **Collections.sort()** method is used to sort the list based on the age and name by passing the **AgeComparator** and **NameComparator** objects respectively. The output of the code is shown below:

```
Sorted by age
3 Mary 21
1 John 23
8 Roger 27
Sorted by name
1 John 23
3 Mary 21
8 Roger 27
```

Figure 7.22: *Sorting with Comparator*

7.10 Java Stream API

Java 8 introduced the Streams API, that is, the **java.util.stream** package which allows parallel processing of elements of Java Collections. Java is inheritably sequential and there is no built-in mechanism to perform parallel processing at the library level. The **Stream** API overcomes this issue. It allows to filter elements of collection on a given criterion. For example, for a **List** of orders, the filter can be performed based on quantity, price, buying, selling, and so on. It supports two popular functional programming functions, map and reduces by providing methods such as **mapToInt(), mapToLong()**, and a **map** function to apply an operation on all elements of **Collections**.

The **Stream** API is not only used for **Collections** but also uses an array, I/O channel, and a generator function as the source. Generally, a **Stream** pipeline in Java 8 consists of a source, followed by zero or more intermediate stream operations, such as **map()** or **filter()**, and a terminal operation such as **reduce()** or **forEach()**.

Consider the following example to understand the use of **Stream** API with Collections:

```
public class Order {
  enum Type {
    PREMIUM, NORMAL;
  }
  private final String id;
  private final int quantity;
```

```
  private double price;
  private final Type type;
  public Order(String id, int quantity, double price, Type type) {
    this.id = id;
    this.quantity = quantity;
    this.price = price;
    this.type = type;
  }
  public double price() {
    return price;
  }
  public void price(double price) {
    this.price = price;
  }
  public String id() {
    return id;
  }
  public int quantity() {
    return quantity;
  }
  public Type type() {
    return type;
  }
}
```

The **Order** class is created with some attributes pertaining to any order of type premium or normal:

```
import java.util.ArrayList;
import java.util.List;
import java.util.stream.Stream;
public class OrderDetails {
  public static void main(String args[]) {
    // Create an ArrayList of type Order
    List<Order> orders = new ArrayList<>();
    Order orderP1 = new Order("P001", 40, 80.50, Order.Type.PREMIUM);
```

```
    Order orderN1 = new Order("N001", 75, 30.30, Order.Type.NORMAL);
    Order orderP2 = new Order("P002", 50, 95, Order.Type.PREMIUM);
    Order orderN2 = new Order("N002", 22, 55, Order.Type.NORMAL);
    Order orderP3 = new Order("P003", 30, 70, Order.Type.PREMIUM);
    orders.add(orderP1);
    orders.add(orderN1);
    orders.add(orderP2);
    orders.add(orderN2);
    orders.add(orderP3);

    // Filtering ArrayList by type of order
    // by using filter() method Stream class
    Stream<Order> stream = orders.stream();
      Stream premium = stream.filter((Order o) -> o.type().equals(Order.Type.
PREMIUM));
    System.out.println("Total Premium Orders: " + premium.count());
    Stream<Order> normal = orders.stream().filter((Order o) -> o.type() == Order.
Type.NORMAL);
    System.out.println("Total Normal Orders: " + normal.count());

    // Calculate total value of all orders
    double value = orders.stream().mapToDouble((Order o) -> o.price()).sum();
    System.out.println("Total amount of orders: " + value);
    long quantity = orders.stream().mapToLong((Order o) -> o.quantity()).sum();
    System.out.println("Total quantity of orders: " + quantity);
  }
}
```

Here, an **ArrayList** of type **Order** is created and initialized. The **Stream** API is used to create a stream over the **ArrayList**. Next, **filter()** method is used to filter orders based on the type. **mapToDouble()** and **mapToLong()** method is used with **sum()** to calculate total order amount and total quantity respectively. Note the use of lambda expressions to reduce the code to one-line statements. The output of the code is shown below:

```
Total Premium Orders: 3
Total Normal Orders: 2
Total amount of orders: 330.8
Total quantity of orders: 217
```

Figure 7.23: Stream API output

Listed below are some important points about **Stream** API:

- Stream operations are mainly of two types, intermediate and terminal. Intermediate operations are further divided into two types, stateless and stateful.
- Intermediate operations like **map()** or **filter()** return a new **Stream**, whereas terminal operations like **Stream.forEach()** produce a result/side effect.
- Once the terminal operation is completed, the stream pipeline is considered consumed, and can no longer be used.
- Stateless operations do not retain the state from a previously processed element. Examples of stateless operations are **filter()** and **map()**.
- Stateful operations retain the state of previously processed elements while processing new elements. Examples of stateful operations are **distinct()** and **sorted()**.
- Stream API can process **Collection** both sequentially and in parallel to support bulk data operations. For example, sequential and parallel streams can be created as follows:

  ```
  List<Order> orders =  getListOfOrders();
  // sequential
  Stream<Order> streamSeq = orders.stream();
  //parallel
  Stream<Order> streamPar = orders.parallelStream();
  ```

  The **Collection** interface now provides stream support through the **stream()** method which returns a sequential **Stream** for the collection used as its source. The stream reference can then be used to perform bulk data operations on the collection.
- Stream does not modify the source/collection. A new **Stream** is created for every operation while the original collection remains unmodified.
- The stream cannot be reused because a closed stream will throw **IllegalStateException** as shown below:

  ```
  Exception in thread "main" java.lang.IllegalStateException: stream has already been operated upon or closed
      at java.util.stream.AbstractPipeline …
  ….
  ```

7.10.1 Improvements of Stream API in Java 9

Java 9 offered some additions and enhancements in the Stream API which are listed below. Java 9 introduced some utility methods to add to those provided by Java 8:

- **takewhile(Predicate Interface) and dropwhile(Predicate Interface) methods**: These two methods accept an argument of type predicate functional interface. As the names suggest, `takewhile()` will accept all values until the predicate returns false and `dropwhile()` will drop all values till the predicate returns false.

  In Java 8, the `filter()` method retains all the elements when it matches the condition whereas `takewhile()` will stop once it encounters an element that does not match the condition. For example, a `Stream` consisting of the longest prefix of elements taken from this `Stream` that matches the given predicate (ordered `Stream`).

  `Dropwhile` will throw away the elements at the beginning where the predicate is true. For example, it will return a `Stream` consisting of the remaining elements of this `Stream` after dropping the longest prefix of elements that match the given predicate (ordered `Stream`). In an unordered case, both return the subset of elements as per their definition.

  The following example explains the working of `takewhile()` and `dropwhile()`:

```
import java.util.stream.Stream;
public class Java9Streams {
  public static void main(String[] args) {
    Stream.of("h", "e", "l", "", "l", "o").takeWhile(s -> !s.isEmpty()).
forEach(System.out::print);
    System.out.println("");
    Stream.of("h", "e", "l", "", "l", "o").dropWhile(s -> !s.isEmpty()).
forEach(System.out::print);
    System.out.println("");
     Stream.of("h", "e", "l", "", "l", "o", "h", "", "i").dropWhile(s ->
!s.isEmpty()).forEach(System.out::print);
    System.out.println("");
  }
}
```

  The output of the code is given below:

```
hel
lo
lohi
```

  In this example, `takewhile()` takes the values `hel` and then finds that the string is empty, so it stops executing because the condition returns false. The `dropwhile()` drops `hel` till it finds an empty string and then takes all the values that match the condition.

- **iterate() method**: The **iterate()** method accepts two arguments, one is the initializer also called a seed and the other is the function to be applied to the previous element to produce the new element. However, this method has a drawback that there are no terminating criteria **for** loop. For example:

  ```
  Stream.iterate(1, count->count+2).forEach(System.out::println);
  ```

  This statement will continue executing infinitely. Java 9 updated the **iterate()** method similar to **for** loop-based iterations to work as a replacement **for** loops. It solves the problem of the earlier iterate method by adding a termination clause.

  Syntax:

  ```
  iterate(initialize section; predicate section(hasNext); next section)
  ```

  This **iterate()** method will stop once the **hasNext** section returns false. The following example shows the use of the **iterate()** method:

  ```
  import java.util.stream.IntStream;
  import java.util.stream.Stream;
  public class Java9Streams {
    public static void main(String[] args) {
     IntStream.iterate(2, x -> x < 8, x -> x+2).forEach(System.out::println);
    }
  }
  ```

  Here, the value is initialized with 2 and increments each time by 2. The predicate condition indicates that **x** should be less than **8**. So, the output will be **2**, **4**, and **6**.

- **ofNullable() method**: The **ofNullable** method is introduced in Java 9 to return empty Optionals if the value is null. This helps to avoid **NullPointerExceptions** and adding null checks in code. It returns the sequential **Stream** containing a single element if the value is not null else it returns the empty **Stream**. For example:

  ```
  Stream.ofNullable(100).count();
    Stream.ofNullable(null).count();
  ```

  ```
  Before Java 8
  Employee e1= getEmployee(empId);
  Stream<Roles> roles=e1== null? Stream.empty(): e1.roles();
  ```

  Here, a null check is performed before the operation because the **getEmployee()** method may return null. In Java 9, this can be avoided by using the **ofNullable()** method as shown below:

  ```
  Employee e1= getEmployee(empId);
  Stream.ofNullable(e1).flatMap(Employee::roles)
  ```

Conclusion

In this chapter you learnt that the **java.util** package provides several utility classes and interfaces for different functionalities. A collection is a container object which helps to group multiple elements into a single unit. The **Iterable** interface belongs to the **java.lang** package and is the top-level interface for classes and interfaces that need the iterator functionality. The **Collection** interface is at the top level of the interfaces and classes belonging to the collections framework. Java 9 introduced factory methods which are a special type of static method used to create unmodifiable/immutable instances of collections. Lists are ordered collections that allow duplicate values and multiple null elements. The **Queue** interface represents the queue data structure where generally the elements are ordered in **First-In-First-Out** (**FIFO**) order. **Set** is a collection of unordered non-duplicate list of object references. A **Map** object stores data in the form of key-value pairs where each key is mapped to a single value. The **java.util.Arrays** class provides methods for performing operations such as sorting, searching, and so on, on arrays. The **Comparable** interface belongs to the **java.lang** package and **Comparator** interface belongs to the **java.util** package, and are used to order the objects of the user-defined class. Java 8 introduced the Streams API, that is, the **java.util.stream** package which allows parallel processing of elements of Java Collections.

In the next chapter, you will learn about Generics and Time API.

Multiple choice questions

1. **Which of the following collection allows duplicate values?**
   a. HashSet
   b. TreeSet
   c. ArrayList
   d. All of these
2. **Consider the below partial code.**

```
public static void main(String[] args) {

   SortedSet<String> names = new TreeSet<>();
   names.add("Brian");
   names.add("Pearl");
   names.add("Vicky");
   names.add("Linda");
   System.out.println("Names: " + names);
}
```

What will be the output of the code?

a. Names: [Brian, Pearl, Vicky, Linda]

b. Names: [Linda, Vicky, Pearl, Brian]

c. Names: [Vicky, Pearl, Linda, Brian]

d. Names: [Brian, Linda, Pearl, Vicky]

3. Consider the below partial code.

```
IntStream.iterate(6, x -> x > 2, x -> x-2).forEach(System.out::print);
```

What will be the output of the code?

a. 64

b. 6

c. 642

d. 65432

4. Which of the following statements is false?

a. The SortedSet interface extends the Set interface.

b. Maps can have duplicate keys.

c. Lists are ordered collections that allow duplicate values.

d. The Comparable interface belongs to the java.lang package.

5. Match the columns.

	Method		Description
a.	`add(E obj)`	1.	Returns the number of elements in this list.
b.	`contains(Object obj)`	2.	Adds the specified element to the end of this list.
c.	`size()`	3.	Trims the size of the ArrayList to the current size of the list.
d.	`trimToSize()`	4.	Returns true if this list contains the specified element.

a. a-2, b-3, c-4, d-1

b. a-3, b-4, c-1, d-2

c. a-4, b-1, c-2, d-3

d. a-2, b-4, c-1, d-3

Answers

1. c

2. d

3. a

4. b

5. d

Assignment

Create a Java program as per the below specifications.

1. Create a class named **`Item`** which contains attributes about a product/item and constructors/methods to accept/return values of the attributes.
2. Create another class called **`Item manager`** that shows a menu to the user for entering, viewing item details as well as to exit the program.
3. When the user selects enter item details, the data should be accepted and saved in a collection of type **`Item`**. [Hint: use a collection that stores data as key-value pairs]
4. When the user selects **view item details**, the program accepts the id of the item and then displays the details of the specific item.
5. If the specific item does not exist, the appropriate message should be displayed to the user.
6. When the user selects view all items, the details of all items in the collection should be displayed.
7. When the collection is empty, the appropriate message should be displayed to the user.
8. When the user selects **exit**, the program should be terminated.

The expected output is shown below. When there are no items in the collection:

```
1. Enter Item Details
2. View Item Details
3. View All Items
4. Exit
Enter your choice: 2
Enter Item id: I001
Item ID does not exist.

1. Enter Item Details
2. View Item Details
3. View All Items
4. Exit
Enter your choice: 3
There are no Items.
```

Figure 7.24: No items

Add items to the collection:

```
1. Enter Item Details
2. View Item Details
3. View All Items
4. Exit
Enter your choice: 1
Enter Item ID:I001
Enter Item Type:Toy
Enter Description:Pink_Teddy
Enter Price ($):40
Enter Quantity:250
1. Enter Item Details
2. View Item Details
3. View All Items
4. Exit
Enter your choice: 1
Enter Item ID:I002
Enter Item Type:Utensil
Enter Description:Steel_Plate
Enter Price ($):10
Enter Quantity:150
```

Figure 7.25: *Items added to collection*

View details of a specific item after adding item data to the collection:

```
1. Enter Item Details
2. View Item Details
3. View All Items
4. Exit
Enter your choice: 2
Enter Item id: I002
ID:I002
Type: Utensil
Description: Steel_Plate
Price ($): 10.0
Quantity:150
```

Figure 7.26: *View a specific item detail*

View all items of the collection and then exit the program:

```
1. Enter Item Details
2. View Item Details
3. View All Items
4. Exit
Enter your choice: 3
ID:I001
Type: Toy
Description: Pink_Teddy
Price ($): 40.0
Quantity:250
ID:I002
Type: Utensil
Description: Steel_Plate
Price ($): 10.0
Quantity:150
1. Enter Item Details
2. View Item Details
3. View All Items
4. Exit
Enter your choice: 4
Good Bye!!
BUILD SUCCESSFUL (total time: 1 minute 21 seconds)
```

Figure 7.27: *View all items*

Join our book's Discord space

Join the book's Discord Workspace for Latest updates, Offers, Tech happenings around the world, New Release and Sessions with the Authors:

https://discord.bpbonline.com

CHAPTER 8
Generics and Time API

Introduction

This chapter introduces the concept of generics in Java which allows a class to use parameters to specify the type of objects it can work with. You will learn to create a generic class to create a general type for a set of related types. Generics can also be used with collections and exceptions. Generics can be implemented with inheritance whereby classes can extend the generic class. You will also be introduced to the new **time** API which provides support for managing date and time in applications.

Structure

In this chapter, we will go through the following topics:

- Generics
- Generic classes and methods
- Type inference
- Using generic constructors with generic and non-generic classes
- Using generics with collections
- Using wildcards with generics
- Using generics with exceptions
- Implementing generics with inheritance

- Type erasure
- Time API

Objectives

In this chapter you will learn about generics and create generic classes and methods. You will also learn to use generics with collection and exceptions. Further you will implement generics with inheritance. You will also understand the concept of type erasure can work with the Time API.

8.1 Generics

Generics in Java allows a class to use parameters to specify the type of objects it can work with. The type/value of these parameters is specified at runtime. Generics allows avoiding type inconsistencies and the need for explicit type casting, thereby, preventing **`ClassCastException`** at compile time. This is because the correctness of the type is checked at compile time.

For a non-generic collection, retrieval of elements requires an explicit type with chances of **`ClassCastException`**. With generics, the collection type is specified to the compiler directly, which helps for consistent checks on elements during insertion and retrieval.

Example of non-generic collection:

```
LinkedList list1 = new LinkedList();
list1.add(1);
Integer num = (Integer) list1.get(0);
```

Here, the instance of the linked list is created, and an **`Integer`** type element is added to it. While retrieving the element, explicit casting is done to avoid exceptions.

Example of generic code:

```
LinkedList<Integer> list = new LinkedList<>();
list.add(1);
Integer num = list.get(0);
```

Here, generics is used to identify the type supported by the collection so that the correctness of the value is checked at compile-time, thereby, avoiding the need for explicit casting during retrieval.

Important points about generics:

- Generics adds type safety to the code.
- Allows dynamic binding.
- It helps to detect and fix errors at compile time.
- Simplifies the code by reducing ambiguity and the need for explicit casting.

- It does not support generic constructors.
- It does not support variables where the key and value are of a different type.

8.2 Generic classes and methods

A generic class is used to create a general type for a set of related types. The actual type is determined during the instantiation of the class. The declaration of a generic class is similar to a non-generic class, followed by a type parameter specified in angular brackets <>.

Syntax:

```
class class-name <Type> {...}
```

The value of type parameter can be a class, interface, or any other type except primitive type. By creating a generic class, different types of objects can be stored. Moreover, a class allows more than one type of parameter separated by a comma, and hence, it can also be termed as a parameterized class.

Generic classes can have generic methods with type parameters. However, generic methods can be part of non-generic classes as well. The use of type arguments supports polymorphism and can be used for method overloading. A method can also return generic data.

Syntax:

```
public<T> void display(T[] val)
```

A `type` variable can be any non-primitive type such as class, array, interface, or even another type variable. The `type` parameter names are usually single, uppercase letters. Listed below are some commonly used `type` parameter names:

- K - Key
- T - Type
- V - Value
- N - Number
- E - Element
- S, U, V, and so on.

In Java SE 7 and later, the required type arguments are replaced to invoke the constructor of a generic class with an empty set of type arguments (`<>`) brackets called the diamond. **Example**:

```
TestClass<String> testObj = new TestClass<>();
```

Following example shows the use of the generic class, method, and return type:

```
import java.util.LinkedList;
public class Toys<T> {
  private LinkedList<T> toyList = new LinkedList<>();
  public void addToy(T item) {
```

```
    toyList.addLast(item);
  }
  public T removeToy() {
    return toyList.removeFirst();
  }
  public boolean checkEmpty() {
    return (toyList.isEmpty());
  }

  public String viewToys(){
    return toyList.toString();
  }
  public static void main(String[] args) {
    Toys<String> toyObj = new Toys<>();
    toyObj.addToy("Barbie");
    toyObj.addToy("Teddy Bear");
    System.out.println("Toy list: "+toyObj.viewToys());
    System.out.println("First Toy: "+toyObj.removeToy());
  }
}
```

Here, a generic class **Toys** is created with a type parameter. The methods, **addToy()** and **removeToy()** are used to accept and return parameters of type **T**. The type is set when an instance of **Toys** class is created with **String** type. The output of the code is shown below:

```
Toy list: [Barbie, Teddy Bear]
First Toy: Barbie
```

***Figure 8.1:** Generic class and generic method*

A generic class can have two or more type parameters, as shown below:

```
import java.util.LinkedList;
public class Toys<T,U> {
  private U title;
  private LinkedList<T> toyList = new LinkedList<>();
  public void addTitle(U title){
    this.title=title;
```

```
    }
    public U showTitle(){
      return title;
    }
    public void addToy(T item) {
      toyList.addLast(item);
    }
    public T removeToy() {
      return toyList.removeFirst();
    }
    public boolean checkEmpty() {
      return (toyList.isEmpty());
    }

    public String viewToys(){
      return toyList.toString();
    }
    public static void main(String[] args) {
      Toys<String,String> toyObj = new Toys<>();
      toyObj.addTitle("Toys List");
      System.out.println(toyObj.showTitle());
      toyObj.addToy("Barbie");
      toyObj.addToy("Teddy Bear");
      System.out.println(toyObj.viewToys());
      System.out.println("First Toy: "+toyObj.removeToy());
    }
}
```

Here, a generic class with two parameters is created and the datatypes are specified during instantiation in the main method. The first parameter **T** is used to specify the type for the **LinkedList**, and the parameter **U**, is used to specify the type of the variable **title**. The output of the code:

```
Toys List
[Barbie, Teddy Bear]
First Toy: Barbie
```

Figure 8.2: Multiple generic parameters

8.3 Type inference

Type inference allows invoking the appropriate generic method by enabling the Java compiler to determine the type of arguments. The inference algorithm determines the following:

- Types of arguments.
- The type of the value being returned.
- The most specific type that works with all of the arguments.

Java SE 7 onwards, the type arguments are no longer needed to be specified for invoking the constructor.

Example:

```
Map<String, List<String>> map1 = new HashMap<String, List<String>>();
Instead, an empty set of type parameters (<>) is used. Example:
Map<String, List<String>> map1 = new HashMap<>();
```

8.4 Using generic constructors with generic and non-generic classes

It is possible to use generic constructors with generic as well as non-generic classes. Example:

```
class Sample<X> {
  // generic constructor
  <T> Sample(T t) {
    // ...
  }
  public static void main(String[] args){
    // instantiate the class
    Sample<Integer> myObject = new Sample<>("");
  }
}
```

Here, the compiler understands that the **Integer** is for the formal type parameter, **X**, of the generic class **Sample<X>** while the type **String** is for the formal type parameter, **T**, of the constructor of the generic class.

The following example shows the use of generic constructor in a non-generic class:

```
public class Sample {
  // generic constructor
  <T> Sample(T t) {
    System.out.println("The value is "+ t);
  }
  public static void main(String[] args) {
    // instantiate the class
    Sample obj = new Sample(10);
    Sample obj1 = new Sample("Hello");
  }
}
```

8.5 Using generics with collections

A collection is an object that manages a group of objects and uses generics for collection implementation. Following example shows the creation of a generic collection:

```
import java.util.List;
import java.util.ArrayList;
import java.util.Iterator;
public class GenericCollection {
  public static void main(String[] args) {
    List<String> items = new ArrayList<>(3);
    items.add("I001");
    items.add("I002");
    items.add("I003");
    System.out.println("Item Numbers");
    Iterator<String> value = items.iterator();
    while (value.hasNext()) {
      String itemObj = value.next();
      System.out.println("" + itemObj);
    }
```

```
    }
}
```

The output of the code is shown below:

```
Item Numbers
I001
I002
I003
```

Figure 8.3: *Generic collection*

Using an invalid value with a generic collection will result in a compile-time error as shown below:

```
public class Generic    no suitable method found for add(int)
                          method Collection.add(String) is not applicable
                            (argument mismatch; int cannot be converted to String)
    public static vo      method List.add(String) is not applicable
        List<String>        (argument mismatch; int cannot be converted to String)
        items.add("I    ----
        items.add("I    (Alt-Enter shows hints)
        items.add(3);
        System.out.println("Item Numbers");
        Iterator<String> value = items.iterator();
        while (value.hasNext()) {
            String itemObj = value.next();
            System.out.println("" + itemObj);
        }
    }
}
```

Figure 8.4: *Invalid value for a generic collection*

8.6 Using wildcards with generics

Java allows the use of wildcards with generics when there is little or no information about the type argument of a parameterized type. It is mainly used as an argument for instances of generic types. The question mark (**?**) symbol is known as a wildcard in generics. It can be used to represent the type of a parameter, field, local variable, and at times as a return type.

Listed below are the types of wildcards used with generics:

- **Upper bounded wildcards**: These wildcards can be used to relax restrictions on variables. For example, to create a method that can operate on different types of lists such as **List <Integer>, List <Double>**, and so on., the upper bound wildcard character ? can be used. It must be succeeded by the **extends** keyword followed by its upper bound.

  Example:

```
public static void add(List<? extends Number> list)
```

The following code demonstrates the use of an upper bounded wildcard:

```
import java.util.Arrays;
import java.util.List;
public class UpBoundWildcard {
  public static void main(String[] args) {
    //Integer List - upper bounded
    List<Integer> intList = Arrays.asList(5, 2, 4, 6);
    System.out.println("Sum is:" + sumList(intList));
    //Double list
    List<Double> doubleList = Arrays.asList(3.5, 2.8, 5.5);
    System.out.println("Sum is:" + sumList(doubleList));
  }
  private static double sumList(List<? extends Number> list) {
    double sum = 0.0;
    for (Number i : list) {
      sum += i.doubleValue();
    }
    return sum;
  }
}
```

Here, two lists named **intList** and **doubleList** are created to hold the collections of the respective type. These objects are passed to the sum method, which has a wildcard '**?**' that extends type **Number**. This indicates that the list passed to the method can be any field or subclass of the field. In this case, **Integer** and **Double** are subclasses of class **Number**.

Output:

```
Total sum is:17.0
Total sum is:11.8
```

Figure 8.5: Upper bounded wildcard

Lower bounded wildcards: These wildcards use the character ('**?**') succeeded by the **super** keyword, followed by its lower bound: **<? super A>.**

```
Collection-type <? super A>
```

The following example shows the use of lower bounded wildcards:

```
import java.util.Arrays;
```

```
import java.util.List;
public class LoBoundWildcard {
  public static void main(String[] args) {
    //Integer List - lower bounded
    List<Integer> intList = Arrays.asList(2, 8, 5, 6);
    displayList(intList);
    //Number list
    List<Number> numList = Arrays.asList(2.5, 8.2, 5.6, 6.4);
    displayList(numList);
  }
  public static void displayList(List<? super Integer> list) {
    System.out.println(list);
  }
}
```

Here, the arguments passed to the **displayList()** method can be an Integer or superclass of **Integer**. In this case, it is the **Number** class. For example, if a **Double** class argument is passed, it will throw a compilation error because **Double** is not a superclass of **Integer** class.

Output:

```
[2, 8, 5, 6]
[2.5, 8.2, 5.6, 6.4]
```

Figure 8.6: Lower bounded wildcard

Note: You can either specify an upper bound or a lower bound for a wildcard, but you cannot specify both.

- **Unbounded wildcard**: An unbounded wildcard type is specified by using the wildcard character (**?**). For example, **List<?>** indicates a list of unknown type.

  The following example shows the use of unbounded wildcard:

```
import java.util.Arrays;
import java.util.List;
public class UnboundWildcard {
  public static void main(String[] args) {
    //Integer List
    List<Integer> intList = Arrays.asList(3, 8, 5);
    //Double list
    List<Double> doubleList = Arrays.asList(2.4, 1.2, 6.5);
```

```
    displayList(intList);
    displayList(doubleList);
  }
  private static void displayList(List<?> list) {
    System.out.println(list);
  }
}
```

Here, a generic list parameter is specified in the **displayList()** method. This means it can accept any type of list. From the **main()** method, an **Integer** and **Double** list are passed as an argument to the **displayList()** method. Both the lists will be processed by the method since the **List** is using an unbounded (**?**) wild card.

Output:

```
[3, 8, 5]
[2.4, 1.2, 6.5]
```

Figure 8.7: Unbounded wildcard

8.7 Using generics with exceptions

Exception handling ensures smooth functioning of code by identifying and handling errors. The **catch** clause of a **try-catch** statement can handle an exception that matches the given type. However, the type of exception parameters specified in the **catch** clause cannot be verified by the compiler to ensure that it matches the exception of unknown type. This is because an exception is thrown and caught only at runtime and the **catch** clause cannot include wildcards or type variables. Further, it is not possible to make a generic subclass of **Throwable** class because a runtime exception cannot be caught with compile-time parameters intact. However, the type parameter can be used in the **throws** clause of the method signature.

The following code demonstrates the use of generic type with exceptions:

```
public interface Calculator<X extends Throwable> {
  public void calc(Integer args) throws X;
}
public class TestCalculator implements Calculator<ArrayIndexOutOfBoundsException>
{
  @Override
  public void calc(Integer args) throws ArrayIndexOutOfBoundsException {
    int arr[] = new int[5];
    for (int i = 0; i < args; i++) {
      arr[i] = i;
```

```
    }
  }
  public static void main(String[] args) {
    TestCalculator obj = new TestCalculator();
    obj.calc(6);
  }
}
```

Here, the code uses a type variable with the **throws** clause of the method signature in the **Calculator** interface. The class **TestCalculator** identifies the type parameter as **ArrayIndexOutOfBoundsException** which will be thrown from the **calc()** method.

The output of the above code snippet is as follows:

```
Exception in thread "main" java.lang.ArrayIndexOutOfBoundsException: 5
        at moduleOne/Sess8Codes.TestCalculator.calc(TestCalculator.java:20)
        at moduleOne/Sess8Codes.TestCalculator.main(TestCalculator.java:26)
C:\Users\Admin3\AppData\Local\NetBeans\Cache\dev\executor-snippets\run.xml:135: The following err
C:\Users\Admin3\AppData\Local\NetBeans\Cache\dev\executor-snippets\run.xml:64: Java returned: 1
```

Figure 8.8: *Exception handling with generics*

8.8 Implementing generics with inheritance

Generics can be used while implementing inheritance. It is possible for classes to extend the generic class and set values for the type parameters as well as add new type parameters. The following are the rules:

- A class cannot inherit from a parametric type.
- Two instantiations of the same generic type cannot be used in inheritance.

The following example shows the use of generics with an inheritance:

```
public class Employee<T> {
  T empObj;
  Employee(T obj) {
    empObj = obj;
  }
  // Return empObj
  T getObj() {
    return empObj;
  }
}
```

```
public class TestEmployee<T, V> extends Employee<T> {
  V valObj;
  TestEmployee(T obj, V obj2) {
    super(obj);
    valObj = obj2;
  }
  V getob2() {
    return valObj;
  }
  public static void main(String args[]) {
    TestEmployee<String, Float> emp1;
    emp1 = new TestEmployee<>("Part Time", 2000f);
    System.out.println("Employee Type: " + emp1.getObj());
    System.out.println("Salary: $" + emp1.getob2());
  }
}
```

Here, the subclass **TestEmployee** is the concrete instance of the generic class **Employee<T>**. The following will be the output:

```
Employee Type: Part Time
Salary: $2000.0
```

Figure 8.9: *Inheritance with generics*

8.9 Type erasure

Java introduced generics to provide a higher type safety during compile time. Generics is implemented by the Java compiler by using type erasure. That is,

- It replaces all type parameters in generic types with their bounds or if the type parameters are unbounded, it is replaced by **Object**
- The bytecode produced thereafter contains only ordinary classes, interfaces, and methods.
- It inserts type casts if necessary to preserve type safety.
- It generates bridge methods to preserve polymorphism in extended generic types.

Type erasure is used to ensure that no new classes are created for parameterized types. This way, generics incur no runtime overhead. For example, a parameterized type such as **List<String>** is converted into **List**. Erasure ensures compatibility is maintained with Java libraries and applications created before generics was introduced.

8.10 Time API

For a long time, Java developers suffered due to inadequate support for date and time in Java API. For example, classes such as **java.util.Date** and **SimpleDateFormatter** are not thread-safe which led to a lot of concurrency issues and a poor API design, which are difficult to deal with for an average developer. This led to the use of third-party date and time libraries. To address these issues and provide better support for date and time, Java introduced the new date and time API with Java SE 8. These features have been incorporated in the new Java SE 8 package, **java.time**.

LocalDate and LocalTime classes

LocalDate and **LocalTime** are the most important classes of the time API. They represent date and time from the context of the observer, for example, a calendar or a clock used on a daily basis. The **LocalDateTime** class is a composite class created by the pairing of **LocalDate** and **LocalTime**.

Important points about **java.time** package:

- **Local**: Date-time API is simplified with no complexity of time zone handling.
- **Zoned**: Date-time API has been specialized to deal with different time zones.

The following example shows the use of **LocalDate, LocalTime**, and **LocalDateTime** classes:

```
import java.time.LocalDate;
import java.time.LocalTime;
import java.time.LocalDateTime;
import java.time.Month;
public class TimeDemo {
  public static void main(String[] args) {
    TimeDemo obj = new TimeDemo();
    obj.displayLocalDateTime();
  }
  public void displayLocalDateTime() {
    // Get the current date and time
    LocalDateTime currentTime = LocalDateTime.now();
    System.out.println("Current Date and Time: " + currentTime);
    LocalDate dt1 = currentTime.toLocalDate();
    System.out.println("Current Date: " + dt1);
    Month month = currentTime.getMonth();
    int day = currentTime.getDayOfMonth();
```

```
    int seconds = currentTime.getSecond();
     System.out.println("Month: " + month + " Day: " + day + " Seconds: " +
seconds);
    LocalDateTime dt2 = currentTime.withDayOfMonth(10).withYear(2017);
    System.out.println("Time with Month and Year: " + dt2);
    //31 May 2017
    LocalDate dt3 = LocalDate.of(2017, Month.MAY, 31);
    System.out.println("Date: " + dt3);
    //20 hour 10 minutes
    LocalTime time1 = LocalTime.of(20, 10);
    System.out.println("Time: " + time1);
    //parsing a string
    LocalTime time2 = LocalTime.parse("20:15:30");
    System.out.println("Time from String: " + time2);
  }
}
```

The code shows the different ways of using the **LocalDate, LocalTime**, and **LocalDateTime** classes. The following will be the output:

```
Current Date and Time: 2018-10-21T19:54:26.933169600
Current Date: 2018-10-21
Month: OCTOBER Day: 21 Seconds: 26
Time with Month and Year: 2017-10-10T19:54:26.933169600
Date: 2017-05-31
Time: 20:10
Time from String: 20:15:30
```

Figure 8.10: Time API

8.10.1 ZonedDateTime API

When time zone needs to be specified, use the **ZonedDateTime** API as shown in the below example:

```
import java.time.ZonedDateTime;
import java.time.ZoneId;
import java.time.LocalTime;
public class ZonedTimeDemo {
  public static void main(String args[]) {
```

```
        ZonedTimeDemo obj = new ZonedTimeDemo();
        obj.displayZonedDateTime();
    }
    public void displayZonedDateTime() {

        ZonedDateTime dt1 = ZonedDateTime.parse("2017-12-20T10:15:30+05:30[Asia/
Bangkok]");
        System.out.println("Date Time of Asia/Bangkok zone: " + dt1);
        ZoneId zid = ZoneId.of("Europe/Berlin");
        LocalTime now1 = LocalTime.now(zid);
        System.out.println("Time in Zone Id " + zid + " is " + now1);
        ZoneId currentZone = ZoneId.systemDefault();
        System.out.println("Current Zone: " + currentZone);
    }
}
```

The code uses zone ID to display the time of the specific zone. The following will be the output:

```
Date Time of Asia/Bangkok zone: 2017-12-20T11:45:30+07:00[Asia/Bangkok]
Time in Zone Id Europe/Berlin is 18:13:17.212133800
Current Zone: Asia/Calcutta
```

Figure 8.11: *Zoned date-time*

8.10.2 ChronoUnit Enum

Java SE 8 added the **`java.time.temporal.ChronoUnit enum`** to replace the integer values used to represent the day, month, and so on. in the old API:

```
import java.time.LocalDate;
import java.time.temporal.ChronoUnit;
public class ChronoUnitDemo {
    public static void main(String args[]) {
        ChronoUnitDemo obj = new ChronoUnitDemo();
        obj.displayChromoUnits();
    }
    public void displayChromoUnits() {
        //Get the current date
        LocalDate today = LocalDate.now();
```

```
    System.out.println("Current date: " + today);
    //add 2 weeks to the current date
    LocalDate next2Week = today.plus(2, ChronoUnit.WEEKS);
    System.out.println("Week after next week: " + next2Week);
    //add 1 month to the current date
    LocalDate nextMonth = today.plus(1, ChronoUnit.MONTHS);
    System.out.println("Next month: " + nextMonth);
    //add 1 year to the current date
    LocalDate nextYear = today.plus(1, ChronoUnit.YEARS);
    System.out.println("Next year: " + nextYear);
    //add 10 years to the current date
    LocalDate nextDecade = today.plus(1, ChronoUnit.DECADES);
    System.out.println("Date after ten years: " + nextDecade);
  }
}
```

The code shows the use of the **ChronoUnit** constants for displaying the date, month, and so on.

Output:

```
Current date: 2018-10-21
Week after next week: 2018-11-04
Next month: 2018-11-21
Next year: 2019-10-21
Date after ten years: 2028-10-21
```

Figure 8.12: ChronoUnit enum

8.10.3 Period and Duration classes

Two special classes were introduced in Java SE 8 to manage time differences:

- **Period**: Manages date-based amount of time.
- **Duration**: Manages time-based amount of time.

The following program shows the use of period and duration in time API:

```
import java.time.temporal.ChronoUnit;
import java.time.LocalDate;
import java.time.LocalTime;
import java.time.Duration;
import java.time.Period;
public class PeriodDurationDemo {
```

```
  public static void main(String args[]) {
    PeriodDurationDemo obj = new PeriodDurationDemo();
    obj.displayPeriod();
    obj.displayDuration();
  }
  public void displayPeriod() {
    LocalDate dt1 = LocalDate.now();
    System.out.println("Current date: " + dt1);
    //add 1 month to the current date
    LocalDate dt2 = dt1.plus(1, ChronoUnit.MONTHS);
    System.out.println("Next month: " + dt2);

    Period period = Period.between(dt2, dt1);
    System.out.println("Period between "+ dt1 +" and "+dt2+" is " + period);
  }
  public void displayDuration() {
    LocalTime time1 = LocalTime.now();
    Duration oneHour = Duration.ofHours(1);

    // add 1 hour to current time
    LocalTime time2 = time1.plus(oneHour);
    Duration duration = Duration.between(time1, time2);
      System.out.println("Duration between "+time1+" and " + time2 +" is "+
duration);
  }
}
```

Here, the **Period** and **Duration** classes are used to identify the difference in the date and time amount between two dates and times. The following will be the output:

```
Current date: 2018-10-21
Next month: 2018-11-21
Period between 2018-10-21 and 2018-11-21 is P-1M
Duration between 22:54:59.751685500 and 23:54:59.751685500 is PT1H
```

Figure 8.13: Period and Duration classes

8.10.4 TemporalAdjusters class

Java time API provides the **TemporalAdjusters** class to perform date mathematics. For example, get the **Third Monday of the Month** or **Next Wednesday**. The following example shows the use of **TemporalAdjusters** class:

```
import java.time.temporal.TemporalAdjusters;
import java.time.DayOfWeek;
import java.time.LocalDate;
public class TemporalAdjustersDemo {
  public static void main(String args[]) {
    TemporalAdjustersDemo obj = new TemporalAdjustersDemo();
    obj.testAdjusters();
  }
  public void testAdjusters() {
    LocalDate today = LocalDate.now();
    System.out.println("Current date is " + today);
    //get the next Wednesday
   LocalDate nextWed = today.with(TemporalAdjusters.next(DayOfWeek.WEDNESDAY));
    System.out.println("Next Wednesday is on " + nextWed);
    //get the second Saturday of the month
    LocalDate firstDay = LocalDate.of(today.getYear(), today.getMonth(), 1);
    System.out.println("First date of the current month: " + firstDay);
    LocalDate secondSaturday = firstDay.with(TemporalAdjusters.nextOrSame(
    DayOfWeek.SATURDAY)).with(TemporalAdjusters.next(DayOfWeek.SATURDAY));
    System.out.println("Second Saturday is on " + secondSaturday);
  }
}
```

Here, the **TemporalAdjusters** class is used to fetch the day of the week and the second **Saturday** of the month. The following will be the output:

```
Current date is 2018-10-28
Next Wednesday is on 2018-10-31
First date of the current month: 2018-10-01
Second Saturday is on 2018-10-13
```

Figure 8.14: *TemporalAdjusters class*

8.10.5 Backward compatibility

Java added the **toInstant()** method to the original **Date** and **Calendar** objects which allows converting them to the new Date-Time API. The **ofInstant(Insant, ZoneId)** method is used to get a **LocalDateTime** or **ZonedDateTime** object.

The following program shows the use of **ofInstant()** method for backward compatibility:

```
import java.time.LocalDateTime;
import java.time.ZonedDateTime;
import java.util.Date;
import java.time.Instant;
import java.time.ZoneId;
public class ToInstantDemo {
  public static void main(String args[]) {
    ToInstantDemo obj = new ToInstantDemo();
      // test Backward Compatibility
    obj.testBC();
  }
  public void testBC() {
     Date today = new Date();
    System.out.println("Current date is " + today);
    //Get the instant of current date in milliseconds
    Instant now = today.toInstant();
    ZoneId thisZone = ZoneId.systemDefault();
    LocalDateTime lDT = LocalDateTime.ofInstant(now, thisZone);
    System.out.println("Local date and time is " + lDT);
    ZonedDateTime zDT = ZonedDateTime.ofInstant(now, thisZone);
    System.out.println("Zoned date and time is " + zDT);
  }
}
```

The code shows the utility of **toInstant()** method for implementing backward compatibility with original **Date** and **Calendar** objects.

Output:

```
Current date is Sun Oct 28 18:42:20 IST 2018
Local date and time is 2018-10-28T18:42:20.567
Zoned date and time is 2018-10-28T18:42:20.567+05:30[Asia/Calcutta]
```

Figure 8.15: Using toInstant() method

Conclusion

In this chapter, you learnt that Java supports the concept of generics by which a class can specify the type of objects it can work with, by using parameters whose type/value is specified at runtime. A generic collection also requires a specific type of element which is indicated by the type parameter. A generic class is used to create a general type for a set of related types. A type variable can be any non-primitive type such as class, array, interface, or even another type variable. Type inference allows invoking the appropriate generic method by enabling the Java compiler to determine the type of arguments. It is possible to use generic constructors with generic as well as non-generic classes. To provide better support for date and time, Java introduced the new date and time API with Java SE 8. **`LocalDate`** and **`LocalTime`** are the most important classes of the time API. They represent date and time from the context of the observer. **`Period`** class manages date-based amount of time, and the **`Duration`** class manages a time-based amount of time. Java added the **`toInstant()`** method to the original **`Date`** and **`Calendar`** objects which allows converting them to the new Date-Time API.

In the next chapter, you will learn about file manipulation in Java.

Multiple choice questions

1. **In Java SE 7 and later, the required type arguments are replaced to invoke the constructor of a generic class with an empty set of type arguments by using ______ brackets.**
   a. `()`
   b. `<>`
   c. `{}`
   d. `[]`
2. **Which concept is depicted in the below code?**

```
Public class Sample {
  <T> Sample(T t) {
    System.out.println("The value is "+ t);
  }
  public static void main(String[] args) {
    Sample obj = new Sample(10);
    Sample obj1 = new Sample("Hello");
  }
}
```

   a. Generic class
   b. Generic method
   c. Generic constructor
   d. None of these

3. **Which of the following is an example of unbounded wildcard?**
    a. `private static void displayList(List<?> list)`
    b. `public static void displayList(List<? Super Integer> list)`
    c. `public static void add(List<? Extends Number> list)`
    d. `public static void displayList(List<? Extends ?> list)`
4. **Consider the below partial code. What will be the output?**

```
Public static void main(String[] args) {
  List<String> items = new ArrayList<>(3);
  items.add("I001");
  items.add(20);
  System.out.println("Item Numbers");
  Iterator<String> value = items.iterator();
  while (value.hasNext()) {
    String itemObj = value.next();
    System.out.print(" " + itemObj);
  }
}
```

    a. I001 20
    b. 20 I001
    c. Compile-time error
    d. None of these
5. **Consider the below partial code. What will be the output?**

```
LocalDate dt = LocalDate.of(2019, Month.JULY, 31);
System.out.println("Date: " + dt);
```

    a. Date: 2019-07-31
    b. Date: 31-07-2019
    c. Date: 2019-31-07
    d. Date: 07-31-2019

Answers

1. b
2. c
3. a
4. c
5. a

Assignment

Create a Java program as per the below specifications.

1. Create an abstract class named **`Shape`** with a method **`draw()`**.
2. Create two or more subclasses of **`Shape`** class, such as **`Circle, Triangle`**, and so on. and override the **`draw()`** method in all the classes.
3. Add print functionality within the overridden **`draw()`** methods of each subclass.
4. Create another class named **`GenericsTest`** with a method named **`drawShape()`**.
5. The **`drawShape()`** method should take a **`List`** as a parameter with an upper bounded wild card extending class **`Shape`**.
6. Within the method, the type of list object should be identified and the appropriate **`draw()`** method should be executed.
7. In the **`main()`** method, create lists of the different subclasses of **`Shape`** class and pass these to the **`drawShape()`** method. [Hint: Use type safety with generics]

The expected output is shown below:

```
Drawing a Rectangle
Drawing a Circle
Drawing a Circle
```

Figure 8.16: *Output*

Join our book's Discord space

Join the book's Discord Workspace for Latest updates, Offers, Tech happenings around the world, New Release and Sessions with the Authors:

https://discord.bpbonline.com

CHAPTER 9
File Manipulation in Java

Introduction

This chapter explains the use of different types of streams. You will learn to work with the `File` class and its members. You will also understand the use of the byte and character streams of `java.io` package. Further, you will learn about serialization, `Console` class, and different classes of packages such as `java.util.zip and java.nio` package.

Structure

In this chapter, we will learn the following topics:

- Files and streams
- DataInput and DataOutput interfaces
- FilenameFilter interface
- ByteStreams
- OutputStream class hierarchy
- Character streams
- Writer class hierarchy
- Console class
- java.util.zip package
- java.nio package

Objectives

In this chapter you will understand data streams and work with the **File** class. You will also learn to work with the **DataInput** and **DataOutput** interfaces. You will understand the different classes of the **java.io** package and the **java.nio** packages. Further, you will learn about serialization as well as the use of the **Console** class.

9.1 Files and streams

Generally, data is stored on a device in the form of files that can be present locally or over a network. To process the data of these files, Java uses the concept of streams. A stream is a sequence of data or a channel that transmits data from source to destination, such as storage media, I/O devices or computers over a network. Java reads from a logical stream created from physical storage. Data can be read byte by byte or character by character. Thus, Java streams can be used to perform different types of I/O operations.

Different types of data are supported by streams, such as bytes, primitive types, localized characters, and so on. The **Stream** class of Java is used to manage the standard I/O operations. The input stream reads data from the source to a program, and the output stream writes data from a program to the destination. Streams can be used to transmit and transform data. Streams also allow managing data on disk files and sharing across the network:

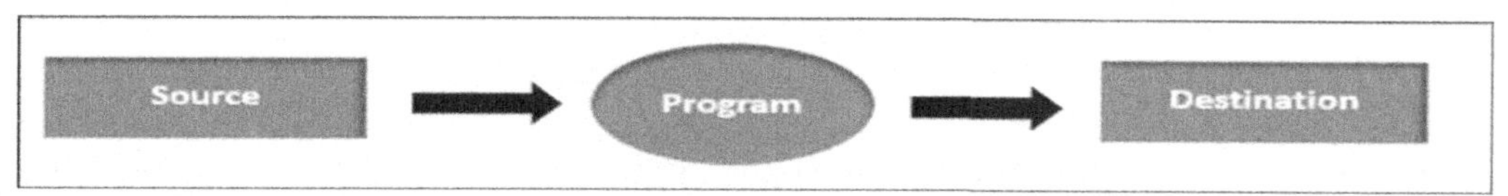

Figure 9.1: *Java streams*

The fields that represent these streams include:

- **in**: Represents the standard input stream that reads characters of data from the standard input devices such as a keyboard or any other input source.

  ```
  public static final InputStream in;
  ```

- **out**: Represents the standard output stream which displays the output on the screen or any other output media.

  ```
  public static final PrintStream out;
  ```

- **err**: Represents the standard error stream which displays errors on the user's console.

  ```
  public static final PrintStream err;
  ```

Following steps need to be performed to read or write data using Input/Output streams:

- Open a stream (The source could be a file, URL, socket, and so on.).
- Read/write data from/to the stream.
- Close the stream.

Java provides a hierarchy of abstract classes and subclasses of Input and Output streams to read and write data in the form of byte streams. The **java.io** package provides the class hierarchy for input and output operations. Some important classes are shown in the following figure:

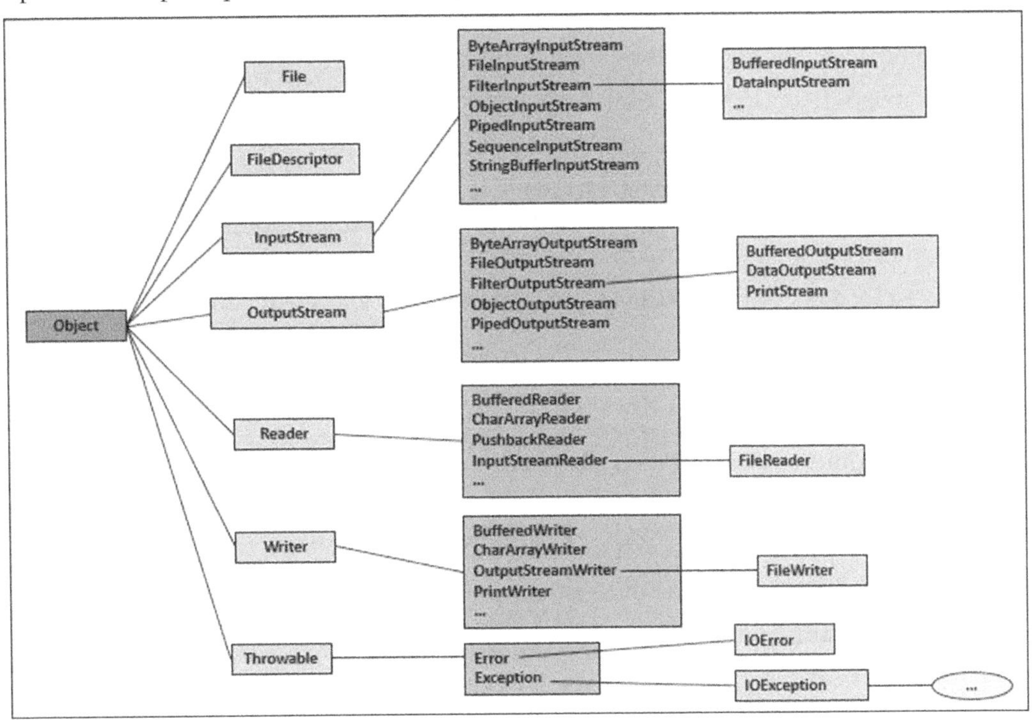

Figure 9.2: Classes of java.io package

Listed below are some important interfaces of **java.io** package.

- **Closeable**
- **DataInput**
- **DataOutput**
- **FileFilter**
- **FilenameFilter**
- **Serializable**

9.1.1 File class

The most important class for manipulating files on a file system directly is the **File** class. The **java.io.File** class is used to create files and directories, search a file, delete a file, and so on. The naming convention of the file is as per the host OS. The pathname of a file can be specified using a relative path or an absolute path. The **getParent()** method helps to resolve the parent of an abstract pathname.

A **File** class instance is immutable, hence, the abstract pathname represented by a **File** object cannot be changed once it is created. The **File** class stores the name and path of a file or directory and allows file manipulation through various access methods. The common operations supported include create, delete, rename, list files, and so on. File permissions need to be determined before performing any operation.

Listed below are some important constructors of the **java.io.File** class:

- **File(String path)**: Creates a **File** object with the specified pathname.
- **File(String parent, String child)**: Creates a **File** object with the specified parent and child parameters for the pathname. Here, the parent points to the directory, and the child refers to a directory or a file.
- **File(File obj, String filename)**: Creates a **File** object from another **File** object and file or directory name.
- **File(URL obj)**: Converts the given URL into a pathname and generates a new **File** object.

Listed below are some methods of the **File** class:

- **boolean exists()**: Checks if the given file or directory exists.
- **boolean isFile()**: Checks if the object is a normal file.
- **String getPath()**: Returns the abstract pathname as a string.
- **boolean mkdir()**: Creates a new directory by the given abstract pathname.
- **boolean createNewFile()**: Creates a new empty file with the given file name, only if a file with a similar name does not exist. The method throws **IOException** exception.
- **boolean renameTo(File newFile)**: Renames an existing **File** object with the new name specified as the parameter.
- **boolean delete()**: Deletes the file pointed by the pathname.
- **Path toPath()**: Returns the **java.nio.file.Path** object from the given path.
- **URI toURI()**: Constructs a file, URI representing the given pathname.

The following code demonstrates the usage of constructors and methods of the **File** class:

```
import java.io.File;
public class FileDemo {
  public static void main(String[] args) {
    File obj = new File("F:/JavaDemos/FirstFile.txt");
    // Below line shows overloaded constructor of File class
    //File obj = new File("F:/JavaDemos", "FirstFile.txt");
    System.out.println("File exists is: " + obj.exists());
    System.out.println("File is: " + obj.isFile());
    System.out.println("Path is: " + obj.getPath());
```

```
    System.out.println("Name is: " + obj.getName());
  }
}
```

The output of the code is shown below:

```
File exists is: false
File is: false
Path is: F:\JavaDemos\FirstFile.txt
Name is: FirstFile.txt
```

Figure 9.3: File class constructor and methods

9.1.2 FileDescriptor class

The operating system maintains file descriptors when the directories and files are accessed. These can be retrieved by using the **FileDescriptor** class.

The **FileDescriptor** class has the following public fields:

- **static final FileDescriptor in**: Acts as a handle to the standard input stream.
- **static final FileDescriptor out**: Acts as a handle to the standard output stream.
- **static final FileDescriptor err**: Acts as a handle to the standard error stream.

Listed below are the constructors of **FileDescriptor** class:

- **FileDescriptor()**: Creates an invalid **FileDescriptor** object.

Listed below are the important methods of the **FileDescriptor** class:

- **sync()**: Clears the system buffers and writes the content that they contain to the actual hardware. It throws the **SyncFailedException**.
- **valid()**: Checks whether the file descriptor is valid. Since the file descriptors are associated with open files, they become invalid when the file is closed.

A file descriptor is generally used to create a **FileInputStream** or **FileOutputStream** to contain it.

For example:

```
public static void main(String[] args) throws IOException {
  FileDescriptor desc = null;  FileOutputStream out = null;
  byte[] buff = {48,28,48,38,29};
  try{    out = new FileOutputStream("File1.txt");    desc = out.getFD();    //
write bytes to file output stream    out.write(buff);    // Sync data to the source
file    desc.sync();    System.out.print("Sync Completed");
  }
```

```
catch(Exception ex){    ex.printStackTrace();  }
finally{
  // release resources    if(out!=null)      out.close();  }}
```

9.2 DataInput and DataOutput interfaces

Data streams implement the **DataInput** and **DataOutput** interfaces to perform I/O operations. The methods of these interfaces allow conversion of binary data to primitive types of Java and UTF 8 to strings and vice-versa.

Listed below are the methods in the **DataInput** interface:

- **readByte()**: Reads one byte from a stream which is a signed value in the range from -128 to 127.
- **readChar()**: Reads two bytes from a stream and returns a **char** value.
- **readInt()**: Reads four bytes from a stream and returns the corresponding **int** value.
- **readDouble()**: Reads eight bytes from a stream and returns the corresponding **double** value.
- **readBoolean()**: Reads an input byte from a stream and returns true if the byte is not zero; else returns false.
- **readLine()**: Reads a line of text from the input stream a byte at a time until it reaches the end of line or end of the file. Each byte is converted to a character, and the characters are returned as a **String**.
- **readUTF()**: Reads a line of text in the modified UTF-8 format from a stream.

If the methods fail to read bytes from the steam or the input stream is closed, an **IOException** is raised. Listed below are the methods in the **DataOutput** interface:

- **writeByte(int value)**: Writes the byte value of the specified integer parameter to an output stream.
- **writeChar(int value)**: Writes the **Char** value of the specified integer parameter to an output stream.
- **writeChars(String value)**: Writes the given string parameter to an output stream.
- **writeInt(int value)**: Writes four bytes representing the specified integer parameter to an output stream.
- **writeDouble(double value)**: Writes eight bytes representing the specified double parameter to an output stream.
- **writeBoolean(boolean b)**: Writes the boolean value specified as a parameter to an output stream. If the value is true, then 1 will be written, else, 0 is written.
- **writeUTF(String value)**: Writes a string in Java modified UTF-8 form given as a parameter to a stream.

If the methods fail to write bytes to the steam or the output stream is closed, an **IOException** is raised.

9.3 FilenameFilter interface

Following code demonstrates the usage of **FilenameFilter** interface to filter files with a specific extension:

```
import java.io.FilenameFilter;
import java.io.File;
public class FilenameFilterDemo {
  public static void main(String[] args) {
    String dirPath = "F:/JavaDemos";
    File fObj = new File(dirPath);
    FilenameFilter filterObj = new FileFilter("txt");
    String[] names = fObj.list(filterObj);
    System.out.println("Files count: " + names.length);
    System.out.println("List of Files Found");
    for (int n = 0; n < names.length; n++) {
      System.out.println(names[n]);
    }
  }
}
class FileFilter implements FilenameFilter {
  String fileExtn;
  public FileFilter(String extn) {
    fileExtn = "." + extn;
  }
  @Override
  public boolean accept(File dir, String fileName) {
    return fileName.endsWith(fileExtn);
  }
}
```

The code filters file names with extension **.txt**. The output of the code is shown below:

```
Files count: 3
List of Files Found
File1.txt
TextDoc.txt
TextFile.txt
```

Figure 9.4: Using FilenameFilter interface

9.4 Byte streams

Java byte streams allow performing input and output of data byte by byte (8-bits). There are several classes supporting byte streams. Broadly these are classified as **InputStream** and **OutputStream**.

9.4.1 InputStream class hierarchy

InputStream class is the superclass of all input streams. It is an abstract class that provides methods for reading bytes, counting number of bytes read, marking locations in streams, and so on:

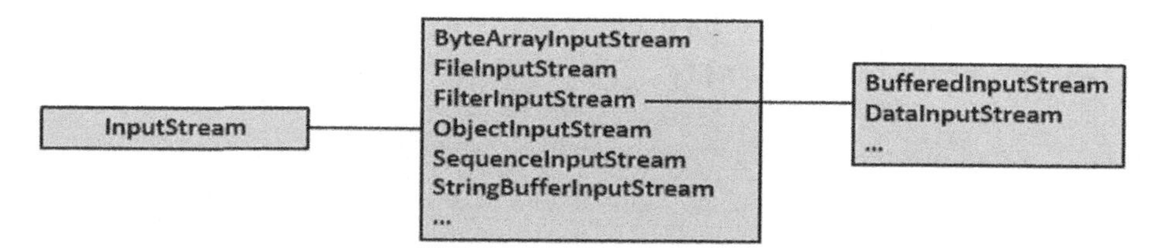

Figure 9.5: InputStream class hierarchy

Listed below are some important methods of **InputStream** class:

- **read()**: Reads the next bytes of data from the input stream and returns an **int** value in the range of 0 to 255. It returns -1 when the end of file is encountered.
- **available()**: Returns the number of available bytes that can be read without blocking.
- **close()**: Closes the input stream and releases the system resources occupied by the stream.
- **mark(int n)**: Marks the current position in the stream and remains valid until the number of bytes specified in the variable, **n**, are read.
- **skip(long n)**: Skips **n** bytes of data while reading from an input stream.
- **reset()**: Rests the reading pointer to the previously set mark in the stream.

Some important subclasses of **InputStream** are explained in the upcoming sections.

9.4.1.1 FileInputStream class

FileInputStream class allows reading bytes from a file. It overrides all methods of **InputStream** class except **mark()** and **reset()**. Listed below are some important constructors of **FileInputStream** class:

- **FileInputStream(String str)**: Creates an **InputStream** object to read bytes from a file at the location specified by the **String** parameter. For example:

  ```
  FileInputStream fis = new FileInputStream("File1.txt");
  ```

- **FileInputStream(File f)**: Creates an **InputStream** object to read bytes from a file pointed by the **File** object parameter.

  ```
  File f = new File("/File1.txt");
  FileInputStream fis = new FileInputStream(f);
  ```

- **FileInputStream(FileDescriptor fd)**: Creates a **FileInputStream** from the specified file descriptor object to represent an existing connection to the file which is there in the file system.

The following code demonstrates the use of **FileInputStream** class:

```
public class FileInputStreamDemo {
  public static void main(String argv[]) {
    try {
      FileInputStream fis = new FileInputStream("D:/Demos/File1.txt");
      int ch;
      while ((ch = fis.read()) > -1) {
        StringBuilder buf = new StringBuilder();
        buf.append((char) ch);
        System.out.print(buf.toString());
      }
    } catch (IOException e) {
      System.out.println(e.getMessage());
    }
  }
}
```

The code reads the data from **File1.txt** and stores it in the **StringBuilder** object, which is then used to display the entire data as a string.

Output:

```
Good Morning!!
This is the content of File1.
```

Figure 9.6: FileInputStream output

9.4.1.2 ByteArrayInputStream class

The **ByteArrayInputStream** class stores bytes that are read from the stream into a buffer. The source of data is usually a byte array. To keep track of the bytes to read, it maintains an internal counter. It overrides several methods of the **InputStream** class, such as **read(), skip(), available()**, and **reset()**.

The constructors of this class are as follows:

- **ByteArrayInputStream(byte[] b)**: Creates a **ByteArrayInputStream** with the specified byte array as the input source.
- **ByteArrayInputStream(byte[] b, int offset, int length)**: Creates a **ByteArrayInputStream** with the specified byte array as the input source. It begins with the character at the index specified by offset until the value specified length.

The following code snippet displays the use of the **ByteArrayInputStream** class:

```
public class ByteArrayISDemo {
  public static void main(String[] args) {
    String content = "Good Morning";
    byte[] bytes = content.getBytes();
    ByteArrayInputStream bais = new ByteArrayInputStream(bytes);
    int i = 0;
    while ((i = bais.read()) != -1) {
      //Convert byte into character
      char ch = (char) i;
      System.out.println("Read character: "+ch);
    }
  }
}
```

The following output of the above code:

```
Read character: G
Read character: o
Read character: o
Read character: d
Read character:
Read character: M
Read character: o
Read character: r
Read character: n
Read character: i
Read character: n
Read character: g
```

Figure 9.7: ByteArrayInputStream output

9.4.1.3 FilterInputStream class

The **FilterInputStream** class allows us to transform data along the way or uses the input stream as a basic source of data to provide additional functionality.

Constructor:

- **protected FilterInputStream(InputStream in)**: Creates a **FilterInputStream** with the value assigned to the field **this.in**.

Listed below are the methods of **FilterInputStream** class:

- **read()**: Reads the next byte of data from the input stream.
- **available()**: Returns a number of bytes that can be read or skipped from the input stream.
- **read(byte[] b)**: Reads bytes of data from the input stream into the specified array of bytes.
- **read(byte[] b, int offset, int length)**: Reads bytes of data from the input stream into the specified array of bytes from the offset to the specified length.
- **mark(int readlimit)**: Identifies the current position in the input stream.
- **markSupported()**: Checks if the input stream supports the mark and resets methods.
- **close()**: Closes the input stream and releases the system resources related to the stream.
- **reset()**: Repositions the pointer to the position in the stream to the mark set earlier.
- **skip(long n)**: Skips and discards **n** number of bytes of data from the input stream.

9.4.1.4 BufferedInputStream

The bytes read from a source can be cached in a temporary storage area to improve performance in read and write operations from streams. Such temporary storage is called a buffer. It allows skip, mark, and reset operations on streams. Any **InputStream** class can be wrapped in the **BufferedInputStream** to cache inputs. Internally, the cached data is stored as an array of bytes.

Constructors:

- **BufferedInputStream(InputStream is)**: Creates a buffered input stream for the specified **InputStream** instance with a default buffer size of 2048 bytes.
- **BufferedInputStream(InputStream is, int size)**: Creates a buffered input stream of specified **InputStream** instance and the given size.

Listed below are some important methods of **BufferedInputStream** class:

- **int available()**: Returns the number of bytes of input that is available for reading.
- **void mark(int num)**: Places a mark at the current position in the input stream.
- **int read()**: Reads data from the input stream.

- **int read(byte [] b, int off, int length)**: Reads bytes into the specified byte array from the given offset to the given length.
- **void reset()**: Repositions the pointer in the stream to the mark set earlier.

Following code demonstrates the use of **FilterInputStream** with **BufferedInputStream**:

```
public class FilterInputStreamDemo {
  public static void main(String[] args) throws Exception {
    InputStream is = null;
    FilterInputStream fis = null;
    try {
      // instantiate input stream objects
      is = new FileInputStream("D:/Demos/File1.txt");
      fis = new BufferedInputStream(is);
      // read and print from filter input stream
      System.out.println("Read character: "+(char) fis.read());
      System.out.println("Read character: "+(char) fis.read());
      // set a mark
      fis.mark(0);
      System.out.println("mark set");
      System.out.println("Read character: "+(char) fis.read());
      System.out.println("Read character: "+(char) fis.read());
    } catch (IOException e) {
      System.out.println("Error: " + e.getMessage());
    } finally {
      if (is != null) {
        is.close();
      }
      if (fis != null) {
        fis.close();
      }
    }
  }
}
```

The following will be the output for the above code:

```
Read character: G
Read character: o
mark set
Read character: o
Read character: d
```

Figure 9.8: FilterInputStream and BufferedInputStream

9.4.1.5 ObjectInputStream class

`ObjectInputStream` class extends the **`InputStream`** class and implements the **`ObjectInput`** interface. This class is used to deserialize objects and primitive data that have been written by using the **`ObjectOutputStream`**. The following figure shows the class hierarchy of **`ObjectInputStream`** class:

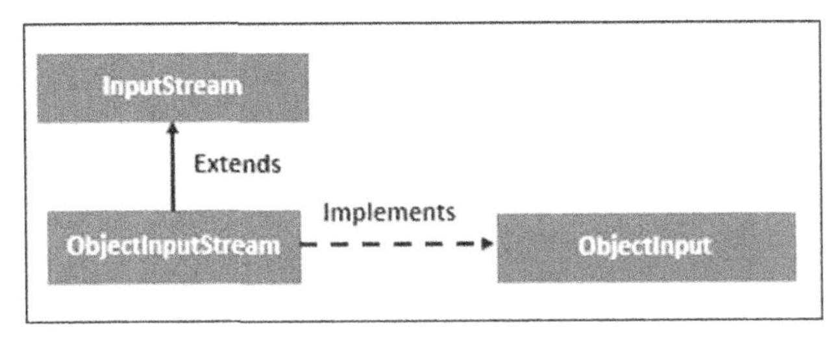

Figure 9.9: ObjectInputStream

Listed below are the constructors of **`ObjectInputStream`** class:

Constructors:

- **`ObjectInputStream()`**: Allows subclasses that completely re-implement **`ObjectInputStream`** to avoid allocating private data recently used by the current implementation of **`ObjectInputStream`**.
- **`ObjectInputStream(InputStream in)`**: Creates an **`ObjectInputStream`** that reads serialized objects from the specified **`InputStream`**.

Listed below are the methods in **`ObjectInputStream`** class:

- **`readByte()`**: The **`readByte()`** method reads and returns a **`byte`** from the input stream.
- **`readChar()`**: The **`readChar()`** method reads and returns a **`char`** from the input stream.
- **`readFloat()`**: The **`readFloat()`** method reads and returns a **`float`** from the input stream.
- **`readBoolean()`**: The **`readBoolean()`** method reads and returns a boolean from the input stream.
- **`readObject()`**: The **`readObject()`** method reads and returns an object from the input stream.

The following code demonstrates the use of **ObjectInputStream** class:

```
...
FileInputStream fis = new FileInputStream("student");
ObjectInputStream ois = new ObjectInputStream(fis);
Student s = (Student) ois.readObject();
ois.close();
...
```

Here, the **FileInputStream** object is passed as a parameter to the **ObjectInputStream** constructor. The **readObject()** method deserializes the previously serialized object from the **ObjectInputStream** and stores it in the Student object **s** after typecasting it to the appropriate type. Lastly, the **ObjectInputStream** is closed.

9.4.2 OutputStream class hierarchy

OutputStreamClass is an abstract class. It provides methods to write bytes or arrays of bytes to streams. The subclasses of **OutputStream** class include **ByteArrayOutputstream**, **FileOutputStream**, and so on as shown in the below figure:

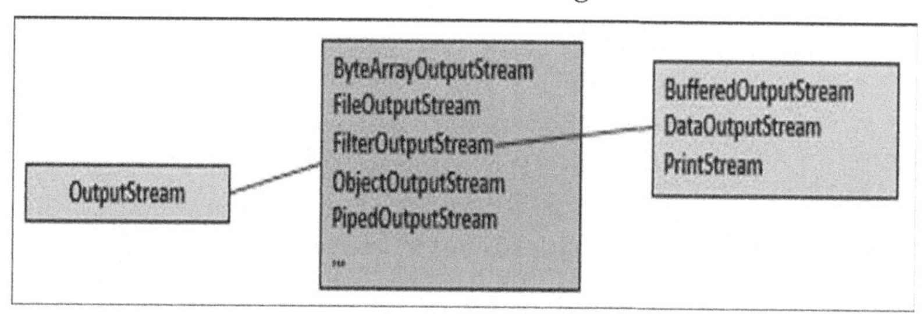

Figure 9.10: *OutputStream class hierarchy*

Listed below are the methods of **OutputStream** class:

- **write(int b)**: The **write(int b)** method writes the specified byte of the integer given as a parameter to an output stream.
- **write(byte[] b)**: Writes the entire specified byte array parameter to an output stream.
- **write(byte[] b, int off, int len)**: Writes bytes from the specified byte array parameter starting from the offset to the specified length to an output stream.
- **flush( )**: Flushes the stream and forcefully writes any buffered output bytes.
- **close()**: Closes the output stream and releases any system resources associated with the output stream.

Some important subclasses of **OutputStream** are explained here.

9.4.2.1 FileOutputStream

FileOutputStream class allows writing bytes to a file or file descriptor. Based on the underlying platform, the file may or may not be created if not available. Some platforms may allow a file to be opened for writing only by a single **FileOutputStream** at a time, resulting in a failed constructor call for an already open file.

Constructors:

- **FileOutputStream(String filepath)**: Creates a **FileOutputStream** object to write bytes to the specified file.
- **FileOutputStream(File name)**: Creates a **FileOutputStream** object to write bytes to the file indicated by the **File** object.
- **FileOutputStream(String filename, boolean flag)**: Creates a **FileOutputStream** object to write bytes to the specified file. If the flag is true, the file is opened in append mode.
- **FileOutputStream(File name, boolean flag)**: Creates a **FileOutputStream** object to write bytes to a file indicated by the **File** object. If the flag is true, the file is opened in append mode.

The following code shows the use of **FileOutputStream** class:

```
import java.io.FileOutputStream;
import java.io.OutputStream;
public class FileOutputStreamDemo {
  public static void main(String[] args) {
    try {
      String str = "This statement will be written to File2";
      byte[] buff = str.getBytes();
      OutputStream os = new FileOutputStream("D:/Demos/File2.txt");
      os.write(buff);
      System.out.println("Data Written to File");
      os.close();
    } catch (Exception e) {
      System.out.println("Error: " + e.getMessage());
    }
  }
}
```

Here, the data from a string is converted into bytes and stored in a byte array. The **FileOutputStream** object is created with the output file path as a parameter. The bytes from the array are then written to the output stream by using the **write()** method.

9.4.2.2 ByteArrayOutputStream class

The **ByteArrayOutputStream** class creates an output stream wherein the data is written into a byte array. The buffer grows dynamically in size as data is written to it. Methods of this class can be accessed even after closing the stream without raising an **IOException**.

Constructors:

- **ByteArrayOutputStream()**: Initializes a new **ByteArrayOutputStream** object with a default buffer size of 32 bytes.
- **ByteArrayOutputStream(int size)**: Initializes a new **ByteArrayOutputStream** object with the specified buffer size.

Listed below are some important methods of **ByteArrayOutputStream** class:

- **reset()**: Resets the byte array output stream to zero and discards all accumulated output from the output stream.
- **size()**: Returns the size of the buffer.
- **toByteArray()**: Creates a newly allocated byte array with the bytes written so far.
- **writeTo(OutputStream out)**: Writes the entire byte array contents of the current output stream to the specified output stream argument.
- **toString()**: Converts the contents of the buffer's contents into a string. The bytes are decoded by using the default character set of the platform.

The following code demonstrates the use of **ByteArrayOutputStream** class:

```
import java.io.ByteArrayOutputStream;
public class ByteArrayOSDemo {
  public static void main(String[] args) {
    try {
      String str = "Good Morning";
      byte[] buff = str.getBytes();
      ByteArrayOutputStream baos = new ByteArrayOutputStream();
      baos.write(buff);
      System.out.println("The string written to buffer is: " + baos.toString());
    } catch (Exception e) {
      System.out.println("Caught exception: " + e.getMessage());
    }
  }
}
```

Here, the contents of a string are converted to bytes and stored in a byte array. The byte array is passed as a parameter to the **write()** method of the **ByteArrayOutputStream** object. The contents of the object are then printed by using the **toString()** method.

9.4.2.3 FilterOutputStream class

The **FilterOutputStream** class overrides all the methods of **OutputStream** class and also includes the protected outfield to represent the underlying output stream to be filtered.

Constructor:

- **FilterOutputStream(OutputStream out)**: Creates an output stream filter on top of the given output stream.

The following code demonstrates the use of **FilterOutputStream** class:

```
import java.io.FileInputStream;
import java.io.FilterOutputStream;
import java.io.FileOutputStream;
import java.io.IOException;
import java.io.OutputStream;
public class FilterOutputStreamDemo {
  public static void main(String[] args) throws Exception {
    OutputStream os = null;
    FilterOutputStream fos = null;
    FileInputStream fis = null;
    FileInputStream filis = null;
    String s="Java Program";
    byte buf[]=s.getBytes();
    int i = 0;
    char c;
    try {
      // creates output stream objects
      os = new FileOutputStream("D://Demos//Write.txt");
      fos = new FilterOutputStream(os);
      // write to the output stream from a byte array
      fos.write(buf);
      // flush all contents of the output stream
      fos.flush();
```

```
        // create an input stream to read from the file
        filis = new FileInputStream("D:/Demos/Write.txt");
        while ((i = filis.read()) != -1) {
          // convert integer to character
          c = (char) i;
          System.out.println("Character read: " + c);
        }
      } catch (IOException e) {
        System.out.print("Error: "+e.getMessage());
      } finally {
        // releases system resources
        if (os != null) {
          os.close();
        }
        if (fis != null) {
          fis.close();
        }
      }
    }
}
```

The following will be the output for the above code:

```
Character read: J
Character read: a
Character read: v
Character read: a
Character read: 
Character read: P
Character read: r
Character read: o
Character read: g
Character read: r
Character read: a
Character read: m
```

Figure 9.11: *FilterOutputStream*

9.4.2.4 BufferedOutputStream class

BufferedOutputStream creates a buffer for an output stream which allows caching data into the buffer to improve performance while writing bytes.

Constructors:

- **BufferedOutputStream(OutputStream os)**: Creates a buffered output stream with a default size of 512 bytes for the specified **OutputStream** instance.
- **BufferedOutputStream(OutputStream os, int size)**: Creates a buffered output stream of the specified size for the given **OutputStream** instance.

Methods:

- **flush()**: Flushes the buffered output stream.
- **write(int b)**: Writes the specified byte to this buffered output stream.
- **write(byte[] b, int off, int len)**: Writes bytes from the specified **byte** array to the buffered output stream starting at offset off to the given length.

The following code demonstrates the use of **BufferedOutputStream** class:

```
import java.io.BufferedOutputStream;
import java.io.FileOutputStream;
public class BufferedOutputStreamDemo {
  public static void main(String args[]) throws Exception {
    try {
      // create an output stream
      FileOutputStream fos = new FileOutputStream("D:\\Demos\\Write1.txt");
      // Wrap the output stream with the buffered stream
      BufferedOutputStream bos = new BufferedOutputStream(fos);
      String str = "Data written to file";
      byte b[] = str.getBytes();
      // write the bytes to output stream
      bos.write(b);
      bos.flush();
      bos.close();
      fos.close();
      System.out.println("Task Completed");
    } catch (Exception e) {
```

```
            System.out.println("Error: " + e.getMessage());
        }
    }
}
```

9.4.2.5 ObjectOutputStream class

ObjectOutputStream class is a subclass of **OutputStream** class. It is used to write objects and primitive types to the output stream.

Constructors:

- **ObjectOutputStream()**: Allows subclasses that are completely re-implementing **ObjectOutputStream** to avoid allocating private data just used by the current implementation of **ObjectOutputStream**.
- **ObjectOutputStream(OutputStream out)**: Creates an **ObjectOutputStream** that writes to the given **OutputStream**.

Listed below are the important methods of **ObjectOutputStream** class:

- **writeFloat(float f)**: Writes a **float** value to the output stream.
- **writeObject (Object obj)**: Writes the specified object to the output stream
- **writeObject()**: Writes non-static and non-transient fields to the underlying output stream.

The following code demonstrates the use of **ObjectOutputStream** class:

```
import java.io.FileInputStream;
import java.io.FileOutputStream;
import java.io.IOException;
import java.io.ObjectInputStream;
import java.io.ObjectOutputStream;
import java.io.Serializable;
public class ObjectOutputStreamDemo {
  public static void main(String[] args) {
    // create input and output streams
    FileInputStream fis = null;
    FileOutputStream fos = null;
    ObjectInputStream ois = null;
    ObjectOutputStream oos = null;
    try {
```

```
    fos = new FileOutputStream("D:\\Demos\\Student.txt");
    oos = new ObjectOutputStream(fos);
    // create a Student object for serialization
    Student s1 = new Student();
    s1.lastName = "Preston";
    s1.firstName = "Clark";
    s1.score = 68.7f;
    // write the object to the output stream
    oos.writeObject(s1);
    oos.close();
    fos.close();
    // initialize the input streams
    fis = new FileInputStream("D:\\Demos\\Student.txt");
    ois = new ObjectInputStream(fis);
    //de-serialize Student object
    Student s = (Student) ois.readObject();
    System.out.println("Deserialized Data:\n" + s.firstName + " "
                  + s.lastName + "\n" + s.score);
  } catch (IOException | ClassNotFoundException e) {
    System.out.println("Exception occurred");
  } finally {
    try {
      if (fis != null) {
        fis.close();
      }
      if (ois != null) {
        ois.close();
      }
    } catch (Exception e) {
      System.out.println("Exception while closing stream");
    }
  }
}
```

```
}
// create a Serailizable class
class Student implements Serializable {
  String lastName;
  String firstName;
  float score;
}
```

The following will be the output for the above program:

```
Deserialized Data:
Clark Preston
68.7
```

Figure 9.12: ObjectOutputStream

9.5 Serialization

Persistence is the process of storing data to permanent storage. Java allows persisting objects as well as reading back from persistent storage.

Serialization is the process of converting the state of an object into a byte stream. When the byte stream is used to recreate the actual Java object in memory, it is termed deserialization. To implement serialization, Java provides the **java.io.Serializable** interface, which must be implemented by a class whose object is to be serialized. The interface does not have any methods; it simply indicates that the object of this class and its subclasses are serializable. However, the static and transient variables cannot be serialized.

9.6 Character streams

The classes of Byte streams allow I/O operations on all types except Unicode characters. Therefore, Java provides the character streams to handle character data I/O. The character streams provide methods for read/write operations on Unicode characters and can also be internationalized. The **Reader** and **Writer** class are the top-level classes of character streams, and they are abstract classes.

9.6.1 Reader class hierarchy

The **Reader** class is an abstract class that provides methods to read character streams. The subclasses need to override the methods with the required functionality:

Figure 9.13: *Reader class hierarchy*

Constructors:

- `Reader()`: Creates a new character-stream reader whose critical sections will synchronize on this reader object.
- `Reader(Object lock)`: Creates a new character-stream reader whose critical sections will synchronize on the specified object.

All methods of `Reader` class throw `IOException`. Listed below are some important methods of the `Reader` class:

- `read()`: Reads a single character. Returns `-1` when the end of file is encountered.
- `read(char[] buffer, int offset, int count)`: Reads characters to the specified array from offset to count and returns the number of characters that are read.
- `read(char[] buffer)`: Reads characters into the specified array and returns the number of characters read.
- `skip(long count)`: Skips a specified number of characters.
- `ready()`: Checks if the reader is ready and returns true if the reader is ready to be read from.
- `close()`: Closes the stream and releases the system resources.
- `markSupported()`: Checks whether mark operation is supported by the stream.
- `mark(int readAheadLimit)`: Marks the current position in the stream.
- `reset()`: Resets the stream.

Some important subclasses of `Reader` class are explained here.

9.6.1.1 CharArrayReader class

The `CharArrayReader` class extends the `Reader` class and allows reading from a character array. It provides two constructors to read from an array of characters.

Constructors:

- `CharArrayReader(char arr[])`: Creates a `CharArrayReader` from the specified character array, `arr`.
- `CharArrayReader(char arr[], int start, int num)`: Creates a `CharArrayReader` from a subset of the character array, `arr`, starting from the character specified by the `index`, `start`, and is `num` characters long.

Listed below are some important methods of the **CharArrayReader** class:

- **read()**: Reads a single character.
- **read(char[] b, int off, int length)**: Reads characters into the specified array from the given offset to the given length.
- **skip(long n)**: Skips **n** number of characters before reading.
- **mark(int num)**: Marks the current position in the stream.
- **reset()**: Repositions the pointer in the stream to the previous **mark()** call or the beginning of the stream if **mark()** was not invoked.
- **ready()**: Checks whether this stream is ready to be read.
- **close()**: Closes the input stream.

The following code demonstrates the use of **CharArrayReader** class:

```
import java.io.CharArrayReader;
public class CharArrayReaderDemo {
  public static void main(String[] args) {
    try {
      // Initialize the character array
      char[] buff = {'W', 'H', 'I', 'T', 'E'};
      // Initialize the character array reader
      CharArrayReader car = new CharArrayReader(buff);
      // check for readiness
      boolean check = car.ready();
      if (check == true) {
        System.out.println("Ready to read");
      } else {
        System.out.println("Not ready");
      }
      int i = 0;
      System.out.println("Reading the array:");
      // invoke the read() method
      while ((i = car.read()) != -1) {
        char c = (char) i;
        System.out.println(c);
        // invoke the skip() method
        long c1 = car.skip(1);
```

```
          System.out.println("Characters Skipped: " + c1);
        }
        CharArrayReader car1 = new CharArrayReader(buff);
        // Read part of the array
        char buff1[] = new char[6];
        // read data into a buffer from offset and number of chars specified
        car1.read(buff1, 1, 3);
        int b = 0;
        System.out.println("Display the remaining array");
        while ((b = car1.read()) != -1) {
          char c2 = (char) b;
          System.out.print(c2);
        }
        System.out.println("");
      } catch (Exception e) {
        System.out.println("Error: " + e.getMessage());
      }
  }
}
```

The following will be the output of the above code:

```
Ready to read
Reading the array:
W
Characters Skipped: 1
I
Characters Skipped: 1
E
Characters Skipped: 0
Display the remaining array
TE
```

Figure 9.14: CharacterArrayReader

9.6.1.2 FileReader class

FileReader class is a subclass of **InputStreamReader** and is used to read character files. It inherits methods of **Reader** class as well as **InputStreamReader** class.

Constructors:

- **FileReader(File file)**: Creates a new **FileReader**, given the **File** to read from.
- **FileReader(FileDescriptor fd)**: Creates a new **FileReader**, given the **FileDescriptor** to read from.
- **FileReader(String fileName)**: Creates a new **FileReader**, given the name of the file to read from.

The following code demonstrates the use of **FileReader** class to read characters from a file:

```
import java.io.FileReader;
public class FileReaderDemo {
  public static void main(String args[]) throws Exception {
    try {
      // initialize the FileReader with the file path
      FileReader fr = new FileReader("D:\\Demos\\File1.txt");
      int i;
      // read character at a time
      while ((i = fr.read()) != -1) {
        System.out.print((char) i);
      }
      System.out.println("");
      fr.close();
    } catch (Exception e) {
      System.out.println("Error: " + e.getMessage());
    }
  }
}
```

The data is read and displayed from the file character by character.

9.6.2 Writer class hierarchy

The **Writer** class is an abstract class that provides methods to write characters to the streams. The subclass needs to override the methods with the required functionality:

Figure 9.15: Writer class hierarchy

Constructors:

- `Writer()`: Creates a new character-stream writer whose critical sections will synchronize on this writer object itself.
- `Writer(Object lock)`: Creates a new character-stream writer whose critical sections will synchronize on the specified object.

The methods of `Writer` class are the same as the methods of `OutputStream` class, and all the methods throw an `IOException`.

Listed below are some important methods of `Writer` class:

- `write(int c)`: Writes a single character.
- `write(char[] text)`: Writes an array of characters to an output stream.
- `write(char[] text, int offset, int length)`: Writes a portion of an array of characters to the output stream starting from the offset and the number of characters specified by length.
- `write(String s)`: Writes a string to the output stream.
- `write(String s, int offset, int length)`: Writes a portion of a string to the output stream starting from the offset and the number of characters specified by length.
- `flush()`: Flushes the output stream to clear the buffers.
- `close()`: Closes the output stream.

9.6.2.1 PrintWriter class

The main utility of the `PrintWriter` class is to output character data to the console, including Unicode characters. It has all the print methods of the `PrintStream` class but additionally provides support for multiple bytes and other character sets.

Constructors:

- `PrintWriter(OutputStream out)`: Creates a new `PrintWriter` from an existing `OutputStream`. It does not support automatic line flushing.
- `PrintWriter(OutputStream out, boolean autoFlush)`: Creates a new `PrintWriter` from an existing `OutputStream` with automatic line flushing.

- **PrintWriter(Writer out)**: Creates a new **PrintWriter** without automatic line flushing.
- **PrintWriter(Writer out, boolean autoFlush)**: Creates a new **PrintWriter** with automatic line flushing.

The class has the following characteristics:

- It overrides the **write()** method of the **Writer** class.
- It tests the printed output for errors by using the **checkError()** method instead of **IOException**.
- It provides the **print()** and **println()** methods to print primitive types, strings, objects, character arrays as well as formatted output.

The **println()** method argument is followed by a platform-dependent line separator. Both **print()** and **println()** are the same, except that the **print()** method does not flush the stream automatically.

Some important methods of **PrintWriter** class are listed below:

- **print(char c)**: Prints a character.
- **print(char[] s)**: Prints an array of characters.
- **print(int i)**: Prints an integer.
- **print(float f)**: Prints a floating-point number.
- **print(long l)**: Prints a long integer.
- **print(double d)**: Prints a double-precision floating-point number.
- **print(boolean b)**: Prints a boolean value.
- **print(Object obj)**: Prints an object and calls the **toString()** method on the argument.
- **print(String s)**: Prints a string.
- **println()**: Terminates the current line by a line separator.
- **println(Boolean x)**: Prints a boolean value and then terminate the line.
- **checkError()**: Flushes the stream if it is open and checks the error state.
- **flush()**: Flushes the output stream to clear the buffers.
- **close()**: Closes the output stream.
- **setError()**: Indicates that an error has occurred.
- **write(char[] buf)**: Writes an array of characters.
- **write(char[] buf, int off, int len)**: Writes a part of an array of characters.
- **write(int c)**: Writes a single character.
- **write(String s)**: Writes a string.
- **write(String s, int off, int len)**: Writes a part of a string.

The **write()** methods of the **PrintWriter** class do not throw an **IOException** as it is caught inside the class, and an **error** flag is set. The following code demonstrates the use of

`PrintWriter` class:

```
import java.io.File;
import java.io.PrintWriter;
public class PrintWriterDemo {
  public static void main(String[] args) {
    try {
      // Write to Console by using PrintWriter
      PrintWriter pw = new PrintWriter(System.out);
      pw.write("Welcome to the World of Java");
      pw.flush();
      pw.close();
      // Write to a File by using PrintWriter
      PrintWriter pw1 = new PrintWriter(new File("D:\\Demos\\PwOut.txt"));
      pw1.write("Welcome to the World of Java");
      pw1.flush();
      pw1.close();
    } catch (Exception e) {
      System.out.println("Error: " + e.getMessage());
    }
  }
}
```

9.6.2.2 CharArrayWriter class

The `CharArrayWriter` class is used to write characters to a character array and the size of the array expands as required.

Constructors:

- `CharArrayWriter()`: Creates a `CharArrayWriter` with a default buffer size of 32 characters.
- `CharArrayWriter(int num)`: Creates a `CharArrayWriter` with a buffer of the specified size.

Listed below are some important methods of `CharArrayWriter` class:

- `write()`: Writes a single character to the array.
- `write(char[] b, int off, int length)`: Writes characters to the given buffer.
- `void write(String str, int off, int len)`: Writes a portion of the string to buffer.

- **writeTo(Writer out)**: Writes the contents of the buffer to a character stream.
- **size()**: Returns current size of the buffer.
- **close()**: Closes the stream.
- **flush()**: Flushes stream.
- **reset()**: Repositions the pointer in the buffer to the last call of the **mark()** method or to the beginning of the buffer if the mark is not set.
- **toCharArray()**: Returns a copy of the data.
- **toString()**: Converts the input data to a string.

The following code demonstrates the use of **CharArrayWriter** class:

```
import java.io.CharArrayWriter;
import java.io.FileWriter;
public class CharArrayWriterDemo {
  public static void main(String args[]) {
    try {
      // Initialize the CharArrayWriter object
      CharArrayWriter cout = new CharArrayWriter();
      cout.write("Welcome to the World of Java");
      // Initialize the FileWriter object
      FileWriter fw1 = new FileWriter("D:\\Demos\\Out1.txt");
      // Write to the file from character array writer
      cout.writeTo(fw1);
      fw1.close();
      System.out.println("Task Completed");
    } catch (Exception e) {
      System.out.println("Error: " + e.getMessage());
    }
  }
}
```

The data from the buffer of **CharArrayWriter** is written to the file **Out1.txt** by using the **writeTo()** method.

9.7 Console class

The **Console** class simplifies the development of command-line applications and allows reading text from the terminal without echoing the characters on the screen. It was introduced in the

java.io package since Java SE 6. It uses the **Reader** and **Writer** classes for I/O operations on character streams.

Console class does not support public constructors and can be accessed with the **System.Console()** method. It returns a **Console** object if available, else returns null.

Listed below are some important methods of the **Console** class:

- **readLine()**: Reads one line of text from the console.
- **readLine(String fmt, Object... args)**: Provides a formatted prompt and reads one line of text from the console.
- **readPassword()**: Reads a password from the console with echoing disabled method. It returns a character array instead of a String to allow modification of the password.
- **format(String fmt, Object... args)**: Writes a formatted string to the output stream of the current console by using the specified format string and given arguments.
- **printf(String fmt, Object... args)**: A convenience method to write a formatted string to the output stream of the current console by using the given format string and arguments.
- **reader()**: Returns the unique **Reader** object that is associated with the console.
- **writer()**: Returns the unique **PrintWriter** object associated with this console.

The **Console** class methods can be invoked only from the command line and not from **Integrated Development Environments** (**IDEs**) like NetBeans, Eclipse, and so on.

The following code demonstrates the use of the **Console** class:

```
import java.io.Console;
import java.io.IOError;
public class ConsoleDemo {
  public static void main(String[] args) {
    Console cons = System.console();
    if (cons == null) {
      System.err.println("Console not available!");
      return;
    }
    try {
      String loginid = cons.readLine("Login id: ");
      char[] pass = cons.readPassword("Password: ");
      if(loginid.equals("admin") && String.valueOf(pass).equals("admin"))
        System.out.println("Welcome!! Admin");
      else
```

```
            System.out.println("Invalid credentials");
        } catch (IOError ioe) {
            cons.printf("I/O Error: %s\n", ioe.getMessage());
        }
    }
}
```

If the program is run from an IDE that does not support a console device, the **`Console not available!`** the message is displayed. When the code is executed in a console device, it accepts the user input through **`readLine()`** and **`readPassword()`** methods. The output is shown below:

```
D:\>java ConsoleDemo
Login id: admin
Password:
Welcome!! Admin

D:\>java ConsoleDemo
Login id: admin
Password:
Invalid credentials
```

Figure 9.16: *Console class*

9.8 java.util.zip package

The JAR tool introduced in Java SE 6 was updated so that the timestamp of extracted files matched the archive time. The **`java.util.zip`** package consists of classes that can be used to compress and decompress files.

Some of the important classes are explained in the upcoming sections.

9.8.1 Deflater class

The **`Deflater`** class is used to compress data present in an input stream by using the ZLIB compression library.

Constructor:

- **`Deflater()`**: Creates a **`Deflater`** instance with the default compression level.

Listed below are some important methods of **`Deflater`** class:

- **`deflate(byte[] buffer)`**: Fills the output buffer with compressed data and returns the actual size of compressed data.

- **deflate(byte[] buffer, int offset, int len)**: Fills the output buffer with compressed data from the given offset and the total number of bytes. It returns the actual size of compressed data.
- **setInput(byte[] buffer)**: Sets the input data present in the buffer for compression.
- **setInput(byte[] buffer, int offset, int len)**: Sets the input data present in the buffer for compression from the given offset to the number of bytes.
- **finish()**: Indicates that the compression should end with the current contents of the input buffer.
- **end()**: Closes the compressor and discards the unprocessed input.

The following code demonstrates the use of **Deflater** class:

```
import java.util.zip.Deflater;
public class DeflaterDemo {
  public static void main(String[] args) {
    try {
      // Convert string to bytes
      String str = "Compressing data by using Deflater class";
      byte[] strInput = str.getBytes("UTF-8");
      byte[] strOutput = new byte[100];
      Deflater deflater = new Deflater();
      deflater.setInput(strInput);
      deflater.finish();
      // Compress the bytes
      int length = deflater.deflate(strOutput);
      System.out.println("Compressed Data Length:"+length);
    } catch (Exception e) {
      System.out.println("Error: " + e.getMessage());
    }
  }
}
```

9.8.2 Inflater class

The **Inflater** class decompresses the compressed data by using the ZLIB compression library.

Constructor:

- **Inflater()**: Creates an instance with the default compression level.

Listed below are some important methods of **Inflater** class:

- **inflate(byte[] buffer)**: Fills the output buffer with decompressed data and returns its actual size.
- **inflate(byte[] buffer, int offset, int len)**: Fills the output buffer with decompressed data from the specified offset and the maximum number of bytes.
- **setInput(byte[] buffer)**: Sets the input data in the buffer for decompression.
- **setInput(byte[] buffer, int offset, int len)**: Sets the input data in the buffer for decompression from the specified offset and the number of bytes.
- **end()**: Closes the decompressor.

The following code demonstrates the use of **Inflater** class:

```
import java.util.zip.Deflater;
import java.util.zip.Inflater;
public class InflaterDemo {
  public static void main(String[] args) {
    try {
      String input = "Example of Inflater";
      // Convert string to byte array
      byte[] inBuff = input.getBytes("UTF-8");
      // Compress the bytes
      byte[] outBuff = new byte[100];
      Deflater d1 = new Deflater();
      d1.setInput(inBuff);
      d1.finish();
      int len = d1.deflate(outBuff);
      System.out.println("Compressed data length: "+len);
      // Decompress the bytes
      Inflater i1 = new Inflater();
      i1.setInput(outBuff, 0, outBuff.length);
      byte[] inflated = new byte[100];
      int inflateLen = i1.inflate(inflated);
      i1.end();
      // Convert bytes to string
      String str = new String(inflated, 0, inflateLen, "UTF-8");
      System.out.println("Decompressed string is: " + str);
```

```
        } catch (Exception e) {
            System.out.println("Error:" + e.getMessage());
        }
    }
}
```

The following will be the output of the above code:

```
Compressed data length: 27
Decompressed string is: Example of Inflater
```

Figure 9.17: *Inflater class*

9.8.3 DeflaterInputStream class

The **DeflaterInputStream** class reads and compresses the source data from an input stream in the 'deflate' compression format.

Constructors:

- **DeflaterInputStream(InputStream in)**: Creates an input stream of bytes with a default compressor and buffer size.
- **DeflaterInputStream(InputStream in, Deflater defl)**: Creates an input stream with a default buffer size and the given compressor.
- **DeflaterInputStream(InputStream in, Deflater defl, int bufLen)**: Creates an input stream with the given buffer size and compressor.

Listed below are some important methods of **DeflaterInputStream** class:

- **read()**: Reads one byte of compressed data from an input stream.
- **read(byte[] buffer, int offset, int buffSize)**: Reads compressed data read into a byte array from the given offset and number of bytes.
- **close()**: Closes the input stream after discarding remaining uncompressed data.
- **available()**: Returns 0 after EOF is reached; else returns 1 every time.
- **long skip(long n)**: Skips and discards the specified amount of data from the input stream.

The following code demonstrates the use of **DeflaterInputStream** class:

```
import java.io.File;
import java.io.FileInputStream;
import java.io.FileNotFoundException;
import java.io.FileOutputStream;
import java.io.IOException;
```

```
import java.util.zip.DeflaterInputStream;
public class DeflaterInputStreamDemo {
  public static byte[] expandBuffer(byte[] temp) {
    byte[] temp1 = temp;
    temp = new byte[temp.length + 1];
    // backup the data
    for (int i = 0; i < temp1.length; i++) {
      temp[i] = temp1[i];
    }
    return temp;
  }
  public static void main(String args[]) throws IOException {
    FileOutputStream fos = null;
    try {
      // set the input stream
      File f1 = new File("D:/Demos/Read.txt");
      FileInputStream fis = new FileInputStream(f1);
      DeflaterInputStream dis = new DeflaterInputStream(fis);
      // byte array to store deflated data
      byte inBuff[] = new byte[0];
      int index = -1;
      // read data from the file
      int read = 0;
      while ((read = dis.read()) != -1) {
        inBuff = expandBuffer(inBuff);
        inBuff[++index] = (byte) read;
      }
      // write compressed data to a file
      fos = new FileOutputStream("D:/Demos/DeflatedFile.txt");
      fos.write(inBuff, 0, inBuff.length);
      System.out.println("Compressed data written to file.");
      fos.close();
      System.out.println("Compressed data size: " + inBuff.length);
```

```
    } catch (FileNotFoundException e) {
      System.out.println("Error: " + e.getMessage());
    }
  }
}
```

The following will be the output of the above program:

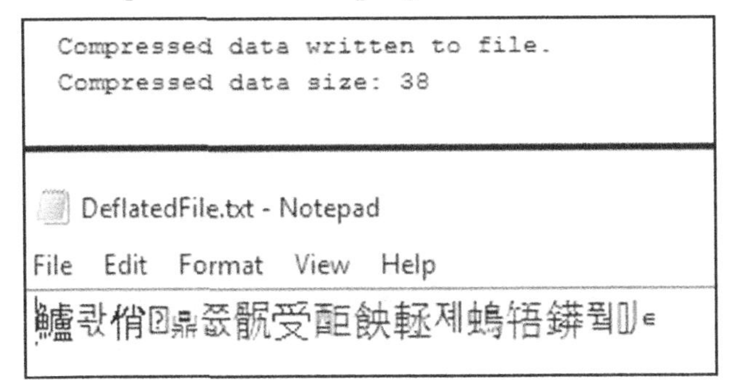

Figure 9.18: DeflaterInputStream class

9.8.4 DeflaterOutputStream class

The **DeflaterOutputStream** class reads and compresses the source data in the *deflate* compression format. Later, it writes the compressed data to an output stream. It is also a base class for compression classes like **GZIPOutputStream** and **ZipOutputStream**.

Constructor:

- **DeflaterOutputStream(OutputStream in)**: Creates an output stream with the default compressor and buffer size.

Listed below are the important methods of **DeflaterOutputStream** class:

- **write(int buffer)**: Writes a byte of compressed data to the output stream.
- **write(byte[] buffer, int offset, int buffSize)**: Writes an array of bytes of compressed data to the output stream from offset to the specified size.
- **deflate()**: Writes the next block of compressed data to the output stream.
- **close()**: Closes the output stream after writing the remaining compressed data.
- **finish()**: Completes the writing of compressed data to the output stream without closing it.

The following code demonstrates the use of **DeflaterOutputStream** class:

```
import java.io.File;
import java.io.FileInputStream;
```

```
import java.io.FileOutputStream;
import java.util.zip.DeflaterOutputStream;
public class DeflaterOutputStreamDemo {
  public static void main(String args[]) {
    try {
      // set the input stream
      File f1 = new File("D:/Demos/Read.txt");
      FileInputStream fin = new FileInputStream(f1);
      System.out.println("Original file size: " + f1.length());
      // set the output stream
      File fout = new File("D:/Demos/DeflatedData.txt");
      FileOutputStream fos = new FileOutputStream(fout);
      DeflaterOutputStream defOs = new DeflaterOutputStream(fos);
      // Read the data and write the
      // compressed data to output file
      int data = 0;
      while ((data = fin.read()) != -1) {
        defOs.write(data);
      }
      defOs.close();
      fin.close();
      System.out.println("Compressed data length: " + fout.length());
    } catch (Exception e) {
      e.printStackTrace();
    }
  }
}
```

9.8.5 InflaterInputStream class

The **InflaterInputStream** class reads compressed data and decompresses it in the *deflate* compression format.

Constructor:

- **InflaterInputStream(InputStream in)**: Creates an input stream with a default decompressor and buffer size.

Listed below are some important methods of the **InflaterInputStream** class:

- **read()**: Reads one byte of decompressed data from the input stream
- **read(byte[] buffer, int offset, int buffSize)**: Reads decompressed data into a byte array from the given offset and of the given size.

The following code demonstrates the use of **InflaterInputStream** class:

```
import java.io.File;
import java.io.FileInputStream;
import java.io.FileOutputStream;
import java.io.IOException;
import java.util.zip.InflaterInputStream;
public class InflaterInputStreamDemo {
  public static void main(String args[]) {
    try {
      // set the output file
      File f1 = new File("D:/Demos/InflatedData.txt");
      // set the output stream
      FileOutputStream fout = new FileOutputStream(f1);
      // set the input stream to read the compressed data
      File f2 = new File("D:/Demos/DeflatedData.txt");
      FileInputStream fis = new FileInputStream(f2);
      InflaterInputStream iis = new InflaterInputStream(fis);
      System.out.println("Compressed file length: " + f2.length());
      // Decompress the file to original size
      // and write the decompressed data to the output file
      int read = 0;
      while ((read = iis.read()) != -1) {
        fout.write(read);
      }
      fout.close();
      System.out.println("Decompressed file size: " + f1.length());
    } catch (IOException e) {
      System.out.println("Error: "+e.getMessage());
    }
  }
}
```

The compressed data is read from the **DeflatedData.txt** file. It is then decompressed by the **InflaterInputStream** and written to the **InflatedData.txt** file. The following will be the output of the above code:

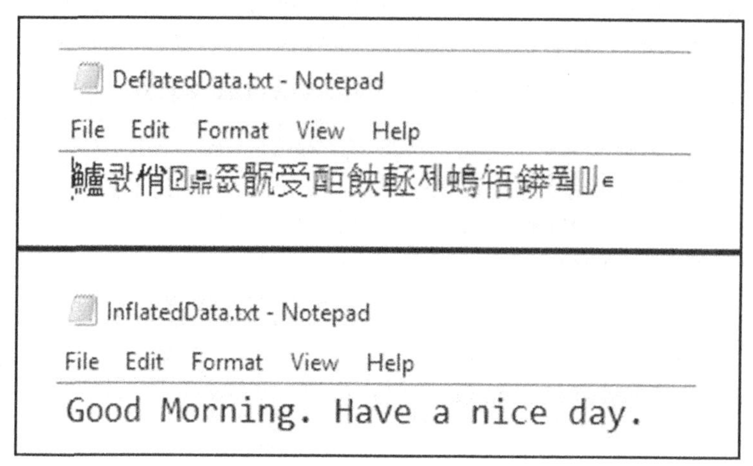

Figure 9.19: InflaterInputStream class

9.8.6 InflaterOutputStream class

The **InflaterOutputStream** class reads the compressed data and decompresses it in the deflate compression format. Later, the decompressed data is written to an output stream.

Constructor:

- **InflaterOutputStream(OutputStream out)**: Creates an output stream with the default decompressor and buffer size.

Listed below are the important methods:

- **write(int buffer)**: Write one byte of decompressed data to the output stream.
- **write(byte[] buffer, int offset, int buffSize)**: Writes an array of bytes to the output stream from the given offset and the size.

The following code demonstrates the use of **InflaterOutputStream** class:

```
import java.io.File;
import java.io.FileInputStream;
import java.io.FileOutputStream;
import java.io.IOException;
import java.util.zip.InflaterOutputStream;
public class InflaterOutputStreamDemo {
  public static void main(String args[]) {
```

```
    try {
      // set the input stream
      File f1 = new File("D:/Demos/DeflatedData.txt");
      FileInputStream fis = new FileInputStream(f1);
      // set the output stream
      File f2 = new File("D:/Demos/InflatedData1.txt");
      FileOutputStream fos = new FileOutputStream(f2);
      InflaterOutputStream ios = new InflaterOutputStream(fos);
      System.out.println("Compressed file size: " + f1.length());
      // Read compressed data and write
      // decompressed data to the output file
      int read = 0;
      while ((read = fis.read()) != -1) {
        ios.write(read);
      }
      ios.close();
      System.out.println("Decompressed file size: " + f2.length());
    } catch (IOException e) {
      System.out.println("Error: " + e.getMessage());
    }
  }
}
```

The following will be the output of the above code:

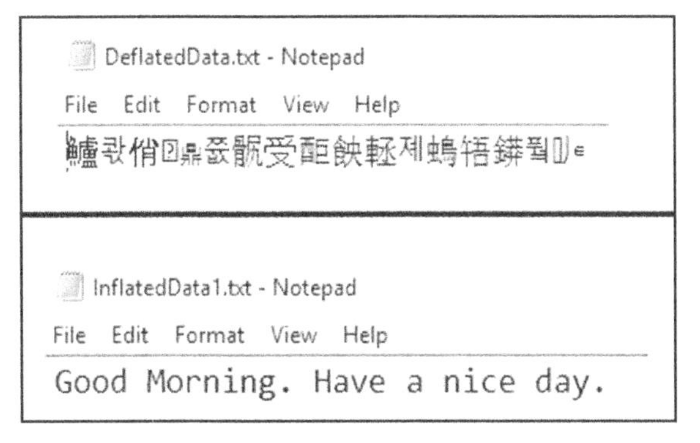

Figure 9.20: InflaterOutputStream class

Java introduced the new **java.nio.file** package to access files easily.

9.9 java.nio package

The **java.nio** package was introduced with J2SE 1.4. NIO stands for New Input/Output. Java SE 7 introduced NIO.2, which has the same objective as NIO, that is, to improve the I/O operations in application development. NIO's ability to improve performance depends on the OS, Data, Mass storage, JVM, and host virtualization. The **java.nio** package defines buffers that act as containers for data.

Listed below are the important features of the NIO APIs:

- **Charsets, decoders, and encoders**: Translate the data between bytes and Unicode characters. The **java.nio.charset** package defines the charset API. It is more flexible than **getBytes()** method, with better performance and easier implementation.
- **Buffers**: Act as containers for data and are used by all NIO APIs. The buffer classes are defined in the **java.nio** package.
- **Channels**: Represent connections to entities that are capable of performing I/O operations. These are abstract files and sockets and support asynchronous I/O.
- **Selectors and Selection Keys**: Define a multiplexed and non-blocking I/O together with selectable channels.

Note: In the case of non-blocking I/O, the I/O operations are event-based. In case of an I/O event, a selector is defined to manage the event, and it wakes up and executes. The channel and selector APIs are defined in the java.nio.channels package.

The **java.nio.file** package and **java.nio.file.attribute** package support file I/O and help to access the default file system. A file system stores and organizes files on storage media such as hard drives. Each file has a path within the file system and can be easily accessed:

- **File systems**: Generally, in a file system, files are stored in a hierarchy with a root node under which other subdirectories and files are created at different levels. There may be more than one root directory and different characteristics for path separators. Files can be accessed by the relative or absolute path. The **java.nio.file.Path** objects in **NIO.2** represent the relative or absolute location of a file or directory. Before JDK 7, files were represented by the **java.io.File** class.
- **Path**: A path identifies the location of a file in the file system starting from the root node. Some OS supports a single root node, such as Solaris, which is separated by a slash '**/**'. Some OS, such as Windows, supports multiple root nodes, each of which maps to a volume, such as **E:**. Each file system uses a different path separator (delimiter) that separates the directory names. For example, Solaris uses a forward slash (**/**), and MS Windows uses a backslash (****).

  Example of path in MS Windows: **C:\user\demos\datafile**

  Example of path in Solaris: **/home/user/demos/datafile**

  - **Absolute path**: Includes the entire directory list from the root node to the file or directory.

For example. **`/home/user/demos/datafile`**

- o **Relative path**: This does not include the entire directory list of the path.

For example. **`user/demos/datafile`**

- **Files**: The new packages and classes included in **`NIO.2`** to access files are as follows:
  - o **`java.nio.file.Path`**: Uses a system-dependent path to locate a file or a directory.
  - o **`Java.nio.file.Files`**: Uses a **`Path`** object to perform operations on files and directories.
  - o **`java.nio.file.FileSystem`**: Provides an interface to a file system and helps to create a **`Path`** object as well as other objects to access a file system.

  With **`java.io.File`**, the methods for path manipulation were in the same package as the methods for reading and writing files. With **`NIO.2`**, these have been separated in the **`Path`** interface and **`Files`** class, respectively. The **`Path`** interface creates and controls the paths while the **`Files`** class performs operations on files.
- **Symbolic links**: A symbolic link or symlink is a reference to another file, also called the target. For example, a shortcut to a file in Windows. Operations on symbolic links are redirected to the target of the link automatically. Read / write operations on a symbolic link are equivalent to read / write on a file or directory. However, deleting or renaming a symbolic link does not affect the target file.

9.9.1 Path interface

The **`java.nio.file.Path`** interface object is used to locate and manipulate a file in a file system. A path consists of directory and file names separated by a delimiter. An empty path is one that has only one element name.

Listed below are some important methods of **`Path`** interface:

- **Methods to access the elements of a path**: **`getRoot()`**, **`getParent()`**, **`subpath()`**, **`getFileName()`**.
- **Methods to combine paths**: **`resolve()`**, **`resolveSibling()`**.
- **Methods to construct a relative path between two paths**: **`relativize()`**.
- **Methods to compare and test paths**: **`startsWith()`**, **`endsWith()`**.

`Path` objects are immutable and cannot be changed once created. Another static and final class of **`java.nio.file`** package is the **`Paths`** class which consists of only static methods that return a **`Path`** object from a path string or URI.

The following code demonstrates the use of **`Path`** interface:

```
import java.nio.file.Path;
import java.nio.file.Paths;
public class PathsDemo {
  public static void main(String[] args) {
```

```
    Path p = Paths.get("D:/Demos/File.txt");
    System.out.println("File Name: " + p.getFileName());
    System.out.println("Parent: " + p.getParent());
    System.out.println("Name Count:" + p.getNameCount());
    System.out.println("Root Directory:" + p.getRoot());
    System.out.print("Is Absolute? ");
    boolean ans = p.isAbsolute();
    if (ans == true) {
      System.out.println("Yes");
    } else {
      System.out.println("No");
    }
    //obtain a portion of the path
    System.out.println("Subpath:" + p.subpath(0, 2));
    //combine two paths
    Path p1 = Paths.get("D:/Demos/");
    System.out.println("Combined path: " + p1.resolve("File.txt"));
    //construct a path from one location of a file system
    // to another location
    Path p2 = Paths.get("user");
    Path p3 = Paths.get("home");
    Path pNew = p2.relativize(p3);
    System.out.println("New path:" + pNew);
  }
}
```

The following will be the output of the above code:

```
File Name: File.txt
Parent: D:\Demos
Name Count:2
Root Directory:D:\
Is Absolute? Yes
Subpath:Demos\File.txt
Combined path: D:\Demos\File.txt
New path:..\home
```

Figure 9.21: *Path interface*

9.9.2 Files class

File operations are performed by the static methods of the **java.nio.file.Files** class for the **Path** objects. The different file operations are explained in the below sections:

9.9.2.1 List the contents of a directory

This is done by using the **DirectoryStream** class. It allows iterating over all the directories and files from any **Path** directory. The **DirectoryIteratorException** is thrown if an I/O error is encountered while iterating over the entries in the specified directory, and **PatternSyntaxException** is thrown if the pattern is invalid.

The following code demonstrates the use of **DirectoryStream** class to iterate:

```
import java.io.IOException;
import java.nio.file.DirectoryIteratorException;
import java.nio.file.DirectoryStream;
import java.nio.file.Files;
import java.nio.file.Path;
import java.nio.file.Paths;
import java.util.Iterator;
public class ListDir {
  public static void main(String[] args) {
    Path p = Paths.get("D:/Demos");
    try (DirectoryStream<Path> ds = Files.newDirectoryStream(p, "*.txt")) {
      for (Iterator<Path> itr = ds.iterator(); itr.hasNext();) {
        Path p1 = itr.next();
        System.out.println(p1.getFileName());
      }
    } catch (IOException | DirectoryIteratorException e) {
      System.err.println(e.getMessage());
    }
  }
}
```

The following will be the output of the above code:

```
DeflatedData.txt
DeflatedFile.txt
File1.txt
File2.txt
InflatedData.txt
InflatedData1.txt
Out1.txt
Out2.txt
PwOut.txt
Read.txt
Student.txt
Write.txt
Write1.txt
```

Figure 9.22: DirectoryStream class

9.9.2.2 Create directories and files

The **createDirectory(Path dir)** method is used to create a new directory. The **createDirectories()** method can be used to create a top-to-bottom hierarchy of directories. For example, to create a directory hierarchy, use the **createDirectories()** method:

```
Files.createDirectories(Paths.get("D:/Demos/dir/sample"));
```

The directory '**dir**' will be created within **Demos,** and the sample directory will be created within dir. Similarly, to create a file, use the **createFile()** method as shown below:

```
Files.createFile(Path dir)
```

9.9.2.3 Check the existence of a file or directory

To check if a path exists, use the below method of **Files** class:

- **exists(Path, LinkOption...opt)**: Checks if the given file exists. By default, it uses symbolic links.
- **notExists(Path, LinkOption...)**: Checks if the file does not exist.

The existence of the file cannot be verified if both **exists()** and **notExists()** return false. In that case, the file's status is unknown. This happens when the program does not have access to the file.

The **isReadable(Path)**, **isWritable(Path)**, and **isExecutable(Path)** methods can be used to check if the program can access a file.

For example:

```
Path file = ...;

boolean isRegularExecutableFile = Files.isRegularFile(file) & Files.isReadable(file)
& Files.isExecutable(file);
```

Note: These tests may not give reliable results.

When a system uses symbolic links, it may locate the same file through two different paths. In such cases, the **isSameFile(Path, Path)** method can be used to compare two paths and verify if they lead to the same file on the file system. For example,

```
Path p1 = ...;
Path p2 = ...;
if (Files.isSameFile(p1, p2)) {
…
}
```

9.9.2.4 Read and write operation on files

The **readAllBytes** or **readAllLines** methods are used to read files.

For example:

```
Path p1 = ….;
byte[] data;
data = Files.readAllBytes(p1);
```

To write files, use the below methods:

- **write(Path p, byte[] b, OpenOption… options)**: Writes bytes to a file. Here, **p** indicates the path to the file, **b** is the byte array that is to be written, and options indicate the mode of opening the file. It throws **IOException**, **UnsupportedOperationException**, and **SecurityException**.

  Listed below are the standard values of **OpenOptions**:

  - **WRITE**: Opens the file for write access
  - **APPEND**: Appends data to the end of the file. It is used with **WRITE** or **CREATE**
  - **TRUNCATE _ EXISTING**: Truncates the file
  - **CREATE _ NEW**: Creates a new file
  - **CREATE**: Creates a new file if the file does not exist or opens the file
  - **DELETE _ ON _ CLOSE**: Deletes the file when the stream closes

- **write (Path p, Iterable<extends CharSequence> lines, CharSet ch, OpenOption… options)**: Writes lines of text to a file. Here, **p** indicates the path to the file, 'lines' specifies an object to iterate over the char sequences, **ch** specifies the charset to be used for encoding, and 'options' indicates the mode of opening the file.

  For example:

  ```
  Path p1 = ...;
  byte[] data = ...;
  Files.write(p1, data);
  ```

Note: The java.nio.file package supports channel I/O, which moves data in buffers and bypasses certain layers that hinder stream I/O.

The **newBufferedWriter(Path, Charset, OpenOption...)** method is used to write to a file using a **BufferedWriter**. The **newBufferedReader(Path, Charset)** method opens a file for reading and returns a **BufferedReader** object that allows reading from a file efficiently.

The following code demonstrates the use of buffered Stream I/O to write and read a file:

```
import java.io.BufferedReader;
import java.io.BufferedWriter;
import java.io.IOException;
import java.nio.charset.Charset;
import java.nio.file.Files;
import java.nio.file.Path;
import java.nio.file.Paths;
public class ReadWriteFiles {
  public static void main(String[] args) {
    Charset c = Charset.forName("US-ASCII");
    String str = "Example of Read Write by using Files class";
    Path p1 = Paths.get("D:/Demos/ReadWrite.txt");
    try {
      BufferedWriter bw = Files.newBufferedWriter(p1, c);
      // write to file
      bw.write(str, 0, str.length());
      bw.close();
      String strRead = null;
      // read from file
      BufferedReader br = Files.newBufferedReader(p1, c);
      while ((strRead = br.readLine()) != null) {
        System.out.println(strRead);
      }
      br.close();
    } catch (IOException e) {
      System.out.println("Error: " + e.getMessage());
    }
  }
}
```

The **newBufferedWriter()** method creates a file encoded in "**US-ASCII**" and the **newBufferdReader()** method reads from the file.

9.9.2.5 Copy a file or directory

The **copy(Path, Path, CopyOption...)** method can be used to copy a file or directory. Listed below are some important points for copying:

- The **REPLACE _ EXISTING** option should be specified if the target file already exists, else the copy operation will fail.
- The files within a directory will not be copied while copying a directory.
- For copying a symbolic link only, use the **NOFOLLOW_LINKS** or **REPLACE_EXISTING** option; else, when copying a symbolic link, the target of the link is copied.

Listed below are the standard options of the **copy()** method:

- **COPY _ ATTRIBUTES**: Copies the file attributes of a file to the target file.
- **NOFOLLOW _ LINKS**: Used when symbolic links are not to be followed. The target of the link is not copied.
- **REPLACE _ EXISTING**: Copies the file even if the target file exists. If the target is a symbolic link, the link is copied, and the target of the link is not copied. If the target is a non-empty directory, the copy fails.

For example:

```
import static java.nio.file.StandardCopyOption.*;

...

Files.copy(source, target, REPLACE_EXISTING);
```

Listed below are methods of the **Files** class to copy between a file and a stream. Following are such methods:

- **copy(InputStream in, Path file, CopyOptions... options)**: Copies all bytes from an input stream to a file. Here, 'options' specifies how the copy should be performed. The exceptions thrown include **IOException**, **SecurityException**, **FileAlreadyExistsException**, **DirectoryNotEmptyException**, and **UnSupportedOperationException**.
- **copy(Path file, OutputStream out)**: Copies all bytes from a file to an output stream. The exceptions thrown include **IOException** and **SecurityException**.

The following code demonstrates the use of **copy()** method to copy an input stream data to a file:

```
import java.io.IOException;

import java.io.InputStream;

import java.net.MalformedURLException;

import java.net.URI;
```

```
import java.nio.file.Files;
import java.nio.file.Path;
import java.nio.file.Paths;
import java.nio.file.StandardCopyOption;
public class CopyDemo {
  public static void main(String[] args) {
    Path p1 = Paths.get("D:/Demos/copy.txt");
    URI uri1 = URI.create("https://www.yahoo.com/");
    try (InputStream is = uri1.toURL().openStream()) {
      //copy input stream to a file
      Files.copy(is, p1, StandardCopyOption.REPLACE_EXISTING);
    } catch (final MalformedURLException e) {
      System.out.println("Error: " + e.getMessage());
    } catch (IOException e) {
      System.out.println("Error: " + e.getMessage());
    }
  }
}
```

The data from the web page is read by the input stream and copied to the file. The following will be the output:

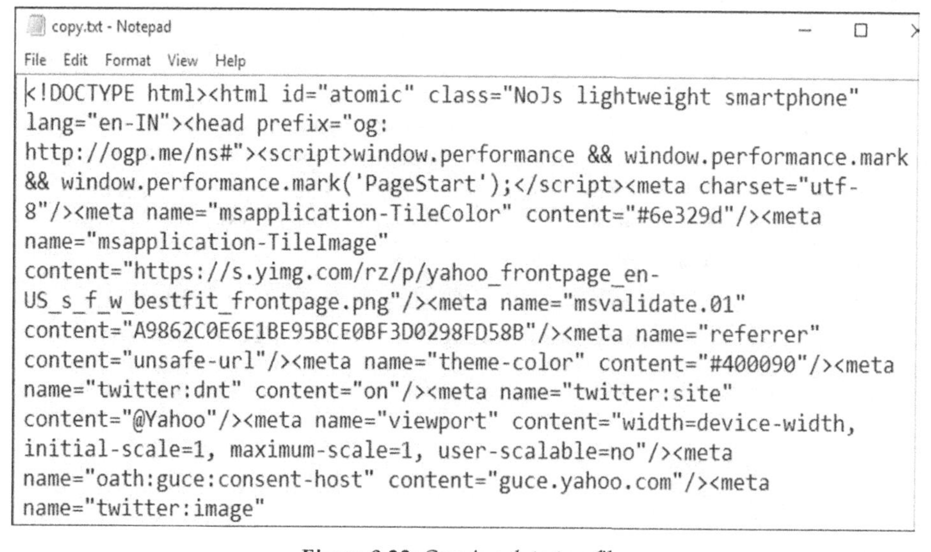

Figure 9.23: Copying data to a file

9.9.2.6 Move a file or directory

The move operation can be done by using **move(Path, Path, CopyOption...)** method. Use the **REPLACE_EXISTING** option if the target file exists, else, the move will fail. A non-empty directory is moved without moving the contents.

Syntax:

```
Files.move(Path source, Path target, CopyOption... options)
```

Here, 'source' is the path to the file to move, 'target' is the path to the target file, and 'options' indicates how the move should be performed.

Listed below are the common **CopyOption** enums:

- **REPLACE_EXISTING**: For a non-empty directory, it replaces the target file even when the target file exists. For a symbolic link, it replaces the symbolic link only, but the target of the link is not replaced.
- **ATOMIC_MOVE**: Moves the files and directories as an atomic file system operation. This option is used to move a file into a directory. If the file system does not support the atomic move, an exception is raised.

Important points for moving files or directories:

- If the target path is an empty directory, the move will succeed if **REPLACE_EXISTING** option is used.
- If the target directory does not exist, then the move will succeed.
- If the target path is an anon-empty directory, then **DirectoryNotEmptyException** is raised.

The following code demonstrates the use of **Files.move()** method:

```
import java.io.IOException;
import java.nio.file.Files;
import java.nio.file.Path;
import java.nio.file.Paths;
import java.nio.file.StandardCopyOption;
public class MoveDemo {
  public static void main(String[] args) {
    Path source = Paths.get("D:/Demos/abc.txt");
    Path destination = Paths.get("F:/Moved/abc.txt");
    try {
      Files.move(source, destination, StandardCopyOption.REPLACE_EXISTING);
      System.out.println("File moved");
```

```
    } catch (IOException e) {
      System.out.println("Move Failed: "+e.getMessage());
      e.printStackTrace();
    }
  }
}
```

9.9.2.7 Delete a file or directory

To delete a file, directory, or link, use the **delete(Path)** method. Delete fails on a non-empty directory, and an exception is raised if the deletion fails. The following code demonstrates the use of **delete** method:

```
import java.nio.file.DirectoryNotEmptyException;
import java.nio.file.Files;
import java.nio.file.NoSuchFileException;
import java.nio.file.Path;
import java.nio.file.Paths;
public class DeleteDemo {
  public static void main(String[] args) {
    try {
      Path p1 = Paths.get("F:/Moved/abc.txt");
      Files.delete(p1);
    } catch (NoSuchFileException ex) {
      System.out.println("No such file or directory: " + ex.getMessage());
    } catch (DirectoryNotEmptyException e) {
      System.out.println("Directory not empty: " + e.getMessage());
    } catch (Exception e) {
      System.err.println("Error: " + e.getMessage());
    }
  }
}
```

The **deleteIfExists(Path)** method deletes the file. In addition, if the file does not exist, no exception is thrown. This is useful when there are multiple threads to delete files.

9.9.2.8 Randomly access a file

The **SeekableByteChannel** interface allows accessing files non-sequentially or randomly. Steps involved in random access include:

- Open the file.
- Seek a specific location.
- Read / Write the file.

Listed below are the important methods of the interface:

- **position()**: Returns the channel's current position.
- **position(long)**: Sets the channel's position as specified by the argument.
- **read(ByteBuffer)**: Reads bytes into the buffer from the channel.
- **write(ByteBuffer)**: Writes bytes from the buffer to the channel.
- **truncate(long)**: Truncates the file connected to the channel. It can also truncate any other entity.

To read or write files with Channel I/O, the **Path.newByteChannel()** method is used to return an instance of **SeekableByteChannel**. For advanced features like locking a region of the file, cast the channel to a **FileChannel**.

Note: Buffers are used along with channels. Buffers act as the source or target of the I/O data transfers that take place through Channels.

The following code demonstrates the use of **FileChannel** for random access:

```
import java.io.IOException;
import java.nio.ByteBuffer;
import java.nio.channels.FileChannel;
import java.nio.file.Path;
import java.nio.file.Paths;
import static java.nio.file.StandardOpenOption.*;
public class RandomAccessDemo {
  public static void main(String[] args) {
    String str = "This is random access example\n";
    byte buff[] = str.getBytes();
    ByteBuffer bufAlloc = ByteBuffer.allocate(10);
    //store the data of the string into the byte buffer
    ByteBuffer bufWrap = ByteBuffer.wrap(buff);
    // set the path of the file to read/write
    Path p1 = Paths.get("D:/Demos/Random.txt");
```

```
    //create a new file if does not exist
    try (FileChannel fc = (FileChannel.open(p1, CREATE, READ, WRITE))) {
      //read the first 10 bytes of the file
      int readC;
      do {
        readC = fc.read(bufAlloc);
        // display the number of characters read
        System.out.println("Total characters read: " + readC);
      } while (readC != -1 && bufAlloc.hasRemaining());
      // write at the beginning of the file.
      fc.position(0);
      while (bufWrap.hasRemaining()) {
        fc.write(bufWrap);
      }
      bufWrap.rewind();
      // Move to the end of the file and
      //copy the first 10 bytes
      long length = fc.size();
      fc.position(length - 1);
      //flip the buffer
      bufAlloc.flip();
      while (bufAlloc.hasRemaining()) {
        fc.write(bufAlloc);
      }
      while (bufWrap.hasRemaining()) {
        fc.write(bufWrap);
      }
    } catch (IOException ex) {
      System.out.println("Error" + ex.getMessage());
    }
  }
}
```

The following will be the output of the above code:

Random.txt - Notepad

File Edit Format View Help

```
This is random access exampleeJava is a This is random access example
```

Figure 9.24: Random access

9.9.3 FileSystem class

The **FileSystem** class is used to access files and other objects in the file system. A file system could have a single hierarchy with a top-level root directory or several distinct file hierarchies, each with its top-level root directory. A **FileSystem** may have read-only or read-write access. A read-only file system throws **ReadOnlyFileSystemException**.

Listed below are some important methods of the class:

- **getUserPrincipalLookupService()**: Returns the **UserPrincipalLookupService** to lookup users or groups by name.
- **newWatchService()**: Creates a **WatchService** that watches objects for changes.
- **getPath()**: Converts a system-dependent path string and returns a Path object to locate and access a file.
- **getPathMatcher()**: Creates a **PathMatcher** that performs match operations on paths.
- **getFileStores()**: Returns an iterator over the underlying file-stores.
- **getRootDirectories()**: Used to iterate over the root directories in the file system.
- **close()**: Closes a file system. Accessing objects in a closed file system will throw **ClosedFileSystemException**.

9.9.4 Watch service

A watch service allows the monitoring of registered objects for events and changes. For example, a file manager can use a watch service to monitor the creation/deletion of files in a directory and update the files list accordingly. It can be used concurrently by multiple consumers.

Following steps explain registering an object to a watch service:

- Invoke the **register()** method to register a **Watchable** object with a watch service.
- The **register()** method returns a **WatchKey** to represent the registration.
- Signal or queue the key to the watch service when a change or event for an object occurs.

- Whenever `poll()` or `take()` methods are invoked, consumers can retrieve the key and process the events.
- After processing the events, the `reset()` method of the key is invoked by the consumer to reset the key.
- Next, the key is signaled and re-queued with other events.

Note: To ensure that only a single consumer processes events at a time, invoke the key's reset() method only after its events are processed. Invoke the close() method to close the service. When any thread is waiting to retrieve the key, a ClosedWatchServiceException is thrown, and the service is closed.

The following steps explain the cancellation of registration with a watch service:

- Invoke the key's `cancel()` method to cancel the registration with a watch service.
- It remains in the queue until it is retrieved.

An indication from an event for a file that is modified in a watched directory does not assure the completion of the program that modified it. The file might be updated by other programs. Hence, it is necessary to coordinate the access of a file by multiple programs and lock the file when it is accessed by one program. This can be achieved by using the methods of `FileChannel` class.

Listed below are the methods of `WatchService` interface:

- `WatchKey poll(long timeout, TimeUnit unit)`: Retrieves and removes the next watch key. This can wait until the specified wait time.
- `WatchKey take()`: Retrieves and removes the next `Watchkey`. This waits if none are yet present.
- `void close()`: Closes the watch service.

9.9.5 PathMatcher interface

To search a file in a file system, `PathMatcher` interface can be used. It provides the match method to check if a `Path` object matches the given string.

Syntax:

```
syntax: pattern
Here, syntax: can be glob or regex
```

The term glob is used to find pathnames that match the specified pattern as per rules of Unix shell.

Listed below are some common patterns:

- `.*.{java,class}`: Identifies a file with an extension, either `.java` or `.class`.
- `Client.?`: Identifies a file name beginning with Client and a single character extension.

- `C:\\*`: Identifies a path beginning with `c:\` followed by any number of characters. For example. `c:\test` or `c:\Java` on the Windows platform.
- `*.java`: Identifies a file name with `.java` extension.
- `*.*`: Identifies a file containing a dot.

Listed below are some rules for interpreting the glob patterns:

- `*`- Indicates a single or zero character.
- `**` -Indicates zero or more characters.
- `?` - Indicates exactly one character.
- `\` - Indicates escape characters that can be used as a special character.
- `[]` - Indicates a single character of a name within the square brackets. For example, [abc] matches a, b, or c.
- `-`: Hyphen indicates a range. For example: [a-g]
- `*, ?` and `\` characters within a bracket match themselves.

Note: The leading period in a file name is considered a regular character while performing a match operation.

- `{}` characters indicate a group of subpatterns where the group matches if any subpattern in the group matches.

The comma is used for separating the subpattern, and groups cannot be nested.

To search a file by recursively traversing a directory, use the match method to check the **`Path`** matches the specified string. To retrieve the **`PathMather`** instance, use the factory methods of **`FileSystems`** class. To traverse a file tree, implement the **`FileVisitor`** interface, which provides methods representing the various situations of a traversal process as under:

- **`preVisitDirectory()`**: Invoked before visiting a directory
- **`postVisitDirectory()`**: Invoked after all entries in a directory are visited
- **`visitFile()`**: Invoked when a file is visited
- **`visitFileFailed()`**: Invoked when a file cannot be accessed

The **`SimpleFileVisitor`** class is an implementation of the **`FileVisitor`** interface. It can be further extended, and only the required methods can be overridden. The following code demonstrates the use of **`PathMatcher`** and the **`SimpleFileVisitor`** class:

```
import java.io.IOException;

import java.nio.file.FileSystems;

import java.nio.file.FileVisitResult;

import static java.nio.file.FileVisitResult.CONTINUE;

import java.nio.file.Files;

import java.nio.file.Path;
```

```
import java.nio.file.PathMatcher;
import java.nio.file.Paths;
import java.nio.file.SimpleFileVisitor;
import java.nio.file.attribute.BasicFileAttributes;
public class SearchFile {
  public static void main(String[] args) throws IOException {
    Path p1;
    p1 = Paths.get("D:/Test");
   PathMatcher pm1 = FileSystems.getDefault().getPathMatcher("glob:" + "*.txt");
    FindFile f1 = new FindFile(p1, pm1);
    try {
      Files.walkFileTree(p1, f1);
      f1.finished();
    } catch (IOException ex) {
      System.out.println(ex);
    }
  }
}
class FindFile extends SimpleFileVisitor<Path> {
  private final PathMatcher matcher;
  private int count;
  public FindFile(Path path, PathMatcher matcher) {
    this.matcher = matcher;
  }
  private void find(Path file) {
    Path pName = file.getFileName();
    // check for matching path
    if (pName != null && matcher.matches(pName)) {
      count++;
      System.out.println(file);
    }
  }
  void finished() {
```

```
    System.out.println("Matched: " + count);
  }
  @Override
  public FileVisitResult visitFile(Path file, BasicFileAttributes attr) {
    find(file);
    return CONTINUE;
  }
  // Pattern matching on each directory
  @Override
  public FileVisitResult preVisitDirectory(Path dir, BasicFileAttributes attrs)
{
    find(dir);
    return CONTINUE;
  }
  @Override
  public FileVisitResult visitFileFailed(Path file, IOException exc) {
    System.err.println(exc);
    return CONTINUE;
  }
}
```

The following will be the output:

```
D:\Test\File1.txt
D:\Test\File2.txt
D:\Test\InflatedData.txt
D:\Test\InflatedData1.txt
D:\Test\Out1.txt
D:\Test\Out2.txt
D:\Test\PwOut.txt
D:\Test\Random.txt
D:\Test\TestDir\Read.txt
D:\Test\TestDir\ReadWrite.txt
D:\Test\TestDir\Student.txt
D:\Test\Write.txt
D:\Test\Write1.txt
Matched: 13
```

Figure 9.25: *PathMatcher output*

Conclusion

In this chapter, you learnt that the operating system maintains file descriptors when the directories and files are accessed. The **DataInput** and **DataOutput** interfaces provide methods to convert binary data into Java primitive types and UTF-8 to strings and vice-versa, respectively. **FileInputStream** class allows reading bytes from a file. **ByteArrayInputStream** uses a buffer to store the bytes that are read from the stream. The **FilterInputStream** class transforms data along the way or provides additional functionality by using an input stream as its basic source of data. To implement serialization, Java provides the **java.io.Serializable** interface. **BufferedOutputStream** creates a buffer for an output stream which allows caching data into the buffer to improve performance while writing bytes. **Reader** class is used to read character streams. The **PrintWriter** class is mainly used to output character data to the console. The **Console** class simplifies the development of command-line applications. The **DeflaterInputStream** class reads and compresses the source data from an input stream in the 'deflate' compression format. The **java.nio** package was introduced with J2SE 1.4. NIO stands for New Input/Output. The **java.nio.file.Path** interface object is used to locate and manipulate a file in a file system. The **FileSystem** class is used to access files and other objects in the file system. To search a file in a file system, **PathMatcher** interface can be used.

In the next chapter, you will learn about Threads and JDBC.

Multiple choice questions

1. **The most important class for manipulating files on a file system directly is the ____ class.**
    a. `File`
    b. `InputStream`
    c. `PathMatcher`
    d. `WatchService`
2. **Identify the incorrect code.**
    a. `FileInputStream fis = new FileInputStream("File1.txt");`
    b. `FileInputStream fis = new File("File1.txt");`
    c. `File f = new File("/File1.txt"); FileInputStream fis = new FileInputStream(f);`
    d. None of these
3. **Consider the below partial code.**

    ```
    PrintWriter pw = new PrintWriter(System.out);
    pw.write("Welcome to the World of Java");
    ```

    What will the code do?

    a. Write the given statement to the system log.
    b. Write the given statement to a system file.

   c. Write the given statement to the console.
   d. Write the given statement to the output stream.

4. **The `Deflater` class is used to compress data present in an input stream by using the ZLIB compression library.**
   a. Inflater
   b. Deflater
   c. Zip
   d. All of these
5. **Consider the below partial code.**

   ```
   Files.copy(source, target, REPLACE_EXISTING);
   ```

   What will the copy option do?
   a. Copies the file even if the target file exists.
   b. Copies the file attributes of a file to the target file.
   c. Used when symbolic links are not to be followed.
   d. Creates a copy of the file.

Answers

1. a
2. b
3. c
4. b
5. a

Assignment

Create a Java program as per the below specifications:

- Create a menu-driven program called `FileManager` which displays a menu to the user with options to **Read, Write, List** files, and Exit the program.
- Based on the choice, the appropriate functionality should be executed.
- If the user selects Read, the program should ask for the full path of the file to be read. The contents of the file should be displayed on the console. (Hint: Use `FileReader`)
- If the user selects `Write`, the program should ask for the full path of the file to be written to. Next, it should ask for the text to be written. The text should be written to the file. (**Hint**: Use `PrintWriter`)
- If the user selects `List files`, the program should ask the full path of the directory whose files need to be listed. Next, it should ask for the file extension. For example txt, java, and so on.

- Based on the values entered, the files of that type should be listed.
- If the user selects `Exit`, the program should be terminated. **The program should display the menu recursively until the user selects Exit.**

The expected output is shown below:

```
Welcome to File Manager
1. Read a file
2. Write a file
3. List files
4. Exit
Select an option (1..4):
2
Enter file path
F:\\Demos\\test.txt
Enter text to be written:
Hello this is a test file
1. Read a file
2. Write a file
3. List files
4. Exit
Select an option (1..4):
1
Enter file path:
F:\\Demos\\test.txt
Hello this is a test file
1. Read a file
2. Write a file
3. List files
4. Exit
Select an option (1..4):
3
Enter directory path:
F:\\Demos
Enter file type eg. txt, java
txt
abc.txt
File1.txt
MyFile.txt
Test.txt
test1.txt
1. Read a file
2. Write a file
3. List files
4. Exit
Select an option (1..4):
4
BUILD SUCCESSFUL (total time: 52 seconds)
```

Figure 9.26: *Output of Read, Write, List and Exit options*

Join our book's Discord space

Join the book's Discord Workspace for Latest updates, Offers, Tech happenings around the world, New Release and Sessions with the Authors:

https://discord.bpbonline.com

CHAPTER 10
Threads and JDBC

Introduction

This chapter introduces threads and Thread class for creating and managing threads. It also explains about thread states, multithreading, concurrency, and deadlocks. Java provides the **Java Database Connectivity (JDBC)** API to connect a Java application to a database. You will learn to use JDBC interfaces to query databases and execute transactions.

Structure

In this chapter, we will go through the following topics:

- Threads
- Thread class
- Runnable interface
- Daemon threads
- Multithreading
- Thread synchronization
- Concurrent Collection APIs
- Atomic variables
- java.util.concurrent.locks package

- Executors and thread pools
- Java Database Connectivity (JDBC)
- DatabaseMetaData
- ResultSetMetaData
- Execute stored procedure with CallableStatement object
- Scrollable ResultSet
- Batch updates
- Transactions
- RowSet interface

Objectives

In this chapter you learn to create and manage threads, understand the thread states as well as work with multiple threads by using multithreading. You will also understand the concepts of concurrency and deadlocks. Further, you will learn about the **Java Database Connectivity (JDBC)** API and work with the JDBC interfaces to query databases.

10.1 Threads

In the context of Java programming, a thread is a path of execution of a program. For each program, there exists at least one thread created by the JVM, called the Main thread. It invokes the `main()` method at the start of the program. A thread runs independently with its own run-time resources. It is the smallest unit of execution for an application to perform a specific task. It is possible to execute multiple threads at a time to manage multiple tasks concurrently in an application.

Threads share CPU time and execute sequentially within a process. At a time, only one thread is active in a single-thread application. However, a multi-threaded application of multiple tasks can be executed simultaneously within one application. A thread can create child threads or sub-threads and if one thread is blocked, another thread can begin execution. Unlike processes, threads are dependent on one another and assist other threads in accomplishing a task.

Threads allow parallel processing of multiple tasks in applications such as scrolling multiple images, patterns, audio with images, and more. Java allows creating threads by extending the `Thread` class or implementing the `Runnable` interface.

10.1.1 Java thread states and lifecycle

A thread goes through different stages in its lifecycle as shown in *Figure 10.1*:

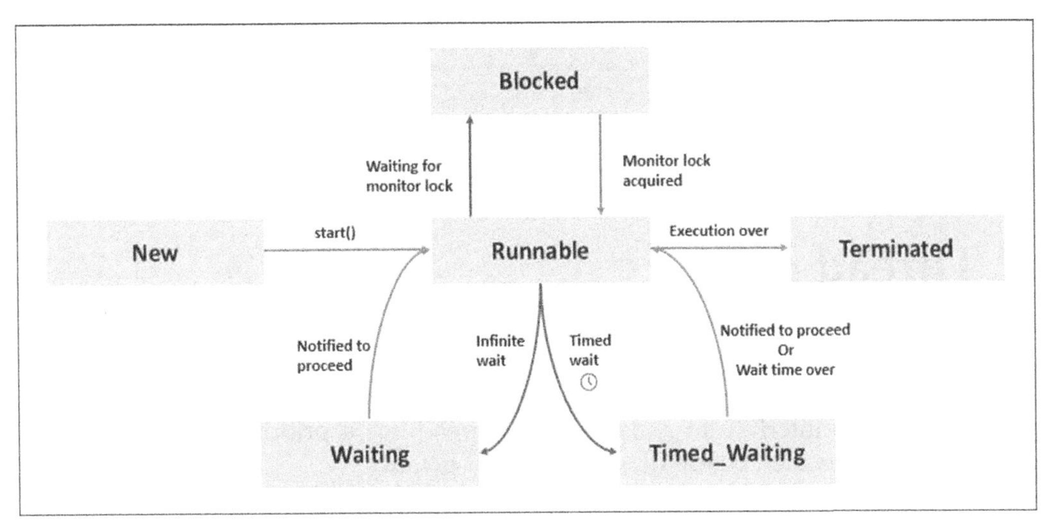

Figure 10.1: Stages of a thread's lifecycle

At a time, a thread can be in only one state.

Note: These states are virtual machine states and do not relate to any operating system thread states.

- **New:** A thread that has been newly created and not yet started, that is, not alive. An attempt to call any method before starting a thread will raise the `IllegalThreadStateException` exception:

```
Thread t = new Thread();
```

- **Runnable:** A thread enters the runnable state when the `start()` method is invoked on it. In this state, the thread is said to be executing in the JVM. Here, the thread is allocated all resources to run as it is eligible to run but may not be running based on its priority assigned by the scheduler. When it is running, it executes the instructions of the `run()` method:

```
ThreadClass t = new ThreadClass();
t.start();
```

- **Blocked:** A thread in the blocked state is alive but cannot run as it is waiting for a monitor lock on some resource. A call to `sleep()`, `wait()`, or `suspend()` methods put the thread in the blocked state.

Note: The monitor is an imaginary box to which only a single thread can have access at a time by acquiring a lock on the shared resource.

- **Waiting**: In this state, a thread waits indefinitely for another thread to perform a particular operation. To put the thread in the waiting state, the `wait()` method is called, and to bring it back to the runnable state, a call to `notify()` or `notifyAll()` methods is made.

- **Timed_Waiting:** In this state, a thread waits for another thread to perform an operation for a specific waiting time.
- **Terminated**: A thread that has completed the execution of `run()` method and exited is in this state. A terminated thread cannot go back to a runnable state. An attempt to call the `start()` method on a terminated thread will throw a run-time exception.

10.2 Thread class

The Thread class belongs to the `java.lang` package and is used to create and control threads. To create a group of threads, the `ThreadGroup` class is used by passing it as a parameter to the constructors of the `Thread` class. Another way of creating threads is by implementing the `java.lang.Runnable` interface in a class. Every thread has a priority and the threads with higher priority are executed before those with lower priority.

The JVM stops thread execution on invoking the `exit()` method or when all the daemon threads of a program have died. Listed below are the important constructors of the `Thread` class:

- `Thread()`: No argument/default constructor.
- `Thread(Runnable r)`: Creates a new T`hread object` whose `run()` method is invoked.
- `Thread(String name)`: Creates a new T`hread object` with the given name.
- `Thread(Runnable r, String name)`: Creates a new T`hread object` with the given name whose `run()` method is invoked.
- `Thread(ThreadGroup group, String threadName)`: Creates a new T`hread object` with the given name within the given thread group.
- `Thread(ThreadGroup group, Runnable r)`: Creates a new T`hread object` within the given `thread group` whose `run()` method is invoked.
- `Thread(ThreadGroup group, Runnable r, String name)`: Creates a new T`hread object` with the given name within the given `thread group`.

Listed below are some important methods of the `Thread` class:

- `static Thread currentThread()`: Returns a reference to the current thread object in execution.
- `static int activeCount()`: Returns the number of active threads in the program.
- `static boolean interrupted()`: Checks if the current thread has been interrupted.
- `boolean isAlive()`: Checks if this thread is alive.
- `boolean isInterrupted()`: Checks if this thread has been interrupted.
- `void join()`: Waits for this thread to die.
- `void setName(String name)`: Changes the name of this thread to the given name.
- `ThreadGroup getThreadGroup()`: Returns the thread group to which this thread belongs.

The following code demonstrates creation of new thread by extending a class from **java.lang. Thread** class:

```
public class ThreadClassDemo extends Thread {
  String threadName;
  public void run() {
    int num = 0;
    while (num <= 3) {
      //Display the number of active threads
      System.out.println("Active thread count:"+Thread.activeCount());
      //Displays the currently running thread
      threadName = Thread.currentThread().getName();
      num++;
      System.out.println("Current thread is "+threadName);
      if (threadName.equals("T1")) {
        System.out.println("This is Thread 1");
      } else {
        System.out.println("Unknown thread");
      }
    }
  }
  public static void main(String args[]) {
    ThreadClassDemo obj = new ThreadClassDemo();
    obj.setName("T1");
    //Checks if threads are alive
      System.out.println("Current thread is alive? "+Thread.currentThread().
isAlive());
    System.out.println("Thread T1 is alive? "+obj.isAlive());
    // invokes the start method on the thread object
    obj.start();
```

```
        System.out.println("Current thread is alive? "+Thread.currentThread().
isAlive());

    System.out.println("Thread T1 is alive? "+obj.isAlive());

  }

}
```

The output of the code is as shown in *Figure 10.2*:

```
Current thread is alive? true
Thread T1 is alive? false
Current thread is alive? true
Thread T1 is alive? true
Active thread count:2
Current thread is T1
This is Thread 1
Active thread count:2
Current thread is T1
This is Thread 1
Active thread count:2
Current thread is T1
This is Thread 1
Active thread count:2
Current thread is T1
This is Thread 1
```

Figure 10.2: *Thread created by using thread class*

10.2.1 Methods of the Thread class

The important **Thread** class methods for manipulating threads and their lifecycle are listed as follows:

- **getName()**: Helps to retrieve the name of the current thread.

  ```
  Thread t = Thread.currentThread();
  System.out.println("Name = " + t.getName());
  ```

- **start()**: Allocates system resources to a newly created thread object and executes its **run()** method. It brings a thread to the runnable state.

  ```
  NewThread t = new NewThread():
  t.start();
  ```

- **run()**: It executes the instructions for the current thread object. The **run()** method does not accept any arguments, does not return any value nor throws any exception:

  ```
  class Thread1 implements Runnable {
  . . .
  public void run() {
  ```

```
System.out.println("Executing run method.");
}
. . .
}
```

- `sleep()`: This method suspends current thread execution for a specific time specified in milliseconds or nanoseconds. This allows other threads to avail processor time for executing their tasks. It throws the **InterruptedException.**

Syntax:

```
void sleep(long millis)
```

For example,

```
try{
t1.sleep (10000);
}
catch (InterruptedException e)
{}
```

The thread has been put to sleep for 10000 milliseconds.

- `interrupt()`: This method interrupts thread execution before the task is completed. It raises **InterruptedException** if the thread is blocked by **wait()**, **join()**, or **sleep()** method.

10.2.2 Thread priority

Java allows setting a priority of thread to ensure that multiple threads in a program can share a resource to accomplish a task. The thread scheduler can determine the order of thread execution with the help of thread priority. All threads have the same priority by default. When a thread is created, it inherits the priority of the parent thread.

It is possible to set the priority of a thread by using the **setPriority()** method. The priority is specified as an integer ranging between, 1 to 10, where 10 is the highest and 1 is the lowest priority. The default priority is 5. Value out of the range raises the **IllegalArgumentException**. The **Thread** class also provides some static constants representing values 1, 5, and 10. These are **MIN_PRIORITY**, **NORM_PRIORITY**, and **MAX_PRIORITY** respectively. The priority of the main thread is 5, that is, **Thread.NORM_PRIORITY**.

The scheduler manages the thread execution with the help of thread priority. Usually, threads with higher priority are executed first.

10.2.3 Methods for thread priority

Java provides methods to assign and retrieve the priority to threads:

- **setPriority()**: This method is used to change the priority of a thread. A newly created thread inherits the priority from the parent thread. The **setPriority()** method changes the current priority by accepting an integer value ranging from 1 to 10. For example:

```
Thread t1 = new Thread("Worker thread");
t1.setPriority(6);
```

- **getPriority()**: This method is used to retrieve the current priority value of any thread. It returns the priority as an integer value. For example:

```
System.out.println("Thread priority is "+t1.getpriority());
```

The following code demonstrates the implementation of thread priority:

```
public class ThreadPriorityDemo {
  public static void main(String[] args) {
  System.out.println("Main thread started");
    One t1 = new One();
    Two t2 = new Two();
    Three t3 = new Three();
    t3.setPriority(Thread.MAX_PRIORITY);  // priority = 10
    t2.setPriority(t1.getPriority() + 1); // default priority + 1 = 6
    t1.setPriority(Thread.MIN_PRIORITY); // priority =1
    t1.start();
    t2.start();
    t3.start();
    try {
      t1.join();
      t2.join();
      t3.join();
    } catch (InterruptedException e) {
    }
  System.out.println("Main Thread Exited");
  }
}
class One extends Thread {
  @Override
```

```
  public void run() {
      System.out.println("Thread One Started with priority: "+ this.
getPriority());
    for (int num = 0; num < 5; num++) {
      System.out.println("\t value of num in Thread One: " + num);
    }
    System.out.println("Thread One Exited");
  }
}
class Two extends Thread {
  @Override
  public void run() {
      System.out.println("Thread Two started with priority: "+ this.
getPriority());
    for (int num = 0; num < 5; num++) {
      System.out.println("\tValue of num in Thread Two: " + num);
    }
    System.out.println("Thread Two Exited");
  }
}
class Three extends Thread {
  @Override
  public void run() {
   System.out.println("Thread Three started with priority: "+ this.
getPriority());
    for (int num = 0; num < 5; num++) {
      System.out.println("\tValue of num in Thread Three: " + num);
    }
    System.out.println("Thread Three Exited");
  }
}
```

The output of the code is as follows, in *Figure 10.3*:

```
Main thread started
Thread Three started with priority: 10
        Value of num in Thread Three: 0
        Value of num in Thread Three: 1
        Value of num in Thread Three: 2
        Value of num in Thread Three: 3
        Value of num in Thread Three: 4
Thread Three Exited
Thread Two started with priority: 6
        Value of num in Thread Two: 0
        Value of num in Thread Two: 1
        Value of num in Thread Two: 2
        Value of num in Thread Two: 3
        Value of num in Thread Two: 4
Thread Two Exited
Thread One Started with priority: 1
        value of num in Thread One: 0
        value of num in Thread One: 1
        value of num in Thread One: 2
        value of num in Thread One: 3
        value of num in Thread One: 4
Thread One Exited
Main Thread Exited
```

Figure 10.3: *Thread priority*

10.3 Runnable interface

The **Runnable** interface is another way of creating a thread. The implementing class must override the **run()** methods. By using the **Runnable** interface, the implementing class gets the flexibility to inherit another class if required.

Steps to create a new **Thread** using **Runnable** interface:

1. Declare a class and implement the **Runnable** interface.
2. Implement the **run()** method.
3. Instantiate the class.
4. Pass its object to the **Thread** class constructor.
5. Invoke the **start()** method on the thread.

The following code demonstrates the creation of a thread by implementing the **Runnable** interface:

```
public class RunnableInterfaceDemo {
  public static void main(String[] args) {
```

```
        // instantiate the class
        Thread1 objT1 = new Thread1();
        // pass its object to Thread class constructor
        Thread t = new Thread(objT1);
        //invoke the start method
        t.start();
    }
}
// Declare a class and implement Runnable interface
class Thread1 implements Runnable {
    String tName; // stores thread name
    // implement the run() method
    @Override
    public void run() {
        int tCount = 1; // stores thread count
        while (tCount < 5) {
            tName = Thread.currentThread().getName();
            System.out.println("Thread name = "+tName);
            tCount++;
        }
    }
}
```

The output of the code is as shown in *Figure 10.4*:

```
Thread name = Thread-0
Thread name = Thread-0
Thread name = Thread-0
Thread name = Thread-0
```

Figure 10.4: *Implementing runnable interface*

10.4 Daemon threads

Daemon thread is a low-priority service provider thread that runs in the background and provides services to the user thread. Characteristics of a **Daemon** thread:

- Dependent on user threads.

- JVM terminates daemon thread after all user threads die.
- Provides services to user threads for background supporting tasks.

Several daemon threads run in the background automatically such as **gc**, **finalizer**, and so on. If there is no user thread, JVM terminates the **Daemon** thread.

Methods of **Thread** class for daemon threads:

- **setDaemon(boolean value)**: It is used to convert a user thread into a **Daemon** thread. When a Boolean value of true is passed as an argument to this method, a default user thread is converted to a **Daemon** thread.
- **isDaemon()**: It is used to verify if the current thread is a **Daemon** thread. It will return true if the thread is a **Daemon** thread, else it will return false.

The following demonstration shows the use of the **Daemon** thread methods:

```
public class DaemonThreadDemo extends Thread {
  public void run() {
    //check for existence of daemon thread
    if (Thread.currentThread().isDaemon()) {
      System.out.println("Daemon thread at work");
    } else {
      System.out.println("User thread at work");
    }
  }
  public static void main(String[] args) {
    // create thread objects
    DaemonThreadDemo t1 = new DaemonThreadDemo();
    DaemonThreadDemo t2 = new DaemonThreadDemo();
    DaemonThreadDemo t3 = new DaemonThreadDemo();
    t1.setDaemon(true);// set t1 as daemon thread

    //start the threads
    t1.start();
    t2.start();
    t3.start();
  }
}
```

The output of the code is as shown in *Figure 10.5*:

```
Daemon thread at work
User thread at work
User thread at work
```

Figure 10.5: Daemon thread

10.5 Multithreading

The concurrent execution of two or more parts of a program is termed as multithreading. It is similar to multitasking. It allows the creation of more than one thread to execute multiple tasks in parallel, that is, concurrently.

Characteristics of multithreading are as follows:

- Execute and manage multiple concurrent tasks
- Differentiate tasks based on priority.
- Allow the user to interact with the application while the program performs background tasks.

Multithreading and multitasking have the following differences:

- Multithreading allows two or more threads to execute simultaneously within the same process. Multitasking allows two processes to execute concurrently.
- Multithreading incurs less overhead as compared to multitasking as threads are lightweight and share address space for execution.
- In multitasking, processes require their own address space.
- Context switching between processes is more expensive than inter-thread communication.

Listed below are some benefits of multithreading:

- Increased performance due to reduced CPU idle time.
- Parallel processing of tasks leading to increased scalability.
- Faster execution of the program as threads share data.

Multithreading can be implemented by using **`Thread`** class and **`Runnable`** interface as demonstrated in the following program:

```
public class MultithreadingDemo extends Thread {
  String name;
  @Override
  public void run() {
    while (true) {
```

```
        name = Thread.currentThread().getName();
        System.out.println(name);
        try {
          Thread.sleep(500);
        } catch (InterruptedException e) {
          break;
        }
      }
    }
  public static void main(String args[]) {
    MultithreadingDemo t1 = new MultithreadingDemo();
    MultithreadingDemo t2 = new MultithreadingDemo();
    t1.setName("Thread1");
    t2.setName("Thread2");
    t1.start();
    t2.start();
    System.out.println("Total threads in execution: " + Thread.activeCount());
  }
}
```

Here, both threads try to access processor time and are managed by using the **sleep()** method which allows another thread to run while the previous thread remains suspended. The code runs infinitely until the user manually stops program execution. The output of the code is as seen in *Figure 10.6*:

```
Total threads in execution: 3
Thread2
Thread1
Thread1
Thread2
Thread2
Thread1
Thread1
Thread2
Thread2
Thread1
```

Figure 10.6: *Multithreading*

Once a thread execution stops, it cannot be restarted by calling the **`start()`** method. An attempt to invoke **`start()`** on an already running thread raises the **`IllegalThreadStateException`** exception.

Note: A thread object will not become eligible for garbage collection if it fails to call the start() method even if the application has removed all references to the thread. Hence, it is advisable to set thread object references to null once thread execution is over.

10.5.1 isAlive() method

The **`isAlive()`** method is used to determine if the current thread is still running. It is important to ensure that all child threads are terminated before the main thread exits. This can be done by calling the **`isAlive()`** method on the thread object. If **`isAlive()`** returns true, the thread is running. A false value indicates that the thread is either in the new or terminated state.

The following code demonstrates the use of **`isAlive()`** method:

```
public class IsAliveDemo extends Thread {
  public void run() {
    System.out.println("Hello");
    try {
      Thread.sleep(300);
    } catch (InterruptedException ie) {
  }
    System.out.println("World");
  }
  public static void main(String[] args) {
    IsAliveDemo t1 = new IsAliveDemo();
    IsAliveDemo t2 = new IsAliveDemo();
    System.out.println("T1 is alive? "+t1.isAlive());
    System.out.println("T2 is alive? "+t2.isAlive());
    t1.start();
    t2.start();
    System.out.println(t1.isAlive());
    System.out.println(t2.isAlive());
  }
}
```

The output of the code is as seen in *Figure 10.7*:

```
T1 is alive? false
T2 is alive? false
true
true
Hello
Hello
World
World
```

Figure 10.7: Using isAlive() method

10.5.2 join() method

The **`join()`** method makes the current thread will simply wait until the thread it is joining terminates:

`void join();`

The following are the two overloaded versions:

- **`void join(long timeInMillis)`**: Puts the current thread on wait for the specified time (milliseconds) or till the thread on which it is called is dead.
- **`void join(long timeout, int nanoseconds)`**: Puts the current thread on wait for the specified time (milliseconds + nanos) or till the thread on which it is called is dead.

The following code demonstrates the use of **`join()`** method:

```
public class JoinMethodDemo extends Thread {
  public void run() {
    System.out.println("Hello");
    try {
      Thread.sleep(300);
    } catch (InterruptedException ie) {
    }
    System.out.println("World");
  }
  public static void main(String[] args) {
    JoinMethodDemo t1 = new JoinMethodDemo();
    JoinMethodDemo t2 = new JoinMethodDemo();
    t1.start();
```

```
    try {
      t1.join(); // Waiting for t1 to finish
    } catch (InterruptedException ie) {
    }
    t2.start();
  }
}
```

Here, the **join()** method is called on thread **t1**. It will ensure that **t1** terminates before **t2** begins execution. The output of the code is as follows, in *Figure 10.8*:

```
Hello
World
Hello
World
```

Figure 10.8: *Using join() method*

10.6 Thread synchronization

At times, when multiple threads try to access a shared resource simultaneously, it leads to a situation called a race condition. For example, when two or more threads try to read/write the same file simultaneously, it leads to a race condition and leaves the file in an inconsistent state. To avoid race conditions, Java provides the synchronized keyword to create synchronized blocks and synchronized methods.

Synchronization of threads in Java is implemented by using a piece of code called monitor which is guarded by a mutex or mutual-exclusion program.

10.6.1 Synchronized block

A synchronized block is a section of code written in curly brackets with the synchronized keyword. Only a single thread can access this code at a time by acquiring a lock on it. Until the current thread releases the lock, no other thread can access the block. This lock is based on the object that acquires it and not on the method.

The following code demonstrates the creation of a synchronized block:

```
public class TestSynchornizedBlock {
  public static void main(String[] args) {
    BankAccount accObj = new BankAccount();
    Transaction t1 = new Transaction(accObj, 30000.00);
    Transaction t2 = new Transaction(accObj, 6000.00);
```

```
    }
}
class BankAccount {
    double balance = 800.0;
    public void depositAmount(double amount) {
        balance = balance + amount;
    }
    public void showBalance() {
        System.out.println("Balance:" + balance);
    }
}
class Transaction implements Runnable {
    double amount;
    BankAccount a1;
    Thread t;
    public Transaction(BankAccount a1, double amt) {
        this.a1 = a1;
        amount = amt;
        t = new Thread(this);
        t.start();
    }
    @Override
    public void run() {
        // Synchronized block
        synchronized (a1) {
            a1.depositAmount(amount);
            a1.showBalance();
        }
    }
}
```

Here, the synchronized block calls the **depositAmount()** method and ensures that the account remains in a consistent state as only one thread can access the method at a time. The output of the code is as follows, in *Figure 10.9*:

```
Balance:30800.0
Balance:36800.0
```

Figure 10.9: Synchronized block

10.6.2 Synchronized method

Synchronization can also be implemented by using a synchronized method that uses the **synchronized** keyword. A thread that accesses the synchronized method acquires the lock and other threads need to wait till the current thread releases the lock.

The following code demonstrates the use of the **synchronized** method to prevent race conditions:

```
public class TestSynchronizedMethod {
  public static void main(String[] args) {
    TrackLine obj = new TrackLine();
    // creating two threads which share same Line Object.
    Train t1 = new Train(obj);
    Train t2 = new Train(obj);
    // both threads start executing
    t1.start();
    t2.start();
  }
}
class TrackLine {
  // if multiple threads(trains) try to access
  // this synchronized method on the same Object
  // only one thread will be able to execute it at a time.
  synchronized public void getLine(Thread t) {
    System.out.println("Thread "+t.getName());
    for (int i = 0; i < 3; i++) {
      System.out.println("Accessing line "+i);
      try {
        Thread.sleep(400);
```

```
        } catch (Exception e) {
          System.out.println(e);
        }
      }
    }
}
class Train extends Thread {
  // Line class object
  TrackLine l1;
  Train(TrackLine line) {
    this.l1 = line;
  }
  @Override
  public void run() {

    l1.getLine(this);
  }
}
```

Here, only one thread can access the **getLine()** method as it has been synchronized. The output of the code is as follows, in *Figure 10.10*:

```
Thread Thread-1
Accessing line 0
Accessing line 1
Accessing line 2
Thread Thread-0
Accessing line 0
Accessing line 1
Accessing line 2
```

Figure 10.10: *Synchronized method*

10.6.3 Wait-notify mechanism

The wait-notify mechanism is a way of making a thread wait for some time to run another thread and then wake it up when done. This is accomplished by using the **wait()** and **notify()** methods to ensure a consistent state of a resource between two competitive threads:

- **wait()**: Puts the current thread on wait until another thread releases the lock on a resource and notifies it. The **wait()** method can be invoked only from a synchronized code.

  Listed below are the overloaded signatures of **wait()** method:

  - **wait()**: Causes the current thread to wait indefinitely until another thread invokes the **notify()** or **notifyAll()** method on this object.
  - **wait(long timeout)**: Allows to specify a timeout after which the waiting thread will be woken up automatically. To wake up the thread before the timeout, use the **notify()** or **notifyAll()**.
  - **wait(long timeout, int nanos)**: Similar to the previous version of **wait()** except that it allows to specify timeout with higher precision. The total timeout period (in nanoseconds) is calculated as **1_000_000*timeout + nanos**.

- **notify()**: Arbitrarily notifies any one of the threads waiting to acquire the lock on a shared resource. The thread selection is non-deterministic and done randomly based on the implementation.
- **notifyAll()**: Wakes all threads that are waiting to acquire the lock on a shared resource.

  The following **Producer-Consumer** example demonstrates the wait-notify mechanism:

```
public class Producer implements Runnable {
  private final List<Integer> queue;
  private final int SIZE;
  public Producer(List<Integer> queue, int size) {
    this.queue = queue;
    SIZE = size;
  }
  @Override
  public void run() {
    int counter = 0;
    while (true) {
      try {
        produce(counter++);
      } catch (InterruptedException ex) {
        ex.printStackTrace();
      }
```

```
            }
        }
        private void produce(int i) throws InterruptedException {
          synchronized (queue) {
            while (queue.size() == SIZE) {
                System.out.println("Queue is full " + Thread.currentThread().
      getName() +  is waiting , size: " + queue.size());
              queue.wait();
            }
            Thread.sleep(3000);
            queue.add(i);
            System.out.println("Produced: " + i);
            queue.notifyAll();
          }
        }
      }
```

The **Producer** class generates a number by incrementing the counter. The **produce()** method has a synchronized block that can be accessed by only one thread at a time. The **wait()** method makes the current thread wait infinitely till it receives the wakeup call from **notify()** or **notifyAll()** method. The **sleep()** method puts the current thread to sleep for 3 seconds. Once the current thread is done executing, the **notifyAll()** method wakes up all threads waiting to access the synchronized block:

```
public class Consumer implements Runnable {
  private final List<Integer> queue;
  public Consumer(List<Integer> queue) {
    this.queue = queue;
  }
  @Override
  public void run() {
    while (true) {
      try {
        consume();
      } catch (InterruptedException ex) {
        ex.printStackTrace();
      }
```

```
    }
  }
  private void consume() throws InterruptedException {
    synchronized (queue) {
      while (queue.isEmpty()) {
        System.out.println("Queue is empty " + Thread.currentThread().getName()
+ " is waiting , size: " + queue.size());
        queue.wait();
      }
      Thread.sleep(1000);
      int i = (Integer) queue.remove(0);
      System.out.println(Thread.currentThread().getName() + " consumed: " + i);
      queue.notifyAll();
    }
  }
}
```

The **Consumer** class also creates a synchronized block on the queue object. The **wait()** and **notifyAll()** methods help to synchronize access to the shared queue:

```
public class TestWaitNotify {
  public static void main(String[] args) {
    List<Integer> queue = new ArrayList<Integer>();
    int SIZE = 5;
    Thread tProducer = new Thread(new Producer(queue, SIZE), "Producer");
    Thread tConsumer1 = new Thread(new Consumer(queue), "Consumer 1");
    Thread tConsumer2 = new Thread(new Consumer(queue), "Consumer 2");
    tProducer.start();
    tConsumer1.start();
    tConsumer2.start();
  }
}
```

Here, one **Producer** and two **Consumer** threads are created on the same queue object. While **Producer** threads attempt to add to the queue, the two consumer threads try to remove values from the queue simultaneously.

Note: The output of the code will be different every time as the threads will randomly get access to the shared resource.

The output of the code is as shown in *Figure 10.11*:

```
Produced: 0
Consumer 2 consumed: 0
Queue is empty Consumer 2 is waiting , size: 0
Queue is empty Consumer 1 is waiting , size: 0
Produced: 1
Produced: 2
Produced: 3
Produced: 4
Produced: 5
Consumer 1 consumed: 1
Consumer 1 consumed: 2
Consumer 1 consumed: 3
Consumer 1 consumed: 4
Consumer 2 consumed: 5
Queue is empty Consumer 2 is waiting , size: 0
Queue is empty Consumer 1 is waiting , size: 0
Produced: 6
Consumer 1 consumed: 6
Queue is empty Consumer 1 is waiting , size: 0
Queue is empty Consumer 2 is waiting , size: 0
Produced: 7
Consumer 2 consumed: 7
Queue is empty Consumer 2 is waiting , size: 0
Queue is empty Consumer 1 is waiting , size: 0
Produced: 8
Consumer 1 consumed: 8
Queue is empty Consumer 2 is waiting , size: 0
Queue is empty Consumer 1 is waiting , size: 0
```

Figure 10.11: *Wait-notify mechanism*

10.6.4 Deadlock

When two or more threads wait for resources locked by each other, the waiting state continues infinitely leading to a situation known as deadlock. A deadlock brings program execution to a halt. *Figure 10.12* depicts a deadlock situation between two threads:

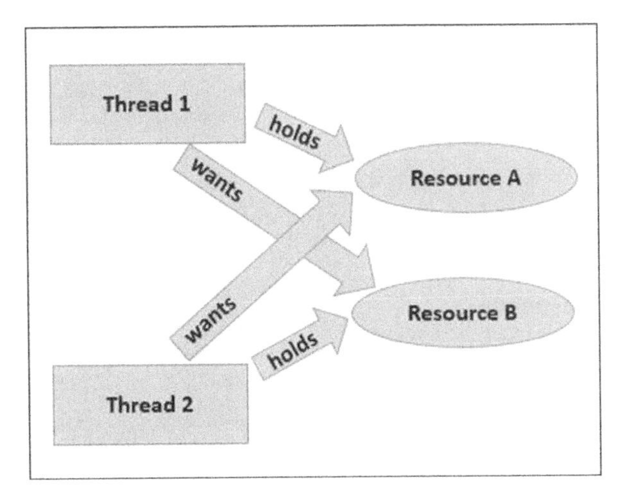

Figure 10.12: *Deadlock*

The following code demonstrates a deadlock situation:

```
public class DeadlockExample {
  public static Object resource1 = new Object();
  public static Object resource2 = new Object();
  public static void main(String args[]) {
    Thread1 t1 = new Thread1();
    Thread2 t2 = new Thread2();
    t1.start();
    t2.start();
  }
  private static class Thread1 extends Thread {
    public void run() {
      synchronized (resource1) {
        System.out.println("Thread 1: Holding Resource 1");
        try {
          Thread.sleep(10);
        } catch (InterruptedException e) {
        }
        System.out.println("Thread 1: Waiting for Resource 2");
        synchronized (resource2) {
          System.out.println("Thread 1: Holding Resource 1 & 2");
```

```
            }
          }
        }
      }
      private static class Thread2 extends Thread {
        public void run() {
          synchronized (resource2) {
            System.out.println("Thread 2: Holding Resource 2");
            try {
              Thread.sleep(10);
            } catch (InterruptedException e) {
            }
            System.out.println("Thread 2: Waiting for Resource 1");
            synchronized (resource1) {
              System.out.println("Thread 2: Holding Resource1 & 2");
            }
          }
        }
      }
    }
```

Here, **Thread 1** acquires **resource1** and then tries to acquire **resource2** whereas **Thread 2** acquires **resource2** and then tries to acquire **resource1**. During execution, the two threads get into a deadlock situation as each waits for the other to release the lock on the resources. The output of the code is as seen in *Figure 10.13*:

```
Thread 2: Holding Resource 2
Thread 1: Holding Resource 1
Thread 1: Waiting for Resource 2
Thread 2: Waiting for Resource 1
```

Figure 10.13: *Deadlock example*

It is important to endure the prevention of deadlock while implementing multithreading. Listed below are some points to prevent deadlocks:

- Acquire locks in a defined order for multiple threads.
- Locking multiple resources at a time should be avoided.

For example, in the above code, if the order of locking is modified for **Thread 2**, deadlock can be avoided. The following code demonstrates the resolution of deadlock encountered in the earlier code:

```
public class DeadlockSolution {
  public static Object resource1 = new Object();
  public static Object resource2 = new Object();
  public static void main(String args[]) {
    Thread1 t1 = new Thread1();
    Thread2 t2 = new Thread2();
    t1.start();
    t2.start();
  }
  private static class Thread1 extends Thread {
    @Override
    public void run() {
      synchronized (resource1) {
        System.out.println("Thread 1: Holding Resource 1");
        try {
          Thread.sleep(10);
        } catch (InterruptedException e) {
        }
        System.out.println("Thread 1: Waiting for Resource 2");
        synchronized (resource2) {
          System.out.println("Thread 1: Holding Resource 1 & 2");
        }
      }
    }
  }
  private static class Thread2 extends Thread {
    @Override
    public void run() {
      synchronized (resource1) {
        System.out.println("Thread 2: Holding Resource 1");
        try {
```

```
          Thread.sleep(10);
        } catch (InterruptedException e) {
        }
        System.out.println("Thread 2: Waiting for Resource 2");
        synchronized (resource2) {
          System.out.println("Thread 2: Holding Resource 1 & 2");
        }
      }
    }
  }
}
```

The order of access to **Resource 1** and **Resource 2** has been modified and made consistent to avoid deadlock. The output of the code is as seen in *Figure 10.14*:

```
Thread 2: Holding Resource 1
Thread 2: Waiting for Resource 2
Thread 2: Holding Resource 1 & 2
Thread 1: Holding Resource 1
Thread 1: Waiting for Resource 2
Thread 1: Holding Resource 1 & 2
```

Figure 10.14: *Deadlock resolution*

10.7 Concurrent collection APIs

Concurrent collection APIs were added since Java 5 within the **java.util.concurrent** package. These APIs allow concurrent access to collections from multiple threads. The APIs support features such as synchronization and locking, concurrent collections, and thread pools. Listed below are some important interfaces of **java.util.concurrent** package:

- **BlockingQueue**: It defines a **First In, First Out (FIFO)** data structure that blocks or times out on an attempt to add to a full queue or retrieve from an empty queue.
- **ConcurrentMap**: It is a subinterface of **java.util.Map**. It consists of important atomic operations to remove or replace a key-value pair only if the key is present or add a key-value pair only if the key is absent. These atomic operations help to avoid synchronization.
- **ConcurrentHashMap**: It is a standard general-purpose implementation of **ConcurrentMap**. It is a concurrent analog of the collection **HashMap**.
- **ConcurrentNavigableMap**: It is a subinterface of **ConcurrentMap**. It supports approximate matches.

- **ConcurrentSkipListMap**: It is the standard general-purpose implementation of **ConcurrentNavigableMap**. It is a concurrent analog of **TreeMap**.

The following code demonstrates the use of concurrent collections:

```
import java.util.Random;
import java.util.concurrent.BlockingQueue;
import java.util.concurrent.LinkedBlockingQueue;
public class ConcurrentCollectionExample {
  static BlockingQueue<Integer> queue1 = new LinkedBlockingQueue<>(5);
  public static void main(String[] args) throws
    InterruptedException {
      int noOfProducers = 7;
      int noOfConsumers = 9;
      for (int i = 0; i < noOfProducers; i++) {
        new Thread(new Producer(), "PRODUCER "+i).start();
      }
      for (int i = 0; i < noOfConsumers; i++) {
        new Thread(new Consumer(), "CONSUMER "+i).start();
      }
      System.exit(0);
    }
    static class Producer implements Runnable {
      Random = new Random();
      @Override
      public void run() {
        try {
          int num = random.nextInt(100);
          queue1.put(num);
           System.out.println(Thread.currentThread().getName()+ " produced: " +
num
                    + " Queue size : "+ queue1.size());
          Thread.sleep(100);
        } catch (InterruptedException ex) {
```

```
          System.out.println("Producer "+ Thread.currentThread().getName() +" is interrupted.");
        }
      }
    }
    static class Consumer implements Runnable {
      @Override
      public void run() {
        try {
          System.out.println(Thread.currentThread().getName()+ " consumed: " + queue1.take()
                        + " Queue size : "+ queue1.size());
          Thread.sleep(100);
        } catch (InterruptedException ex) {
          System.out.println("Consumer "+Thread.currentThread().getName()+" is interrupted.");
        }
      }
    }
  }
```

Here, multiple **Producer** and **Consumer** objects try to access the **BlockingQueue** object simultaneously. Note that the queue full and queue empty conditions have not been checked as the **BlockingQueue** object manages it intrinsically. The output of the code is as follows, in *Figure 10.15*:

```
PRODUCER 0 produced: 83 Queue size : 2
PRODUCER 2 produced: 19 Queue size : 3
PRODUCER 1 produced: 51 Queue size : 2
PRODUCER 4 produced: 25 Queue size : 4
PRODUCER 3 produced: 45 Queue size : 5
PRODUCER 5 produced: 12 Queue size : 5
CONSUMER 0 consumed: 51 Queue size : 5
PRODUCER 6 produced: 14 Queue size : 5
CONSUMER 1 consumed: 83 Queue size : 4
CONSUMER 2 consumed: 19 Queue size : 4
CONSUMER 3 consumed: 25 Queue size : 3
```

Figure 10.15: *Concurrent collections*

10.8 Atomic variables

In multithreading, access to a shared variable by multiple threads can lead to inconsistent reads and writes. Therefore, it is important to synchronize access to shared data. Consider the codes given below:

`public class Counter {`
`    private int count;`
`    public int getCount(){`
`        return count;`
`    }`
`    public int getNextCount(){`
`        return count++;`
`    }`
`    public int getPreviousCount()`
`{`
`        return count--;`
`    }`
`}`
	`public class SynchronizedCounter {`
	`    private int count;`
	`    public synchronized int getCount()`
	`{`
	`        return count;`
	`    }`
	`        public    synchronized    int`
	`getNextCount(){`
	`        return count++;`
	`    }`
	`        public    synchronized    int`
	`getPreviousCount(){`
	`        return count--;`
	`    }`
	`}`

The class **Counter** works well in a single-thread scenario but when multiple threads try to access the shared variable **count**, it leads to an inconsistent state of data. The problem can be resolved by using the **synchronized** keyword to lock the variable when one thread accesses it so that no other threads can access/modify the data. This is depicted in the **SynchronizedCounter** class.

However, the locking mechanism is expensive especially when the critical section is small. Firstly, other threads remain in the suspended mode when one thread acquires the lock. Secondly, the context-switching overhead is very heavy for a small piece of code when the lock is acquired very often and there are a lot of conflicts.

This problem can be resolved by using non-blocking algorithms which do not block threads and improve performance too. The non-blocking algorithms use atomic low-level machine instructions to ensure the atomicity of high-level operations. The most common operation used by processors to implement non-blocking algorithms is the **Compare-And-Swap (CAS)** operation. The three parameters taken by this operation include:

- The memory address of the variable
- The expected current value

- The new value which needs to be set

The value at the given memory address is atomically updated with the new value, if it matches the expected value else, it will do nothing. In either case, the value at the address is returned after the operation.

In case multiple threads attempt to execute the CAS operation, any one of the threads gets access while other threads either retry or do something else. However, the threads are not blocked. The same approach is used with the compare-and-set operation except that it returns a boolean indicating whether the operation succeeded or not.

10.8.1 java.util.concurrent.atomic package

Support for atomic operations on single variables was added from Java 5 by providing the **java.util.concurrent.atomic** package. All classes of this package contain the getter and setter methods that work similarly to read and write on volatile variables. In Java 5.0 several atomic variables were added for **int**, **long**, Boolean, and reference values. Listed below are the classes:

- **AtomicInteger**
- **AtomicLong**
- **AtomicBoolean**
- **AtomicReference**

These classes support the compare-and-set operation with the help of methods such as **get()**, **set()**, **getAndSet()**, and **compareAndSet()**. The modified counter example by using an **AtomicInteger** is as follows:

```
public class AtomicCounter {
  private final AtomicInteger count = new AtomicInteger(0);
  public int getCount(){
    return count.get();
  }
  public int getNextCount(){
    return count.incrementAndGet();
  }
  public int getPreviousCount(){
    return count.decrementAndGet();
  }
}
```

This code is faster in execution than the synchronized version and is also thread-safe. The **incrementAndGet()** and **decrementAndGet()** methods are numeric operations supported by

AtomicLong and **AtomicInteger** classes. These methods increment and decrement the count by one respectively.

Listed below are other important methods:

- **getAndDecrement()**: Atomically decrements the current value by one.
- **getAndIncrement()**:Atomically increments the current value by one.
- **getAndAdd(int i)**: Atomically adds the given value to the current value.
- **addAndGet(int i)**: Atomically adds the given value to the current value.

The code to increment counter by using **compareAndSet** as shown below:

```
public void increment(AtomicInteger integer){
  while(true){
    int counter = integer.get();
    int next = counter + 1;
    if(integer.compareAndSet(counter, next)){
      return;
    }
  }
}
```

The code becomes complex but that is how it is with non-blocking algorithms. Detect collision and retry until the operation completes successfully. The following code demonstrates the use of **AtomicInteger** accessed by multiple threads:

```
import java.util.concurrent.atomic.AtomicInteger;
public class AtomicExample {
  public static void main(String[] args) throws InterruptedException {
    Threads t = new Threads();
    Thread t1 = new Thread(t, "Thread 1");
    t1.start();
    Thread t2 = new Thread(t, "Thread 2");
    t2.start();
    t1.join();
    t2.join();
    System.out.println("Thread counter = " + t.getCounter());
  }
}
class Threads implements Runnable {
```

```
    private AtomicInteger counter = new AtomicInteger();
    @Override
    public void run() {
      for (int i = 1; i < 5; i++) {
        doSomething(i);
        counter.incrementAndGet();
      }
    }
    public int getCounter() {
      return this.counter.get();
    }
    private void doSomething(int i) {
      System.out.println("Processing...");
      try {
        Thread.sleep(i * 1000);
      } catch (InterruptedException e) {
        e.printStackTrace();
      }
    }
}
```

Here, multiple threads try to access the atomic variable counter to increment its value by using the **incrementAndGet()** method. The output of the code is as shown in *Figure 10.16*:

```
Processing...
Processing...
Processing...
Processing...
Processing...
Processing...
Processing...
Processing...
Thread counter = 8
```

Figure 10.16: *Atomic variables*

10.9 java.util.concurrent.locks package

Java provides another thread synchronization mechanism with the **java.util.concurrent.locks** package. It is similar to synchronized blocks but provides more flexibility than a **synchronized** block.

Listed below are some differences of **synchronized** block and **Lock**:

- A sequence in which threads may get access to a synchronized block is not guaranteed.
- Arguments cannot be passed to a synchronized block. Therefore, it is not possible to set a timeout for trying access to the synchronized block.
- The synchronized block must be fully contained within a single method whereas, a **Lock** can place calls to **lock()** and **unlock()** in separate methods.

Listed below are the methods of the **Lock** interface:

- **lock()**: Acquires the lock.
- **lockInterruptibly()**: Acquires the lock unless the current thread is interrupted by another thread.
- **newCondition()**: Returns a new **Condition** instance that is bound to this **Lock** instance.
- **tryLock()**: Acquires the lock only if it is free at the time of invocation.
- **tryLock(long time, TimeUnit unit)**: Acquires the lock if it is available within the given waiting time and the current thread has not been interrupted.
- **unlock()**: Releases the lock.

Lock implementing classes:

ReentrantLock

ReentrantReadWriteLock.ReadLock

ReentrantReadWriteLock.WriteLock

Lock is an interface; hence, it can be used through one of its implementations as shown below:

```
Lock lock = new ReentrantLock();

lock.lock();

//critical section

lock.unlock();
```

The **Lock** instance is created and locked by calling the **lock()** method. Other threads will be blocked until **unlock()** is called. Finally, **unlock()** is called, and the **Lock** is now available for other threads.

The following table shows locks applied by using a **synchronized** block and **Lock** interface:

<pre>public class Counter{
  private int count = 0;
  public int updateCount(){
    synchronized(this){
      return ++count;
    }
  }
}</pre>
	<pre>public class Counter{
	  private Lock lock = new Lock();
	  private int count = 0;
	  public int updateCount(){
	    lock.lock();
	    int count1 = ++count;
	    lock.unlock();
	    return count1;
	  }
	}</pre>

In the first example, the **synchronized(this)** block in the **updateCount()** method ensures that only one thread can execute the **return ++count** statement at a time. In the second example, the code has been written by using a **Lock** instead of a synchronized block.

10.10 Executors and thread pools

JDK 5 introduced the Java executor framework to run the **Runnable** objects without having to create new threads every time and reuse the already created threads. Listed below are the executor interfaces defined in the **java.util.concurrent** package:

- **Executor**: A simple interface that supports launching new tasks. The only method that the **Executor** interface provides is **execute()** as a drop-in replacement of the standard thread-creation method.

That is, you can **replace (new Thread(r)).start();** with **e.execute(r)**, where **r** is a **Runnable** object and **e** is the **Executor** object. The executor implementations make use of advanced **ExecutorService** and **ScheduledExecutorService** interfaces. Depending on the **Executor** implementation, **execute()** method uses an existing worker thread to run the **Runnable** object **r**. It can also place the **Runnable** object in a queue to wait for a worker thread to become available.

- **ExecutorService**: A subinterface of **Executor** interface which provides features that help in managing the lifecycle of the individual tasks as well as the executor itself. The **execute()** method has a more versatile supplement called the **submit()** method. In addition to accepting **Runnable** objects, **submit()** also accepts **Callable** objects, thereby, allowing a task to return a value.

The **Future** object returned by **submit()** method allows retrieving the **Callable** return value. It also manages the status of **Callable** and **Runnable** tasks. **ExecutorService** also provides methods for:

- o Submitting large collections of **Callable** objects.
- o Managing the shutdown of the executor.

To support the immediate shutdown, interrupts should be handled correctly by all tasks.

- **ScheduledExecutorService**: A subinterface of **ExecutorService** that supports the future and/or periodic execution of tasks.

It supplements the methods of **ExecutorService** with a schedule in order to execute a **Callable** or **Runnable** task after a specified delay. It also defines **scheduleAtFixedRate** and **scheduleWithFixedDelay** to execute specified tasks repeatedly, at defined intervals.

10.10.1 Thread pools

Multiple active threads created by JVM can consume system resources at a rapid rate due to which the system may run out of memory. It is therefore important to limit the number of threads being created. A thread pool reduces the thread cycle overhead by reusing existing threads to execute new tasks. This eliminates the delay caused by thread creation and makes the application more responsive.

The thread pools can be used as follows:

- Create an object of **ExecutorService** and pass a set of tasks to it.
- Set the core and maximum pool size by using **ThreadPoolExecutor** class.

The **Runnable** objects that are executed by a particular thread are executed sequentially. Listed below are the **Executor** Thread Pool factory methods:

- **newFixedThreadPool(int)**: Creates a fixed-size thread pool.
- **newCachedThreadPool()**: Creates a thread pool that creates new threads when required, but will reuse previously constructed threads when they are available.

newSingleThreadExecutor(): Creates an executor that executes a single thread at a time.

A fixed pool is the most common type of thread pool that allows a specific number of running threads. If all the threads in the pool are occupied, the pending tasks are placed in a queue till a thread becomes idle. The following code demonstrates the use of **Executors**:

```
import java.util.concurrent.ExecutorService;
import java.util.concurrent.Executors;
import java.util.concurrent.Future;
public class ExecutorDemo {
  private static ExecutorService exe1 = null;
  private static volatile Future task1 = null;
  private static volatile Future task2 = null;
  private static volatile Future task3 = null;
  public static void main(String[] args) {
```

```
      exe1 = Executors.newFixedThreadPool(2);
      while (true) {
        try {
          taskStatus();
          Thread.sleep(2000);
        } catch (Exception e) {
          System.err.println("Error: " + e.getMessage());
        }
      }
    }
    private static void taskStatus() throws Exception {
      if (task1 == null || task1.isDone() || task1.isCancelled()) {
        task1 = exe1.submit(new ThreadClass1());
      }
      if (task2 == null || task2.isDone() || task2.isCancelled()) {
        task2 = exe1.submit(new ThreadClass2());
      }
       if (task3 == null || task3.isDone() || task3.isCancelled()) {
        task3 = exe1.submit(new ThreadClass2());
      }
    }
  }
  class ThreadClass1 implements Runnable {
    public void run() {
      while (true) {
        System.out.println("Executing task one");
        try {
          Thread.sleep(1000);
        } catch (Throwable e) {
          e.printStackTrace();
        }
      }
    }
  }
```

```
class ThreadClass2 implements Runnable {
  public void run() {
    while (true) {
      System.out.println("Executing task two");
      try {
        Thread.sleep(1000);
      } catch (Throwable e) {
        e.printStackTrace();
      }
    }
  }
}
class ThreadClass3 implements Runnable {
  public void run() {
    while (true) {
      System.out.println("Executing task three");
      try {
        Thread.sleep(1000);
      } catch (Throwable e) {
        e.printStackTrace();
      }
    }
  }
}
```

Here, three tasks are created and the thread pool size is fixed to 2. The threads are utilized by the first two tasks. The third task cannot be executed until one of the two threads becomes idle. The output is as follows, in *Figure 10.17*:

```
run:
Executing task one
Executing task two
Executing task two
Executing task one
Executing task one
Executing task two
Executing task one
Executing task two
Executing task one
Executing task two
Executing task two
Executing task one
Executing task one
Executing task two
Executing task two
Executing task one
Executing task two
Executing task one
Executing task one
Executing task two
Executing task two
```

Figure 10.17: *Executors and thread pool*

10.10.2 ForkJoinPool

Java 7 introduced the **`ForkJoinPool`** class, an extension of the **`AbstractExecutorService`**, which is similar to the **`ExecutorService`** interface. However, **`ForkJoinPool`** allows tasks to split the job into smaller subtasks recursively that can be submitted again to the **`ForkJoinPool`**. This allows working with multiple processors and can give a major boost to application performance.

The Fork and **Join** principle involves two steps namely, fork and join which are performed recursively:

Fork: In this step, the task is split into multiple smaller subtasks that are executed concurrently on multiple processors or by different threads on the same processor (*Figure 10.18*):

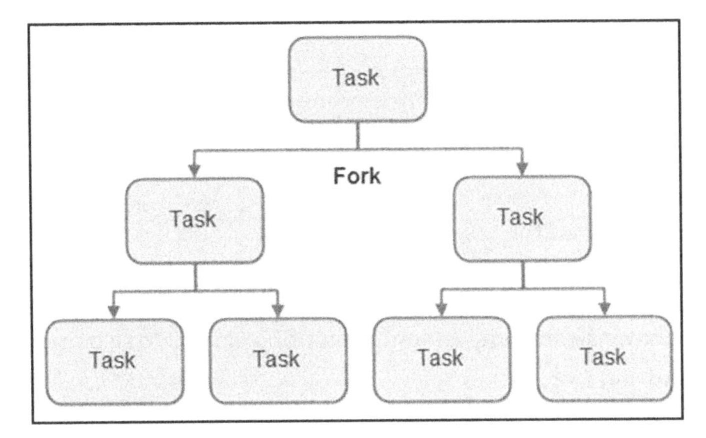

Figure 10.18: Fork

- **Join**: In this step, the subtasks that finished executing may join (merge) into one result. All types of tasks may not return a result. In that case, the task waits for the subtasks to complete and a no result merging takes place. (see *Figure 10.19*):

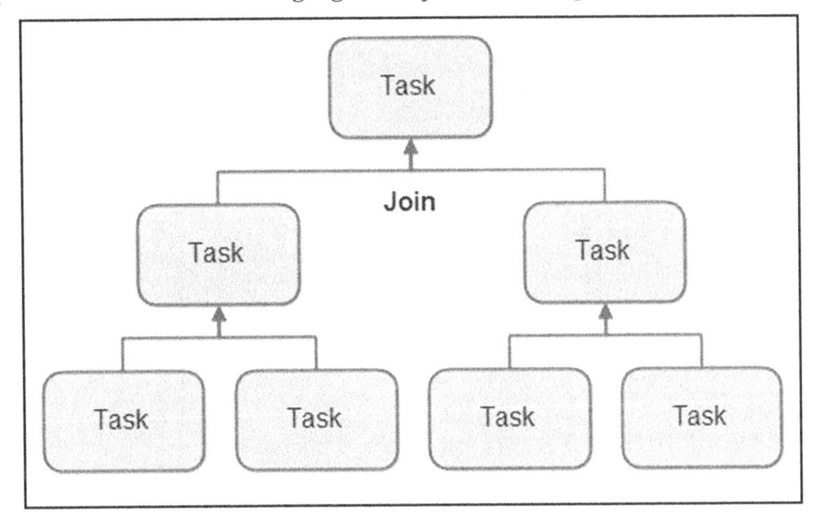

Figure 10.19: Join

Note: The limit at which forking a task into subtasks is justified is also called a threshold. It depends on the kind of work being done.

Listed below are the steps to implement the `Fork` and `Join` concept:

- Write the code that performs a segment of the work.

```
if (task is greater than threshold)
  split the task into subtasks
  invoke the subtasks and wait for the results
```

```
  else
    execute the task
```

- Use one of the subclasses of **ForkJoinTask** to wrap the code in a **ForkJoinTask** subclass. For example, **RecursiveTask** that returns a result or **RecursiveAction** that does not return a result.
- Create the object for all the tasks to be executed.

Pass the objects to the **invoke()** method of a **ForkJoinPool** instance.

The following code demonstrates implementation of **Fork** and **Join** principle:

```
import java.util.ArrayList;
import java.util.List;
import java.util.concurrent.ForkJoinPool;
import java.util.concurrent.RecursiveAction;
public class ForkJoinDemo extends RecursiveAction {
  private long task = 0;
  public ForkJoinDemo(long task) {
    this.task = task;
  }
  @Override
  protected void compute() {
    try {
      //if workload is above threshold value 16,
      //break the task into smaller subtasks
      if (task > 16) {
        System.out.println("Splitting task: " + task);
        List<ForkJoinDemo> lstSubtasks = new ArrayList<>();

        lstSubtasks.addAll(createSubtasks());
        for (RecursiveAction subtask : lstSubtasks) {
          subtask.fork();
        }

      } else {
        System.out.println("Executing task: " + task);
      }
    } catch (Exception e) {
```

```
            System.out.println("Exception:" + e.getMessage());
            e.printStackTrace();
        }
    }
    private List<ForkJoinDemo> createSubtasks() {
        List<ForkJoinDemo> subtasks = new ArrayList<>();
        //create subtasks
        ForkJoinDemo subtask1 = new ForkJoinDemo(task / 2);
        ForkJoinDemo subtask2 = new ForkJoinDemo(task / 2);
        subtasks.add(subtask1);
        subtasks.add(subtask2);

        return subtasks;
    }
    public static void main(String[] args) {
        try {
            // submit the task to the pool with parallelism 4
            final ForkJoinPool pool = new ForkJoinPool(4);
            final ForkJoinDemo obj = new ForkJoinDemo(40);

            //call invoke() method. It calls the compute() method
            System.out.println(pool.invoke(obj));
        } catch (Exception e) {
            System.out.println("Error: " + e.getMessage());
            e.printStackTrace();
        }
    }
}
```

Here, a fictitious number of tasks are passed to the constructor of **ForkJoinDemo** class. If the number of tasks is greater than the threshold of 16, the task is split else the task is directly executed. The output of the code is as seen in *Figure 10.20*:

```
Splitting task: 40
Splitting task: 20
Splitting task: 20
Executing task: 10
Executing task: 10
Executing task: 10
Executing task: 10
```

Figure 10.20: *Fork and join*

10.11 Java Database Connectivity (JDBC)

Databases are used to store data for an application. Java provides the **Java Database Connectivity (JDBC) Application Programming Interface (API)** to connect a Java application to a database. JDBC API provides a set of libraries and database drivers that are platform-independent in their implementation. **Open DataBase Connectivity (ODBC)** and JDBC are two widely used APIs for such activities.

ODBC API is a Microsoft product that uses **Structured Query Language (SQL)** for accessing, querying, and manipulating databases from an application. To connect to multiple databases, a driver manager is used which manages the different database drivers and ensures that calls are directed to the correct **Database Management System (DBMS)**. Each DBMS has a specific driver software, for example, SQL Server driver, Oracle driver, and so on. JDBC is a Java API used to manipulate database(s) from a Java program to perform the following activities:

- Connect to the database
- Query and update the database
- Retrieve data from the database

It uses JDBC drivers to connect with the database as shown in *Figure 10.21*:

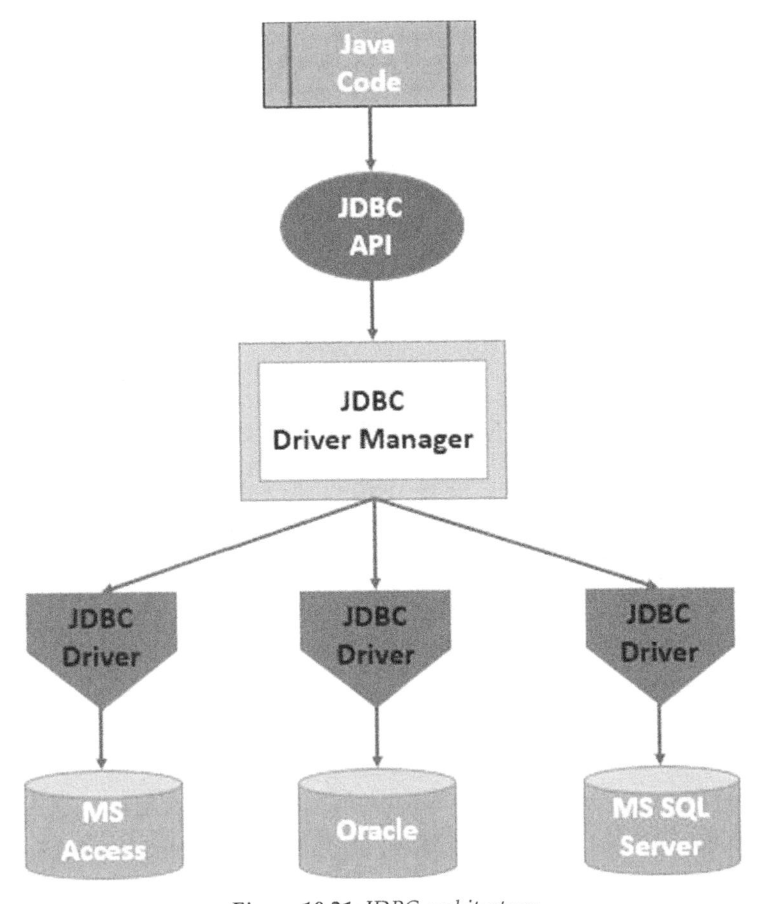

Figure 10.21: JDBC architecture

There are four types of JDBC drivers which are listed below:

- **Type I, JDBC-ODBC Bridge driver**: Bridges access to JDBC drivers to the database via ODBC drivers. Majorly used to access Microsoft DBMS products such as MS Access and MS SQL Server.
- **Type II, Native API-Java/ Partly Java driver**: Accesses native methods of a particular database through JDBC calls. It is faster than type-I as JDBC calls are converted to database-specific calls. However, it requires the configuration of native database codes on client machines.
- **Type III, JDBC Network-All Java driver**: Translates JDBC calls to an intermediate DBMS-independent network protocol, which is then converted by a middle-tier server to database-specific calls. No requirement of native software or service installation on the client machine. However, on the middle-tier, the database-specific code needs to be executed with the additional overhead of implementing security in the middle-tier.
- **Type IV, Native Protocol-All Java:** Converts JDBC calls directly to database-specific network protocol with no requirement of middleware or native library installation on

the client machine. It is the fastest driver of all four drivers. However, since it is DBMS specific, any change in the database requires the deployment of a new Type 4 driver specific to that database.

Listed below are some of the advantages of JDBC:

- Platform independent and vendor independent as it supports any DBMS used as backend storage.
- Easy to use as it hides the complexity of connecting a program with the backend database.
- Allows using existing data with different DBMS.

10.11.1 JDBC API classes and interfaces

Java provides a set of classes and interfaces defined in the **`java.sql`** package to connect and manipulate databases. Listed below are some of the interfaces of the **`java.sql`** package:

- **`Connection`**: Used to connect to and monitor database connections.
- **`DatabaseMetaData`**: Provides information about databases such as version, table names, and more. It has methods to get information about schemas, number of tables, and so on.
- **`Driver`**: Used to create **`Connection`** objects.
- **`PreparedStatement`**: Used to execute pre-compiled SQL statements.
- **`ResultSet`**: Provides methods for retrieving data returned by a SQL statement.
- **`ResultSetMetaData`**: Used to get information about the last **`ResultSet`** object.
- **`Statement`**: Used to execute SQL statements and retrieve data into the **`ResultSet`**.

Listed below are some of the classes of the **`java.sql`** package:

- **`Date`**: Provides methods to convert SQL date formats to Java Date formats.
- **`DriverManager`**: Used to handle the loading and unloading of drivers and establish a connection with the database.
- **`DriverPropertyInfo`**: Provides methods to retrieve or insert driver properties.
- **`Time`**: Provides operations for formatting and parsing time values.

Listed below are the exceptions defined by the **`java.sql`** package:

- **`SQLException`**: Provides information on database access errors or other errors.
- **`SQLWarning`**: Provides information on database access warnings.
- **`DataTruncation`**: Raised when a data value is truncated.
- **`BatchUpdateException`**: Raised when an error occurs during the batch update operation.

10.11.2 Connecting to a database from a Java program

Figure 10.22 shows the steps involved in connecting and accessing a database from a Java program:

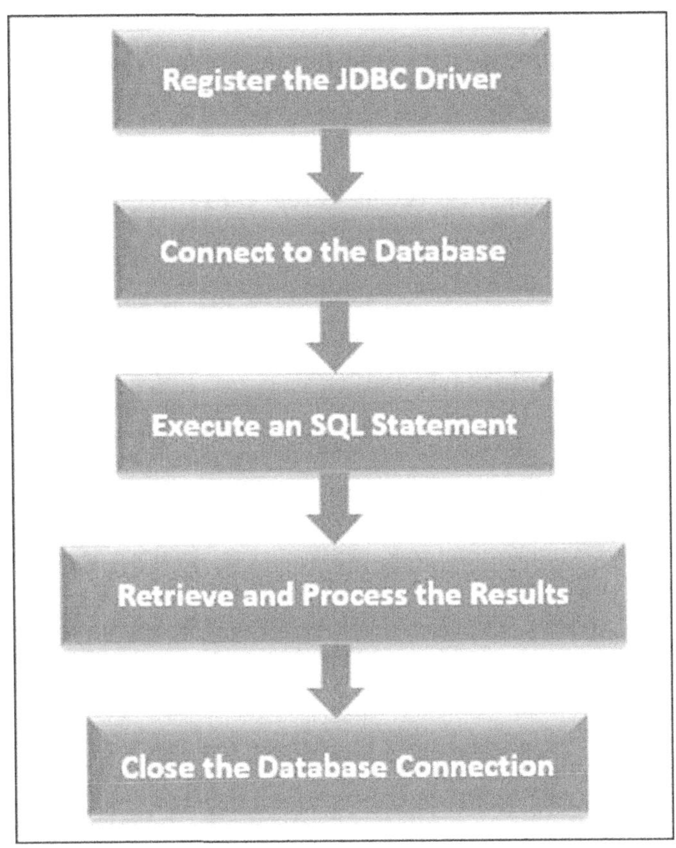

Figure 10.22: *Steps for connecting to a database*

Let us understand each step one-by-one.

Register the JDBC driver

To register a driver, use the **`DriverManager`** class. It manages all references to different driver objects that are available to a JDBC client. Earlier **`Class.forName()`** was used to load the driver class and register it with **`DriverManager`**. However, with JDBC 4.0 drivers, this is no longer required since JDBC 4.0 (JDK 6) drivers available in the classpath are automatically loaded.

Syntax:

```
Class.forName(<protocol>)
```

For example,

```
Class.forName("com.microsoft.sqlserver.jdbc.SQLServerDriver")
```

Once the driver is successfully loaded, the connection with a database can be established.

Connect to the database

To establish a database connection, use the **DriverManager.getConnection()** method. It checks for all available drivers and/or the specific driver whose URL is specified.

Syntax:

```
Connection con = DriverManager.getConnection(<url>, <username>,<password>);
```

Here,

- **Connection**: The object that holds the reference to the connection details.
- **url**: Specifies the connection properties such as protocol, sub-protocol, and more.

  protocol:<subprotocol>:<subname>

For example:

```
jdbc:odbc:sample
```

- **username**: The user login name
- **password**: The password to validate the user

For example:

```
Connection con = DriverManager.getConnection("jdbc:odbc:sample",
"sa","sa");
```

Execute an SQL statement

An SQL statement can be created to retrieve, insert, update, or delete data from the database. This is done by using the **Statement** object which allows to execute non-parameterized queries. The **Connection.createStatement()** method is used to create a **Statement** object.

For example:

```
Connection con = DriverManager.getConnection("jdbc:odbc:sample", "sa","sa");
Statement stmt = con.createStatement();
```

An SQL query can be created by using the below three types of **Statement** objects:

- **Statement** interface to execute non-parameterized queries.
- **PreparedStatement** interface to execute precompiled SQL statements with or without **IN** parameters.
- **CallableStatement** interface to execute a call to the stored procedure.

Listed below are the methods used for executing SQL statements:

- **`executeQuery()`**: Executes an SQL statement with a **`SELECT`** clause. Returns the result in the form of a **`ResultSet`** object. The SQL query string is passed as a parameter to the method.

For example:

```
ResultSet rs = stmt.executeQuery("SELECT Name FROM Student");
```

- **`executeUpdate()`**: Executes **`INSERT`**, **`DELETE`**, **`UPDATE`**, and other **Data Definition Language** (DDL) statements such as **`CREATE TABLE`**, **`DROP TABLE`**, and so on. Returns an integer value that indicates the number of rows affected.

Syntax:

```
public int executeUpdate(String sql) throws SQLException
```

- **`execute()`**: Execute SQL statements that return more than one result set. It returns true if a **`ResultSet`** object is generated by the SQL statements.

  Syntax:

  ```
  public boolean execute (String sql) throws SQLException
  ```

Retrieve and process the results

The results received from SQL statements are extracted from the **`ResultSet`** object. It provides methods to retrieve and process the data.

Syntax:

```
public ResultSet executeQuery(String sql) throws SQLException
```

The **`ResultSet`** object stores data in a tabular format with the cursor positioned before the first row. To traverse the **`ResultSet`**, the **`next()`** method is used which moves the cursor one row forward. The **`next()`** method returns a true if the cursor is at a valid position. It returns false if the curse is positioned after the last row.

For example:

```
ResultSet rs = stmt.executeQuery("SELECT Name FROM Student");
while (rs.next()) {
  String studName=rs.getString("Name");
  System.out.println(studName);
}
```

Here, the names of students are retrieved from the **`Student`** table in a **`ResultSet`** object. The **`ResultSet`** is then traversed by using the **`next()`** method and data is displayed by using the **`getString()`** method.

Listed below are the different getter methods to retrieve the different types of data:

- **getString()**: Retrieves string values (SQL type **VARCHAR**) that are assigned to a **String** object.
- **getInt()**: Retrieves integer values that are assigned to an integer variable.
- **getFloat()**: Retrieves float values that are assigned to a **float** variable.
- **getObject()**: Retrieves values as an object that is assigned to **Object** type of variable.

For example:

```
while (rs.next()) {
  String name=rs.getString("Name");
  int id=rs.getInt("StudId");
  float score=rs.getFloat("Percentage");
  System.out.println(id + " " name + score);
}
```

Different types of values are extracted from the **ResultSet** in appropriate variables and displayed.

Close the database connection

Once data processing is completed, a database connection must be closed along with all the statement objects in the reverse order of their creation. For example,

```
stmt.close();
con.close();
```

Here, **stmt** is a **Statement** object and **con** is a **Connection** object.

Note: To ensure resources are released even though an exception may be thrown, database connections should always be closed within a finally block.

10.11.3 Parameterized queries

To create dynamic queries with parameters that users can specify at runtime, use the **PreparedStatement** object. Similar to **Statement** object, **PreparedStatement** is also created by using the **preparedStatement()** method of **Connection** object. This method accepts the SQL query as a parameter. To create the dynamic query, a placeholder **?** is used for the value to be passed at runtime.

For example:

```
String query = "UPDATE Student SET Name = ? WHERE StudId = ?";
```

```
PreparedStatement pStmt = con.preparedStatement(query);
The query is pre-compiled.
```

The appropriate **setXXX()** method must be used to specify the values for the placeholders.

For example:

```
pStmt.setString(1, "Roger");
pStmt.setInt(2, 25);
```

Here, the first placeholder is replaced by the word **Roger** and the second by the number **25**. Hence, the final query will be **UPDATE Student SET Name = Roger WHERE StudId = 25**. To execute the update, use the **executeUpdate()** method. It is used with both **Statement** and **PreparedStatement** for insert, update, and delete queries. It will return an integer indicating the number of rows affected.

For example:

```
pStmt.executeUpdate();
```

10.11.4 Manage SQL exceptions

To manage exceptions in database transactions, Java provides appropriate exception classes to handle the specific type of exception:

- **ClassNotFoundException**: This exception can be raised when a driver that does not exist in the package is specified in the **Class.forName()** method. To handle the exception, the **Class.forName()** statement should be wrapped in a **try** block and the exception is mentioned in the **catch** block.

For example:

```
try {
  Class.forName("<name of driver>");
} catch(ClassNotFoundException e) {
  System.out.println ("Error: "+ e.getMessage());
}
```

- **SQLException**: This exception may arise from any method defined by JDBC objects such as **Connection**, **Statement**, **ResultSet**, and so on. To manage this exception, the method calls should be wrapped within the **try** block and the exception should be specified in the **catch** block.

For example:

```
try {
  // statement that may generate SQL exception
}
catch(SQLException e)
```

```
{
  System.out.println("Exception: " + e.getMessage());
  System.out.println("ErrorCode: " + e.getErrorCode ());
}
```

10.11.5 Connect to a database with Type 4 driver

Java applications can be connected to different databases through Type 4 JDBC driver.

Syntax:

```
<protocol>:<subprotocol>://<server-name>;instanceName:portNumber;property=valu
e[;property=value]
```

```
jdbc:sqlserver://serverName;instanceName:portNumber;property=value[;property
=value]
```

For example:

```
jdbc:sqlserver://SQLS:1433; databaseName=MyDB;integratedSecurity=true;
```

Here, protocol and subprotocol are constant, `serverName` and `instanceName` are variable and optional. They indicate the server address and instance name on the server. Server name can be localhost or the IP address of the computer. Port number identifies the port to connect to the specified `serverName`. Default value of port is `1433`. Property is the login information such as username and password or `integratedSecurity` in case of Windows authentication.
For example:

```
jdbc:sqlserver://localhost;user=Admin;password=******;
```

10.11.6 Execute queries with Statement object

The following code demonstrates the use of a `Statement` object for creating and executing queries.

Note: The database used in the demo is MS SQL Server. The database driver sqljdbc42.jar has been loaded into the project as shown in the *Figure 10.23*:

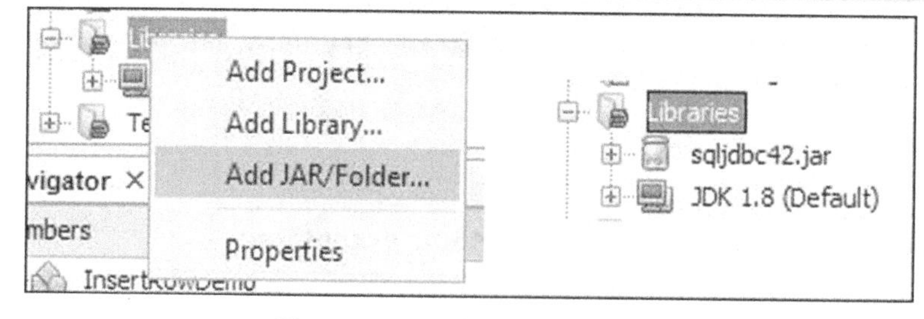

***Figure 10.23:** Add driver to project*

Note: The .jar file of the driver is selected and added to the libraries folder as shown in the figure. The specific driver for a DBMS must be downloaded from the official website to connect to the DBMS from Java code.

```
import java.sql.Connection;
import java.sql.DriverManager;
import java.sql.ResultSet;
import java.sql.SQLException;
import java.sql.Statement;
public class JDBCDemo {
  public static void main(String[] args) {
    Connection conn;
    //Since Windows authentication is used, integratedSecurity is set to true
    // the url has protocol:subprotocol:server-name:port number, database name
    // and authentication details.
                    String      dbURL      =      "jdbc:sqlserver://SQLS:1433;
databaseName=MyDB;integratedSecurity=true;";
    try {
      conn = DriverManager.getConnection(dbURL);
      Statement stmt = conn.createStatement();
      ResultSet rs = stmt.executeQuery("SELECT StudId, StudName, Percentage FROM
Student");
      System.out.println("ID \t Name \t Percentage");
      while(rs.next()){
        System.out.println(rs.getInt("StudId")+"\t"+rs.getString("StudName")+"\
t"+rs.getFloat("Percentage"));
      }
    } catch (SQLException e) {
      System.out.println("Exception: " + e.getMessage());
    }
  }
}
```

The **executeQuery()** method is used to extract data from the database. The **ResultSet** object stores the extracted data and the getter methods are used to display the data. The output of the code is as shown in *Figure 10.24*:

ID	Name	Percentage
1	Maddy	45.0
2	Mary	54.0
3	Clara	77.5
4	Peter	40.0
5	Mark	70.0

Figure 10.24: *Output of SELECT query*

The following code shows the example of **executeUpdate()** method for inserting data into the table:

```
import java.sql.Connection;
import java.sql.DriverManager;
import java.sql.Statement;
public class QueryDemo {
  public static void main(String[] args) {
    Connection conn;
    try{
                          String    dbURL    =    "jdbc:sqlserver://SQLS:1433;
databaseName=MyDB;integratedSecurity=true;";
      conn = DriverManager.getConnection(dbURL);
      Statement stmt = conn.createStatement();
             int   result   =   stmt.executeUpdate("insert  into  Student  values
(6,'Roger','78.6')");
      if(result >0){
        System.out.println("Data Inserted");
      }else{
        System.out.println("Insert Failed");
      }

    }catch(Exception e){
      System.out.println("Error:"+e.getMessage());
    }
  }
}
```

Here, the **createStatement()** method is used to create the **Statement** object. The **executeUpdate()** method is used to execute an **Insert** statement. The result is an integer indicating the number of rows affected. Based on the execution result, the appropriate message is displayed to the user. The output of the code is as under. The data inserted in the table is also shown in *Figure 10.25*:

```
run:
Data Inserted
```

	StudId	StudName	Percentage
1	1	Maddy	45
2	2	Mary	54
3	3	Clara	77
4	4	Peter	40
5	5	Mark	70
6	6	Roger	78.6

Figure 10.25: Result of INSERT query

Similarly, **`Update`** and **`Delete`** queries can also be executed by using **`executeUpdate()`** method.

10.11.7 Execute queries with PreparedStatement object

The following code demonstrates the use of **`PreparedStatement`** object for creating and executing queries:

```
import java.sql.Connection;
import java.sql.DriverManager;
import java.sql.PreparedStatement;
import java.sql.ResultSet;
import java.sql.SQLException;
public class JDBCExample {
  public static void main(String[] args) {
    Connection conn;
    //Since Windows authentication is used, integratedSecurity is set to true
    // the url has protocol:subprotocol:server-name:port number, database name
    // and authentication details.
                         String      dbURL       =      "jdbc:sqlserver://SQLS:1433;
databaseName=MyDB;integratedSecurity=true;";
    try {
      conn = DriverManager.getConnection(dbURL);
```

```
        String query = "SELECT * FROM Student where StudName like ?";
        PreparedStatement pstmt = conn.prepareStatement(query);
        pstmt.setString(1, "M%");
        ResultSet rs = pstmt.executeQuery();
        System.out.println("ID \t Name \t Percentage");
        while(rs.next()){
          System.out.println(rs.getInt("StudId")+"\t"+rs.getString("StudName")+"\
t"+rs.getFloat("Percentage"));
        }
      } catch (SQLException e) {
        System.out.println("Exception: " + e.getMessage());
      }
    }
}
```

Here, **prepareStatement()** method is used to create a **PreparedStatement** object. A parameterized **SELECT** query is created to retrieve all students whose name begins with **M** by using the **LIKE** wildcard of SQL. The placeholder **?** is replaced by the value given in the **setString()** method. The output of the code is as shown in *Figure 10.26*:

ID	Name	Percentage
1	Maddy	45.0
2	Mary	54.0
5	Mark	70.0

***Figure 10.26:** Parameterized SELECT query*

The following code shows the example of **executeUpdate()** method for inserting data into the table by using a parameterized **INSERT** statement:

```
import java.sql.Connection;
import java.sql.DriverManager;
import java.sql.PreparedStatement;
public class QueryDemo1 {
  public static void main(String[] args) {
    Connection conn;
    try{
                        String    dbURL    =    "jdbc:sqlserver://SQLS:1433;
databaseName=MyDB;integratedSecurity=true;";
      conn = DriverManager.getConnection(dbURL);
```

```
      String query = "insert into Student values (?,?,?)";
      PreparedStatement pstmt = conn.prepareStatement(query);
      pstmt.setInt(1,7);
      pstmt.setString(2, "Victor");
      pstmt.setFloat(3,76.8f);
      int result = pstmt.executeUpdate();
      if(result >0){
        System.out.println("Data Inserted");
      }else{
        System.out.println("Insert Failed");
      }

    }catch(Exception e){
      System.out.println("Error:"+e.getMessage());
    }
  }
}
```

Here, the placeholder **?** is replaced by the actual values specified in the setters. The output of the code is shown in *Figure 10.27*. The data is inserted in the table:

	StudId	StudName	Percentage
1	1	Maddy	45
2	2	Mary	54
3	3	Clara	77
4	4	Peter	40
5	5	Mark	70
6	6	Roger	78.6
7	7	Victor	76.8000030517578

Figure 10.27: *Parameterized INSERT query*

10.12 DatabaseMetaData

Metadata is data about data. JDBC allows access to metadata of a database by using the **`DatabaseMetaData`** interface. It has methods that provide information about a database such as a database product name, product version, total number of tables, driver name, names of tables, the total number of views, and so on.

The **getMetaData()** method of **Connection** interface fetches information about the metadata of the database. For example:

```
DatabaseMetaData dmd = cn.getMetaData();
```

Listed below are some important methods of **DatabaseMetaData** interface:

- **getDriverName()**: Returns the name of the currently used JDBC driver as a string.
- **getDriverVersion()**: Returns the version number of the currently used JDBC driver as a string.
- **getDriverMajorVersion()**: Returns the major version number of the currently used JDBC driver as an integer.
- **getURL()**: Returns the URL for the current DBMS as a **String**.
- **getUserName()**: Returns the user name of the database as a **String**.
- **getConnection()**: Returns the connection object that produced this metadata object.
- **getSearchStringEscape()**: Returns the string to escape wildcard characters.
- **getDatabaseProductName()**: Returns the name of the database product as a **String**.
- **getDatabaseProductVersion()**: Returns the version number of the database product as a **String**.
- **isReadOnly()**: Returns a boolean value of true if the database is read-only, else returns false.
- **supportsTransactions()**: Returns a Boolean value of true if the database supports transactions else, returns false.

The following code demonstrates the use of **DatabaseMetaData**:

```
import java.sql.Connection;
import java.sql.DatabaseMetaData;
import java.sql.DriverManager;
import java.sql.SQLException;
public class DBMetaData {
  public static void main(String args[]) throws SQLException {
    Connection conn = null;
    try {
                       String    dbURL    =    "jdbc:sqlserver://SQLS:1433;
databaseName=MyDB;integratedSecurity=true;";
      conn = DriverManager.getConnection(dbURL);
      DatabaseMetaData dbmd = conn.getMetaData();
      System.out.println("Driver Name: " + dbmd.getDriverName());
      System.out.println("Driver Version: " + dbmd.getDriverVersion());
```

```
      System.out.println("UserName: " + dbmd.getUserName());
   System.out.println("Database Product Name: " + dbmd.getDatabaseProductName());
                  System.out.println("Database   Product   Version:    "    +    dbmd.
getDatabaseProductVersion());
    } catch (Exception e) {
      System.out.println(e);
    } finally {
      conn.close();
    }
  }
}
```

The output of the code is as follows, in *Figure 10.28*:

```
Driver Name: Microsoft JDBC Driver 6.0 for SQL Server
Driver Version: 6.0.8112.200
UserName:UV\sqls
Database Product Name: Microsoft SQL Server
Database Product Version: 11.00.2100
```

Figure 10.28: *DatabaseMetaData*

10.13 ResultSetMetaData

ResultSetMetaData interface provides information about the data within a **ResultSet** object such as the number of columns, column names, and type, and so on. The **getMetaData()** method of **ResultSet** object is used to retrieve the required information.

For example:

```
ResultSetMetaData rmd = rs.getMetaData();
```

Some important methods of **ResultSetMetaData** interface are listed below:

- **getColumnName()**: Returns the name of the specified column as a **String**.
- **getColumnCount()**: Returns the number of columns in the **ResultSet** object as an integer.
- **getColumnType()**: Returns the SQL type of the specified column as a **String**.
- **getTableName(int index)**: Returns the table name for the specified column index as a **String**.

The following code demonstrates the use of **ResultSetMetaData**:

```
import java.sql.Connection;
```

```
import java.sql.DriverManager;
import java.sql.PreparedStatement;
import java.sql.ResultSet;
import java.sql.ResultSetMetaData;
public class RSMetaData {
  public static void main(String args[]) {
    Connection conn;
    try {
      String dbURL = "jdbc:sqlserver://SQLS:1433;
databaseName=MyDB;integratedSecurity=true;";
      conn = DriverManager.getConnection(dbURL);
      PreparedStatement pstmt = conn.prepareStatement("select * from Student");
      ResultSet rs = pstmt.executeQuery();
      ResultSetMetaData rsmd = rs.getMetaData();
      System.out.println("Total columns: " + rsmd.getColumnCount());
      System.out.println("Name of 1st column: " + rsmd.getColumnName(1));
      System.out.println("Type of 1st column: " + rsmd.getColumnTypeName(1));
      conn.close();
    } catch (Exception e) {
      System.out.println(e);
    }
  }
}
```

The output of the code is as shown in *Figure 10.29*:

```
Total columns: 3
Name of 1st column: StudId
Type of 1st column: int
```

***Figure 10.29:** ResultSetMetaData*

10.14 Execute stored procedure with CallableStatement object

A stored procedure is a set of SQL statements that are stored in the database as a group with an assigned name so it can be reused and shared by multiple programs. Listed below are some characteristics of a stored procedure:

- A stored procedure can accept input parameters and return values as output parameters to the calling program.
- It may call other procedures.
- It may contain code to perform operations in the database.
- Returns a status value to the calling code indicating success or failure
- A stored procedure is compiled only once and then reused. This improves performance.
- It can be executed locally as well as remotely.

Listed below are the parameters used in the stored procedure:

- **IN**: Used to pass input values to a stored procedure.
- **OUT**: It is passed out of the stored procedure module, back to the calling code.
- **IN/OUT**: It is an **IN** or an **OUT** parameter or both. Its value is passed in the stored procedure and the value returned can be assigned to the same parameter and passed out of the module.

The following code demonstrates the creation of stored procedure by using the **Statement** object:

```
import java.sql.Connection;
import java.sql.DriverManager;
import java.sql.Statement;
public class SPDemo {
  public static Connection conn = null;
  public static void main(String[] args) {
    try {
      String dbURL = "jdbc:sqlserver://SQLS:1433;
databaseName=MyDB;integratedSecurity=true;";
      conn = DriverManager.getConnection(dbURL);
      Statement st = conn.createStatement();
      String myProcedure = "Create Procedure Show_Students as select * from
Student order by StudName";
      // Execute the stored procedure
      int result = st.executeUpdate(myProcedure);
      if(result==0)
        System.out.println("Stored Procedure Created");
      else
        System.out.println("Stored Procedure Creation Failed");
      } catch (Exception e) {
```

```
            System.out.println("");
            e.printStackTrace();
        }
    }
}
```

The stored procedure is created in the database.

10.14.1 CallableStatement interface

The **CallableStatement** object is used to call a stored procedure. The procedure can be called with or without a result parameter which is similar to the **OUT** parameter of the procedure. The question mark **?** placeholder is used to represent the parameters.

Syntax:

```
{call procedure_name}
```

Syntax:

```
{call procedure_name[(?, ?, ...)]}
```

Syntax:

```
{? = call procedure_name[(?, ?, ...)]}
```

> **Note: The code within the curly braces is the escape syntax for stored procedures. It is converted by the driver into native SQL used by the database.**

The **CallableStatement** inherits from the **Statement** and **PreparedStatement** interfaces. The getter method, that is, **get<Type>** is used to retrieve the **OUT** parameter values. The **prepareCall()** method is used to create the **CallableStatement** object.

Syntax:

```
CallableStatement cst = cn.prepareCall("{call functionname(?, ?)}");
```

For example:

```
CallableStatement cs = cn.prepareCall( "{call empSalaries(?)}");
```

Here, **empSalaries(?)** stored procedure is called with a single placeholder which could be an **IN**, **OUT**, or **IN/OUT** parameter. It does not have any result parameter. The setter methods, that is, **set<Type>** are used to specify values for the **IN** parameters.

The **OUT** parameters need to be registered by using the method, **registerOutParameter()**, before calling the stored procedure. The following code demonstrates the use of **CallableStatement** to invoke the **Show_Students** stored procedure:

```
import java.sql.CallableStatement;
```

```
import java.sql.Connection;
import java.sql.DriverManager;
import java.sql.ResultSet;
public class SPDemo {
  public static Connection conn = null;
  public static void main(String[] args) {
    try {
                              String    dbURL    =    "jdbc:sqlserver://SQLS:1433;
databaseName=MyDB;integratedSecurity=true;";
      conn = DriverManager.getConnection(dbURL);
      CallableStatement cst = conn.prepareCall("{call Show_Students}");
      ResultSet rs = cst.executeQuery();
      System.out.println("StudId\tStudName\tPercentage");
      while (rs.next()) {
          System.out.println(rs.getInt(1) + "\t" + rs.getString(2) + "\t\t" +
rs.getFloat(3));
      }
    } catch (Exception e) {
      System.out.println("");
      e.printStackTrace();
    }
  }
}
```

Here, the **prepareCall()** method is used to invoke the **Show_Students** stored procedure. The output of the code is shown in *Figure 10.30*:

StudId	StudName	Percentage
3	Clara	77.0
1	Maddy	45.0
5	Mark	70.0
2	Mary	54.0
4	Peter	40.0
6	Roger	78.6

Figure 10.30: *CallableStatement output*

The following code demonstrates the use of **registerOutParameter()** method:

```
/*
--Create a below parameterized procedure in your database
--The procedure uses max function to find the maximum percentage
--and returns it to caller as OUT parameter
Create procedure findMaxPer
@per_max float OUT
as
select @per_max = max(Percentage) from Student
*/
import java.sql.CallableStatement;
import java.sql.Connection;
import java.sql.DriverManager;
public class SPDemo1 {
  public static void main(String[] args) {
    try {
      Connection conn;
      String dbURL = "jdbc:sqlserver://SQLS:1433;
databaseName=MyDB;integratedSecurity=true;";
      conn = DriverManager.getConnection(dbURL);
      CallableStatement cstmt = conn.prepareCall("{call findMaxPer(?)}");
      cstmt.registerOutParameter(1, java.sql.Types.FLOAT);
      cstmt.execute();
      float maxPer = cstmt.getFloat(1);
      System.out.println("Maximum Percentage is " + maxPer);
    } catch (Exception e) {
      System.out.println("");
      e.printStackTrace();
    }
  }
}
```

Here, the **?** placeholder is for the **OUT** parameter, which is the maximum percentage returned by the query in the stored procedure. The **execute()** method is used to execute the query. The output will be as follows:

`Maximum Percentage is 78.6`

Listed below are some more examples of Stored procedures with **`IN`** and **`OUT`** parameters.

- Example with IN parameter:

```
/*
--Create a below parameterized procedure in your database---
--The procedure takes student id as parameter
--and returns the student details of that student
Create Procedure Display_Student (@Stud_Id Integer)
as
select StudName, Percentage
from Student
where StudId=@Stud_Id
*/
…
CallableStatement cstmt = conn.prepareCall("{call Display_Student (?)}");
   cstmt.setInt(1, 5);
   ResultSet rs = cstmt.executeQuery();
   while (rs.next()) {
      System.out.println("Name:" + rs.getString(1));
      System.out.println("Percentage:" + rs.getFloat(2));
   …
```

- Example with IN and OUT parameters:

```
/*
--Create below parameterized procedure in your database---
--The procedure takes a baseline value as parameter
--and returns the smallest percentage greater than the baseline
Create procedure [dbo].[findPercent]
@baseline int, @per_min int OUT
as
select @per_min = min(Percentage) from Student where Percentage > @
baseline
*/
…
   CallableStatement cstmt = conn.prepareCall("{call findPer(?,?)}");
   cstmt.setInt(1, 40);
```

```
    cstmt.registerOutParameter(2, java.sql.Types.INTEGER);
    cstmt.execute();
    int per = cstmt.getInt(2);
    System.out.println("Smallest Percentage greater than 40 is " + per);
...
```

10.15 Scrollable ResultSet

The **ResultSet** object contains data returned by the query in the form of rows and columns. By default, **ResultSet** can be traversed only once in the forward direction from the first to the last row. However, it is possible to traverse a **ResultSet** one row at a time, in the backward direction as well as move the cursor to a specific row. Also, it is possible to insert, update, and delete rows in a **ResultSet** object.

Listed below are the characteristics of the **ResultSet** object:

- **Scrollable**: Cursor can move forward as well as backward through a result set.
- **Updatable**: **ResultSet** object can be updated, and the changes can be saved to the database. This includes inserting new rows, updating, and deleting existing rows.
- **Holdable**: Can check if the cursor remains open after a **COMMIT**.

Listed below are the methods for creating a scrollable **ResultSet**:

1. **public Statement createStatement(int resultSetType, int resultSetConcurrency) throws SQL Exception**

   Here,

   - **resultSetType**: A constant value that can be **ResultSet.TYPE_FORWARD**, **ResultSet.TYPE_SCROLL_SENSITIVE**, or **ResultSet.TYPE_SCROLL_INSENSITIVE**.
   - **resultSetConcurrency**: Indicates whether a result set is read-only or updatable. The constant values can be **ResultSet.CONCUR_READ_ONLY** or **ResultSet.CONCUR_UPDATABLE**

     For example:

     ```
     Statement stmt = conn.createStatement(
     ResultSet.TYPE_SCROLL_INSENSITIVE,ResultSet.CONCUR_READ_ONLY);
     ResultSet rs = stmt.executeQuery("SELECT * FROM STUDENT");
     ```

2. **public CallableStatement prepareCall(String sql, int resultSetType, int resultSetConcurrency) throws SQLException**

   For example:

   ```
   CallableStatement cstmt = conn.prepareCall("? =call StudentDetail(?, ?)",
   ResultSet.TYPE_SCROLL_INSENSITIVE, ResultSet.CONCUR_READ_ONLY);
   ```

Listed below are the different static constants for the result set type:

- **TYPE_FORWARD_ONLY**: Cursor can move only in a forward direction in a **ResultSet**. This is the default type. This type of cursor is not sensitive to changes made to a database while it is open.

  For example:

  ```
  PreparedStatement pstmt = cn.prepareStatement
  ("SELECT * FROM STUDENT WHERE STUDID = ?",
  ResultSet.TYPE_FORWARD_ONLY, ResultSet.CONCUR_READ_ONLY);
  ```

- **TYPE_SCROLL_INSENSITIVE**: Cursor can scroll through the result set in various ways. This type of cursor is insensitive to changes made to the database while it is open.

  For example:

  ```
  PreparedStatement pstmt = cn.prepareStatement
  ("SELECT * FROM STUDENT WHERE STUDID = ?", ResultSet.TYPE_SCROLL_
  INSENSITIVE, ResultSet.CONCUR_READ_ONLY);
  ```

- **TYPE_SCROLL_SENSITIVE**: The cursor can scroll through the result set in various ways. This type of cursor is sensitive to changes made to the database while it is open. The changes will reflect when the cursor scrolls back and forth.

  For example:

  ```
  PreparedStatement pstmt = cn.prepareStatement
  ("SELECT * FROM STUDENT WHERE STUDID = ?",ResultSet.TYPE_SCROLL_SENSITIVE,
  ResultSet.CONCUR_ READ_ONLY);
  ```

Concurrency indicates two or more events occurring in parallel. The concurrency type of a **ResultSet** object can be set to indicate whether it is updatable. Listed below are the constant values for specifying the concurrency types:

- **CONCURRENCY.READ_ONLY**: Result set cannot be modified and hence, not updatable.
- **CONCURRENCY.UPDATABLE**: Allows to perform insert, update, and delete operations on the result set, and the changes are saved to the database.

Listed below are the important cursor positioning methods for scrollable result set:

- **next()**: Moves the cursor forward by one row from the current position in the **ResultSet**. Returns true if the cursor is positioned on a valid row, else returns false.
- **previous()**: Moves the cursor backward by one row from the current position in the **ResultSet**. Returns true if the cursor is positioned on a valid row, else returns false.
- **first()**: Moves the cursor to the first row in the **ResultSet**. Returns true if the cursor is positioned on the first row. Returns false if the **ResultSet** is empty.
- **last()**: Moves the cursor to the last row in the **ResultSet**. Returns true if the cursor is positioned on the last row. Returns false if the **ResultSet** is empty.
- **beforeFirst()**: Moves the cursor immediately before the first row in the **ResultSet**.

- **afterLast()**: Moves the cursor immediately after the last row in the **ResultSet**.
- **relative(int rows)**: Moves the cursor relative to its current position in the **ResultSet**. Returns true if the cursor is positioned on a valid row, else returns false. For row value 0, this method has no effect. For a positive row value, it moves the cursor forward by that many rows. For a negative row value, it moves the cursor backward by that many rows. If the number of rows is less than the specified count, it operates like **afterLast()** method.
- **absolute(int row)**: Moves the cursor to the row specified by row value. Returns true if the cursor is positioned on a valid row, else returns false. For row value 0, this method operates like **beforeFirst** method. For a positive row value, the cursor is positioned that many rows from the beginning of the **ResultSet**. The first row is numbered 1, the second is 2, and so on. For a negative row value, the cursor is positioned that many rows from the end of the **ResultSet**. The last row is numbered -1, the second to last is -2, and so on.

10.15.1 Insert, update, delete operations on a ResultSet object

A scrollable and updatable result set allows traversing, inserting, and modifying rows in a **ResultSet** object. The **updateXXX()** methods are used to modify data in an existing row. Insert, Update, Delete operations on a **ResultSet** object can be done by using the below steps:

1. Positioning the cursor
2. Updating the columns
3. Commit the row

The following example demonstrates how to insert a row in a **ResultSet** object:

```
import java.sql.Connection;
import java.sql.DriverManager;
import java.sql.ResultSet;
import java.sql.Statement;
public class InsertRowExample {
  public static void main(String[] args) {
    try {
      Connection conn;
      String dbURL = "jdbc:sqlserver://SQLS:1433;
databaseName=MyDB;integratedSecurity=true;";
      conn = DriverManager.getConnection(dbURL);
      //Create an updatable result set
```

```
        Statement stmt = conn.createStatement(ResultSet.TYPE_SCROLL_SENSITIVE,
ResultSet.CONCUR_UPDATABLE);
      ResultSet rs = stmt.executeQuery("SELECT StudId, StudName, Percentage FROM
Student");
        rs.moveToInsertRow();
        // Set values for the new row
        rs.updateInt(1, 7);
        rs.updateString(2, "William");
        rs.updateFloat(3, 10.5f);
        //Commit appending of new row to the result set
        rs.insertRow();
      } catch (Exception e) {
        e.printStackTrace();
        System.out.println("Exception" + e.getMessage());
      }
    }
}
```

The new row is inserted and saved into the database as shown in *Figure 10.31:*

StudId	StudName	Percentage
1	Maddy	45
2	Mary	54
3	Clara	77
4	Peter	40
5	Mark	70
6	Roger	78.6
7	Florence	79

Figure 10.31: *Insert row in a ResultSet*

The following code demonstrates how to update a row in a **ReslutSet** object:

```
import java.sql.Connection;
import java.sql.DriverManager;
import java.sql.ResultSet;
import java.sql.Statement;
public class UpdateRowExample {
  public static void main(String[] args) {
```

```
    // TODO code application logic here
    try {
      Connection conn;
      String dbURL = "jdbc:sqlserver://SQLS:1433;
databaseName=MyDB;integratedSecurity=true;";
      conn = DriverManager.getConnection(dbURL);
      //Create an updatable result set
         Statement st = conn.createStatement(ResultSet.TYPE_SCROLL_SENSITIVE,
ResultSet.CONCUR_UPDATABLE);
       ResultSet rs = st.executeQuery("SELECT StudId, StudName, Percentage FROM
Student where StudId=4");
      // Move to the first row in the result set
      rs.first();
      rs.updateString(2, "Patrick");
      rs.updateFloat(3, 85.6f);
      // commit the update
      rs.updateRow();
    } catch (Exception e) {
      System.out.println("");
      e.printStackTrace();
    }
  }
}
```

The row for the student with **StudID** 4 is updated and saved into the database as shown in *Figure 10.32*:

StudId	StudName	Percentage
1	Maddy	45
2	Mary	54
3	Clara	77
4	Patrick	85.5999984741211
5	Mark	70
6	Roger	78.6
7	Florence	79

Figure 10.32: *Update row in a ResultSet*

The following code demonstrates how to delete a row in a **ResultSet** object:

```
import java.sql.Connection;
import java.sql.DriverManager;
import java.sql.ResultSet;
import java.sql.Statement;
public class DeleteRowDemo {
  public static void main(String[] args) {
    try {
      Connection conn;
      String dbURL = "jdbc:sqlserver://SQLS:1433;
databaseName=MyDB;integratedSecurity=true;";
      conn = DriverManager.getConnection(dbURL);
      //Create an updatable result set
         Statement st = conn.createStatement(ResultSet.TYPE_SCROLL_SENSITIVE,
ResultSet.CONCUR_UPDATABLE);
      ResultSet rs = st.executeQuery("SELECT * FROM Student");
      // Move to the last row in the result set
      rs.last();
      // Commit the delete
      rs.deleteRow();
    } catch (Exception e) {
      System.out.println("");
      e.printStackTrace();
    }
  }
}
```

The last row (in this case **StudId**=7), is deleted and changes saved into the database as shown in *Figure 10.33*:

StudId	StudName	Percentage
1	Maddy	45
2	Mary	54
3	Clara	77
4	Patrick	85.5999984741211
5	Mark	70
6	Roger	78.6

Figure 10.33: *Delete row in a ResultSet*

10.16 Batch updates

A batch is a set of statements grouped together for processing at the same time. The batch update feature allows the processing of multiple update commands as a single unit or batch. The **Statement**, **PreparedStatement** as well as **CallableStatement** objects, can be used to submit batch updates. Batch updates essentially help to improve performance. The steps to implement batch updates using the **Statement** interface are:

- Disable the auto-commit mode

  conn.setAutoCommit(false);

- Create a Statement/PreparedStatement/CallableStatement instance

  Statement stmt = conn.createStatement();

- Add query statements to the batch

  stmt.addBatch("INSERT INTO STUDENT VALUES (10, 'Michael')");

  stmt.addBatch("INSERT INTO STUDENT VALUES (11, 'Willy')");

- Execute the batch

  int[] count = stmt.executeBatch();

- Commit the changes in the database

  conn.commit();

  conn.setAutoCommit(true);

- Remove commands from the batch

  stmt.clearBatch();

The following demonstration shows how to execute batch updates by using **Statement** object:

```
import java.sql.Connection;
import java.sql.DriverManager;
import java.sql.Statement;
public class StmtBatchUpdate {

  public static void main(String[] args) {
    try {
      Connection conn;
      //Get a connection
                    String    dbURL    =    "jdbc:sqlserver://SQLS:1433;
databaseName=MyDB;integratedSecurity=true;";
      conn = DriverManager.getConnection(dbURL);
      conn.setAutoCommit(false);
      Statement st = conn.createStatement();
```

```
        st.addBatch("INSERT INTO Student VALUES (7, 'Stephen',65.8)");
        st.addBatch("INSERT INTO Student VALUES (8, 'Vereonica',77.2)");
        st.addBatch("INSERT INTO Student VALUES (9, 'Stella',58.6)");
        int[] updateCount = st.executeBatch();
        conn.commit();
        for (int i = 0; i <updateCount.length; i++) {
            System.out.println("Update count for statement "+ (i+1) +" is "+
updateCount[i]);
        }

        conn.setAutoCommit(true);
          st.clearBatch();
        }catch(Exception e){
          e.printStackTrace();
        }
      }
}
```

The **batch** statements are inserted into the database. The output of the code is as shown in *Figure 10.34*:

```
date count for statement 2 is
date count for statement 3 is
```

StudId	StudName	Percentage
1	Maddy	45
2	Mary	54
3	Clara	77
4	Patrick	85.5999984741211
5	Mark	70
6	Roger	78.6
7	Stephen	65.8
8	Vereonica	77.2
9	Stella	58.6

***Figure 10.34:** Batch update with Statement object*

The following demonstration shows how to execute batch updates by using **PreparedStatement** object:

```
import java.sql.Connection;
import java.sql.DriverManager;
import java.sql.PreparedStatement;
public class PstmtBatchUpdate {

  public static void main(String[] args) {
    try {
      Connection conn;
      //Get a connection
                    String    dbURL    =    "jdbc:sqlserver://SQLS:1433;
databaseName=MyDB;integratedSecurity=true;";
      conn = DriverManager.getConnection(dbURL);
      conn.setAutoCommit(false);

      PreparedStatement pst = conn.prepareStatement("INSERT INTO Student VALUES
(?,?,?)");
      // set the parameter values
      pst.setInt(1, 10);
      pst.setString(2, "Michael");
      pst.setFloat(3, 78f);
      pst.addBatch();

      pst.setInt(1, 11);
      pst.setString(2, "Cooper");
      pst.setFloat(3, 66.6f);
      pst.addBatch();
      int[] updateCount = pst.executeBatch();
      for (int i = 0; i <updateCount.length; i++) {
           System.out.println("Update count for statement "+ (i+1) +" is "+
updateCount[i]);
      }
      conn.commit();
      conn.setAutoCommit(true);
```

```
            pst.clearBatch();
        } catch (Exception e) {
            e.printStackTrace();
        }
    }
}
```

The parameterized **batch** statements are inserted into the database. The output of the code is shown in *Figure 10.35*:

```
Update count for statement 1 is 1
Update count for statement 2 is 1
```

StudId	StudName	Percentage
1	Maddy	45
2	Mary	54
3	Clara	77
4	Patrick	85.5999984741211
5	Mark	70
6	Roger	78.6
7	Stephen	65.8
8	Vereonica	77.2
9	Stella	58.6
10	Michael	78
11	Cooper	66.5999984741211

Figure 10.35: *Batch update with PreparedStatement object*

The following demonstration shows how to execute batch updates by using **CallableStatement** object:

```
/*
        Create the below-stored procedure in SQL Server
        Create procedure addStudent
        @id int, @name varchar(50), @per float
        as
        insert into Student values (@id,@name,@per)
  */
import java.sql.CallableStatement;
import java.sql.Connection;
```

```
import java.sql.DriverManager;
public class CstmtBatchUpdate {

  public static void main(String[] args) {
    try {
      Connection conn;
      //Get a connection
                          String    dbURL    =    "jdbc:sqlserver://SQLS:1433;
databaseName=MyDB;integratedSecurity=true;";
      conn = DriverManager.getConnection(dbURL);
      conn.setAutoCommit(false);

      CallableStatement cst = conn.prepareCall("{call addStudent(?,?,?)}");
      // Set the query parameter values
      cst.setInt(1, 12);
      cst.setString(2, "Stewart");
      cst.setFloat(3, 69.7f);
      cst.addBatch();

      cst.setInt(1, 13);
      cst.setString(2, "Kevin");
      cst.setFloat(3, 55.5f);
      cst.addBatch();

      int[] updateCount = cst.executeBatch();
      for (int i = 0; i < updateCount.length; i++) {
        System.out.println("Update count for statement " + (i + 1) + " is " +
updateCount[i]);
      }
      conn.commit();
      conn.setAutoCommit(true);
      cst.clearBatch();
    } catch (Exception e) {
      e.printStackTrace();
```

```
        }
    }
}
```

The **batch** statements are inserted into the database. The output of the code is shown in *Figure 10.36*:

```
Update count for statement 1 is 1
Update count for statement 2 is 1
```

StudId	StudName	Percentage
1	Maddy	45
2	Mary	54
3	Clara	77
4	Patrick	85.5999984741211
5	Mark	70
6	Roger	78.6
7	Stephen	65.8
8	Vereonica	77.2
9	Stella	58.6
10	Michael	78
11	Cooper	66.5999984741211
12	Stewart	69.6999969482422
13	Kevin	55.5

Figure 10.36: *Batch update with CallableStatement object*

10.17 Transactions

Transaction refers to a set of statements executed together as a unit. The lock mechanism of transactions allows preserving data integrity in a table. A transaction can be committed or rolled back.

Listed below are the ACID properties of a transaction:

- **Atomicity**: This property guarantees that either all or none of the tasks in the transaction will be executed successfully.
- **Consistency**: This property ensures that data integrity is maintained by applying integrity constraints on data. For example, the score of a student cannot be negative, hence, the transaction will be aborted if the statement fails to adhere to this constraint.
- **Isolation**: This property ensures that there are no conflicts between concurrent transactions and the transactions should execute in isolation.
- **Durability**: This property ensures that the database can recover committed transactions in case of system or storage media failures.

Listed below are the important steps to implement transactions in Java:

1. **Start the Transaction**: The first step is to start the transaction. By default, a new connection is in auto-commit mode. To disable auto-commit mode, use the **`setAutoCommit()`** method as shown below:

   ```
   cn.setAutoCommit(false);
   ```

2. **Perform Transactions**: Specify the transaction statements.
3. **Use SavePoint**: **`Savepoint`** allows saving transactions up to the given point when a rollback is performed. Transaction before the **`savepoint`** will not be rolled back.

   ```
   Savepoint svpt = cn.setSavepoint("SAVEPOINT_1");
   ```

   To remove a **`savepoint`** from the transaction, the method **`cn.releaseSavepoint`** is used that takes a **`savepoint`** object as a parameter.

4. **Close the Transaction**: A transaction can end either with a commit or with a rollback. With a commit, changes will be saved in the database, while with rollback, changes will be undone till the last **`savepoint`** (if any).

   ```
   cn.commit();
   ```

   OR

   ```
   cn.rollback(svpt);
   ```

The following demonstration shows the implementation of the transaction with **`Savepoint`** in Java:

```
import java.sql.Connection;
import java.sql.DriverManager;
import java.sql.PreparedStatement;
import java.sql.SQLException;
import java.sql.Savepoint;
public class TransactionExample {
  public static void main(String[] args) throws SQLException {
    Connection conn = null;
    Savepoint svpt = null;
    try {
                    String   dbURL   =   "jdbc:sqlserver://SQLS:1433;
databaseName=MyDB;integratedSecurity=true;";
      conn = DriverManager.getConnection(dbURL);
      conn.setAutoCommit(false);
      PreparedStatement pst = conn.prepareStatement("INSERT INTO Student
VALUES (?,?,?)");
```

```
      pst.setInt(1, 14);
      pst.setString(2, "Paul");
      pst.setFloat(3, 46.7f);
      pst.executeUpdate();
      svpt = conn.setSavepoint("SAVEPOINT_1");
      pst.setInt(1, 15);
      pst.setString(2, "Jennifer");
      pst.setFloat(3, 68.9f);
      pst.executeUpdate();
      pst.setInt(1, 16);
      pst.setString(2, "Katie");
      pst.setFloat(3, 70.5f);
      pst.executeUpdate();
      conn.commit();
      pst.close();
      conn.close();
    } catch (Exception e) {
      try {
        if (svpt == null) {
          // SQLException occurred in saving into Student table
          conn.rollback();
         System.out.println("JDBC Transaction rolled back successfully");
        } else {
          // exception occurred in inserting second record into Student
table
          // we can ignore it by rollback to the savepoint
          conn.rollback(svpt);
         System.out.println("JDBC Transaction rolled back to savepoint");
          //let's commit now
          conn.commit();
        }
        e.printStackTrace();
      } catch (SQLException e1) {
        System.out.println("SQLException in rollback" + e.getMessage());
      }
```

```
            }
        }
    }
```

Here, the code executes three insert statements in a transaction. A **Savepoint** is created after the first statement. In case any exception occurs in the second or third statement, it will be caught by the **catch()** block and the rollback will happen till the **Savepoint** and only the first statement will be committed. If all statements execute successfully, the table will be updated with the new records as shown in *Figure 10.37*:

StudId	StudName	Percentage
1	Maddy	45
2	Mary	54
3	Clara	77
4	Patrick	85.5999984741211
5	Mark	70
6	Roger	78.6
7	Stephen	65.8
8	Vereonica	77.2
9	Stella	58.6
10	Michael	78
11	Cooper	66.5999984741211
12	Stewart	69.6999969482422
13	Kevin	55.5
14	Paul	46.7000007629395
15	Jennifer	68.9000015258789
16	Katie	70.5

Figure 10.37: *JDBC transaction*

10.18 RowSet interface

The **RowSet** interface is an addition to the **javax.sql** package and is derived from the **ResultSet** interface. Similar to **ResultSet**, a **RowSet** also contains a set of rows from a tabular data source. A field/property in a **RowSet** can be manipulated by using the appropriate getter and setter methods.

The **RowSet** event model allows notifications to be sent to all components that implement the **RowSetListener** interface and are registered to listen for **RowSet** object events such as update, delete, and more.

Listed below are some points of comparison between **RowSet** and **ResultSet** objects:

- Some vendors do not provide scrollable/updatable result set support in the DBMS or the drivers. Instead, the **RowSet** object provides scrollability and updatability for any kind of DBMS or driver.

- Since a **RowSet** object is like a JavaBeans component, it can be used to notify other registered GUI components of a change.

Characteristics of a **RowSet** object:

- The cursor can be moved to a specific row.
- Allows using Java commands instead of SQL.

10.18.1 Types of RowSets

RowSets are broadly classified as connected or disconnected based on the duration of connection to the database. These are discussed below:

- Disconnected **RowSet**: **RowSet** object connects to a data source only to read or write data from a **ResultSet** to the data source. Once the read / write operation is completed, the **RowSet** object disconnects from the data source.
- Connected **RowSet**: **RowSet** object connects to a relational database by using a JDBC driver and the connection is maintained throughout the lifespan of the **RowSet** object.

Listed below are the important sub-interfaces of the **RowSet** interface:

- **JdbcRowSet**
- **CachedRowSet**
- **WebRowSet**
- **JoinRowSet**
- **FilteredRowSet**

Figure 10.38 shows the **RowSet** hierarchy:

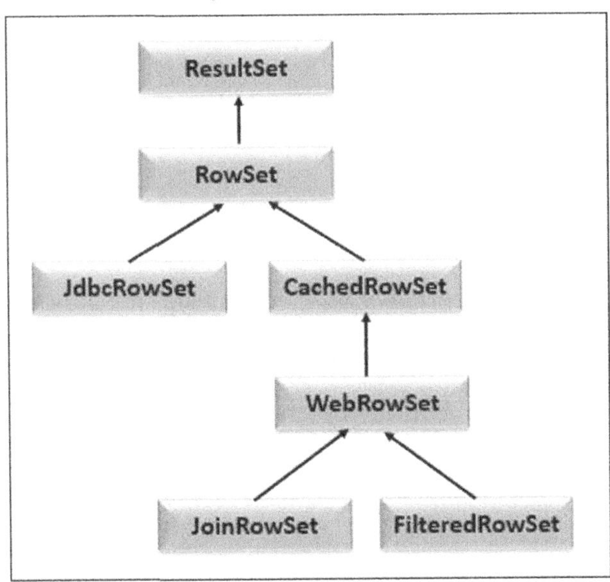

***Figure 10.38:** RowSet hierarchy*

The **RowSetFactory** and **RowSetProvider** interfaces introduced in **javax.sql.rowset** package since JDK 7 allow creating different **RowSet** implementations:

```
RowSetFactory rowsetFactory = RowSetProvider.newFactory();
```

Listed below are the methods of the **RowSetFactory** interface to create various **RowSet** implementations:

- **createJdbcRowSet()**
- **createCachedRowSet()**
- **createWebRowSet()**
- **createJoinRowSet()**
- **createFilteredRowSet()**

10.18.2 Connected RowSets

The only connected **RowSet** implementation is **JdbcRowSet**. It provides several methods to connect to a database and allows converting a non-scrollable read-only **ResultSet** into a scrollable and updatable object.

Listed below are some important methods of **JdbcRowSet** interface:

- **setUserName(String user)**: Sets the username to the specified value.
- **setPassword(String pass)**: Sets the database password to the specified value.
- **setURL(String url)**: Sets the URL to the specified value to establish a connection.
- **setCommand(String sql)**: Sets the command property to the given SQL query.
- **execute()**: Uses the **RowSet** object's properties to establish a connection to the database. It executes the query set in the command property and reads the data from the resulting result set object into the row set object.
- **commit()**: Saves all changes that are made since the last commit / rollback call permanent. It releases all database locks currently held by the connection object wrapped within the **RowSet** object.
- **rollback()**: Reverses all the changes done in the current transaction. It releases any database locks held by the connection object contained in the **RowSet** object.

The standard implementation of the **JdbcRowSet** interface is the **JdbcRowSetImpl** class.

```
JdbcRowSet jrs = new JdbcRowSetImpl(rs);
```

Listed below are the constructors of **JdbcRowSetImpl** class:

- **JdbcRowSetImpl()**: Creates a default **JdbcRowSet** object.
- **JdbcRowSetImpl(Connection con)**: Creates a default **JdbcRowSet** object for a valid connection. The **RowSet** object serves as a proxy for the result set object created.
- **JdbcRowSetImpl(String url, String user, String password)**: Creates a **JdbcRowSet** object with the specified URL, user name, and password.

- `JdbcRowSetImpl(java.sql.ResultSet res)`: Creates a **JdbcRowSet** object as a wrapper around the specified result set object.

Note: All constructors throw the java.sql.SQLException in case of invalid JDBC driver properties or database access error.

Listed below are some characteristics of the default **JdbcRowSet** object:

- It does not show deleted rows in its data.
- No limit on the time taken by a driver to execute the **RowSet** command.
- No limit for the number of rows that a **RowSet** may contain.
- No limit on the number of bytes a column of the **RowSet** may contain.
- It has a scrollable cursor and does not show the changes made by other users to the database.
- It does not show uncommitted data, hence eliminates the problem of dirty reads.

Uses an empty **HashTable** object to store parameters that are set.

Listed below are some ways to create a **JdbcRowSet** object:

- Using a default constructor

  ```
  JdbcRowSet jrs = new JdbcRowSetImpl();
  jrs.setUsername("admin");
  jrs.setPassword("admin");
  jrs.setUrl("jdbc:protocolName:datasourceName");
  jrs.setCommand("Select * from Student");
  jrs.execute();
  ```

  The default constructor of **JdbcRowSetImpl()** class is used and all the properties for a database connection are set. The command is specified and **execute()** is invoked with populates the **RowSet** object with data from the resulting **ResultSet** object.

- Using a **ResultSet** object

  ```
  Statement stmt = conn.createStatement();
  ResultSet rs = stmt.executeQuery(Select * from Student);
  JdbcRowSet jrs = new JdbcRowSetImpl(rs);
  ```

  A query is executed by using the **Statement** object and the resultant **ResultSet** object is passed to the **JdbcRowSetImpl** constructor. The constructor creates a new **JdbcRowSet** object which is initialized with the data in **ResultSet** object.

- Using the **RowSetFactory** interface

  ```
  RowSetFactory  rsFactory = RowSetProvider.newFactory();
  JdbcRowSet  jrs = myRowSetFactory.createJdbcRowSet();
  jrs.setUrl("jdbc:driver-name:<attributes,>");
  ```

```
jrs.setUsername(username);
jrs.setPassword(password);
jrs.setCommand("select * from Student");
jrs.execute();
```

An instance of the **RowSetFactory** interface is used to create a **JdbcRowSet** object.

Listed below are some important methods of the **JdbcRowSetImpl** class:

- **absolute(int row)**: Moves the cursor to the specified row in the **RowSet**.
- **first()**: Moves the cursor to the first row of the **RowSet** object.
- **last()**: Moves the cursor to the last row in the **RowSet**.
- **beforeFirst()**: Moves the cursor to the start of the **RowSet** object just before the first row.
- **afterLast()**: Moves the cursor to the end of the **RowSet** object just after the last row.
- **isFirst()**: Returns true if the cursor is on the first row of the **RowSet**.
- **isLast()**: Returns true if the cursor is on the last row of the **RowSet**.
- **isBeforeFirst ()**: Returns true if the cursor is before the first row of the **RowSet**.
- **isAfterLast()**: Returns true if the cursor is after the last row of the **RowSet**.
- **insertRow()**: Inserts the contents of the insert row into the **RowSet** as well as the database. An event notification is sent to all the listeners that a row has changed.
- **updateRow()**: Updates the database with the new contents of the current row of the **RowSet**. An event notification is sent to all the listeners that a row has changed.
- **deleteRow()**: Deletes the current row from the **RowSet** object as well as the database. An event notification is sent to all the listeners that a row has changed.
- **previous()**: Moves the cursor to the previous row above the current row in the **RowSet**.
- **next()**: Moves the cursor to the next row after the current row in the **RowSet**.
- **moveToCurrentRow()**: Moves the cursor to the remembered position. Used mainly while inserting a new row in the **RowSet** object.
- **moveToInsertRow()**: Moves the cursor to the insert row of a **RowSet** object.
- **updateInt(int column, int i)**: Updates the specified column with the given int value.
- **updateString(int column, String str)**: Updates the specified column with the given string value.
- **updateDate(int column, java.sql.Date date)**: Updates the specified column with the date value given in the parameter.

The following code demonstrates how to insert data by using **JdbcRowSet** object:

```
import com.sun.rowset.JdbcRowSetImpl;
import java.sql.Connection;
```

```
import java.sql.DriverManager;
import java.sql.ResultSet;
import java.sql.Statement;
import javax.sql.rowset.JdbcRowSet;
public class JdbcRowSetExample {
  public static Statement stmt;
  public static Connection conn;
  public static void main(String[] args) {
    try {
                          String    dbURL    =    "jdbc:sqlserver://SQLS:1433;
databaseName=MyDB;integratedSecurity=true;";
      conn = DriverManager.getConnection(dbURL);
        Statement stmt = conn.createStatement(ResultSet.TYPE_SCROLL_SENSITIVE,
ResultSet.CONCUR_UPDATABLE);
      ResultSet rs = stmt.executeQuery("Select * from Student");
      JdbcRowSet jrs = new JdbcRowSetImpl(rs);

//    insert row using JdbcRowSet
      jrs.moveToInsertRow();
      jrs.updateInt("StudId", 17);
      jrs.updateString("StudName", "Rosie");
      jrs.updateFloat("Percentage", 77.4f);
      jrs.insertRow();

    } catch (Exception e) {
      System.out.println(e.getMessage());
      e.printStackTrace();
    }
  }
}
```

The new row will be inserted into the table. Similarly, rows can be updated and deleted as shown below:

```
// update row using JdbcRowSet
jrs.absolute(3); // jump to row 3 in the RowSet
```

```
jrs.updateFloat(3, 67.5f);  //update percentage (column number 3) of student in
row 3
jrs.updateFloat("Percentage", 77.5f); //update percentage of student in row 3
jrs.updateRow();
// delete row using JdbcRowSet
jrs.last();
jrs.deleteRow();
```

10.18.3 Disconnected RowSets

Database connectivity may get interrupted due to low bandwidth networks and limited resources. In such cases, a disconnected **RowSet** is useful as it is not required to remain connected with the database and can be manipulated offline. A disconnected **RowSet** operates on data stored in memory/cache and not on the database directly. An example of a disconnected **RowSet** is the **CachedRowSet**. All other disconnected **RowSets** are derived from **CachedRowSet**. It can read/store data to a relational database as well as any other tabular format data source that has a key column.

In addition to the features of **JdbcRowSet**, it can operate on data when disconnected. Internally, it uses reader and writer objects for performing read/write operations on a data source using **SyncProvider** implementation. Listed below are the ways for creating a **CachedRowSet** object:

- Using the default constructor

  ```
  CachedRowSet crs = new CachedRowSetImpl();
  ```

  The **CachedRowSetImpl** class is a standard implementation of the **CachedRowSet** interface. Here, the default **SyncProvider** is passed to **CachedRowSet** instance by the **CachedRowSetImpl** default constructor:

  ```
  crs.setUsername("admin");
  crs.setPassword("admin");
  crs.setUrl("jdbc:protocolName:datasourceName");
  crs.setCommand("Select * from Student");
  crs.execute();
  ```

  The **username**, **password**, **url**, and **command** properties are set and the **execute()** method is invoked to process the command.

- Using the **SyncProvider** implementation

  ```
  CachedRowSet crs = new CachedRowSetImpl(com.myJava.providers.
  HighAvailabilityProvider);
  ```

  The fully qualified name of a **SyncProvider** implementation is passed as an argument to the **CachedRowSetImpl** constructor. The connection properties are set by using appropriate setter methods along with the command:

```
crs.setCommand("select * from STUDENT");
```

In case of updates, the key column also must be set. For example:

```
int[] keys = {2, 3};
crsStudent.setKeyColumns(keys);
```

After invoking the **execute()** method, the changes in the disconnected **RowSet** object must be saved to the data source. This accomplished by invoking the **acceptChanges()** method on the **CachedRowSet** object.

A **CachedRowSet** object is scrollable and updatable. It uses methods such as **next()**, **previous()**, **last()**, **absolute()**, and **first()** to move forward and backward.

The following demonstration shows the use of **CachedRowSet**:

```
import com.sun.rowset.CachedRowSetImpl;
import javax.sql.rowset.CachedRowSet;
import java.sql.Connection;
import java.sql.DriverManager;
public class CachedRowSetDemo {
  public static Connection conn;
  public static void main(String[] args) {
    try {
                      String    dbURL    =    "jdbc:sqlserver://SQLS:1433;
databaseName=MyDB;integratedSecurity=true;";
      conn = DriverManager.getConnection(dbURL);
      //Get a connection
      conn = DriverManager.getConnection(dbURL);
      CachedRowSet crs = new CachedRowSetImpl();
      String query = "Select * from Student";
      crs.setCommand(query);
      crs.execute(conn);
      System.out.println("Connection opened and data retrieved");
      conn.close(); //close the connection
      System.out.println("Connection Closed");
      System.out.println("\nList of all students before updation");
      System.out.println("ID\t Name \tPercentage");
      while (crs.next()) {
        System.out.println(crs.getInt(1) + "\t" + crs.getString(2) + "\t"
+ crs.getFloat(3));
      }
```

```
            crs.first();
            crs.updateString("StudName", "Melissa");
            crs.updateRow();
            // Save the changes from rowset to the database
            System.out.println("\nConnection Reopened");
            conn = DriverManager.getConnection(dbURL);
            crs.acceptChanges(conn);
            System.out.println("\nList of all students after updation");
            crs.beforeFirst();
            System.out.println("ID\t Name \tPercentage");
            while (crs.next()) {
              System.out.println(crs.getInt(1) + "\t" + crs.getString(2) + "\t"
    + crs.getFloat(3));
            }
          } catch (Exception e) {
            System.out.println(e);
          }
        }
    }
```

The connection is opened, and data is retrieved in the **CachedRowSet** object. Next, the update is performed on the first row of the **RowSet** and then the row is committed to the database by using the **acceptChanges()** method. The output of the code is as shown in *Figure 10.39*:

```
Connection opened and data retrieved
Connection Closed

List of all students before updation
ID      Name    Percentage
1       Maddy   45.0
2       Mary    54.0
3       Clara   77.0
4       Patrick 85.6
5       Mark    70.0
6       Roger   78.6
7       Stephen 65.8
8       Vereonica       77.2
9       Stella  58.6
10      Michael 78.0
11      Cooper  66.6
12      Stewart 69.7
13      Kevin   55.5
14      Paul    46.7
15      Jennifer        68.9
16      Katie   70.5
17      Rosie   77.4

Connection Reopened

List of all students after updation
ID      Name    Percentage
1       Melissa 45.0
2       Mary    54.0
3       Clara   77.0
4       Patrick 85.6
5       Mark    70.0
6       Roger   78.6
7       Stephen 65.8
8       Vereonica       77.2
9       Stella  58.6
10      Michael 78.0
11      Cooper  66.6
12      Stewart 69.7
13      Kevin   55.5
14      Paul    46.7
15      Jennifer        68.9
16      Katie   70.5
17      Rosie   77.4
```

Figure 10.39: *CachedRowSet*

Similarly, insert and delete operations can be performed by using **CachedRowSet**. For example:

```
while (crs.next()) {
  if (crs.getInt("StudId") == 10) {
    crs.deleteRow();
    break;
  }
}
```

This will delete the row with student id as 10 from the row set.

Conclusion

In this chapter you learnt that Java allows creating threads by extending the **Thread** class or implementing the **Runnable** interface. Daemon thread is a low priority service provider thread that runs in the background and provides services to the user thread. When two or more threads wait for resources locked by each other, the waiting state continues infinitely leading to a situation known as deadlock. JDBC API provides a set of libraries and database drivers that are platform-independent in their implementation. Java provides a set of classes and interfaces defined in the **java.sql** package to connect and manipulate databases. **PreparedStatement** object is created by using the **preparedStatement()** method of the **Connection** object. JDBC allows access to the metadata of a database by using the **DatabaseMetaData** interface. A scrollable and updatable result set allows traversing, inserting, and modifying rows in a **ResultSet** object. Transaction refers to a set of statements executed together as a unit. **Savepoint** allows saving transactions up to the given point when a rollback is performed. Connected **RowSet** object connects to a relational database by using a JDBC driver and the connection is maintained throughout the lifespan of the **RowSet** object.

In the next chapter, you will learn about design patterns and internationalization.

Multiple choice questions

1. **Which method allocates system resources to a newly created thread object?**
    a. start
    b. run
    c. sleep
    d. interrupt ()
2. **Consider the below partial code.**

```
try{
  t1.sleep (10000);
}
```

For how many seconds will the thread be suspended?

a. 100
b. 10
c. 1
d. 10000

3. **Which type of driver accesses native methods of a particular database through JDBC calls?**
    a. Type I, JDBC-ODBC Bridge driver
    b. Type II, Native API-Java/ Partly Java driver
    c. Type III, JDBC Network-All Java driver
    d. Type IV, Native Protocol-All Java
4. **Which of the following is used to execute the stored procedure from Java code?**
    a. `PreparedStatement`
    b. `Statement`
    c. `Transaction`
    d. `CallableStatement`
5. **Consider the below partial code.**

```
...
Statement st = conn.createStatement();
st.addBatch("INSERT INTO Student VALUES (7, 'Stephen',65.8)");
st.addBatch("INSERT INTO Student VALUES (8, 'Vereonica',77.2)");
st.addBatch("INSERT INTO Student VALUES (9, 'Stella',58.6)");
int[] updateCount = st.executeBatch();
conn.commit();
...
```

It is an example of which concept?

a. Transaction
b. Concurrency
c. Batch Update
d. Multi-threading

Answers

1. a
2. b
3. b
4. d
5. c

Assignment

Create a Java program as per the below specifications:

1. Create a class named **Student** with attributes id, name, and percentage.
2. Create a constructor to set the values of these attributes.
3. Create another class called **StudentDetails** with the **main()** method.
4. Create a connection to the **Student** table.
5. Use appropriate logic and programming constructs to achieve the following:
    a. The program should ask the user to add id, name, and percentage of three students.
    b. The details of each student should be passed to a **Student** object.
    c. Each **Student** object should then be stored in a collection of type Student.
    d. After all three students' details are received, traverse the collection and add each row of data into a batch.
    e. Execute the batch and commit the data to the database.
    f. The update count should be displayed to the user for each row that was inserted.

Expected output (see *Figure 10.40*):

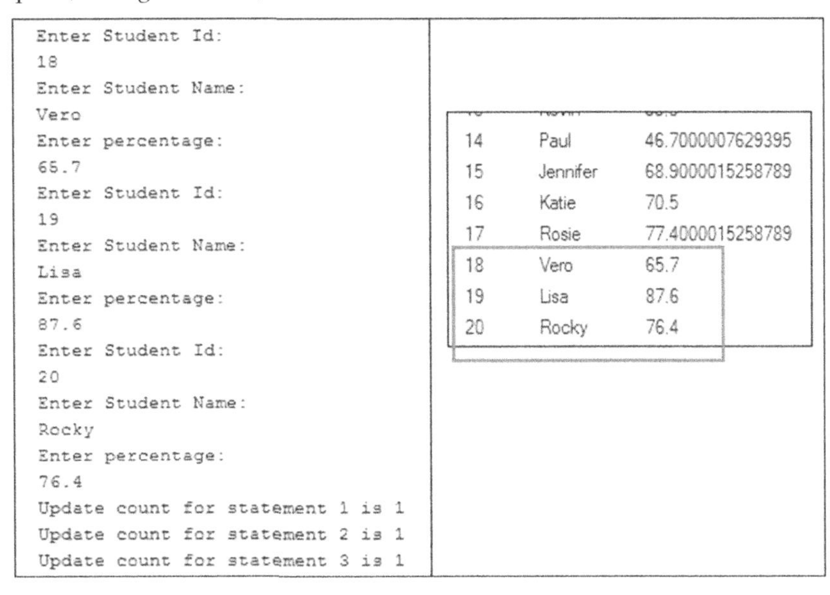

Figure 10.40: *Output*

CHAPTER 11
Design Patterns and Internationalization

Introduction

This chapter explains the implementation of polymorphism in Java. You will learn about the different types of design patterns. You will also learn to implement internationalization and localization in Java.

Structure

The following chapter contains the following topics:

- Design patterns and polymorphism
- Design patterns
- Structural patterns
- Behavioral patterns
- Other design concepts
- Internationalization and localization
- Implementing internationalization and localization
- Internationalization elements

Objectives

In this chapter, you will understand and implement polymorphism in Java. You will learn about design patterns and understand different types of design patterns. Internationalization and localization will be discussed in this chapter. You will also learn how to implement internationalization in Java.

11.1 Design patterns and polymorphism

A design pattern can be described as a solution, best practice, or a template to solve a frequently encountered problem. Programming for such problems is then done based on the design pattern. Most of the popular design patterns are based on the concept of polymorphism.

In object-oriented programming, the most common implementation of polymorphism is through method overloading and overriding. In the case of method overloading, a method with the same name is re-used with a modified signature. In method overriding, a child class modifies the functionality, as per requirement, of a method inherited from the parent class or interface with the same signature.

The following code demonstrates the implementation of polymorphism through method overloading and overriding:

<table>
<tr><th>Method overloading</th><th>Method overriding</th></tr>
<tr><td>

```
public class Calculator {
    public static void main(String[] args) {

        Calculator c = new Calculator();
        c.add(1,2);
        c.add(4,5,6);
        System.out.println("a+b = "+c.add(4,
5.5f));
    }

    public void add(int a, int b){
        System.out.println("a+b = "+(a+b));
    }

    public float add(int a, float b){
        return (a+b);
    }

    public void add(int a, int b, int c){
        System.out.println("a+b+c = "+(a+b+c));
    }

}
```

</td><td>

```
public class DrawShape {
    public static void
main(String[] args) {
        Shape s = new
Circle();
        s.drawShape();
    }
}
class Shape{
    public void drawShape(){
        System.out.
println("Drawing Shape");
    }
}
class Circle extends Shape{
    @Override
    public void drawShape(){
        System.out.
println("Drawing Circle");
    }
}
```

</td></tr>
</table>

Method overloading	Method overriding

Output:
`a+b = 3`
`a+b+c = 15`
`a+b = 9.5`
	Output:
	`Drawing Circle`

Table 11.1: *Implementation of polymorphism through method overloading and overriding*

Here,

- The **add()** has been overloaded to allow addition of different types of numbers.
- The **drawShape()** method has been overridden in **Circle** class and the functionality is modified as per requirement.

The following code demonstrates how to override **toString()** method of **Object** class:

```
public class Student {
  int id;
  String name;
  public Student(int id, String name) {
    this.id = id;
    this.name = name;
  }
  @Override
  public String toString() {
    return String.format(id + "\t" + name);
  }
  public static void main(String[] args) {
    Student s = new Student(1, "Roger");
    System.out.println("Student Detail:\n" + "ID \t Name");
    System.out.println(s);
  }
}
```

Output:

```
Student Detail:
ID  Name
1  Roger
```

11.1.1 instanceOf operator

The **instanceOf** operator is used to compare and object with another instance to check if it is of the same type. Null is not considered as an instance of any type.

The following code demonstrates the use of **instanceOf** operator:

```
import java.util.Scanner;
public class CheckBonus {
  public static void main(String[] args) {
    Employee emp = new Employee();
    Scanner sc = new Scanner(System.in);
    System.out.println("Enter Employee Details");
    System.out.println("Emp Id: ");
    emp.empid = sc.nextLine();
    System.out.println("Emp Name: ");
    emp.name = sc.nextLine();
    Employee ef = new FullTime();
    System.out.println("Full Time Employee");
    System.out.println("Emp Id: ");
    ef.empid = sc.nextLine();
    System.out.println("Emp Name: ");
    ef.name = sc.nextLine();
    if (emp instanceof Employee) {
      emp.bonus = 5000;
      System.out.println(emp.name + " received bonus of $" + emp.bonus);
    }
    if (emp instanceof FullTime) {
      emp.bonus = 7000;
      System.out.println(emp.name + " received bonus of $" + emp.bonus);
    }
    if (ef instanceof Employee) {
      ef.bonus = 7000;
      System.out.println(ef.name + " received bonus of $" + ef.bonus);
    }
    if (ef instanceof FullTime) {
```

```
            ef.bonus = 12000;
            System.out.println(ef.name + " received bonus of $" + ef.bonus);
        }
    }
}
class Employee {
    String empid;
    String name;
    String type;
    int bonus;
}
class FullTime extends Employee {
    String shift;
}
class PartTime extends Employee {
    String hours;
}
```

Here, **emp** is an instance of **Employee** but not of **FullTime** class. However, the **ef** instance is of type **FullTime** as well as **Employee** because **FullTime** is a child class of **Employee** class.

Output:

```
Enter Employee Details
Emp Id:
E001
Emp Name:
Jack
Full Time Employee
Emp Id:
FE001
Emp Name:
Richard
Jack received bonus of $5000
Richard received bonus of $7000
Richard received bonus of $12000
```

Figure 11.1: *instanceOf operator*

11.2 Design patterns

Design patterns are solutions to common problems encountered by software developers during software development. Over the years, certain popular design patterns have been used by developers to solve commonly encountered programming issues. A design pattern is a handy tool for beginners to reduce the learning curve and increase code maintainability.

Note: A design pattern is not an implementation or a framework and cannot be installed using code.

Listed below is a broad level classification of design patterns:

- Creational patterns:
  - Singleton pattern
  - Factory pattern
  - Abstract factory pattern
  - Builder pattern
  - Prototype pattern
- Structural patterns:
  - Adapter pattern
  - Composite pattern
  - Proxy pattern
  - Flyweight pattern
  - Facade pattern
  - Bridge pattern
  - Decorator pattern
  - DAO pattern
- Behavioral patterns:
  - Template method pattern
  - Mediator pattern
  - Chain of responsibility pattern
  - Observer pattern
  - Strategy pattern
  - Command pattern
  - State pattern
  - Visitor pattern
  - Iterator pattern
  - Memento pattern

11.2.1 Creational patterns

The creational patterns provide different ways to create objects without using the new operator and hiding the logic of creation. Some important creational patterns are explained in detail here:

11.2.1.1 Singleton pattern

The singleton pattern is used when a class needs to be restricted to have only one instance. The following code demonstrates the implementation of the singleton pattern:

```
public class TestSingleton {
  public static void main(String[] args) {
    SingletonDemo obj = SingletonDemo.getInstance();
    obj.message();
    SingletonDemo obj1 = new SingletonDemo(); // shows error


  }
}
class SingletonDemo {
  private static SingletonDemo objSingle = null;
  private SingletonDemo() {
  }
  public static SingletonDemo getInstance() {
    if (objSingle == null) {
      objSingle = new SingletonDemo();
    }
    return objSingle;
  }
  public void message() {
    System.out.println("This is singleton pattern demo");
  }
}
```

To implement a singleton design pattern, perform the following steps:

1. A static field reference, **objSingle**, is created to point to a single instance.
2. A single private constructor is added to the singleton class to prevent direct instance creation.

3. A public static factory method, **getInstance()**, is defined to instantiate and return the static field reference.

The following figure shows the error generated when the attempt is made to create a new object by using the **new** keyword:

```
public class TestSingleton {

    public static void main(String[] args) {
        SingletonDemo obj = SingletonDemo
        obj.message();
        SingletonDemo obj1 = new SingletonDemo(); // shows error

    }
}
```

SingletonDemo() has private access in SingletonDemo

(Alt-Enter shows hints)

Figure 11.2: Singleton pattern

11.2.1.2 Factory pattern

A factory pattern is used to create different objects without making direct constructor calls. Note that the logic is hidden from the user and a common interface is used for all types of objects that are created.

The following *Figure 11.3* shows an example of a factory pattern:

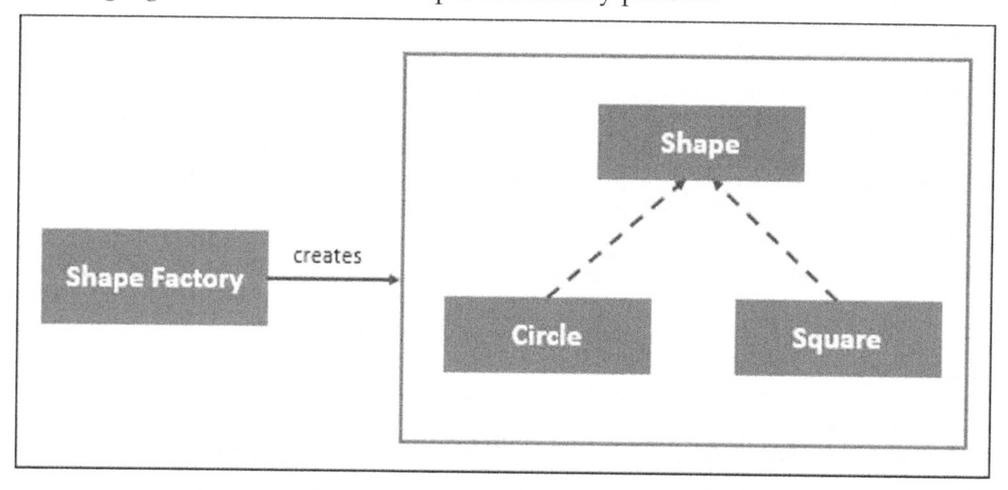

Figure 11.3: Factory pattern

The following code demonstrates the implementation of the factory pattern:

```
public class ShapeFactory {
  public static void main(String[] args) {
    ShapeFactory sFactory = new ShapeFactory();
    //get an object of Circle
```

```
    Shape objCircle = sFactory.getShape("Circle");
    //call the drawShape method of Circle class
    objCircle.drawShape();
    //get an object of Square
    Shape objSquare = sFactory.getShape("Square");
    //call the drawShape method of Square class
    objSquare.drawShape();
  }
  public Shape getShape(String shapeType) {
    if (shapeType == null) {
      return null;
    }
    if (shapeType.equalsIgnoreCase("Circle")) {
      return new Circle();
    } else if (shapeType.equalsIgnoreCase("Square")) {
      return new Square();
    }
    return null;
  }
}
interface Shape {
  public void drawShape();
}
class Circle implements Shape {
  @Override
  public void drawShape() {
    System.out.println("Drawing Circle");
  }
}
class Square implements Shape {
  @Override
  public void drawShape() {
    System.out.println("Drawing Square");
  }
}
```

Here, an interface **`Shape`** has been created with a method **`drawShape()`** which is overridden in the implementing classes **`Circle`** and **`Square`**. The **`ShapeFactory`** class creates a **`Shape`** instance and based on the reference assigned to it, the appropriate implementing class's **`drawShape()`** method is invoked.

11.3 Structural patterns

Structural patterns deal with the composition of class and objects. Inheritance is used to compose interfaces and different ways are defined to compose objects for different functionalities. Some important structural patterns are explained in detail here.

11.3.1 Data Access Object (DAO) pattern

The **Data Access Object (DAO)** design pattern is suitable in a scenario where the application data needs to be persisted. Here, there is a separation of the business logic from the data persistence logic, thereby making the code more maintainable. DAO pattern can be used with databases as well as any other type of data source such as XML files.

Listed below are some common data objects that DAOs can support:

- **Memory-based DAOs**: These represent temporary solutions.
- **File-based DAOs**: These may be required for an initial release.
- **JDBC based DAOs**: These support database persistence.
- **Java persistence API based DAOs**: These also support database persistence.

Listed below are the main components of an application using the DAO pattern:

- **Interface**: Defines the standard operations or methods for a model object to be used for persistence.
- **Concrete class**: Implements the interface and retrieves data from a data source.
- **Model / value object**: Defines the getter and setter methods that store data retrieved by the concrete class.

The following figure shows an example of DAO pattern:

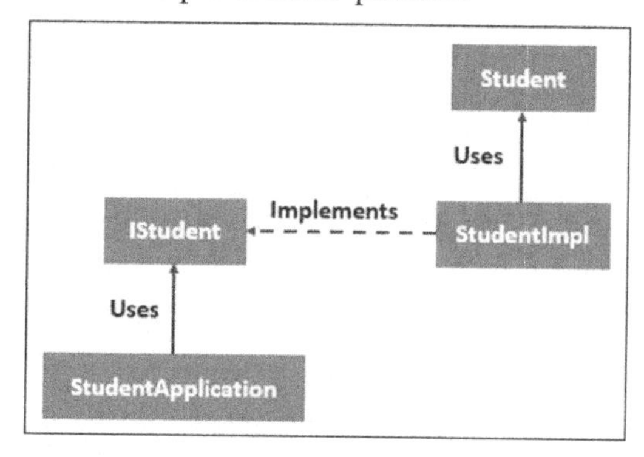

Figure 11.4: DAO pattern

Here,

- **Student** object is the Model/Value Object
- **IStudent** is the DAO interface
- **StudentImpl** is the concrete class that implements the **IStudent** interface
- **StudentApplication** is the main class which will use **IStudent** interface to demonstrate the use of the DAO pattern

The following code demonstrates the implementation of the DAO pattern [assumptions: Student ID begins with 1 and increments serially only]:

```
public class StudentApplication {

  public static void main(String[] args) {
    IStudent objStudent = new StudentImpl();
    System.out.println("Student Details");
    //display all students details
    System.out.println("ID\tName");
    for (Student objS : objStudent.getAllStudents()) {
      System.out.println(objS.getID() + "\t" + objS.getName());
    }
    //update student detail
    objStudent.updateStudent(1, "Roger");

    //get a specific student's detail
    Student s1 = objStudent.getStudent(1);
    System.out.println("Student: [ID : " + s1.getID() + ", Name:" + s1.getName()
+ " ]");
//
    //display all students details after update
    System.out.println("Student Details after Update");
    System.out.println("ID\tName");
    for (Student objS : objStudent.getAllStudents()) {
      System.out.println(objS.getID() + "\t" + objS.getName());
    }

    //delete student detail
    objStudent.deleteStudent(1);
```

```
        //display all students details after update
      System.out.println("Student Details after Delete");
      System.out.println("ID\tName");
      for (Student objS : objStudent.getAllStudents()) {
        System.out.println(objS.getID() + "\t" + objS.getName());
      }
    }
}
// DAO Model
class Student {
    private String name;
    private int ID;
    Student(int ID, String name) {
      this.ID = ID;
      this.name = name;
    }
    public int getID() {
      return ID;
    }
    public void setID(int ID) {
      this.ID = ID;
    }
    public String getName() {
      return name;
    }
    public void setName(String name) {
      this.name = name;
    }
}
// DAO interface
interface IStudent {
    public java.util.List<Student> getAllStudents();
    public Student getStudent(int ID);
```

```
  public void updateStudent(int ID, String name);
  public void deleteStudent(int ID);
}
// DAO implementation class
class StudentImpl implements IStudent {
  // list is used as a datasource
  java.util.List<Student> lstStudent;
  public StudentImpl() {
    lstStudent = new java.util.ArrayList<>();
    Student s1 = new Student(1, "Jack");
    Student s2 = new Student(2, "Mary");
    lstStudent.add(s1);
    lstStudent.add(s2);
  }

  // retrieve list of students from the data source
  @Override
  public java.util.List<Student> getAllStudents() {
    return lstStudent;
  }
  @Override
  public Student getStudent(int ID) {
    // ID-1 done to get the correct index position
    return lstStudent.get(ID-1);
  }
  @Override
  public void updateStudent(int ID, String name) {
    lstStudent.get(ID-1).setName(name);
    System.out.println("Student: ID " + ID + ", updated in the database.");
  }

  @Override
  public void deleteStudent(int ID) {
    lstStudent.remove(ID-1);
```

```
    System.out.println("Student: ID " + ID + ", deleted from database.");
  }
}
```

Output:

```
Student Details
ID      Name
1       Jack
2       Mary
Student: ID 1, updated in the database.
Student: [ID : 1, Name:Roger ]
Student Details after Update
ID      Name
1       Roger
2       Mary
Student: ID 1, deleted from database.
Student Details after Delete
ID      Name
2       Mary
```

Figure 11.5: *DAO pattern output*

11.4 Behavioral patterns

The behavioral patterns deal with communication between various objects. The following are the behavioral patterns. Some important behavioral patterns are explained in detail in this section.

11.4.1 Observer pattern

The observer pattern is implemented in cases when it is required to observe the change in state/property or other such behavior of objects. For example, in an online shopping site, the status of items can be monitored/observed, and notifications can be generated when an item is available or out of stock.

Listed below are the main components of the observer pattern:

- **`Subject`**: Manages a collection of observers and provides an interface to attach/detach to/from the observer object at runtime. It can have any number of observers.
- **`Observer`**: Provides an updated interface to receive notification from the subject.
- **`ConcreteSubject`**: Stores and indicates status to the **`ConcreteObserver`** as well as sends notifications.
- **`ConcreteObserver`**: Preserves a reference to an object of **`ConcreteSubject`** type and observer state. It also implements the update tasks.

Whenever the subject changes, it notifies the observers, and the status change will also be reflected in the observer's state. Java provides the **java.util.Observable** and **java.util.Observer** interfaces to implement the observer pattern. The following code demonstrates the use of the observer pattern to implement a messaging service.

Create the **Subject** and **Observer** interfaces:

```
public interface ISubject {
  //methods to register and unregister observers
  public void registerObserver(IObserver obj);
  public void unregisterObserver(IObserver obj);
  //method to notify observers of change
  public void notifyAllObservers();
  //method to get updates from subject
  public Object getSubjectUpdate(IObserver obj);
}
public interface IObserver {
  //method to update the observer, will be used by subject
  public void updateObserver();
  //method to attach observer with subject to observe
  public void attachToSubject(ISubject sub);
}
```

Create the implementation class for the **subject** interface:

```
import java.util.ArrayList;
import java.util.List;
public class MsgService implements ISubject {
  private List<IObserver> lstObserver;
  private String message;
  private boolean changed;
  private final Object SYNC = new Object();
  public MsgService() {
    lstObserver = new ArrayList<>();
  }
  //implement all overridden methods
  @Override
  public void registerObserver(IObserver obj) {
```

```
        if (obj == null) {
            throw new NullPointerException("Unknown Observer");
        }
        synchronized (SYNC) {
            if (!lstObserver.contains(obj)) {
                lstObserver.add(obj);
            }
        }
    }
    @Override
    public void unregisterObserver(IObserver obj) {
        synchronized (SYNC) {
            lstObserver.remove(obj);
        }
    }
    @Override
    public void notifyAllObservers() {
        List<IObserver> observersLocal = null;
        //synchronization ensure that an observer registered
        // after message is received is not notified
        synchronized (SYNC) {
            if (!changed) {
                return;
            }
            observersLocal = new ArrayList<>(this.lstObserver);
            this.changed = false;
        }
        for (IObserver obj : observersLocal) {
            obj.updateObserver();
        }
    }
    @Override
    public Object getSubjectUpdate(IObserver obj) {
```

```
    return this.message;
  }
  //method to send message to the MsgService
  public void sendMessage(String msg) {
    System.out.println("Message Sent to Messenger Service:" + msg);
    this.message = msg;
    this.changed = true;
    notifyAllObservers();
  }
}
```

Create the implementation class for the observer interface:

```
public class SubscriberMsgService implements IObserver {
  private final String name;
  private ISubject msgServ;
  public SubscriberMsgService(String name) {
    this.name = name;
  }
  // implement all overridden methods
  @Override
  public void updateObserver() {
    String msg = (String) msgServ.getSubjectUpdate(this);
    if (msg == null) {
      System.out.println(name + ":: No new message");
    } else {
      System.out.println(name + ":: Received message::" + msg);
    }
  }
  @Override
  public void attachToSubject(ISubject sub) {
    this.msgServ = sub;
  }
}
```

Create an application which will use the messaging service:

```
public class TestObserver {
  public static void main(String[] args) {
    //create subject
    MsgService msgs = new MsgService();
    //create observers
    IObserver obs1 = new SubscriberMsgService("Observer 1");
    IObserver obs2 = new SubscriberMsgService("Observer 2");
    IObserver obs3 = new SubscriberMsgService("Observer 3");
    //register observers to the subject
    msgs.registerObserver(obs1);
    msgs.registerObserver(obs2);
    msgs.registerObserver(obs3);
    //attach observer to subject for changes
    obs1.attachToSubject(msgs);
    obs2.attachToSubject(msgs);
    obs3.attachToSubject(msgs);
    //check if any update is available
    obs1.updateObserver();
    //now send message to subject
    msgs.sendMessage("Good Morning!!");
  }
}
```

The observers are notified every time a new message is generated. The following will be the output as given in *Figure 11.6*:

```
Observer 1:: No new message
Message Sent to Messenger Service:Good Morning!!
Observer 1:: Received message::Good Morning!!
Observer 2:: Received message::Good Morning!!
Observer 3:: Received message::Good Morning!!
```

Figure 11.6: *Observer pattern output*

11.5 Other design concepts

Besides the design patterns categorized earlier, there are other concepts such as delegation, composition, and aggregation that can be used to address specific types of problems.

11.5.1 Delegation

Delegation is a concept that allows an object to forward tasks to another object of similar type which is called the delegate. This promotes code reusability and gives the flexibility of changing delegate at run-time.

The following code demonstrates the use of delegation. Create the interface and implementation classes:

```
public interface IPrinter {
  void printFile(final String message);
}
public class Printer1 implements IPrinter {
  @Override
  public void printFile(String message) {
    System.out.println("Printer1 is printing: " + message);
  }
}
public class Printer2 implements IPrinter {
  @Override
  public void printFile(String message) {
    System.out.println("Printer2 is printing: " + message);
  }
}
```

Create a class that will manage the printers:

```
public class PrintManager implements IPrinter {
  private final IPrinter printer;
  public PrintManager(IPrinter printer) {
    this.printer = printer;
  }

  @Override
  public void printFile(String message) {
    printer.printFile(message);
  }

}
```

Create an application that will use the printers:

```
public class TestPrinter {
  public static final String MSG = "Good Morning";
  public static void main(String[] args) {

    // PrintManager delegates work to Printer1 and Printer2
    PrintManager printer1 = new PrintManager(new Printer1());
    PrintManager printer2 = new PrintManager(new Printer2());
    printer1.printFile(MSG);
    printer2.printFile(MSG);
  }
}
```

Here, the **PrintManager** instance delegates the task of printing to the instances of **Printer1** and **Printer2** classes. The following will be the output:

```
Printer1 is printing: Good Morning
Printer2 is printing: Good Morning
```

11.5.2 Composition and aggregation

Composition allows composing a class from references of other classes which act as fields of the containing class. This way, a complex object can be created from multiple objects. Aggregation is also a similar concept except that in composition, once the container object is destroyed, all inner objects are also destroyed. This does not happen in aggregation.

For example, a house is composed of rooms and each room has certain furniture. If the house is destroyed, the rooms also will no longer exist. However, the furniture will still exist. Thus, the house is a composition of rooms, whereas the rooms have an aggregation of furniture. Further, a piece of furniture can be placed in different rooms as per requirement. But a room of a house cannot be shifted to another house.

The following code demonstrates the use of composition:

```
class House{
  private Door dr;
  private Window wi;
}
class Door{
  string type;
  string material;
```

```
}
class Window{
  int shape;
  string color;
}
```

Here, the class **House** is composed of **Door** and **Window** classes. When the object of **House** class is destroyed, the instances of **Door** and **Window** classes are also destroyed.

11.6 Internationalization and localization

With the globalization of software comes the challenge of making it available to all countries and different locales across the world. The software must overcome the barriers of language, currency, date, time, symbols, and even spellings of words across countries. Two possible solutions could be, to develop the entire product in the desired language or to translate the product in the required language.

The first option will clearly prove to be time-consuming and costly while the second option is difficult since it is not possible for a developer, or a translator will have linguistic as well as coding skills. Thus, to make a software specific to different locales and user preferences, internationalization and localization can be used:

- **Internationalization**: It is also referred to as i18n for the first letter **I**, last letter **n**, and the 18 letters in between. Java provides built-in support for internationalization. I18N allows making an application available to the international market by making the user operations specific to different locales and as per user preferences. This is done without making any changes to the internal code.
- **Localization**: It is also referred to as l10n for the first letter **l**, last letter **n**, and the 10 letters in between. Unlike internationalization which deals with different locales and preferences, l10n deals with a specific region or language. Here, the locale-specific components are added and text (including date, currency, and so on.) and other user interface elements such as images, and so on. are translated/localized to suit a specific region or language.

Note: If an application is internationalized in an efficient manner, then it will be easier to localize it for a particular language and character encoding scheme.

Listed below are some advantages of I18N and L10N:

- New languages can be incorporated without recompiling the code.
- Single executable runs in any locale as localized data is incorporated within the application.
- GUI components are not hardcoded and hence can be retrieved and updated dynamically.

- User preferences such as currencies, dates, numbers, and so on. are applied as per the specific region and language. That is, the application can be easily and quickly localized.

11.6.1 ISO Codes

ISO codes are used to represent a language for implementing internationalization and localization. Language is represented in lower case, that is, alpha-2 or alpha-3 ISO 639 codes such as **es** for Spanish and **en** for English. The country is represented in the upper case by using the ISO 3166 alpha-2 code or UN M.49. For example, **US99** for the USA and **IN** for India. A properly internationalized application can be easily localized.

11.6.2 Unicode

Unicode is a computing standard for encoding characters and symbols of different languages by using hexadecimal values. Originally, it was designed to use 16 bits encoding which supported values from 0x0000 to 0xFFFF. However, this is not sufficient for Java as it is difficult to convert 16 bits to 32 bits. Special escape sequences such as **\uXXXX** (where X is a hexadecimal digit) are used to represent Unicode characters that cannot be represented in ASCII.

In Unicode character encoding, the hexadecimal value is prefixed with the string U+ and the valid code point range is U+0000 to U+10FFFF.

11.7 Implementing internationalization and localization

By using internationalization, messages need not be hardcoded in a specific language. The application becomes usable worldwide without recompilation as the language code is specified at runtime.

An internationalized application can be created as follows:

- Create the properties files: A properties file is a plain text file that stores the information about the program. It can be used to store the text that needs to be translated. The default properties file, **MessagesBundle.properties**, includes the default text to be displayed. It is specified as a key-value pair. For example:

```
greetings = Hello
farewell = Goodbye
inquiry = How are you?
```

  To translate this text into a specific language, for example, French, create a properties file named **MessagesBundle_fr_FR.properties** and specify the French text for the default text as under:

```
greetings = Bonjour
```

```
farewell = Au revoir
inquiry = Comment allez-vous?
```

Note that the keys on the left must not change as these are referred to during translation to fetch the appropriate text. Also, the file name prefix should remain the same followed by the language and country code.

- **Specify the locale**: The `java.util.Locale` object identifies a specific language and country. For example, a number, date, time, and so on. can be displayed as per the specific region or country by using the **Locale** object.

  Listed below are the constructors of the **Locale** object:

  public Locale(String language, String country): Creates a Locale object with the specified language and country.

Note: Language code is specified in lower case and country code in upper case.

```
lus = new Locale("en","US");    // Locale object for English language of USA
lfr = new Locale("fr","FR");    // Locale object for French language of France
les = new Locale("es","CR");    // Locale object for Spanish language of Costa Rica
```

public Locale(String language): Creates a locale object with the specified language.

Locale objects can be further used to format dates, numbers, and other locale-specific data. For example, a **ResourceBundle** is a locale-sensitive object.

Listed below are some important methods of the **Locale** class:

- o **public static Locale getDefault()**: Returns the default **Locale** object.
- o **public final String getDisplayCountry()**: Returns the name of the country for the current **Locale** object as a **String**.
- o **public final String getDisplayLanguage():** Returns the name of the language for the current **Locale** as a **String**. For example, if the default locale is **en_US**, the method returns English.

Create a **ResourceBundle**: **ResourceBundle** objects contain locale-specific objects and are used to retrieve locale-specific information from the properties file. This makes it easy for the application to be used for different languages and locales simultaneously and more can be added later.

The static and final method **getBundle(String, Locale)**, is used to retrieve locale-specific information from a given properties file. It takes two arguments, the name of the resource bundle as a **String** and an object of **Locale** class.

For example:

```
messages = ResourceBundle.getBundle("mybundles/MessagesBundle", currentLocale);
```

Here, the first argument identifies the properties file that will be accessed. It will be used to access the appropriate **MessagesBundle** file based on the locale specified. For example,

MessagesBundle_en_US.properties

MessagesBundle_fr_FR.properties

Listed below are the important methods of **ResourceBundle** object to retrieve the locale-specific data from the properties file:

- **public final String getString(String key):** Retrieves the value of the key specified as an argument from the properties file.
- **public abstract Enumeration <String> getKeys():** Returns an **Enumeration** object representing all the available keys in the properties file.
- **Retrieve the text from the appropriate ResourceBundle class**: The properties file contains the key-value pairs of the text to be translated as per that specific locale. The **getString()** method allows extracting the text from the specified keys.

  For example,

  ```
  String msg = messages.getString("greetings");
  ```

Here, the value of the key greetings is retrieved from the properties file.

The following example demonstrates the use of properties files and **ResourceBundles** to implement internationalization and localization. Create a **MessageBundle.properties** file with below content in a new package named **mybundles**:

```
greetings = Hello
farewell = Goodbye
inquiry = How are you?
```

Create the **locale-specific** properties files:

```
// MessageBundle_en_US.properties (English - USA)
greetings = Hello
farewell = Goodbye
inquiry = How are you?
// MessageBundle_fr_FR.properties (French - France)
greetings = Bonjour
farewell = Au revoir
inquiry = Comment allez-vous
// MessageBundle_es_CR.properties (Spanish - Costa Rica)
greetings = Hola
farewell = Chao
inquiry = ¿Cómo estás?
```

Create the application that will use the internationalization feature:

```
import java.util.Locale;
import java.util.ResourceBundle;
import java.util.Scanner;
public class I18NExample {
  public static void main(String[] args) {
    String language;
    String country;
    Scanner s = new Scanner(System.in);
    System.out.print("Enter language code: ");
    String lCode = s.next();
    System.out.print("Enter country code: ");
    String cCode = s.next();

    // set the default value for language and country
    if (lCode.equals("") || cCode.equals("")) {
      language = "en";
      country = "US";
    } else {
      language = lCode;
      country = cCode;
    }

    Locale currentLocale;
    ResourceBundle messages;

    // set the Locale object
    currentLocale = new Locale(language, country);

    // create the ResourceBundle object
  messages = ResourceBundle.getBundle("mybundles/MessagesBundle", currentLocale);
    // extract and display the translated text from
    // the resource bundle
    System.out.println("Greeting: "+messages.getString("greetings"));
```

```
    System.out.println("Inquiry: "+messages.getString("inquiry"));
    System.out.println("Farewell: "+messages.getString("farewell"));
  }
}
```

The following will be the output of the above code:

```
Enter lanugage code: es
Enter country code: CR
Greeting: Hola
Inquiry: ¿Cómo estás?
Farewell: Chao
```

Figure 11.7: output

11.8 Internationalization elements

In an internationalized application, it is important that the different GUI component captions such as date, time, numbers, text, and so on. are modified as per the culture, region, and language.

11.8.1 Formatting number

Java provides the **NumberFormat** calls with methods to identify and format the number as per the locale. Listed below are the important methods of this class:

- **public static final NumberFormat getNumberInstance():** Returns an object of the class **NumberFormat**.
- **public final String format(double number)**: Returns the **String** form of the formatted number.
- **public static NumberFormat getNumberInstance(Locale inLocale):** Returns an object of the class **NumberFormat** for the specified **Locale**.

The following code demonstrates the use of **NumberFormat** class:

```
import java.text.NumberFormat;
import java.util.Locale;
import java.util.Scanner;
public class FormatNumber {
  static public void displayNumber(Locale currentLocale) {
    Integer num1 = 123374;
    Double num2 = 343847.474;
    NumberFormat numObj;
```

```
    String value1;
    String value2;
    numObj = NumberFormat.getNumberInstance(currentLocale);
    value1 = numObj.format(num1);
    value2 = numObj.format(num2);
   System.out.println("Number Format as per " + currentLocale + " is " + value1);
   System.out.println("Number format as per " + currentLocale + " is " + value2);
  }
  public static void main(String[] args) {
    String language;
    String country;
    Scanner s = new Scanner(System.in);
    System.out.print("Enter language code: ");
    String lCode = s.next();
    System.out.print("Enter country code: ");
    String cCode = s.next();
    if (lCode.equals("") || cCode.equals("")) {
      language = "en";
      country = "US";
    } else {
      language = lCode;
      country = cCode;
    }
    Locale l;
    l = new Locale(language, country);
    displayNumber(l);
  }
}
```

The following will be the output:

```
Enter lanugage code: fr
Enter country code: FR
Number Format as per fr_FR is 123 374
Number format as per fr_FR is 343 847,474
```

Figure 11.8: Format number for a specific locale

11.8.2 Formatting percentage

The **NumberFormat** class provides methods to format percentages as per the specified locale. Listed below are some important methods of **NumberFormat** class:

- **public final String format(double percent):** Returns the formatted percentage in **String** form.
- **public static final NumberFormat getPercentInstance():** Returns an instance of the **NumberFormat** class.
- **public static NumberFormat getPercentInstance(Locale inLocale):** Returns an instance of the **NumberFormat** class for the specified `Locale`.

The following code demonstrates formatting of percentage values as per a specific locale:

```
import java.text.NumberFormat;
import java.util.Locale;
import java.util.Scanner;
public class FormatPercentage {
  public static void main(String[] args) {
    String language;
    String country;
    Scanner s = new Scanner(System.in);
    System.out.print("Enter language code: ");
    String lCode = s.next();
    System.out.print("Enter country code: ");
    String cCode = s.next();
    if (lCode.equals("") || cCode.equals("")) {
      language = "en";
      country = "US";
    } else {
      language = lCode;
      country = cCode;
    }
    Locale l;
    l = new Locale(language, country);
    displayPercentage(l);
  }
  public static void displayPercentage(Locale l) {
```

```
    NumberFormat percentFormatter;
    String strPercent;
    // Create an object of a wrapper class Double
    Double percent = 48.74;
    // Retrieve the NumberFormat instance
    percentFormatter = NumberFormat.getPercentInstance(l);
    // Format the percent figure
    strPercent = percentFormatter.format(percent);
    System.out.println("Percent format as per " + l + " is " + strPercent);
  }
}
```

Output:

```
Enter lanugage code: fr
Enter country code: FR
Percent format as per fr_FR is 4 874 %
```

Figure 11.9: *Format percentage for a specific locale*

11.8.3 Formatting currency

The **NumberFormat** class provides methods to format currencies as per the specified locale. Listed below are some important methods of **NumberFormat** class:

- **public final String format(double currency):** Returns the formatted currency as a **String**.
- **public static final NumberFormat getCurrencyInstance():** Returns an instance of the **NumberFormat** class.
- **public static NumberFormat getCurrencyInstance(Locale inLocale):** Returns an instance of **NumberFormat** class for the specified **Locale**.

The following code demonstrates formatting of currencies as per a specific locale:

```
import java.text.NumberFormat;
import java.util.Locale;
import java.util.Scanner;
public class FormatCurrency {
  public static void main(String[] args) {
    String language;
```

```
        String country;
        Scanner s = new Scanner(System.in);
        System.out.print("Enter language code: ");
        String lCode = s.next();
        System.out.print("Enter country code: ");
        String cCode = s.next();
        if (lCode.equals("") || cCode.equals("")) {
          language = "en";
          country = "US";
        } else {
          language = lCode;
          country = cCode;
        }
        Locale l;
        l = new Locale(language, country);
        displayCurrency(l);
    }
    public static void displayCurrency(Locale l) {
        NumberFormat currencyFormatter;
        String strCurrency;
        // Create an object of a wrapper class Double
        Double currency = 3847.78;
        // Retrieve the NumberFormat instance
        currencyFormatter = NumberFormat.getCurrencyInstance(l);
        // Format the currency
        strCurrency = currencyFormatter.format(currency);
        System.out.println("Currency as per " + l + " is " + strCurrency);
    }
}
```

Output:

```
Enter lanugage code: fr
Enter country code: FR
Currency as per fr_FR is 3 847,78 €
```

***Figure 11.10:** Format currency for a specific locale*

11.8.4 Formatting date

Java provides the **DateFormat** and **SimpleDateFormat** classes to format date and time as per the specified locale. The **format()** method of the **NumberFormat** class is used with the date to be formatted as an argument.

The **getDateInstance()** method returns an instance of the **DateFormat** class.

Syntax:

public static final DateFormat getDateInstance(int style, Locale locale)

Here,

- **Style**: Specifies the style of the date as an integer constant.
- **locale**: An object of the **Locale** class.

Listed below are the possible integer constants for **DateFormat** object:

- **SHORT:** Completely numeric, for example, 12.20.44 or 5:20 pm
- **MEDIUM:** A medium format, for example, Feb 22, 2019
- **LONG:** Longer format, for example, February 22, 2019
- **FULL:** Full specification format, for example, Friday, February 22, 2019 AD

The following code demonstrates formatting of dates as per a specific locale:

```
import java.text.DateFormat;
import java.util.Date;
import java.util.Locale;
import java.util.Scanner;
public class FormatDate {

  public static void main(String[] args) {
    String language;
    String country;
    Scanner s = new Scanner(System.in);
    System.out.print("Enter language code: ");
    String lCode = s.next();
    System.out.print("Enter country code: ");
    String cCode = s.next();
    if (lCode.equals("") || cCode.equals("")) {
      language = "en";
      country = "US";
```

```
    } else {
      language = lCode;
      country = cCode;
    }
    Locale l;
    l = new Locale(language, country);
    displayDate(l);
  }
  public static void displayDate(Locale l) {
    Date today;
    String strDate;
    DateFormat dateFormatter;
    dateFormatter = DateFormat.getDateInstance(DateFormat.FULL, l);
    today = new Date();
    strDate = dateFormatter.format(today);
    System.out.println("Date format as per "+ l + " is "+strDate);
  }
}
```

Output:

```
Enter lanugage code: es
Enter country code: CR
Date format as per es_CR is miércoles 30 de octubre de 2019
```

***Figure 11.11**: Format date for a specific locale*

11.8.5 Formatting messages

For static messages, translation is easy but for messages with dynamic data, translation to different languages is difficult as the statements might not be grammatically correct.

For example, consider the following message in English:

"Her birthday is on 05/02/2007"

French translation of this statement:

"Son anniversaire est le 05/02/2007"

Spanish translation of this statement:

"Su cumpleaños es el 05/02/2007"

The order of verbs and dynamic data differs in different languages and hence, forming a grammatically correct statement by concatenation is difficult in such cases. Java provides the `MessageFormat` class to create such dynamic compound messages. To use the `MessageFormat` class, it is important to identify the static and variable parts of a message.

For example, consider the following message:

Her birthday party is on February 05, 2019, at 6:30 PM and 10 people are invited.

Here, there are three variable parts indicated as bold text.

Next, a template with placeholders like `{0}`, `{1}`, and so on. for the variable parts needs to be created as per their position in the text. These placeholders will be replaced by the actual values at runtime by using `Object` array.

The elements that require translation should be fetched from the `ResourceBundle` with the `getString()` method. The `MessageFormat` instance is used with the desired locale to format the message.

The following code demonstrates formatting of messages as per a specific locale. Create the below message bundles/properties files:

```
MessageFormatBundle.properties

template = Her birthday party is on {0,date,long} at {1,time,short} and
{2,number,integer} people are invited.

MessageFormatBundle_es_CR.properties  (for Spanish of Costa Rica)

template = Su fiesta de cumpleaños es el {0,date,long} a las {1,time,short} y
están invitadas {2,number,integer} personas.

MessageFormatBundle_ja_JP.properties  (for Japanese of Japan)

template = Kanojo no tanjōbi pātī wa {0,date,long} no gogo {1,time,short} de,
{2,number,integer} ga shōtai sa remasu.
```

Note that the variable data in each properties file is substituted with an index and data type placeholder. Create the code to use the internationalization feature:

```
import java.util.Scanner;
import java.text.MessageFormat;
import java.util.Date;
import java.util.Locale;
import java.util.ResourceBundle;
public class MsgFormatDemo {
  public static void main(String[] args) {
    try {
      MessageFormat formatter = new MessageFormat("");
```

```
      String language;
      String country;
      Scanner s = new Scanner(System.in);
      System.out.print("Enter language code: ");
      String lCode = s.next();
      System.out.print("Enter country code: ");
      String cCode = s.next();
      if (lCode.equals("") || cCode.equals("")) {
        language = "en";
        country = "US";
      } else {
        language = lCode;
        country = cCode;
      }
      Locale currentLocale;
      currentLocale = new Locale(language, country);
      formatter.setLocale(currentLocale);
            ResourceBundle messages = ResourceBundle.getBundle("mybundles/
MessageFormatBundle", currentLocale);
      // set values of variables for template at position 0, 1 and 2
      Object[] messageArguments = {new Date(), new Date(), 7};
      formatter.applyPattern(messages.getString("template"));
      String output = formatter.format(messageArguments);
      System.out.println(output);
    } catch (Exception e) {
      System.out.println("Error:" + e.getMessage());
    }
  }
}
```

Output:

```
Enter language code: es
Enter country code: CR
Su fiesta de cumpleaños es el 31 de octubre de 2019 a las 12:48 PM y están invitadas 7 personas.
```

***Figure 11.12**: Formatting messages for specific locale*

Similarly, other messages can also be formatted for a specific region and locale.

Conclusion

In this chapter you learnt that a design pattern is a solution, best practice, or a template to solve a frequently encountered problem. The **instanceOf** operator is used to compare and object with another instance to check if it is of the same type. The creational patterns provide different ways to create objects without using the new operator and hiding the logic of creation. Structural patterns deal with the composition of class and objects. The behavioral patterns deal with communication between various objects. Delegation is a concept that allows an object to forward tasks to another object of similar type which is called the delegate. Composition allows composing a class from references to other classes that act as fields of the containing class. To make a software specific to different locales and user preferences, internationalization and localization can be used. Internationalization is also referred to as i18n for the first letter i, last letter n, and the 18 letters in between. **ResourceBundle** objects contain locale-specific objects and are used to retrieve locale-specific information from the properties file.

In the next chapter, you will learn about more features of JDK 8, 9, and 10.

Multiple choice questions

1. **A _________ is a handy tool for beginners to reduce the learning curve and increase code maintainability.**
   a. Program
   b. Design pattern
   c. Algorithm
   d. Diagram
2. **A factory pattern is used to create different objects without making direct constructor calls.**
   a. Observer
   b. Singleton
   c. Factory
   d. DAO
3. **Which of the following is a component of the Observer pattern?**
   a. Subject
   b. Observer
   c. Concrete Subject
   d. All of these
4. **Identify the correct format to initialize a `Locale` object for the English language of the USA.**
   a. `Locale l = new Locale("en", "US");`
   b. `Locale l = new Locale("US", "en");`

c. `Locale l = new Locale("en-US");`

d. `Locale l = new Locale("US-en");`

5. **Which of the following constant is not part of the `DateFormat` class?**

   a. `LONG`

   b. `SHORT`

   c. `MEDIUM`

   d. `COMPLETE`

Answers

1. b
2. c
3. d
4. a
5. d

Assignment

Create a Java program as per the below specifications:

1. Create a program by using **`FactoryPattern`** as under:

   a. Create an interface named **`IVehicle`** with a **`move()`** method that takes speed and locale as parameters. Use appropriate datatypes for the parameters.

   b. Implement two classes named **`Car`** and **`Bus`** from the **`IVehicle`** interface.

   c. Create different **`MessageBundles`** properties files to store and display dynamic text as per the locale selected by the user. [Hint: Create a template in properties file]

   d. Use the appropriate message bundle in the **`move()`** method of **`Car`** and **`Bus`** class to display a message to the user. [Hint: Use **`MessageFormat`** class]

2. Create a **`VehicleFactory`** class with a **`getVechicle()`** method that takes the vehicle type as a **`String`** parameter and returns the appropriate **`Vehicle`** object of **`Car`** or **`Bus`** as per the user's selection.

3. Create a **`VehicleFactoryTest`** class with the **`main()`** method as under:

   a. Display a list of **`Vehicles`** to the user to select the vehicle type.

   b. Take the language and country as input from the user.

   c. Create the **`Locale`** object based on the user's entry.

   d. Create the **`VehicleFactory`** object.

4. Create the **Vehicle** object and pass the vehicle type as a parameter to the **getVehicle()** method of the **VehicleFactory** object created earlier.
   a. Invoke the **move()** method of the **Vehicle** object with the speed and **Locale** object as the parameter.
   b. Run the **main()** method.

The expected output is in *Figure 11.13*:

```
Select vehicle
1.Car
2.Bus
Enter your choice:
1
Enter language code: es
Enter country code: CR
Car se mueve a una velocidad de 50 km / h.
```

```
Select vehicle
1.Car
2.Bus
Enter your choice:
2
Enter language code: en
Enter country code: US
Bus is moving at a speed of 50 kmph.
```

***Figure 11.13**: Output*

Join our book's Discord space

CHAPTER 12
More about JDK 8, 9, and 10

Introduction

This chapter explains some more features of Java 8 to 10. It explains about `forEach()` method, `StringJoiner`, and parallel array sorting introduced in Java 8. Further, it explains the **Java Platform Module System** (**JPMS**), interactive Java REPL named JShell, and JLink tool introduced in Java 9. Finally, it introduces you to local variable type inference and API changes in Java 10.

Structure

- Features of Java 8
- Features of Java 9
- Features of Java 10

Objectives

In this chapter, you will be introduced to the prominent features and syntax of Java 8, 9 and 10. These features help to create simple and effective code. You will also learn about local variable type inference and API changes in Java 10.

12.1 Features of Java 8

Earlier, we have seen some important new features of Java 8 and 9, such as functional interfaces, lambda expressions, and static/default/private methods of an interface. There are a few more prominent features that were added in Java 8 which are explained as under.

forEach() method

The new **forEach()** method was introduced in Java 8 to iterate the elements. It is defined in the **Stream** and **Iterable** interfaces. In the **Iterable** interface, **forEach()** is defined as a default method that can be used by the collection classes that extend **Iterable** to iterate elements.

Syntax:

```
default void forEach(Consumer<super T> action)
```

This method takes a single parameter which is a functional interface, hence, a lambda expression can be passed as an argument. The **forEachOrdered()** will always maintain the order of elements as they were added. The following example shows the use of the **forEach()** method:

```
import java.util.ArrayList;
import java.util.List;
public class forEachDemo {
  public static void main(String[] args) {
    List<String> lstColors = new ArrayList<>();
    lstColors.add("Red");
    lstColors.add("Green");
    lstColors.add("Blue");

    // traditional enhanced-for loop
    System.out.println("Iterate with enhanced for loop");
    for (String obj : lstColors) {
      System.out.println(obj);
    }
    //new forEach() method
    System.out.println("Iterate with Lambda Expression as parameter");
    lstColors.forEach(obj -> System.out.println(obj));
    System.out.println("Iterate with Method reference as paramenter");
    lstColors.forEach(System.out::println);
```

```
        // new forEachOrdered() method
        System.out.println("Iterate with Lambda Expression as parameter");
        lstColors.stream().forEachOrdered(colors -> System.out.println(colors));
        System.out.println("Iterate with Method reference as paramenter");
        lstColors.stream().forEachOrdered(System.out::println);
    }
}
```

The following *Figure 12.1* shows the output of the above code:

```
Iterate with enhanced for loop
Red
Green
Blue
Iterate with Lambda Expression as parameter
Red
Green
Blue
Iterate with Method reference as paramenter
Red
Green
Blue
Iterate with Lambda Expression as parameter
Red
Green
Blue
Iterate with Method reference as paramenter
Red
Green
Blue
```

Figure 12.1: *Using forEach() method*

StringJoiner class

The **StringJoiner** class was added to the **java.util** package to construct a sequence of characters separated by a delimiter such as a comma **,**, hyphen **-**, and so on. It also allows us to specify the prefix and suffix for the character sequence.

StringJoiner versus StringBuilder

With **StringBuilder**, you need to append each string and delimiter in an alternate sequence. Also, the delimiter needs to be removed from the end if present. However, with **StringJoiner**, the delimiter is mentioned in the constructor, so it gets added automatically and you need to focus only on adding the strings to be joined.

StringJoiner is very useful for joining strings in a stream. The following example shows the use of **StringJoiner** to join strings by using a comma**,** as a delimiter:

```
import java.util.StringJoiner;
public class StringJoinerDemo {
  public static void main(String[] args) {
      StringJoiner joinNames = new StringJoiner(","); // passing comma(,) as
delimiter

    // Adding values to StringJoiner
    joinNames.add("Roger");
    joinNames.add("Victor");
    joinNames.add("Mary");
    joinNames.add("Clara");

    System.out.println(joinNames);

  }
}
```

The following will be the output of the above code:

Roger,Victor,Mary,Clara

StringJoiner provides the **add(String str)** method that allows concatenating strings based on the delimiter, prefix, and suffix specified in the constructor. The following example shows the use of **StringJoiner** and **StringBuilder** for joining strings with a delimiter and specifying the prefix and suffix:

```
import java.util.StringJoiner;
public class StringJvsStringB{
  public static void main(String[] args){
    String str[] = {"John","Roger","Clark"};

    // Initialize StringJoiner instance with
    // required delimiter, prefix and suffix
    StringJoiner sj = new StringJoiner(":", "[", "]");

    // join the strings
```

```
    sj.add("John").add("Roger").add("Clark");

    // convert StringJoiner to String
    String joinedString = sj.toString();

    System.out.println("Joined Strings with StringJoiner: "+joinedString);

    // Using StringBuilder class

    // Instantiate StringBuilder object
    StringBuilder sb = new StringBuilder();

    // append the prefix
    sb.append("[");

    // check for empty string array
    if(str.length>0)
    {
      // append the first element
      sb.append(str[0]);

      // iterate the string array
      // and append required delimiter before each string
      for (int i = 1; i < str.length; i++)
      {
        sb.append(":").append(str[i]);
      }
    }

    // append the sufix
    sb.append("]");

    // convert StringBuilder to String
    String finalStr = sb.toString();

    System.out.println("Joined strings with StringBuilder: "+finalStr);
  }
}
```

With **StringJoiner**, the delimiter, prefix, and suffix are specified in the constructor. However, with **StringBuilder** first, the prefix is appended, then you iterate through string array and append the delimiter before each element. In the end, the suffix is appended.

The following *Figure 12.2* will be the output of the above code:

```
run:
Joined Strings with StringJoiner: [John:Roger:Clark]
Joined strings with StringBuilder: [John:Roger:Clark]
BUILD SUCCESSFUL (total time: 0 seconds)
```

***Figure 12.2:** StringJoiner versus StringBuilder*

Parallel array sorting

This new feature is introduced in the **Arrays** class for sorting array elements in parallel. It is done by using the new method called **parallelSort()** which has been overloaded for all primitive types and **Comparable** objects. This method uses the JSR 166 Fork/join common thread pool to execute parallel tasks. The following *Figure 12.3* shows the different **parallelSort()** methods:

```
parallelSort(T[] a)                                              void
parallelSort(byte[] a)                                           void
parallelSort(char[] a)                                           void
parallelSort(double[] a)                                         void
parallelSort(float[] a)                                          void
parallelSort(int[] a)                                            void
parallelSort(long[] a)                                           void
parallelSort(short[] a)                                          void
parallelSort(T[] a, Comparator<? super T> cmp)                   void
parallelSort(T[] a, int fromIndex, int toIndex)                  void
parallelSort(byte[] a, int fromIndex, int toIndex)               void
parallelSort(char[] a, int fromIndex, int toIndex)               void
parallelSort(double[] a, int fromIndex, int toIndex)             void
parallelSort(float[] a, int fromIndex, int toIndex)              void
parallelSort(int[] a, int fromIndex, int toIndex)                void
parallelSort(long[] a, int fromIndex, int toIndex)               void
parallelSort(short[] a, int fromIndex, int toIndex)              void
```

***Figure 12.3:** Overloaded parallelSort() methods*

The algorithm used for parallel sorting is parallel sort-merge which breaks the array into subarrays and then these are sorted and merged. The following example shows the use of the **parallelSort()** method:

```
import java.util.Arrays;
public class ParallelSortDemo {
  public static void main(String[] args) {
```

```
    // Create an integer array
    int[] arr = {2,7,5,8,1,0,6,9};
    // Iterate array elements
    for (int i : arr) {
      System.out.print(i+" ");
    }
    System.out.println("");

    // Parallel Sort of array elements
    Arrays.parallelSort(arr);

    System.out.println("\nSorting using Arrays.parallelSort()");
    // Iterate and print the array elements
    for (int i : arr) {
      System.out.print(i+" ");
    }
  }
}
```

The **`parallelSort()`** method improves the performance of code. The following *Figure 12.4* will be the output of the above code:

```
run:
2 7 5 8 1 0 6 9

Sorting using Arrays.parallelSort()
0 1 2 5 6 7 8 9
BUILD SUCCESSFUL (total time: 0 seconds)
```

Figure 12.4: *Parallel array sorting*

There are few more features that were added in Java 8 which are explained in the below section.

12.2 Features of Java 9

Java 9 was a major release that introduced a lot of features for developers. Listed below are some important new features which were added to Java 9.

Java Platform Module System

The **Java Platform Module System** (**JPMS**) introduces a new coding paradigm in Java 9 for creating reusable components called modules. It allows the development of components with clearly defined dependencies on other modules. It allows grouping of types and packages into modules with necessary information such as the name of the module, dependencies, outputs, exports, and so on.

What is a module?

A module is a collection of packages, types such as classes, interfaces, abstract classes which are related and contain code as well as data and resources. It is a self-describing collection of resources that support the **Single Responsibility** (functionality) **Principle** (**SRP**).

With Java 9, the JDK jars and Java SE Specifications have been separated by Oracle Corporation into two sets of modules:

- JDK modules that start with `jdk.*`
- Java SE modules which start with `java.*`

An independent base module named `java.base` has been created on which all JDK modules and user-defined modules depend by default. Thereby, is also called *The Mother of Java 9 Modules*. Java 9 introduced the concept of a modular code by the creation of components called modules. These modules contain related packages and types. Also, a module contains a new component called module descriptor file, that is, `module-info.java`. The remaining application is the same as Java 8 or earlier versions.

Listed below are the components of Java 9 module:

- One module with a unique name
- One module descriptor
- Set of packages
- Set of types and resources

Listed below are some important points about Java 9 modules:

- A module name must be unique and must have a single module descriptor.
- The module descriptor is a plain `.java` file with the name `module-info.java` by convention.
- The module descriptor file must be placed in the top-level or root directory of a module.
- There can be multiple packages and types in a module. But you cannot have modules within another module.
- The JDK 9 EA **Early Access** (**EA**) had 95 modules.
- User-defined modules can be created, and a module can depend on several modules.

Like package names, the reverse domain name pattern can also be applied to module names.

For example, if you are developing modules for **www.abc.com**, then the module name can be `com.abc.mod1`.

Java 9 module descriptor

The module descriptor is a plain `.java` file that contains module metadata which is a description of the module. It is also compiled into `module-info.class` file by using `javac` command.

Syntax:

```
module <module-name> {
  // Module metadata
}
```

For example: Contents of `module-info.java` file of the module `com.abc.mod1`.

```
module com.abc.mod1 {
 // metadata
}
```

Module metadata

The module metadata is present in the module descriptor file. It contains the following details:

- **Exports clause**: This clause is used to indicate the packages that the module exports to other modules.

  For example:

  ```
  module com.abc.mod1 {
     exports com.abc.pkg1;
  }
  ```

- **Requires clause**: This clause indicates the packages that a module imports from other modules.

  For example:

  ```
  module com.abc.mod2 {
     requires com.abc.pkg1;
     exports com.abc.pkg2;
  }
  ```

  The `module com.abc.mod2` imports the `com.abc.pkg1` package exported by the `com.abc.mod1` module. It also exports the `com.abc.pkg2` package.

Note: A module descriptor can have zero, one or more exports clause and/or requires clause.

In earlier versions, when a project is created in an IDE, a lot of JDK JARs get added to the project's **CLASSPATH**. With Java 9, when a project is created in an IDE, a lot of JDK modules get added to the project's **MODULEPATH**. Java 9 supports both **MODULEPATH** and **CLASSPATH**.

A **CLASSPATH** is the location of built-in or user-defined classes and packages (or JARs) which the JVM or Java compiler requires for compiling and executing the application. A **MODULEPATH** is the location of modules provided in a folder format, that is, exploded module format or JAR format also called **Modular JAR**.

Readability and accessibility

When a module, says **Mod2** is dependent on another module say **Mod1**, it is said that *Mod2 reads Mod1* or *Mod1 is readable by Mod2*. Such a relationship is called the Readability relationship between the two modules. When **Mod2** has a readability relationship with **Mod1**, it means that **Mod2** can access all public API of **Mod1**. This is called the accessibility relationship between two modules.

Note: A Module can have only Public API or both Public and Private API.

The main purpose of readability and accessibility is to achieve reliable configuration and strong encapsulation. The readability and accessibility relationships can be implemented between modules using **export** clause, **requires** clause, public modifier and **to** clause.

Implied readability

If **Mod2** reads **Mod1** and **Mod3** reads **Mod2**, then **Mod3** also reads **Mod1**. This type of transitive dependency is called *implied readability* form **Mod1** to **Mod3**. It is also known as *implied dependency*. Module dependency can be resolved in two ways as shown in the below *Figure 12.5*, that is direct readability or implied readability:

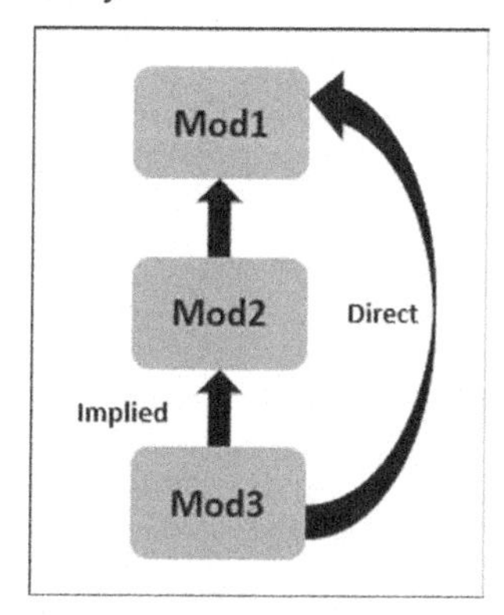

Figure 12.5: *Implied readability*

The following code in *Table 12.1* demonstrates the structure of the **module-info.java** file of the three modules for direct readability and implied readability:

Direct readability	Implied readability

module Mod1{
  exports pkg1;
}
module Mod2{
   requires Mod1;
   exports pkg2;
}
module Mod3{
   requires Mod1;
   requires Mod2;
   exports pkg3;
}
	module Mod1{
	  exports pkg1;
	}
	module Mod2{
	   requires public Mod1;
	   exports pkg2;
	}
	module Mod3{
	   requires Mod2;
	   exports pkg3;
	}

Table 12.1: *The structure of the module-info.java file*

In the first case, the transitive dependency between modules is resolved without using implied readability. This means, that **Mod3** needs to import both **Mod1** and **Mod2** by using the requires clause. However, it is unnecessary since **Mod2** already imports **Mod1**. So, when **Mod3** imports **Mod2**, it would be ideal if it could implicitly import **Mod1** also.

In the second case, the transitive dependency between modules is resolved by using *implied readability*. Thereby, **Mod3** imports only **Mod2** by using the **requires** clause whereas, **Mod1** is implicitly imported due to the usage of public modifier in **Mod2** when it imports **Mod1**.

The following demonstration shows how to implement module dependency:

1. Create a new modular project in Netbeans IDE from **File | New Project | Java | Java Modular Project** as shown below in *Figure 12.6*:

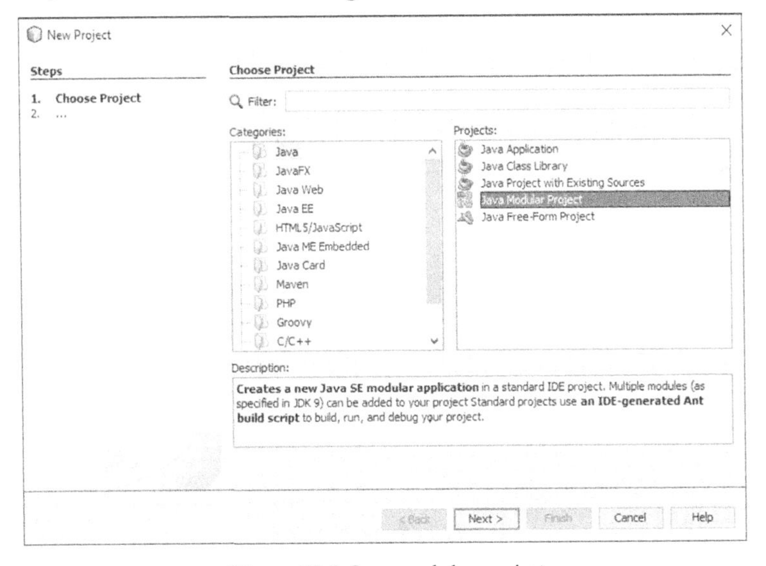

Figure 12.6: *Java modular project*

2. Click **Next** and enter the name of the project as shown below and click **Finish**.

New Java Modular Application

Steps

1. Choose Project
2. **Name and Location**

Name and Location

Project Name: ModularProjectExample

Project Location: F:\java10codes

Browse...

Project Folder: F:\java10codes\ModularProjectExample

Platform: JDK 10 (Default)

Manage Platforms...

< Back | Next > | Finish | Cancel | Help

Figure 12.7: Project name

An empty modular project will be created and opened in the **Projects** tab.

3. To create a new module, right-click the project and select **New** | **Module** as shown below in *Figure 12.8*:

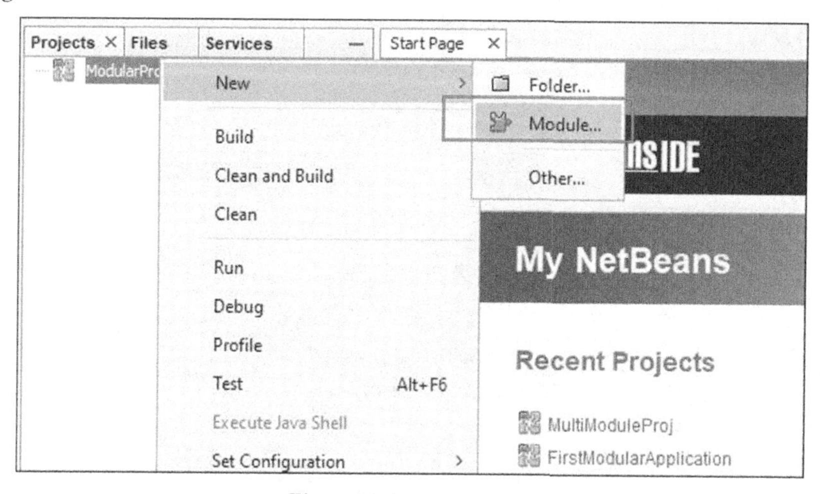

Figure 12.8: New module

4. Give the name of the module as shown below and click **Finish** as shown in Figure 12.9:

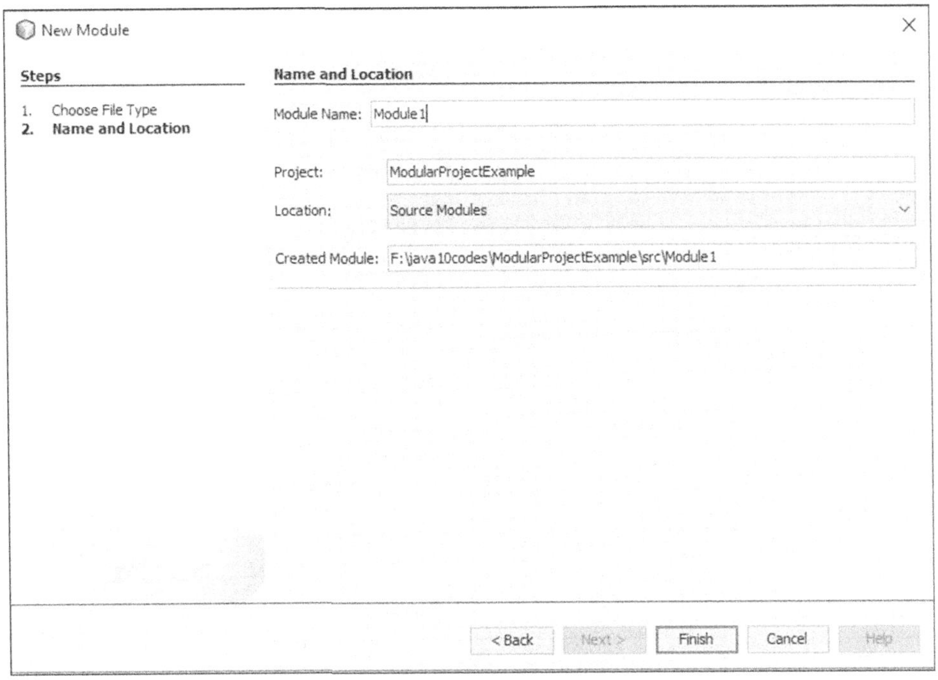

Figure 12.9: *Module name*

5. The module **`Module1`** is created and the **`module-info.java`** file is opened in the editor as shown below in *Figure 12.10*:

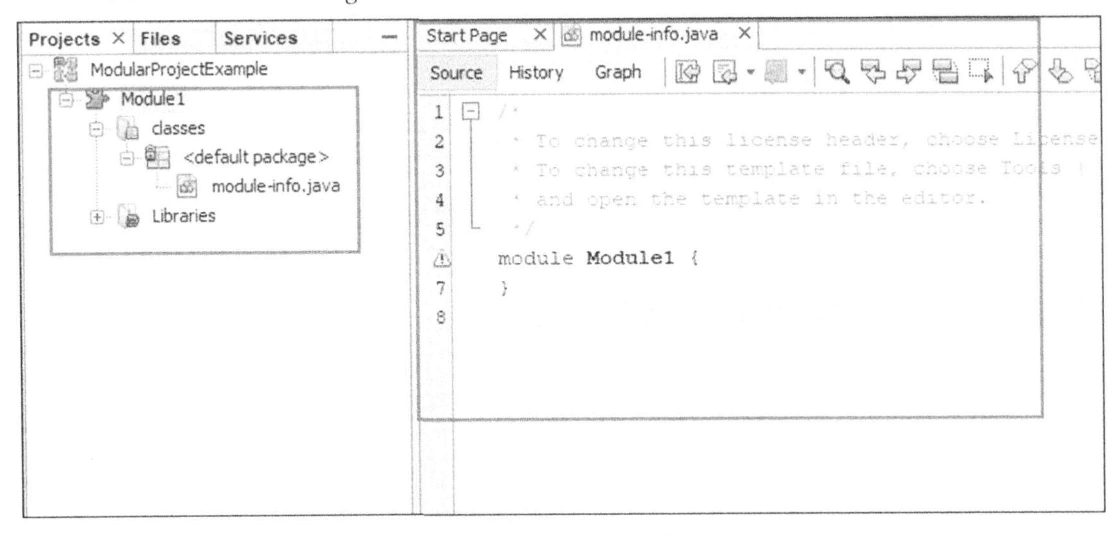

Figure 12.10: *Module1*

6. Right-click **`Module1`** and select **New | Java Class** as shown in the *figure 12.11*:

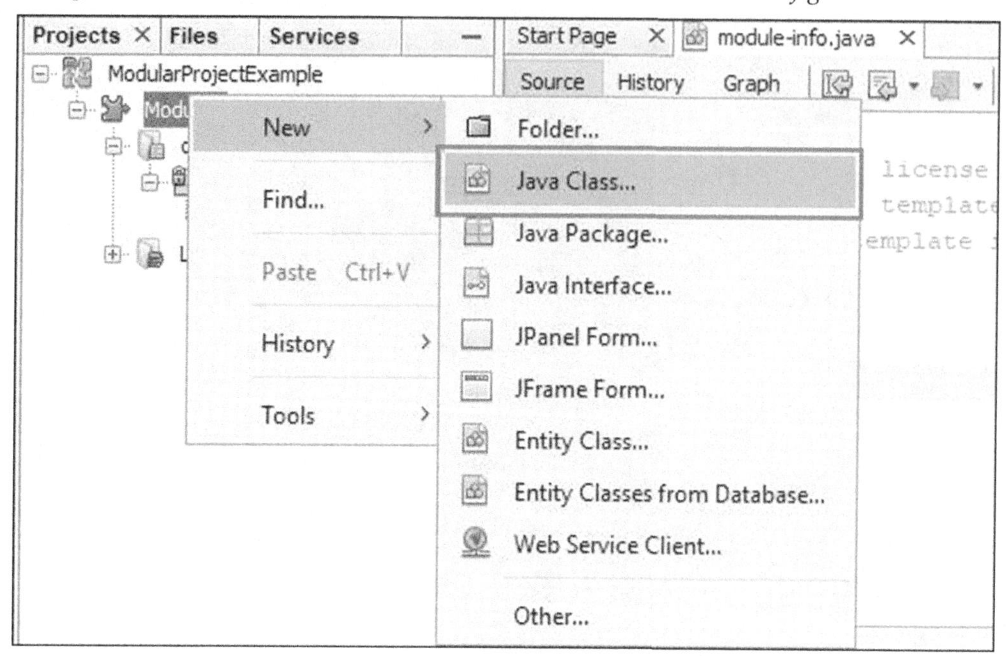

Figure 12.11: *New Java class*

7. Enter the class name and package name as shown in following image and click **Finish**:

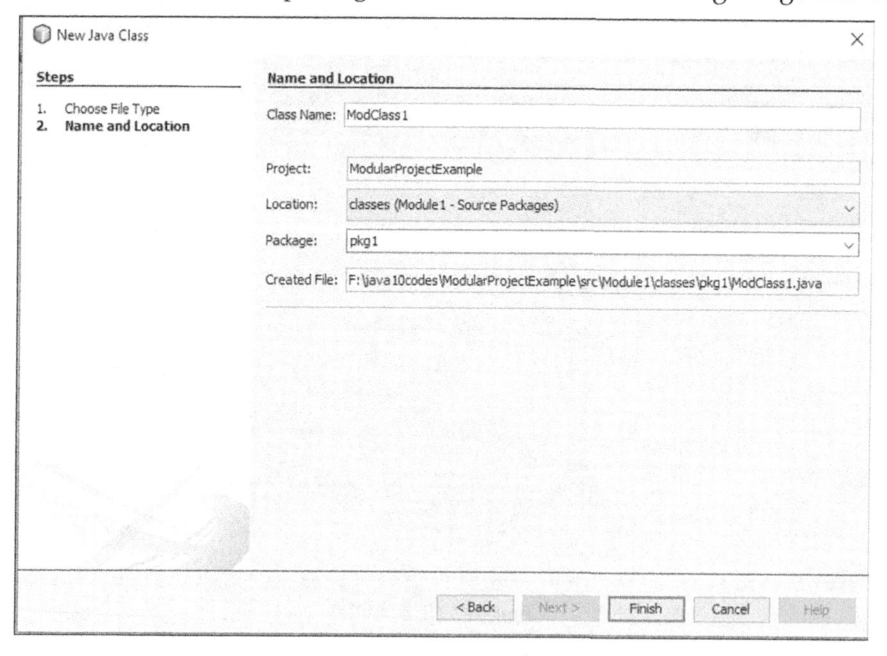

Figure 12.12*: New Java class*

8. A new package and new class are created in the module as shown below *Figure 12.13*:

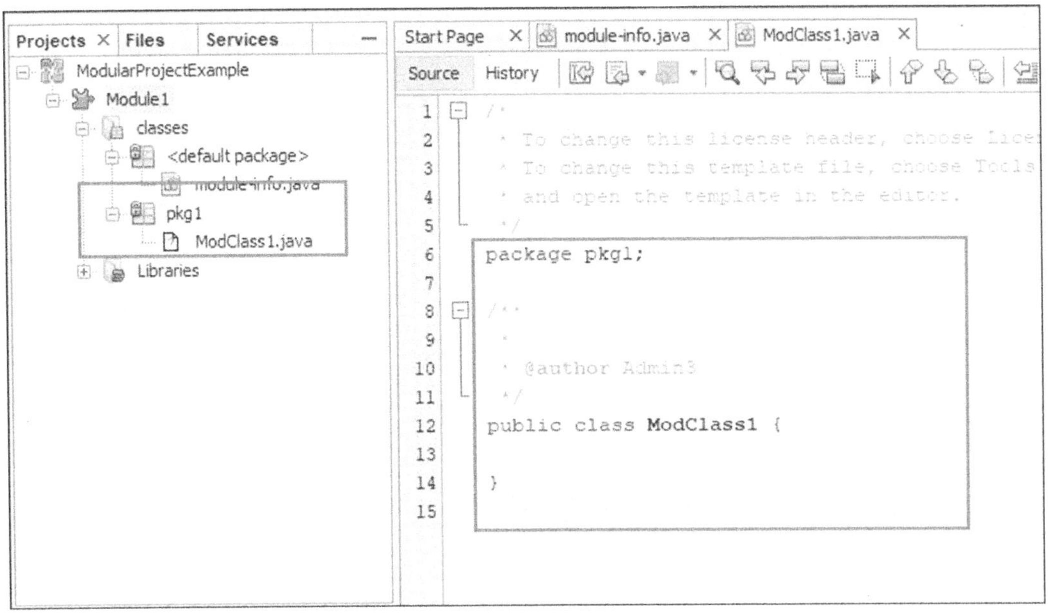

Figure 12.13: New package and new class

9. Add the following code in the class, **ModClass1**:

```
package pkg1;
public class ModClass1 {
  public String getMod1Msg() {
    return "Module1 Message";
  }
}
```

10. Add the following code in the **module-info.java** file of **Module1**:

```
module Module1 {
  exports pkg1;
}
```

The module descriptor indicates that **Module1** exports **pkg1** for access to other modules.

11. Similarly, create **Module2** in the project with **ModClass2** as shown below *Figure 12.14*:

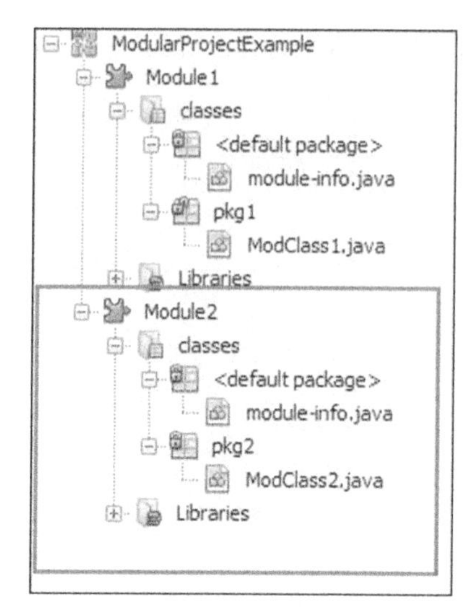

Figure 12.14: Module2 with package and class

12. Add the below code in the class, **ModClass2**:

```
public class ModClass2 {
  public String getMod2Msg() {
    return "Module2 Message";
  }
}
```

13. You can create another class called **TestMod2** and add the below code to it:

```
import pkg1.ModClass1;

public class TestMod2 {
  public String getModMessages() {
    ModClass1 objMod1 = new ModClass1();
    ModClass2 objMod2 = new ModClass2();
    return objMod1.getMod1Msg() + " " + objMod2.getMod2Msg();
  }
}
```

Here, the **pkg1** package of **Module1** is imported in the **TestMod2** class and the **ModClass1** object is created to access its **getMod1Msg()** method.

14. Add the below code to the **module-info.java** file of **Module2** module:

```
module Module2 {
  requires Module1;
  exports pkg2;
}
```

Here, the dependency of **Module2** on **Module1** is mentioned by using the **requires** clause. Also, **Module2** exports the package **pkg2**.

15. Now create another module named **Module3** with a package and class as shown below *Figure 12.15*:

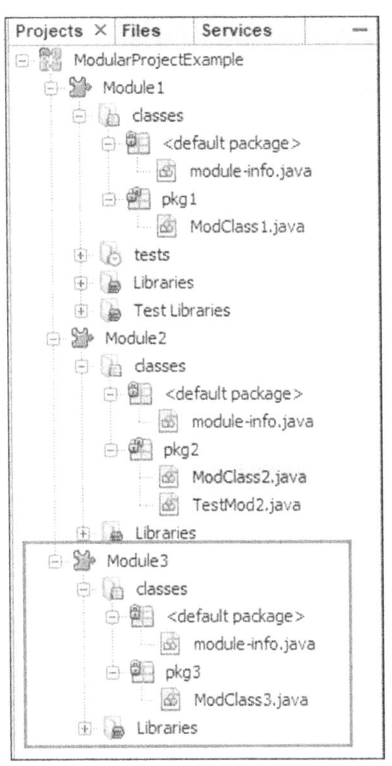

***Figure 12.15:** Module3 with package and class*

16. Add the below code to the **ModClass3.java** file:

```
public class ModClass3 {
  public String getMod3Msg() {
    return "Module3 Message";
  }
}
```

17. Add the below code to the **module-info.java** file of **Module3**:

```
module Module3 {
  requires Module1;
  requires Module2;
  exports pkg3;
}
```

Here, the module descriptor indicates that **Module3** is dependent on **Module1** and **Module2** by using the **requires** clause. Also, it exports the package **pkg3** for access by other modules.

18. You can create another class named **TestMod3** as shown below:

```
import pkg1.ModClass1;
import pkg2.ModClass2;
public class TestMod3 {
  public String getAllMessages() {
    ModClass1 objMod1 = new ModClass1();
    ModClass2 objMod2 = new ModClass2();
    ModClass3 objMod3 = new ModClass3();
     return objMod1.getMod1Msg() + ", " + objMod2.getMod2Msg()  + ", " +
objMod3.getMod3Msg();
  }
}
```

Here, the classes **ModClass1** and **ModClass2** are imported and the methods **getMod1Msg()** and **getMod2Msg()** methods are invoked. This is possible as the dependency is mentioned in the **module-info.java** file of **Module3** module.

19. Now create a test module to test execution of all the modules as shown below in *figure 12.16*. Also, create a class **TestAllModules.java** in a package as shown below:

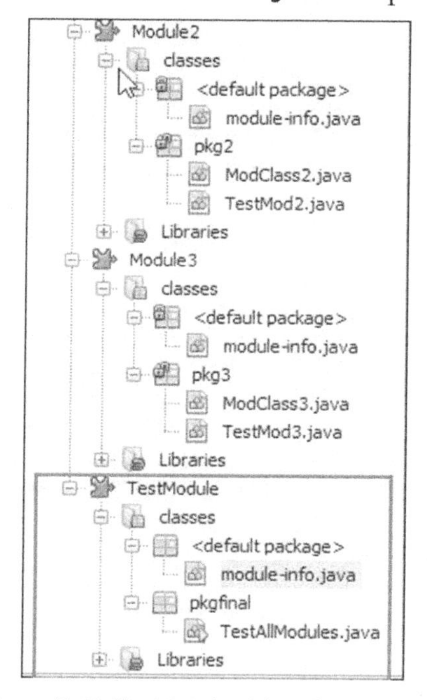

Figure 12.16: *TestModule with package and class*

20. Add the below code to **module-info.java** file:

```
module TestModule {

  requires Module3;
}
```

The module imports only **Module3**.

21. Add the below code to the **TestAllModule.java** file:

```
import pkg3.TestMod3;
public class TestAllModules {
  public static void main(String a[]){
    TestMod3 obj = new TestMod3();
    System.out.println("All messages: " + obj.getAllMessages());
  }
}
```

Here, the **TestMod3** class object is created and the **getAllMessages()** method is called. The following will be the output of the above code:

```
Output - ModularProjectExample (run)
run:
All messages: Module1 Message, Module2 Message, Module3 Message
BUILD SUCCESSFUL (total time: 0 seconds)
```

Figure 12.17: Output of modular Java program

Note that the module dependencies were resolved without using implied readability. To use implied readability, you can modify the **module-info.java** file of **Module2** as shown below:

```
module Module2 {
  requires public Module1;
  exports pkg2;
}
```

The use of public modifier indicates that any module that reads **Module2** will also be able to read **Module1** and will not need to use **requires** clause. Similarly, you can modify the **module-info.java** file of **Module3** as shown below:

```
module Module3 {
  requires Module2;
  exports pkg3;
}
```

Note that the `requires` clause for `Module1` has been removed as `Module2` has used public modifier to allow accessibility of `Module1` to all other modules that import `Module2`.

Interactive Java REPL named JShell

The new **Read Evaluate Print Loop (REPL)** tool or JShell was introduced by Oracle Corp in Java 9. It allows for easy execution and testing of Java constructs such as classes, interfaces, objects, `enum`, and so on. The following *Figure 12.18* shows the JShell window. You can start JShell in the command window from the bin folder of JDK path of version 9 or above:

```
C:\Program Files\Java\jdk-10.0.1\bin>jshell
|  Welcome to JShell -- Version 10.0.1
|  For an introduction type: /help intro

jshell> int num = 20
num ==> 20

jshell> System.out.println("Value of num is " + num)
Value of num is 20

jshell>
```

Figure 12.18: JShell

The support for REPL was added in Java to allow integration of Scala features into Java. REPL is one of the best features of Scala. It is a command-line interface and interpreter to execute Scala programs. The advantage of REPL is that it reduces the learning curve by allowing to execute and test basic programs. Java REPL is named JShell which is short for Java Shell. It is an interactive tool that allows the execution and evaluation of simple programs in Java.

The following *Figure 12.19* shows some more examples of JShell:

```
jshell> System.out.println("Value of num is " + num)
Value of num is 20

jshell> String str = "REPL is interactive";
str ==> "REPL is interactive"

jshell> str
str ==> "REPL is interactive"

jshell> System.out.println(str)
REPL is interactive

jshell> int count = 0
count ==> 0

jshell> count++
$7 ==> 0

jshell> count
count ==> 1

jshell> count+8
$9 ==> 9

jshell> count
count ==> 1

jshell> count=count+8
count ==> 9
```

Figure 12.19: JShell examples

As shown in the above Java REPL examples, it is easy to test Java statements without having to create a class or **main()** method. Also, you do not need to use semicolon for simple statements. REPL also allows defining and executing class methods in the JShell as shown in the below *Figure 12.20*:

```
jshell> class Hello{
   ...> public static void message(){
   ...> System.out.print("Hello user");
   ...> }
   ...> }
|  created class Hello

jshell> Hello.message()
Hello user
jshell>
```

***Figure 12.20**: Define a class*

To view the JShell tool help section, **use /help** command as shown in the below *Figure 12.21*:

```
jshell> /help
|  Type a Java language expression, statement, or declaration.
|  Or type one of the following commands:
|  /list [<name or id>|-all|-start]
|       list the source you have typed
|  /edit <name or id>
|       edit a source entry
|  /drop <name or id>
|       delete a source entry
|  /save [-all|-history|-start] <file>
|       Save snippet source to a file
|  /open <file>
|       open a file as source input
|  /vars [<name or id>|-all|-start]
|       list the declared variables and their values
|  /methods [<name or id>|-all|-start]
|       list the declared methods and their signatures
|  /types [<name or id>|-all|-start]
|       list the type declarations
|  /imports
|       list the imported items
|  /exit [<integer-expression-snippet>]
```

***Figure 12.21**: Help command*

To exit from JShell, **use /exit** command or *Ctrl + D:*

```
jshell> /exit
|  Goodbye
```

***Figure 12.22:** Exit command*

JLink tool for linking

The **JLink** command-line tool was introduced to create a customized JRE. Generally, to execute a Java program, you would use the default JRE which comes with innumerable predefined Java **.class** files.

For example, consider the below simple program:

```
class Hello{
  public static void main(String[]args) {
    System.out.prinltn("Hello World");
  }
}
```

Now, to run this small program, you would need to install the default JRE with a bulk of **.class** files. However, to run this small program, the only **.class** files required are **Hello.class**, **String.class**, **System.class**, and **Object.class**.

If the small *hello world* program is executed with default JRE, all 4300+ predefined Java .class files will be loaded which is not required in this case. Also, the size of JRE will be 203 MB for a simple 1 KB code. This is an unnecessary wastage of memory and impacts performance. Moreover, it is not suitable for developing microservices which have very little memory and are not useful for IoT devices.

However, with Java 9, the **jlink** tool was introduced to create a small customized JRE with only the relevant class(es) required to execute the application. This helps to save memory and improve performance. With **Jlink**, you can link only required modules and create your own JRE.

For example, assume that the **Hello.java** file is in a folder **pkg** in the module named **Module1**. Now, we only need **String.class**, **System.class**, and **Object.class** files. These **.class** files are part of the **java.lang** package which is present in the **java.base** module. So, to execute your program, you only need two modules, **Module1**, and **java.base**, and you can create your own minimal JRE to run the application. The **java.base** module is present in the **java\jdk-9\jmods** path.

So, to create a minimal JRE, you need to copy the **java.base** module into the folder that has the **Hello.class** file. Now create your own JRE by using the command:

```
jlink -module-path out -add-modules module1,java.base -output myjre
```

This command creates the **myjre** folder which is the minimal customized JRE which can be used to execute the program with the **java** command:

```
cd myjre
cd bin
java -m module1/pkg.Test
```

12.3 Features of Java 10

Java 10 was the fastest release in terms of scope, impact, and futuristic changes. Listed below are some important new features of Java 10.

Local variable type inference

Local variable type inference feature was added in Java 10 to support type inference for local variables with initializers. The use of local type inference is restricted to the below scenarios:

- Local variable with an initializer
- Indexes of enhanced **for** loop or indexes
- A local variable declared in **for** loop

The following example explains the use of local type inference:

```
var digits = List.of(4, 3, 5, 2, 6); // inferred value
// Index of Enhanced For Loop
for (var num : digits) {
  System.out.println(num);
}
// Local variable declared in a loop
for (var i = 0; i < digits.size(); i++) {
  System.out.println(numbers.get(i));
}
```

Here, the type of variable **var** is inferred from the type of data that is assigned to it. Thus, type inference refers to the compiler's ability to determine the type argument by looking at the method invocation and declaration. The reserved type name **var** is used for local variable declarations with initializer.

For local variable declarations with initializer, we can now use a reserved type name **var**.

For example:

```
var lst = new ArrayList<String>(); // infers ArrayList<String>
var str = list.stream();            // infers Stream<String>
```

Manifest typing is the explicit identification of the type of a variable that is declared. This was done in Pre Java 10 versions. For example:

```
List<Fruits> fruit = List.of(new Fruit());
```

Here, **List<Fruit>** is the manifest type which must be declared to identify the type of the variable.

Manifest type: Explicit identification of type for each variable being declared is called manifest typing. For example, if a variable **`actors`** is going to store a **`List`** of Actors, then its type **`List<Actor>`** is the manifest type and it must be declared (as mentioned below) prior to Java 10:

However, with Java 10, this can be done as shown below with the reserved type of name **`var`**:

```
var fruit = List.of(new Fruit());
```

Understand the working of local variable type inference

When the compiler parses a **`var`** statement, it looks at the right side of the declaration, referred to as the *initializer*. Based on this **Right-Hand Side** (**RHS**) expression, it infers the type. However, this does not mean that Java is dynamically typed now. It is still a statically typed language.

For example, consider the below code:

```
private static void read() throws IOException {
  var fname = "Test.txt";
  var line = "";
  var fread = new FileReader(fname);
  var bread = new BufferedReader(fread);
...
}
```

`Now, when the type inference happens, the decompiled code looks as shown below:`

```
private static void read() throws IOException {
  String fname = "Test.txt";
  String line = "";
  FileReader fread = new FileReader(fname);
  BufferedReader bread = new BufferedReader(fread);
  ...
}
```

Here, the compiler is able to infer the type of the variable from the RHS expression and which is then added to the bytecode. Here, **`var`** is not a keyword but a reserved type name, which means you can also create a variable with the name **`var`** as shown below:

```
var var = 5; // this is correct
```

You can also create a method with the name **`var`** as shown below:

```
public static void var() {       // this is correct
}
```

A package with the name **var** is also allowed:

```
package var; // this is correct
```

However, you cannot create a class or interface with the name **var**. You will get the below error if a class with name **var** is created:

```
class var{ } // Compile Error
LocalTypeInference.java:45: error: 'var' not allowed here
class var{
      ^
  as of release 10, 'var' is a restricted local variable type and cannot be used
for type declarations
1 error
```

Similarly, it is not allowed for creating interfaces:

```
interface var{ } // Compilation Error
```

As mentioned earlier, usage of local variable type inference is limited to a local variable with initializer, Indexes of enhanced **for** loop or indexes, and local variable declared in a **for** loop.

Listed below are some limitations of using **var**:

- **var** cannot be used without an initializer statement because the compiler cannot infer the type without initializer.

  ```
  var num;
  ```

  The above statement will give the error:

  ```
  LocalTypeInference.java:37: error: cannot infer type for local variable
  num
                  var num;
                      ^
    (cannot use 'var' on variable without initializer)
  1 error
  ```

  var cannot be used to declare multiple variables in a sequence as shown below:

  ```
  var x = 5, y = 10;
  ```

  The above statement will generate error as shown below:

  ```
  LocalTypeInference.java:41: error: 'var' is not allowed in a compound
  declaration
                  var x = 5, y = 10;
                      ^
  1 error
  ```

- **var** cannot be initialized with Null because Null is not a type and the compiler will not be able to infer the type of the RHS expression as shown below:

  ```
  var message = null;
  ```

  The above statement will generate error as shown below:

  ```
  LocalTypeInference.java:47: error: cannot infer type for local variable message
                      var message = null;
                          ^
    (variable initializer is 'null')
  1 error
  ```

- **var** cannot be used with arrays.

  ```
  var fruitArr[] = new Fruit[10];
  ```

  The above statement will generate error as shown below:

  ```
  LocalTypeInference.java:52: error: 'var' is not allowed as an element type of an array
                      var fruitArr[] = new Fruit[10];
                          ^
  1 error
  ```

- **var** does not have support for poly expressions that consist of method references, array initializers, and lambdas. These too will trigger an error. This is because, for resolving the type of Lambda expressions, **Array** initializers, and method references, the compiler refers to the Left-hand side expression or the argument definition of the method where the expression is passed. But **var** uses the RHS expression. This leads to cyclic reference and compile-time error is generated.

Lambda expression

```
var min = (a, b) -> a < b ? a : b;
```

```
Error:
LocalTypeInference.java:59: error: cannot infer type for local variable min
                var min = (a, b) -> a < b ? a : b;
                    ^
  (lambda expression needs an explicit target-type)
1 error
```

Method reference

```
var minimum = Math::min;
```

```
Error:
LocalTypeInference.java:65: error: cannot infer type for local variable minimum
                var minimum = Math::min;
                    ^
  (method reference needs an explicit target-type)
1 error
```

Array initializers

```
var numbers = {4,5,2,6,3};
Error:
LocalTypeInference.java:71: error: cannot infer type for local variable numbers
                var nums = {4,5,2,6,3};
                    ^
  (array initializer needs an explicit target-type)
1 error
```

- **var** can be used with anonymous class types. Anonymous class types cannot have a name and the use of variable for anonymous class type allows a shorthand for declaring a singleton instance of a local class. Below example shows the variable **runThread** used for anonymous class implementing **Runnable**:

```
var t1 = new Runnable() {
  @Override
  public void run() {
    var digits = List.of(4, 3, 5, 2, 6);
    for (var num : digits) {
      System.out.println(num);
    }
  }
};
runThread(t1);
```

Thus, the introduction of **var** helped to reduce code, increase code clarity, and improve the developer experience.

API changes

Java 10 added and removed several APIs. In Java 9, enhance deprecation was introduced whereby several APIs were marked for removal in future releases. Listed below are some APIs that were removed in Java 10.

Fields

java.lang.SecurityManager.inCheck

Methods

java.lang.Runtime.getLocalizedInputStream(java.io.InputStream)

java.lang.Runtime.getLocalizedOutputStream(java.io.OutputStream)

java.lang.SecurityManager.inClass(java.lang.String)

java.lang.SecurityManager.classDepth(java.lang.String)

java.lang.SecurityManager.getInCheck()

java.lang.SecurityManager.inClassLoader()

java.lang.SecurityManager.classLoaderDepth()

java.lang.SecurityManager.currentClassLoader()

java.lang.SecurityManager.currentLoadedClass()

Total 73 new APIs were added in Java 10. Some prominent additions are explained below. The **copyOf(Collection)** method was added to the **List**, **Map** and **Set** interfaces that return an immutable **List**, **Map** and **Set** with the given entries. That is, if the **List** is modified later, the changes will not reflect.

Methods were introduced in **Collectors** class for collecting unmodifiable collections such as **Set**, **List**, and **Map**. The following example shows the use of the **copyOf()** method:

```
List<String> seasons = new ArrayList<>();
seasons.add("Winter");
seasons.add("Summer");
System.out.println(seasons); // prints [Winter, Summer]
// New API - Creates an UnModifiable List from a List.
List<String> copySeasons = List.copyOf(seasons);
System.out.println(copySeasons); // prints [Winter, Summer]
// copySeasons.add("Spring");  //Generates
 UnsupportedOperationException
seasons.add("Spring");
System.out.println(seasons);// prints [Winter, Summer, Spring]
System.out.println(copySeasons); // prints [Winter, Summer]
```

The following example shows the use of **toUnmodifiableList()**:

```
// New API - Collectors.toUnmodifiableList
List<String> lstCollect = seasons.stream().collect(Collectors.
```

```
toUnmodifiableList());
// lstCollect.add("Autumn"); // Generates
UnsupportedOperationException
```

Several other new features such as time-based release versioning, Optional API `orElseThrow()` method, heap allocation on alternative memory devices, and so on. were introduced which are beyond the scope of this book.

Conclusion

In this chapter you learnt that the new **`forEach()`** method was introduced in Java 8 to iterate the elements. It is defined in the **`Stream`** and **`Iterable`** interfaces. The **`StringJoiner`** class was added to the **`java.util`** package to construct a sequence of characters separated by a delimiter such as a comma , ; hyphen -, and so on. Parallel Array Sorting feature is introduced in the **`Arrays`** class for sorting array elements in parallel. The **Java Platform Module System** (JPMS) introduces a new coding paradigm in Java 9 for creating reusable components called modules. The Module Descriptor is a plain .java file that contains Module Metadata that is a description of the module. The Readability and Accessibility Relationships can be implemented between modules using **`export`** clause, **`requires`** clause, public modifier and **`to`** clause. If **`Mod2`** reads **`Mod1`** and **`Mod3`** reads **`Mod2`**, then **`Mod3`** also reads **`Mod1`**. This type of Transitive dependency is called "Implied Readability" from **`Mod1`** to **`Mod3`**. The new **Read Evaluate Print Loop** (REPL) tool or JShell was introduced by Oracle Corp in Java 9 for easy execution and testing of Java constructs such as classes, interfaces, objects, enum, and so on. The JLink command-line tool was introduced to create a customized JRE. Local variable type inference feature was added in Java 10 to support type inference for local variables with initializers. Usage of local variable type inference is limited to Local Variable with initializer, Indexes of enhanced **`for`** loop, and local variable declared in a **`for`** loop. The **`copyOf(Collection)`** method was added to the **`List`**, **`Map`**, and **`Set`** interfaces that return an immutable **`List`**, **`Map`**, and **`Set`** with the given entries.

In the next chapter, you will learn about Java 11 (LTS) and new updates till Java 16.

Multiple choice questions

1. **Identify the correct full form of REPL.**
   a. Read Eliminate Print Loop
   b. Read Evaluate Prompt Loop
   c. Read Evaluate Print Loop
   d. Raise Evaluate Print Loop
2. **Which of the following cannot be part of a Module?**
   a. Java Class
   b. Module
   c. Package
   d. Interface

3. **Match the Columns:**

	Clause		Description
a.	Requires	1.	It indicates that the module is accessible to other modules that access this module.
b.	Exports	2.	Indicates the modules imported by this module
c.	Public	3.	Indicates the packages exported by this module

   a. a-2, b-3, c-1
   b. a-1, b-2, c-3
   c. a-3, b-1, c-2
   d. a-2, b-1, c-3

4. **Identify the correct code for using `var`.**
   a. `var x = 5, y = 10;`
   b. `var message = null;`
   c. `var fruitArr[] = new Fruit[10];`
   d. `var var = 5;`

5. **On which of the following module do all JDK modules and user-defined modules depend by default?**
   a. `java.sql`
   b. `java.base`
   c. `java.naming`
   d. `java.logging`

Answers

1. c
2. b
3. a
4. d
5. b

Assignment

1. Create a modular Java program with two modules with the below specifications.
   a. In the first module, **`ConnectorModule`** should have a package, **`pkg1`** with a class, **`Connector`** that contains the code to connect with a database, and returns the **`Connection`** object. You can use any DBMS. [Assumption: The database has a table called **`UserDetails`**.]

b. The **ConectorModule** should export the package **pkg1**.

c. In the second module, **UserModule** should import the package, **pkg1** exported by the first module. It should have a package, **pkg2** with a class, **UserInfo** that has a method to display data from a table, **UserDetails**. It should use the **Connector** class of **ConnectorModule** to establish the connection. The **UserModule** should export the package **pkg2**.

d. Create a module, **TestModule** that imports the **UserModule** and has a **Test** class with the main method to execute the **UserInfo** class.

2. Research on the other features introduced in Java 9 and Java 10 on the official site of Oracle Corp.

CHAPTER 13

Java 11 (LTS) and New Updates

Introduction

Java 11 is the first **Long Term Support (LTS)** version after Java 8. It added a few new features and removed and deprecated some features of earlier versions. Java 12 to 16 were also released with some new features, while the earlier preview features were standardized and made production ready.

Structure

Following are the topics that are covered in this chapter:

- Introduction to Java 11 (LTS)
- New features of Java 11 (LTS)
- Features of Java versions 12 to 16

Objectives

In this chapter, you will learn about Java 11 and the new features added to the JDK, such as string and file methods, HTTPClient, garbage collectors, and so on. You will also learn about the different JDK providers. Finally, you will understand the new features launched in the preview version as well as standardized in Java 12 to 16.

13.1 Introduction to Java 11 (LTS)

JDK 11 was released in September 2018, only 6 months after Java 10, and is the first **Long-Term Support (LTS)** after Java 8. Although, from a developer perspective, Java 11 was a relatively smaller release, it introduced several new features, which we will discuss in this chapter. However, several features from earlier releases, such as Java applets, Java Web Start, JavaFX, and so on were removed from the JDK.

The last free version of OracleJDK, which could be used commercially without a license, was Java 10. Java 11 onward Oracle does not provide free Long-Term Support (LTS).

However, Oracle still provides OpenJDK releases that can be downloaded and used without charge. Apart from Oracle, there are also other OpenJDK providers.

Adoptium's Eclipse Temurin (earlier known as AdoptOpenJDK)

In 2017, a new community called AdoptOpenJDK was created by a group of Java User Group members, vendors, and developers, including RedHat, Microsoft, Pivotal, Amazon, and a few others. Since August 2021, the AdoptOpenJDK project has been termed as the Eclipse Adoptium project.

Adoptium's free OpenJDK build named Eclipse Temurin has longer availability and updates for different operating systems, versions, and architectures.

You can download the latest JDK from Oracle's official site or from the Adoptium site.

https://www.oracle.com/in/java/technologies/

https://adoptium.net/

Download the executable for JDK 11 installer for Windows and install it in your system. The following image shows the installation of JDK 11:

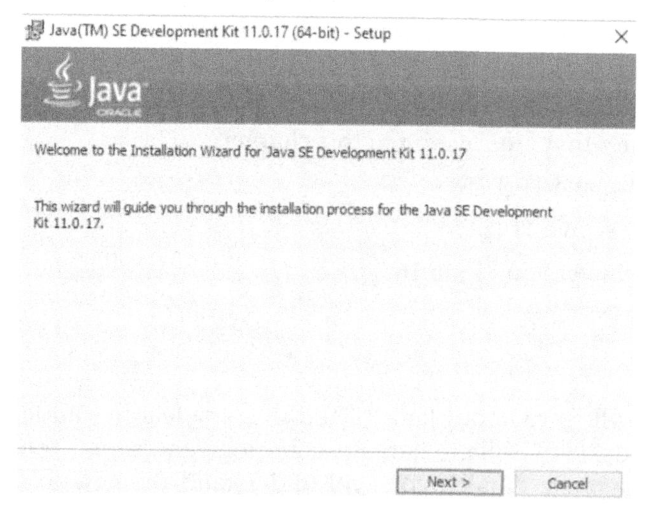

Figure 13.1: *JDK 11 installation wizard*

Note: You can use any IDE for creating the Java application. Here, we will be using Apache NetBeans IDE 17. You can download it from the Apache NetBeans official site.

13.1.1 Oracle versus OpenJDK

Oracle and OpenJDK differ in several aspects, as listed in the following table:

Oracle	OpenJDK
Delivers releases every three years	Delivers releases every six months
Provides long-term support for the releases	Provides support only for the changes in a release till the next version is launched
Oracle JDK was licensed under the Oracle Binary Code License Agreement	OpenJDK has the GNU General Public License (GNU GPL) version 2 with a linking exception
Oracle's platform has licensing implications such that public updates of releases for Java SE 8 after Jan 2019 cannot be used for business or commercial purposes without license	OpenJDK is fully open source and free for usage
Oracle focuses more on stability, considering its enterprise customers. Hence, Oracle's performance is better regarding responsiveness and JVM performance.	OpenJDK encounters more problems with stability due to frequent releases, and hence, users face performance issues.
Oracle offers features such as Flight Recorder, Application Class-data sharing, and Java Mission Control	OpenJDK offers the Font Renderer feature.
Delivers releases every three years	Delivers releases every six months
Provides long-term support for the releases	Provides support only for the changes in a release till the next version is launched
Oracle JDK was licensed under the Oracle Binary Code License Agreement	OpenJDK has the GNU General Public License (GNU GPL) version 2 with a linking exception
Oracle's platform has licensing implications such that public updates of releases for Java SE 8 after Jan 2019 cannot be used for business or commercial purposes without license	OpenJDK is fully open source and free for usage

Oracle	OpenJDK
Oracle focuses more on stability, considering its enterprise customers. Hence, Oracle's performance is better regarding responsiveness and JVM performance.	OpenJDK encounters more problems with stability due to frequent releases, and hence, users face performance issues.
Oracle offers features such as Flight Recorder, Application Class-data sharing, and Java Mission Control	OpenJDK offers the Font Renderer feature.

***Table 13.1:** Oracle versus OpenJDK*

Moreover, Oracle offers more options for garbage collection and better renderers.

It is important to note that with so many new versions released, several real-world usage scenarios arise. Several legacy projects are still stuck with earlier versions like Java 8 or even Java 1.5 and Java 1.6.

However, the speciality of Java is that it ensures backward compatibility. That is, a program created in Java 5 or 8 will still run with a Java 8 to 19 virtual machine.

But it will not work the other way around, that is, a program created with Java 19 features will not run with Java 8 JVM since these features are not available in the earlier versions.

So, if you want to use the latest IDEs and build tools, you can use the latest versions of Java, such as Java 17 (LTS) or Java 19.

An exception is Android app development, which still needs Java 7 support. But you can also switch to the Kotlin programming language for Android app development.

13.2 New features of Java 11 (LTS)

Java 11 provides several new features, such as new methods in `String` and `Files` class, Local-variable type inference (`var`) for lambda parameters, final and non-preview versions of the HttpClient of Java 9, Flight Recorder, and so on.

Let us explore some of the new features of Java 11.

13.2.1 New String class methods

Following are some useful String methods added in Java 11. These methods help to reduce the amount of boilerplate code required for string manipulation:

- `boolean isBlank()`

  This method will return true if a string is empty or consists of only white space codepoints, else it will return false.

For example:

```
System.out.println("JavaBeans".isBlank());
System.out.println(" ".isBlank());
```

Output:

```
False
true
```

- `String strip()`

  This method will return a String after removing all the leading and trailing white spaces from the given string value.

  For example:

  ```
  System.out.println("  JavaBeans  ".strip());
  ```

  Output:

  ```
  JavaBeans
  ```

  Similarly, the methods **`stripLeading()`** and **`stripTrailing()`**, will remove the leading and trailing whitespaces, respectively.

  The strip methods function similar to the **`trim()`** method but with a finer control and Unicode support.

- `Stream<String> lines()`

  This method returns a stream of lines extracted from the string, separated by line terminators.

  A line terminator can be one of the following: "**\n**", "**\r**", or "**\r\n**".

  For example:

  ```
  String multiline = "Java 11 \n \n added \n new string methods.";
  List<String> lines = multiline.lines()
  .filter(line1 -> !line1.isBlank())
  .map(String::strip)
  .collect(Collectors.toList());
  System.out.println(lines);
  ```

  Output:

  ```
  [Java 11, added, new string methods.]
  ```

  The stream will hold lines in the order in which they occur. The line terminator will be removed from each line.

  The **`lines()`** method is a better option over **`split()`** as it will provide better performance for splitting multi-line output.

- `String repeat(int n)`

  This method will return a string which is the concatenation of the given string repeated n times. (Here, n is the number mentioned in the parameter of the repeat method)

For example:

```
String song = "Jingle Bells ".repeat(2) + "Jingle all the way..";
System.out.println(song);
```

Output:

```
Jingle Bells Jingle Bells Jingle all the way..
```

The **repeat()** method will return an empty string if the given string is empty or the count is zero.

13.2.2 New Files class methods

Java 11 introduced new static methods **readString** and **writeString** in the Files class to make it easier to read-write Strings from files.

For example:

```
try {
     Path path1 = Paths.get("F:\\Data");
    // Create a temporary file in a specified directory.
       Path tempFile = Files.writeString(Files.createTempFile(path1,"hello",
".txt"),"Sample file");
    System.out.println("Temp file: " + tempFile);
    // Read from the file
    String fileContent = Files.readString(tempFile);
    System.out.println("File content: "+fileContent);
} catch (IOException ex) {
    System.out.println("Exception occurred");
}
```

Output:

```
Temp file: F:\Data\hello18360941495042199847.txt
File content: Sample file
```

13.2.3 Collection to an array

A new default method named **toArray(IntFunction)** has been added to the **java.util.Collection** interface. It allows a collection's elements to be transferred to a newly created array of a desired type at runtime.

For example:

```
List<String> list1 = Arrays.asList("Java 10", "Java 11");
```

```
String[] sample = list1.toArray(String[]::new);
System.out.println(Arrays.toString(sample));
```

Output:

```
[Java 10, Java 11]
```

13.2.4 The static 'not' method

Java 11 introduced a static 'not' method to the Predicate interface to negate an existing predicate. It is similar to the **negate()** method.

To understand the need of the 'not' method, let us first understand how a negation was achieved before the **Predicate.not()** method.

For example:

Consider a class **Employee** with a sales property and the **isEligible()** method.

```
public class Employee {
    private static final int MIN_SALES = 1500;
    public int sales;
    public Employee(int sales) {
        this.sales = sales;
    }
 // an employee is eligible for bonus if sales is greater than or equal to min
sales value
    public boolean isEligible() {
        return sales >= MIN_SALES;
    }
}
```

Now suppose there is a list of employees with their sales records.

```
List<Employee> emp = Arrays.asList(
                new Employee(3000),
                new Employee(1200),
                new Employee(900),
                new Employee(4000)
        );
```

To retrieve the list of all eligible employees, we can do the following:

```
// getting sales values which are greater than minimum sales
```

```
        List<Employee> eligible = emp.stream()
                .filter(Employee::isEligible)
                .collect(Collectors.toList());
        for (Employee eligible1 : eligible) {
            System.out.println(eligible1.sales);
        }
```

Output:

```
3000
4000
```

However, to retrieve the not-eligible ones, we must negate the predicate as under by using the logical NOT '`!`' operator.

```
// managing negation without Predicte.not method
// getting sales values which are lesser than minimum sales
        List<Employee> noteligible = emp.stream()
                .filter(Employee -> !Employee.isEligible())
                .collect(Collectors.toList());
        for (Employee noteligible1 : noteligible) {
            System.out.println(noteligible1.sales);
        }
```

Output:

```
1200
900
```

Here, we have to let go of the method reference as shown above or use a workaround by creating another **`isNotEligible()`** method in the class as under.

```
emp.stream()
  .filter(Employee::isNotEligible)
  .collect(Collectors.toList());
```

However, we might not want to create a new method or may not be able to create, if the class is not created by us.

This is where the new **`Predicate.not()`** method comes to support. We can modify the above example and use **`Predicate.not()`** to negate an existing predicate as under. Instead of using a lambda or creating a new method on the **`Employee`** class, we can just use this new method:**`// managing negation with Predicate.not method`**

```
// getting sales values which are lesser than minimum sales
```

```
        List<Employee> noteligible2 = emp.stream()
                .filter(Predicate.not(Employee::isEligible))
                .collect(Collectors.toList());
        for (Employee noteligible3 : noteligible2) {
            System.out.println(noteligible3.sales);
        }
```

Output:

```
1200
900
```

This helps to avoid any modification to the existing class and improves the readability of method references.

13.2.5 Local-variable type inference for lambda parameters

Java 11 added the feature for using the local variable (**var** keyword) syntax in lambda parameters.

For example:

```
(var fName, var lName) -> fName + lName
```

This feature allows to apply modifiers to local variables, such as defining a type annotation.

For example:

```
List<String> list1 = Arrays.asList("Java 10", "Java 11");
String result = list1.stream()
  .map((@Nonnull var x) -> x.toUpperCase())
  .collect(Collectors.joining(", "));
System.out.println(result);
```

The local variable type inference feature was introduced in Java 10, which allowed using **var** as a type for a local variable. The actual type was inferred by the compiler based on the value assigned to the variable.

But, the **var** keyword could not be used with lambda parameters, and the types had to be explicitly specified as under:

```
(String s1, String s2) -> s1 + s2
```

However, it is allowed to skip the parameter types and rewrite the lambda as:

```
(s1, s2) -> s1 + s2
```

Even Java 8 supported this, and in Java 10, we would have expected a logical extension to this by using **var** keyword.

```
(var s1, var s2) -> s1 + s2
```

However, Java 10 did not support this, but Java 11 provides support for the above syntax. This ensures uniformity in the usage of **var** in both local variables and lambda parameters.

Though we can simply skip the types, the benefit of this uniformity is that it allows applying modifiers to local variables and lambda formals without losing brevity.

For example, below is the usage with type annotation, which is a common modifier:

```
(@Nonnull var s1, @Nullable var s2) -> s1 + s2
```

Such annotations cannot be used without specifying the types.

The **var** keyword usage in lambda also has certain limitations, as follows:

- We cannot use **var** for some parameters and skip for others.

  ```
  (var s1, s2) -> s1 + s2   // this will give compilation error
  ```

- We cannot mix **var** with explicit types

  ```
  (var s1, String s2) -> s1 + s2   // this will give compilation error
  ```

- We can skip the parentheses in single parameter lambda, but we cannot skip them while using var.

  ```
  s1 -> s1.toUpperCase()  // this is allowed
  var s1 -> s1.toUpperCase()  // this will give compilation error
  ```

13.2.6 HttpClient

The HttpClient class of **java.net.http** package introduced in Java 9 is now in its final, non-preview version and a standard feature in Java 11.

The new HTTP API provides support for both HTTL/1.1 and HTTP/2 with overall improved performance.

Following code shows the use of the standardized HttpClient class:

```
HttpClient httpClient = HttpClient.newBuilder()

  .version(HttpClient.Version.HTTP_2)

  .connectTimeout(Duration.ofSeconds(20))

  .build();

HttpRequest httpReq = HttpRequest.newBuilder()

  .GET()
```

```
  .uri(URI.create("http://localhost:" + port))
  .build();
HttpResponse httpRes = httpClient.send(httpReq, HttpResponse.BodyHandlers.ofString());
assertThat(httpRes.body()).isEqualTo("Message from the server!");
```

13.2.7 Run source files

Java source files can now be executed without having to compile them first.

For example:

Earlier, we need to compile a **.java** file by using the **javac** command and then run it with the java command as under:

```
$ javac Hello.java
$ java Hello
```

However, now we can directly run the **.java** file with the java command under:

```
$ java Hello.java
```

13.2.8 No-Op garbage collector

Java 11 introduced a new garbage collector called Epsilon. It allocates memory but does not actually collect any garbage. Hence, it is called No-Op (no operations) and is applicable for simulating out-of-memory errors.

It will not be suitable for production, but there are some use-cases where it will be useful:

- Performance testing
- Memory pressure testing
- VM interface testing
- Extremely short-lived jobs

You can enable it by using the **-XX:+UnlockExperimentalVMOptions -XX:+UseEpsilonGC** flag.

13.2.9 Flight Recorder

Java Flight Recorder (JFR) was earlier a commercial product in Oracle JDK, but now it is open source in Open JDK. JFR is a profiling tool that helps to gather profiling and diagnostic data from a running Java application.

JFR can be used in production as its overhead is generally below 1%. After the recording time is over, the recorded data will be saved in a JFR file.

For example:

To start a 60 second JFR recording, we can use the following parameter:

```
-XX:StartFlightRecording=duration=60s,settings=profile,filename=java-test-app.
jfr
```

To view and analyze the data, we need another tool called **JDK Mission Control (JMC).**

13.2.10 Removed and deprecated modules

With new versions getting released, we cannot use the removed features and should stop using the deprecated features as well.

Certain modules of Java EE and CORBA had been deprecated in Java 9. With Java 11, these have been completely removed. Since Java EE technologies are available on third-party sites, it is not required to include them in Java SE.

Listed below are the removed modules:

- Java API for XML-Based Web Services (`java.xml.ws`)
- Java Architecture for XML Binding (`java.xml.bind`)
- JavaBeans Activation Framework (`java.activation`)
- Common Annotations (`java.xml.ws.annotation`)
- Common Object Request Broker Architecture (`java.corba`)
- JavaTransaction API (`java.transaction`)

Both **JDK Mission Control (JMC)** and JavaFX are now available as standalone/separate sets of modules. Hence, these have been removed from the JDK.

Furthermore, Java 11 also deprecated the following modules:

- Nashorn JavaScript engine, including the JJS tool
- Pack200 compression scheme for JAR files

13.3 Features of Java versions 12 to 16

Java 11 (LTS) was followed by several smaller releases. Let us look at the features of Java versions 12 to 16.

13.3.1 Java 12

Java 12 introduces some new features and a few clean-ups. The most prominent are the Unicode 11 support and a new switch expression in the preview version. The finalize methods were removed from `FileInputStream` and `FileOutputStream`.

13.3.2 Java 13

A complete list of features of Java 13 can be referred on Oracle's official site. The most important are the Unicode 12.1 support and improved preview versions of two features as under:

- **Switch Expression (Preview)**

  Now a switch expression can also return a value. Further, the lambda-style syntax can be used for the expressions without the fall-through/break issues:

  For example:

  Before Java 13, switch statements were created as under:

```
switch(status) {
  case PAID:
    // code statements
    break;
  case FREE:
    // code statements
    break;
  default:
    // code statements
}
```

  With Java 13, switch statements can be created as under:

```
String type = "PAID";
boolean value = switch (type) {
    case "PAID" ->
       true;
    case "FREE" ->
       false;
    default ->
       throw new IllegalArgumentException("Incorrect Option");
};
System.out.println("Selected PAID? " + value);
```

  Output:

```
Selected PAID? true
```

- **Multiline strings (Preview)**

  Java allows creating multiline string as under:

```
// Multiline string before Java 13
String beforeJava13 = "<html>\n" +
```

```
                "    <body>\n" +
                "        <p>Hello, world</p>\n" +
                "    </body>\n" +
                "</html>\n";
System.out.println(beforeJava13);
// Multiline string with Java 13
String withJava13 = """
                <html>
                    <body>
                        <p>Hello, world</p>
                    </body>
                </html>
                """;
System.out.println(withJava13);
```

Output:

```
<html>
    <body>
        <p>Hello, world</p>
    </body>
</html>
<html>
    <body>
        <p>Hello, world</p>
    </body>
</html>
```

Both versions of the multiline string will give the same output. However, the Java 13 version is more convenient to use.

13.3.3 Java 14

Java 14 standardized the preview versions of features of Java 12 and 13 and introduced new preview features. Let us look at some prominent features:

- **Switch Expression (Standard)**

  The preview versions of switch expressions of Java 12 and 13 are now standardized.

```
String day = "TUESDAY";
        int count = switch (day) {
```

```
            case "MONDAY", "FRIDAY", "SUNDAY" ->
                6;
            case "TUESDAY" ->
                7;
            default -> {
                String s = day;
                int result = s.length();
                yield result;
            }
        };
System.out.println("Letter count "+count);
```

Output:

```
Letter count 7
```

- **Records (Preview)**

  Java 14 introduced new record classes to reduce the writing of a lot of boilerplate code. Before Java 14, a class contained data, getter / setters, **toString()**, and equals / hashcode. For example:

```
final class Calculator {
    public final int a;
    public final int b;
    public Calculator(int a, int b) {
        this.a = a;
        this.b = b;
    }
}
// state-based implementations of equals, hashCode, toString
```

  With records, the code can be written as under:

```
record Calculator(int x, int y) { }
```

Note: This is a preview feature which may be modified in future releases.

- **Useful NullPointerExceptions**

  The **NullPointerExceptions** now describe exactly which variable was null.

  For example:

```
participant.age = 35;
---
```

```
Exception in thread "main" java.lang.NullPointerException:
    Cannot assign field "age" because "participant" is null
```

- **Pattern matching for `Instanceof` (Preview)**

  In earlier versions, we could cast the objects inside an **`instanceof`** as under:

  ```
  if (val instanceof String) {
      String s = (String) val;
      // use s
  }
  ```

  This can be done effectively without the cast.

  ```
  if (val instanceof String s) {
      System.out.println(s.contains("Java14"));
  }
  ```

- **Other features**

  Packaging Tool (Incubator): Allows packaging the Java application into platform-specific packages along with all necessary dependencies by using the new incubating jpackage tool.

  - **Linux**: deb and rpm
  - **macOS**: pkg and dmg
  - **Windows**: msi and exe

  Garbage Collectors: Java 14 added the experimental Z Garbage Collector and removed the **Concurrent Mark Sweep (CMS)** garbage collector.

13.3.4 Java 15

Listed below are some features of Java 15:

- **Text-Blocks / Multiline strings**

  Java 15 standardized the experimental feature of multiline strings introduced in Java13.

  For example:

  ```
  String text = """
          Java is an object-oriented programming language.
          It has several versions.
          The latest version is Java 19.
            Java 20 will be released in Mar 2023.
        """;
  System.out.println(text);
  ```

- **Sealed classes - Preview**

  Java 15 introduced the preview version of sealed class feature to provide a tighter control on who is allowed to subclass your classes.

  For example:

  ```
  public abstract sealed class Vehicle
      permits TwoWheeler, FourWheeler {...}
  ```

  The above code means that while the Vehicle class is public, it can be subclassed by only the `TwoWheeler` and `FourWheeler` classes.

- Records and pattern matching

  The records and pattern matching features from Java 14 are still in preview and not yet finalized.

- **Nashorn JavaScript Engine removed**

  The Nashorn Javascript Engine, which was deprecated in Java 11, was finally removed in JDK 15.

- **Z Garbage collect is production ready**

  The Z Garbage Collector is now made production-ready.

13.3.5 Java 16

Listed below are some prominent features of Java 16:

- **Pattern matching for `instanceof`**: Traditionally, the `instanceof` operator is used to check the type of object, usually followed by a cast. This helps to extract the type of our variable before doing any further processing.

  For example:

  Consider a simple hierarchy of Vehicle objects as under:

  ```
  if (vehicle instanceof TwoWheeler) {
      TwoWheeler bike = (TwoWheeler) vehicle;
      bike.accelerate();
     // other bike operations
  } else if (vehicle instanceof FourWheeler) {
      FourWheleer car = (FourWheeler) vehicle;
      car.brake();
      // other car operations
  }
  // More conditional statements for different vehicles
  ```

Here, for each conditional block, we are checking the type of the vehicle parameter and converting it by using a cast and declaring a local variable. Later, we can perform the relevant operations for that vehicle type.

This approach works however, it has several drawbacks:

- This type of code involves testing the type and repeatedly making a cast for each conditional block.
- The type name is also repeated for every if block.
- Poor readability due to the prominence of the casting and variable declaration code

The improved version of the **instanceof** operator in Java 16 does both tasks of testing the parameter and assigning it to a binding variable of the proper type.

Hence, the previous vehicle example can be written in a much more concise way as under:

```
if (vehicle instanceof TwoWheeler bike) {
  bike.accelerate();
} else if (vehicle instanceof FourWheeler car) {
    car.brake();
}
```

Here, in the first if block, the vehicle object is matched with the pattern type **TwoWheeler** bike. First, we are testing if the vehicle is an instance of **TwoWheeler**. If yes, it will be cast to the **TwoWheeler** type and then, we will assign the result to bike.

- **Foreign linker API – Preview**: This is a planned replacement for **Java Native Interface (JNI)**, that will allow binding to native libraries (think C).
- **Records and pattern matching**: Both the preview features of earlier versions are now production-ready.
- **Sealed classes**: Sealed Classes introduced in Java 15 are still in preview.

You can refer to the other features of versions 12 to 16 on Oracle's official site.

Conclusion

In this chapter, you learnt that Java 11 was the first **Long Term Support (LTS)** version after Java 8. Java 11 was a smaller release but added some useful methods to the String and Files classes. The static 'not' method of Predicate and local-variable type inference (**var**) for lambda parameters helped to reduce boilerplate. Versions 12 to 16 introduced several features, including new switch expressions, multiline strings, pattern matching, instanceof operator, new garbage collectors, records, and sealed classes. Several deprecated features of Java 9 were removed from Java 11.

In the next chapter, you will learn about Java 17 (LTS) and new updates till Java 19.

Multiple choice questions

1. **JDK 11 was released in the year _______.**
    a. 2016
    b. 2020
    c. 2018
    d. 2022
2. **Which of the following is a preview feature of Java 13?**
    a. Switch expression
    b. `NullPointerExceptions`
    c. Sealed class
    d. Records
3. **What does the below code indicate?**

```
public abstract sealed class Vehicle
    permits TwoWheeler, FourWheeler {...}
```

    a. Vehicle class is public, and it can be subclassed by only the `TwoWheeler` and `FourWheeler` classes
    b. Vehicle class be subclassed by any class
    c. Vehicle class can subclass from only `TwoWheeler` and `FourWheeler` classes
    d. Vehicle class cannot be subclassed
4. **Identify the correct format to run a Hello.java file Java 11.**
    a. `$ javac Hello.java`
       `$ java Hello`
    b. `$ javac Hello.java`
       `$ java Hello.java`
    c. `$ javac Hello`
    d. `$ java Hello.java`
5. **The improved version of the `instanceof` operator in Java 16 does both tasks of testing the parameter and assigning it to a binding variable of the proper type.**
    a. True
    b. False

Answers

1. c
2. a
3. a
4. d
5. a

Assignment

1. Download and install JDK 11 and the latest NetBeans IDE. Create a new Java application. Create a new file and write a string to it. Read the string from the same file and check if the string is blank.

   (Hint: Use the new static methods of the Files class and the new String class methods)
2. Consider a scenario where a user needs to book a movie ticket. There are three options 'Morning', 'Afternoon', and 'Evening'. Create a program to allow a user to specify the movie slot and book a ticket accordingly.

   (Hint: Use the new switch expression. Download and install JDK 13 or 17)
3. Create a sealed class called Shape that can be subclassed by only Circle and Square classes.

   (Hint: Download and install JDK 17 and set the platform in the NetBeans IDE)

CHAPTER 14
Java 17 (LTS) and New Updates

Introduction

Java 17 is the first **Long Term Support (LTS)** version after Java 11. It added a few preview features and finalized some features of earlier versions. Java 18 and 19 were also released with some high-level feature enhancements.

Structure

Following are the topics that are **covered in this chapter:**

- Introduction to Java 17 (LTS)
- Features of Java versions 18 and 19

Objectives

In this chapter, you will learn about Java 17 and the new features added to the JDK, such as pattern matching for switch. You will also learn the new features and enhancements in Java versions 18 and 19.

14.1 Introduction to Java 17 (LTS)

After Java 11, the next LTS release was Java 17. It introduced a few new features in the preview version and finalized the preview features of earlier versions. Listed below are some prominent features of Java 17.

14.1.1 Pattern matching for switch (Preview)

The switch statement of Java has evolved a lot. Earlier, you could compare only integers in Java 7 and strings and enums in Java 8. However, with Java 12, the switch case became more versatile as it allowed returning values from a switch block. This converted the switch statements into switch blocks. A value can be returned from a switch block through the "**break**" keyword or through the arrow (->) operator. Further, multiple values were allowed in a case label.

Later, Java 13 introduced the "**yield**" keyword instead of the break keyword for returning values.

Java 17 introduced the pattern matching feature for switch, which allows passing Objects to the switch functions to identify a particular type.

For example, consider the below code:

```
public class Session14Code {
    public static void main(String[] args) {
      // test the object type

        System.out.println(testcase(56));
        System.out.println(testcase("This is Java 17"));
        System.out.println(testcase(true));

        Vehicle car = new Vehicle(4584, 4);
        System.out.println(testcase(car));
    }
    public static String testcase(Object obj) {
    // switch expression to check the object type
        return switch (obj) {
            case Integer i ->
                "An integer";
            case String s ->
                "A string";
            case Vehicle v ->
```

```
                "It is a vehicle";
            default ->
                "Not sure";
        };
    }
}
```

Here, an object is passed to the switch condition, and then, this object is checked for its type, and a value is returned accordingly from the switch case.

The statement,

```
case Integer i -> "An integer";
```

checks if the object passed is of type "**Integer**" and then assigns to "**i**" if it is an integer. With the use of the arrow operator, the string "**An integer**" will be returned.

We can also use the **yield** keyword introduced in Java 13 to return values from switch expressions, for the above statement, as shown below:

```
case Integer i :
  yield  "An integer";
```

We can also create a custom object and pass it to the switch statements/expressions. For example, in the above code, we are passing an object of the **Vehicle** class, which is created as shown below:

```
public class Vehicle {
    private int id;
    private int noOfWheels;
    public Vehicle(int id, int noOfWheels) {
        this.id = id;
        this.noOfWheels = noOfWheels;
    }
    public int getId() {
        return id;
    }
    public int getNoOfWheels() {
        return noOfWheels;
    }
}
```

A case label for "**Vehicle**" object type has been added in the switch block earlier.

When the above code is executed with the test statements in the **main()** method, the output is as under.

Output:

```
An integer
A string
Not sure
It is a vehicle
```

PN: For executing the above program, you need to enable preview in the IDE that you are using, or you can enable it at the command line by using **--enable-preview** option.

In NetBeans 17, you need to add **--enable-preview** as VM Options, as shown in the following image:

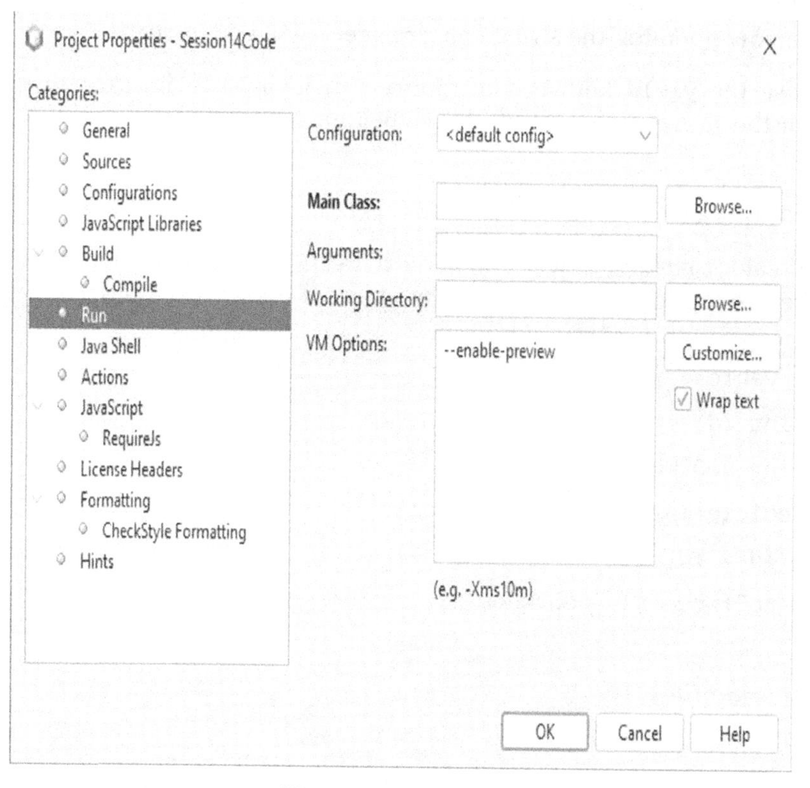

Figure 14.1: VM options

Also modify the **pom.xml** file to add the **--enable-preview** argument tag, as shown in the following image:

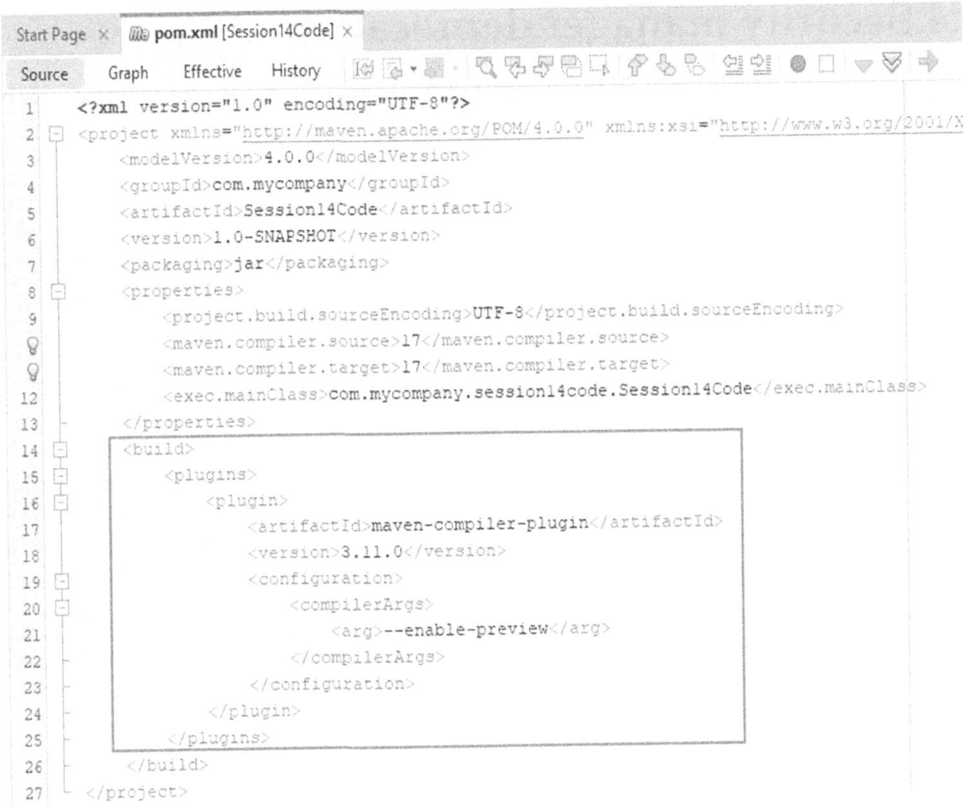

Start Page × pom.xml [Session14Code] ×

Source Graph Effective History

```
<?xml version="1.0" encoding="UTF-8"?>
<project xmlns="http://maven.apache.org/POM/4.0.0" xmlns:xsi="http://www.w3.org/2001/X
    <modelVersion>4.0.0</modelVersion>
    <groupId>com.mycompany</groupId>
    <artifactId>Session14Code</artifactId>
    <version>1.0-SNAPSHOT</version>
    <packaging>jar</packaging>
    <properties>
        <project.build.sourceEncoding>UTF-8</project.build.sourceEncoding>
        <maven.compiler.source>17</maven.compiler.source>
        <maven.compiler.target>17</maven.compiler.target>
        <exec.mainClass>com.mycompany.session14code.Session14Code</exec.mainClass>
    </properties>
    <build>
        <plugins>
            <plugin>
                <artifactId>maven-compiler-plugin</artifactId>
                <version>3.11.0</version>
                <configuration>
                    <compilerArgs>
                        <arg>--enable-preview</arg>
                    </compilerArgs>
                </configuration>
            </plugin>
        </plugins>
    </build>
</project>
```

Figure 14.2: Modified pom.xml

14.1.2 Sealed classes (Finalized)

The sealed class feature which was introduced in Java 15, is now finalized in Java 17. Sealed class allows you to put restriction on who can subclass your classes.

For example,

```
public abstract sealed class Vehicle

  permits TwoWheeler, FourWheeler {…}
```

The above code indicates that the public class vehicle can only be subclassed by the **`TwoWheeler`** and **`FourWheeler`** classes.

14.1.3 Foreign function and Memory API - Incubator

This API is a replacement for the **Java Native Interface (JNI),** and it allows calling native functions and accessing memory outside the JVM. For now, it supports Think C but may support additional languages such as C++, Fortran, and so on eventually.

14.1.4 Security manager deprecated

The security manager which had been existent since Java 1.0, has now been deprecated and will be removed in a future version.

14.2 Features of Java 18 and Java 19

Java 18 and Java 19 were smaller releases and introduced some higher-level features.

14.2.1 Features of Java 18

Listed below are some features of Java 18.

- **UTF-8 by default**

  Earlier, when any file operations were performed on files without explicitly specifying the character encoding, the operating system encoding was used, for example, UTF-8 on Linux and macOS, and Windows-1252 on Windows. With Java 18, this has been set to UTF-8 by default.

- **Simple Web Server**

  Java 18 has introduced a rudimentary HTTP server, that can be started with the **`jwebserver`** command.

  You can refer to more features on the official website of Oracle.

14.2.2 Features of Java 19

Java 19 added several features, such as the new Foreign Function and Memory API, Virtual Threads, Vector API, and Structured Concurrency. However, all these features are in preview mode and are subject to change in future releases.

Conclusion

In this chapter, you learnt that Java 17 was the first LTS version after Java 11. Java 17 added preview features such as pattern matching for switch statement and finalized features of earlier versions. The Java 18 and Java 19 versions were smaller releases and introduced some higher-level features such as UTF-8 by default, simple web server, Virtual threads, and so on.

Multiple choice questions

1. **Which Java version introduced the "`yield`" keyword?**
   a. Java 12
   b. Java 15
   c. Java 17
   d. Java 13

2. **Which of the following features is deprecated in Java 17?**
    a. Records
    b. Sealed class
    c. Security manager
    d. Switch expression
3. **The Foreign function and memory API supports which of the following languages in Java 17?**
    a. Think C
    b. C++
    c. Fortran
    d. None of these
4. **Which of the following is not an LTS version?**
    a. **`Java 17`**
    b. **`Java 7`**
    c. **`Java 8`**
    d. **`Java 11`**
5. **The Sealed classes of Java 15 are still in the preview version in Java 17.**
    a. True
    b. False

Answers

1. d
2. c
3. a
4. b
5. b

Assignment

Extend the example given in the session for switch expression. Add two new parameters in the Vehicle class named **`noOfDoors`** and **`noOfWindows`**. Create a new constructor and respective getters. Print the number of doors and windows in the **`Vehicle`** object as specified by the user in the switch expression.

Join our book's Discord space

Join the book's Discord Workspace for Latest updates, Offers, Tech happenings around the world, New Release and Sessions with the Authors:

https://discord.bpbonline.com

Index

U

V

W

Z

Made in the USA
Middletown, DE
27 November 2023